The Witch in History

A symbol of everything that is dark about the past and woman, the witch continues to fascinate us in the late twentieth century. *The Witch in History* explores that fascination and its manifold forms through court records, early modern dramas and the modern histories and fictions that draw upon them.

This book argues that in early modern England, the witch was a woman's fantasy and not simply a male nightmare. Through witch-beliefs and stories about witches, early modern women were able to express and manage powerful and passionate feelings that still resonate for us today, feelings that could not be uttered in a seventeenth-century context: unconscious fears of and fury with children and mothers.

In our own era, groups as diverse as women writers, academic historians and radical feminists have found in the witch a figure who justifies and defines their own identities. Then too, there are those who still call themselves witches in 1990s Britain, who still practise magic and who invent their own histories of witchcraft to sustain them. Constantly reworked and debated, the witch is central to all these groups.

Looking at texts from colonial narratives to court masques, trial records to folktales, and literary texts from Shakespeare to Sylvia Plath, this book shows how the witch acts as a carrier for the fears, desires and fantasies of women and men both now and in the early modern period.

Diane Purkiss is Lecturer in English at the University of Reading.

The Witch in History

Early Modern and Twentieth-century Representations

Diane Purkiss

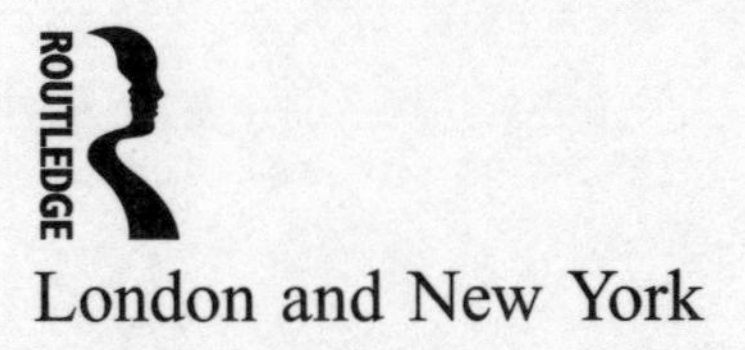

London and New York

First published 1996
by Routledge
11 New Fetter Lane, London EC4P 4EE

Simultaneously published in the USA and Canada
by Routledge
29 West 35th Street, New York, NW 10001

Typeset in Times by LaserScript, Mitcham, Surrey
Printed and bound in Great Britain by Clays Ltd, St. Ives PLC

British Library Cataloguing in Publication Data

A catalogue record for this book is available from the British Library

Library of Congress Cataloging in Publication Data

Purkiss, Diane, 1961–
The witch in history: early modern and twentieth-century representations / Diane Purkiss.
p. cm.
Includes bibliographical references and index.
1. Witchcraft – History. 2. Witchcraft in literature – History 3. Witchcraft in art – History. I. Title.
BF1571.P87 1996
133.4′3′09–dc20

ISBN 0–415–08761–9 (Hbk)
ISBN 0–415–08762–7 (Pbk)

Contents

Deeds which populate the dimensions of space and which reach their end when someone dies may cause us wonderment, but one thing, or an infinite number of things, dies in every final agony, unless there is a universal memory as the theosophists have conjectured. In time there was a day that extinguished the last eyes to see Christ.

Jorge Luis Borges, 'The Witness'

Acknowledgements

This is cross-disciplinary book which wanders across many well-defended boundary lines. I have to thank a very large number of resourceful, intelligent and generous guides. Julia Briggs, Tony Watkins and Marina Warner were kind and helpful on fairy tales, and Julia Briggs was, as always, a fairy godmother in other respects as well. Edith Hall provided an abundance of classical references and advice on the ancients' understanding of ethnicity. Historians of witchcraft were hospitable to the interloper from another discipline: I am especially grateful to Amy Erickson, Alison Gill, Lyndal Roper, Jim Sharpe, Malcolm Gaskill and Tom Robisheaux. I was introduced to Miranda Chaytor in August 1995; since then she has been a paragon of intelligent and knowledgeable kindness. Many modern witches talked to me and answered my questions patiently. I cannot give their names, but I am grateful to them. The staff of the Inner Bookshop, Oxford, provided a steady stream of New Age and neo-Pagan references.

The Oxford 'Women, Text and History' seminars from 1988 to 1990 gave me a sense that there might be an audience for the kind of work I wanted to do, and gave me a rich store of ideas about how to do it. Among scholars in my own discipline I have received help and encouragement in various forms from David Aers, Ros Ballaster, Cedric Brown, John Carey, Hero Chalmers, Kate Chedgzoy, Danielle Clarke, Jacqueline Fear-Segal, Lorraine Fletcher, Helen Hackett, Elizabeth Heale, Coral Howells, Carolyn Lyle, Jonny Morris, David Norbrook, Eleanor Porter, Roger Sales, Nigel Smith, Martin Wiggins, Helen Wilcox and Peter Womack. I am especially grateful to those who read and commented on drafts, including Andrew Gurr, Lorna Hutson and Marion Wynne Davies; all were constructive and encouraging. I have probably forgotten somebody, because this has been a fortunate project for receiving help and forging links.

Audiences in Oxford, Norwich, Reading and London produced helpful comments, questions and interventions. I have taught students on witchcraft at Oxford, UEA and Reading; all the groups I taught enlightened me, but I would particularly like to thank Tom Betteridge, Fiona Breckenridge, Linda Morgan, the entire 1993 'Gender and the Body' group at UEA, Karen Britland, Heike Bruton and Amber Caravéo. My first editor at Routledge, and later my colleague at UEA, Sue Roe, and my subsequent editor, Talia Rodgers, have been brave, thoughtful and supportive.

Witches come from family dramas. My mother, Fay Purkiss, comes from what may be the last generation genuinely to love Shakespeare as a popular playwright and dramatist rather than as a badge of education or elitism. She gave me *Lamb's Tales* when I was eight, and I am hugely grateful to her for making Shakespeare a mother tongue for me. Michael Tobias Dowling, my son, has, by virtue of his being, inflected the sections of this book which concern motherhood and the maternal body, and has given me much delight. For reasons explained in this book, I dare not write down what I really think of him. Claire Gettings disproved all early modern myths about the malice of nurses and nannies; I would never have finished this book without her help. Ivan Dowling is the centre of my life; everything that I do is really his doing, and this book is no exception.

This is a book about women and the often strong and problematic connections between them. Frances Boyle has been my friend for nearly twenty years. She taught me what female solidarity really means, and what women's involvement in medicine might really be like. She was always brave enough to see the limitations of male medicine and also wise enough to see and seize its extraordinary power as beneficently as possible. Without her, I would have written a different and more blinkered book. Clare Brant gave me the kind of intellectual nourishment that is rare indeed these days, the courage to be myself. She supported me by her intelligence, generosity and faith. Without her, I would not have written a book at all. This book is for both of them.

Introduction

When I was a small girl, I was fascinated by *The Wizard of Oz* – not the celebrated MGM musical, but the original book by L. Frank Baum. What intrigued me was not only its child's paradise of bright, flat colours, small people, pretty fairies, easy magic and good food, but the way this painted nursery world was always precarious, subject to corruption by a spectacularly dark figure who seemed to have strayed in from another kind of story. To me, the Wicked Witch of the West did not seem to 'belong' to the bright and pretty world of Oz; she overwhelmed its illusory harmony; her presence was too strong to be contained within its fictional and discursive borders. She did not make sense taken together with the dainty china milkmaids and cute Munchkins; in some way, she therefore came to stand for the irruption of chilly but exhilarating reality into the artificial security of a comfortably privileged childhood. My identification with such a figure was a secret even from me; I wanted to be her partly so that I would not have to be afraid of her.

At the age of four, *The Wizard of Oz* was my favourite Let's Pretend game, specifically the moment when Dorothy melts the Wicked Witch of the West by throwing a bucket of water over her. In Baum's book, as in the film, Dorothy does not mean to kill, but Baum does make her hurl the water in anger at the Witch; she at least means to wet her. I, always cast as Dorothy, was even more knowing; I could relish my knowledge of what was to come, exult in my power, while playing at being a wholly innocent child-victim. Dorothy's awesome power to destroy reality and adulthood and fold herself back into dependent childhood could indeed be relished by a child born, as I was, in the early 1960s, for never before had the children of the middle classes had it so good. Baum's narrative, reshaped as my own sadistic little psychodrama, became the story of the child's emotional power over its apparently all-powerful parents. For I always cast my long-suffering mother as the Witch, as if in an early effort to prove the connections between witch-stories and images of maternity. As she gamely went through the motions of melting many times a day, she too could hardly help but reflect on the connections between witch stories, power and maternity. Feebly, I hasten to add that I did not use a bucket with real water in it; my mother had, however, quite enough knowledge of child psychology to grasp what was afoot, and not enough to avoid being hurt by its rather cruel meanings. Baum's *Wizard of Oz* thus became for a time my own witch-story, shaped by me to present and stage the splits and contradictions in my own role as child in a manner I evidently found consoling. In shaping such a story for such a purpose, I was unknowingly following in the footsteps of the many people, especially women, who had invented, reinvented and retold stories of witches which affirmed and denied their own problematic identities, allowing them to express and manage desires, fears and anxieties otherwise denied legitimate expression.

Rather than making new claims to offer the occulted 'truth' about witches, I have assembled evidence of a number of different investments in the figure of the witch, trying to tell or retell the rich variety of stories told about her and to analyse the way those stories work. Beginning with the histories told by radical feminists and modern witches, and showing how the maverick narratives of such figures unexpectedly intersect with those of more orthodox academic historians, I present the centrality of stories about witches to the identities of all three groups, revealing the witch herself to be a created myth. The resulting female figure has had considerable appeal for women writers, whose engagements with her are briefly discussed. This approach means that I am often criticising groups of which I am myself a member. I write of the inadequacies of some radical feminist histories, though I am a feminist historian indebted to my predecessors in the field. I write of the way psychoanalysis can block apprehension of the supernatural, though I use psychoanlysis to analyse witchcraft. These are not contradictions, but attempts to clarify what is clouded and confused, or, alternatively, attempts to historicise or analyse patterns of thought which for me too are well-nigh inescapable. I think this will be clear to everyone who shares my view that feminism has never been a monolith; to criticise our predecessors is not incompatible with following in their footsteps, since they too criticised a still-earlier generation of scholars.

I then examine the way early modern villagers, and especially women, themselves fashioned stories about the figure of the witch, stories which helped to define their identities. I argue that the witch is not solely or simply the creation of patriarchy, but that women also invested heavily in the figure as a fantasy which allowed them to express and manage otherwise unspeakable fears and desires, centring on the question of motherhood and children. I look at the way the idea of a maternal body, which is both an object of desire and a source of pollution, becomes the basis for an understanding of the witch's magic as that unseen and infinitely extended aspect of her body which can do harm beyond her apparent bounds. I examine the way the women accused of witchcraft used the opportunity of supernatural agency and confession to shape an identity for themselves which represented a compromise between their understanding of the world and the categories developed by more educated people.

Finally, this book looks at the presentation of the witch on the early modern stage. I examine the way in which these village stories were taken up and reshaped by early modern dramatists, who turned them into stage spectaculars and interpretative challenges leading to moral homilies; the effect was to give the witch public meaning in defining the place of the stage and the notion of good order in the political and social realms. At the same time, the witch became a figure in sceptical narratives which divided modernity from the rural past, and scientific skill from supernatural and providential narrations. Even though such narratives did great violence to the actual stories told by ordinary early modern people, it was they that influenced historians, especially psychoanalysts and anthropologists. Beginning with the complex and contestatory relations between gender and power exemplified in the connections between Elizabeth I and the figure of the witch, this book looks at the way those high tensions were both evaded and addressed by dramatists as diverse as Lyly and Shakespeare. The playfulness that accompanies the witch's presence on stage is noted in relation to both Dipsas and the 'witch' of Brainford. The complex and twisted roots of the early modern witch-story are constantly modified by the generic and class expectations of the dramatists, who make little effort to understand or represent the concerns of village believers, content pragmatically to deploy the stories told to them as tropes for something else. Shakespeare's predominance in shaping the figure of the witch is reflected in the emphasis on his plays here, though these are compared with the works of other dramatists: fantasists such as Marston, Middleton and Jonson, and 'realists' such as Dekker, Ford and Rowley, and Heywood and Brome. The section on drama closes with a reading of the interaction between the witches of the Old World and the experience of the New World in relation to *The Tempest*, not usually seen as a witch-play.

This book discusses texts from diverse periods, but it makes no attempt at 'coverage'. Hidden in it are the shadows of many stories which do not get told, stories by both women and men. In the modern world: the story of the witch in canonical literature, from Shelley to Yeats; the story of the witch in art, from Dürer to Burne-Jones; the place of the witch in pornography, and her centrality to S/M; the witch on film, from the silent Swedish classic *Häxan* to *The Witches of Eastwick*. In the early modern period: the story of learned demonological discourses about the witch, their growth and dissemination, and the lack of progress in acculturation in England; the relations between the witch- and fairy-beliefs, ghost-beliefs, and other ideas about the supernatural; generic stories, about witches in medieval romances and Renaissance tragedies; stage stories, about the lost witch-plays and why they were lost, about the staging of the cauldron and apparitions and about hovering through the fog and filthy air; school stories, about the absolute canonical status of *Macbeth* as a 'set text'; the 'cunning women' plays like *The Wise Woman of Hogsdon*, and *The Alchemist*; finally, and most regrettably, the stories of many unknown early modern women, which do not get told here in full or at all.

By the same token, there are questions which I do not address, partly because I am not very interested in them, partly because they seem to me unanswerable. I do not try to explain the larger global issues involved in witchcraft, or account for the 'rise' and 'fall' of witch-persecution, except perhaps to note that its fall, at any rate, is a fall only among the elite. I do not try to answer the empirical questions that preoccupy many of my contemporaries. I am not interested in asking why Ursula Kempe, say, and not some other village woman, became the blank screen onto which the fantasies of her neighbours were projected. No doubt there were reasons, and sometimes one might feel one understands them. I am more interested in the fantasies projected onto Ursula than in why she was chosen as their vehicle. The range of stories I seek to tell, of fantasies I seek to unravel, are not chosen because of their centrality to some overall empirical purpose. The absence of all this material (some of which of course I intend to include in some future work, but probably will not) is itself strong testimony to the impossibility of defining the witch, of getting to the bottom of her, of organising her taxonomically, by name, kind and country. As long as she continues thus to elude us, we shall be seduced into improper curiosity by her very unavailability. And I too hope to beguile the reader, at least a little.

Part I

The histories of witchcraft

1 A Holocaust of one's own

The myth of the Burning Times

> Popular history, and also the history taught in schools, is influenced by this Manichaean tendency, which shuns half-tints and complexities; it is prone to reduce the river of human occurrences to conflicts, and the conflicts to duels – we and they, the good guys and the bad guys respectively, because the good must prevail, else the world would be subverted.
>
> Primo Levi, *The Drowned and the Saved*

Here is a story. Once upon a time, there was a woman who lived on the edge of a village. She lived alone, in her own house surrounded by her garden, in which she grew all manner of herbs and other healing plants. Though she was alone, she was never lonely; she had her garden and her animals for company, she took lovers when she wished, and she was always busy. The woman was a healer and midwife; she had practical knowledge taught her by her mother, and mystical knowledge derived from her closeness to nature, or from a half-submerged pagan religion. She helped women give birth, and she had healing hands; she used her knowledge of herbs and her common sense to help the sick. However, her peaceful existence was disrupted. Even though this woman was harmless, she posed a threat to the fearful. Her medical knowledge threatened the doctor. Her simple, true spiritual values threatened the superstitious nonsense of the Catholic church, as did her affirmation of the sensuous body. Her independence and freedom threatened men. So the Inquisition descended on her, and cruelly tortured her into confessing to lies about the devil. She was burned alive by men who hated women, along with millions of others just like her.

Do you believe this story? Thousands of women do. It is still being retold, in full or in part, by women who are academics, but also by poets, novelists, popular historians, theologians, dramatists.[1] It is compelling, even horrifying. However, in all essentials it is not true, or only partly true, as a history of what happened to the women called witches in the early modern period. Thousands of women were executed as witches, and in some parts of Europe torture was used to extract a confession from them; certainly, their gender often had a great deal to do with it; certainly, their accusers and judges were sometimes misogynists; certainly, by our standards they were innocent, in that to a post-Enlightenment society their 'crime' does not exist. However, the women who died were not quite like the woman of the story, and they were not killed for quite the same reasons. There is no evidence that the majority of those accused were healers and midwives; in England and also in some parts of the Continent, midwives were more likely to be found helping witch-hunters. Most women used herbal medicines as part of their household skills, some of which were quasi-magical, without arousing any anxiety. There is little evidence that convicted witches were invariably unmarried or sexually 'liberated' or lesbian; many (though not most) of those accused were married women with young families. Men were not responsible for all accusations: many, perhaps even most, witches were accused by women, and most cases depend at least partly on the evidence given by women witnesses. Persecution was as severe in Protestant as in Catholic areas. The Inquisition, except in a few areas where the local inquisitor was especially zealous, was more lenient about witchcraft cases than the secular courts; in Spain, for example, where the Inquisition was very strong, there were few deaths. Many inquisitors and secular courts disdained the *Malleus Malificarum*, still the main source for the view that witch-hunting was women-hunting; still others thought it ridiculously paranoid about male sexuality. In some countries, torture was not used at all, and in England, witches were hanged rather than burned.[2]

All this has been known for some time. Yet in the teeth of the evidence, some women continue to find this story believable, continue to circulate it. Some women are still so attached to the story that they resist efforts to disprove it. The myth has become important, not because of its historical truth, but because of its mythic significance. What is that significance? It is a story with clear oppositions. Everyone can tell who is innocent and who guilty, who is good and who bad, who is oppressed and who the oppressor. It offers to identify oppression, to make it noticeable. It legitimates identification of oppression with powerful institutions, and above all with Christianity. This is, above all, a narrative of the Fall, of paradise lost. It is a story about how perfect our lives would be – how perfect we women would be, patient, kind, self-sufficient – if it were not for patriarchy and its violence. It is often linked with another lapsarian myth, the myth of an originary matriarchy, through the themes of mother–daughter learning and of matriarchal religions as sources of witchcraft. This witch-story explains the origins and nature of good and evil. It is a religious myth, and the religion it defines is radical feminism.[3]

How did radical feminists come to need a Holocaust of their own? In order to understand this myth fully, we need to look in more detail at its history. Around 1968, the 'action wing' of New York Radical Women formed, and they chose a striking new name: WITCH. The name exploited the negative associations of the witch as woman of dark power, but the group's members also played with the signification of the term in their presentation of it as an acronym for Women's International Terrorist Conspiracy from Hell. The meaning discovered in the term 'witch' by that acronymic rendering is interesting because it goes beyond any simple reclamation of the witch as a foresister in order to assign explicit meaning to the figure. 'Woman' names the witch as gendered, while 'international' asserts the ubiquity of witches, and 'terrorist' marks witches as violent. 'Conspiracy' deliberately flirts with fears of a secret organisation of subversive women, while 'from Hell' draws attention to the origin of witches' otherness while pointing to women's oppression. This adds up to an image of the witch as violent and empowered woman. WITCH's members hexed the Chase Manhattan bank, and invaded the Bride Fair at Madison Square Gardens dressed as witches. Despite the disjunction between self and role implied by such flagrant theatricality, WITCH also inaugurated many of the myths of witchcraft which have become central to many radical feminists and most modern witches. Describing witches, the collective wrote:

> They bowed to no man, being the living remnant of the oldest culture of all – one in which men and women were equal sharers in a truly cooperative society before the death-dealing sexual, economic, and spiritual oppression of the Imperialist Phallic Society took over and began to destroy nature and human society.[4]

This image owed a great deal to Engels's history of the pre-capitalist family: it was attractive to WITCH's original members and enabling for radical feminism. However, it was also subject to less helpful change and reformulation.

This reformulation began with WITCH itself. 'Violence', 'Conspiracy' and even 'Hell' were eliminated, and more harmless-sounding acronyms were formed. Women Incensed at Telephone Company Harassment; Women Indentured to Traveller's Corporate Hell (a coven who worked at an insurance company); Women Intent on Toppling Consumer Holidays; Women's Independent Taxpayers, Consumers and Homemakers; Women Infuriated at Taking Care of Hoodlums; Women Inspired To Commit Herstory; the acronym increasingly meant only a mild-mannered bunch of consumer-rights groups. While the final group, Women Inspired To Commit Herstory, continue to use the rhetoric of crime, committing herstory is significantly less threatening than committing terrorist acts. This also identifies academic pursuits such as writing and lecturing with magic and with witchcraft as objects of persecution. This is an obvious way to romanticise what might otherwise seem dull or bookish, but it also incises the myth deeply into radical feminist identity.

These examples, however, stand for the extraordinary flexibility of the term 'witch' as a signifier within all feminist discourse. Constantly cast and recast as the late twentieth century's idea of a protofeminist, a sister from the past, the witch has undergone transformations as dramatic as those in any pantomime. The figure of the witch has been central to the revival of women's history over the past two decades. That revival has been carried out by academic historians, but not only by them; the original impetus behind the attempt to uncover women's past came from activists in the women's liberation movement, and partly from the fact that witches were among the few women given any space whatever in pre-feminist history. The witch has consequently been caught up in virtually all of feminist history's debates about itself and its own project. The enormous changes in the standard feminist narrative of the witch and her place in history reflect feminism's attempt to ask and answer questions about what history is, what feminist history is, what might count as authority and authenticity, and where the intersections are between history and textuality, history and politics. The figure of the witch mirrors – albeit sometimes in distorted form – the many images and self-images of feminism itself. Originally, women's history was inspired by the wish to uncover the truth about women, and this led to a yearning to find oneself in the past, to locate real women who share our natures and problems. The witch offers opportunities for both identification and elaborate fantasy, standing in a supportive or antagonistic relation to the contemporary feminist-activist-historian inscribing her. To remark this is not to side with those notorious critics of women's history who see feminist historians as unreasonably 'biased'; feminist histories are no more 'biased' than those male historians who have taken up the figure of the witch and reformulated it according to their needs and fantasies.[5] It is, however, true that many radical feminist figurations of witches and narratives about witches set out to challenge or question the 'rules' by which academic historians have operated, and these challenges can involve a refusal of the professional authority and discursive strategies which have for long defined authentic or 'true' history. While doing this, radical feminist historians make truth-claims of their own, some of which are very easy to refute using the methods of historical scholarship as usually conceived, and in particular the 'rules' of evidence.[6] Usually this has nothing to do with poststructuralism or even solipsism: the more flagrant a radical feminist writer's disregard for the rules of evidence, the more dogmatic her own truth-claims are likely to be. However, I am less interested in engaging with the 'truth' of various figurations of the witch, or even in legitimating or delegitimating various strands of feminist historical scholarship, than in examining radical feminist figurations of the witch to see what kinds of investment produced them.

Like other histories, then, though more egregiously than some, radical feminist histories of witches and witchcraft remember the past according to a variety of myths, ideas and political needs, and often they refer explicitly to the needs and desires which brought them into being. Equally often, however, radical feminist figurations of the witch, again like other histories, seek to erase the traces of their own historicity, in the interests of offering themselves as a means of access to a transparent, unmediated past. Gesturing away from its own immediate past and towards the stories it narrates, the radical feminist history of witches often appears to offer a static, finished vision of the witch. However, feminist histories of witchcraft are not finished artefacts, but stages in a complicated, conflictual series of processes within the public sphere, processes which involve both the writing of women's past and the rewriting of their present and future. Since all feminist histories offer to ask – and sometimes answer – the question 'What is a woman?', all feminist histories of witchcraft are caught up in contemporary questions of authority, authenticity and public politics.

Where the shaping power of those questions in determining radical feminist historical narratives is acknowledged, the acknowledgement often takes the form of a *refusal* of historicity, an insistence that the past must be mapped in a certain way because such a map still applies in and to the present. This tension between past and present is experienced in all feminist histories, but only radical feminism resolves it by denying the difference. Radical feminism offers its narrative not as a reconstruction of the past, but an account of the way things *always* are. This stance is ironically close to traditional humanist scholarship, with its insistence on eternal verities. It constitutes a challenge to the traditions of academic history not because of the explicitness of its political agenda, but – more importantly – because its ahistorical stance allows the complete overthrow of the rules of reading and interpreting evidence. Yet what is significant about these histories is not only unprofessional 'indiscipline', but the way this exposes the extent to which orthodox (male) history suppresses the emotions invested in it in favour of a discourse of objectivity. Radical feminist histories make more conventional historians uncomfortable because of their closeness to what we wish to hide.

Radical feminist history refuses the various positions of detachment which define the historian in a judging, criticising, evaluative relation to the traces of the past. It values highly emotional, involved, 'personal' pleasure and engagement: fear, hatred, love and solidarity are evoked. Emotion is evoked by the fact that the story told by this kind of feminist history is a story of *sameness*; conversely, it is produced as a story of sameness by the relentless repetition of figures of emotional identification.[7] This emotion is often figured as the eruption of 'feminine' values into the masculine terrain of history. The priority given to personal engagement with texts from the past also means a lack of interest in other 'rules' of evidence, especially rules about comprehensiveness and balance. For instance, male historians never tire of observing that radical feminist histories of witchcraft use almost no early modern texts as a source for views about witchcraft except the *Malleus Maleficarum*, refusing to undertake any demonstration of the centrality of the *Malleus*.[8] There are many reasons for this, but one reason is the *Malleus*'s ability to arouse strong feelings in the reader. Passages are quoted from it not for their centrality to witch-beliefs, but for their striking qualities, hence the more or less constant reiteration of the passage about the stolen *phalloi*, a belief rarely recorded elsewhere but striking as an illustration of rabid misogyny. Radical feminist historians are not deluded into thinking that the *Malleus* is central (although they do write as if it is); their criteria are those of the storyteller, in search of the most striking illustration or anecdote. In this sense, J.A. Sharpe's remark that 'it takes more than just a sense of indignation and a knowledge of the *Malleus*' misses the point.[9] As a feeling, and a feeling of identification, indignation is highly valued by radical feminist historians; that is *why* they like the *Malleus*. On the other hand, they do not value wide knowledge of trial records in manuscript and thus would not feel inspired by Sharpe's work. Sharpe assumes that everyone shares his sense of what is important, but radical feminist historians pose a direct and very aggressive challenge to his methodological assumptions.

All this is exemplified by Robin Morgan's well-known poem 'The Network of the Imaginary Mother'. Poems and fictional texts also offer historical narratives, narratives that are often more influential than those of professional historians, and narratives which often depend crucially on precisely the processes of identification and emotional investment which I have been discussing. Morgan's poem offers itself as a kind of litany or lament, a memorial process which willy-nilly involves the reader:

> Repeat the syllables
> before the lesson hemorrhages through the brain:
> Margaret Barclay, crushed to death with stones, 1618.
> Mary Midgeley, beaten to death, 1646.
> Peronette, seated on a hot iron as torture
> and then burned alive, 1462.
> Sister Maria Renata Sanger, sub-prioress
> of the Premonstratensian Convent of Unter-Zell,
> accused of being a lesbian;
> the document certifying her torture
> is inscribed with the seal of the Jesuits,
> and the words *Ad Majorem Dei Gloriam* –
> To the Greater Glory of God.
> What have they done to us?[10]

Beginning with an imperative verb means the poem can insist on the reader's participation. Thereafter, the emphasis is on directing the reader's eye to a memorial, a list of names, means of death, and dates. Such a list symbolises untold stories, lost persons: death or persecution reduces the individual person to a name, a death, a date. The poem borrows this tactic from memorials to more recent events (war memorials, Holocaust memorials), apparently oblivious of the fact that such memorials can afford the luxury of synecdoche and ellipsis because they were intended to *remind* those who already knew the names and stories. This tactic seems inappropriate for commemorating an atrocity which has been forgotten, yet it is part of Morgan's point that the dead witches have been buried in oblivion. However, the poem has to assume that the reader is ignorant of the names and events which it discloses, one who will not recognise the cunning woman Mary Midgeley, for example, or being crushed to death with stones as *peine forte et dure* rather than capital punishment.[11] Such recognitions trouble the central idea that these women are the same by drawing attention to signficant differences among them; to know these women is to reject Morgan's attempt to commemorate them. Paradoxically it is Morgan's use of the discourse of memorialisation that allows her to begin to present the witches as if they were a modern atrocity. This presentation is reinforced by the final line, 'What have they done to *us*?'; the whole poem has been about making it possible to say 'us', to invite – or rather bully – the reader into a group which contains dead witches as exemplars of oppression. This seems impertinent if you actually care about the women mentioned. In the face of a degree of fear and suffering which most of us cannot even imagine, a more humble and less eager identification might be advisable. Again, it is because we do not know or understand these stories as history that they can stand as tropes for the ahistoricity of history; that is, for a commonality of experience which a more exact feminist historicisation might deny.[12] That is, the witches can only represent all oppressed women if we know very little about them. The more witch-history the myth of the Burning Times attempts, the more damage it does to its own mythic status.

A similar lack of interest in specificity informs Mary Daly's *Gyn/Ecology.* Witchcraft persecution is enlisted alongside Chinese footbinding, Indian suttee, genital mutilation in the Arab world, American gynaecology and Mengele's medical experiments to illustrate Daly's thesis that patriarchy means the relentless persecution of women by physical torture. This agenda involves a great deal of conflation of cultures, but the figure of the witch is central to the narrative, owing to Daly's rewriting of the term hagiography as Hag-ography. Daly explicitly invokes the hag as a role model: 'our foresisters were the Great Hags whom the institutionally powerful but privately impotent patriarchs found too threatening for coexistence . . . For women who are on the journey of radical be-ing, the lives of the witches, of the Great Hags of hidden history are deeply intertwined with our own process. As we write/live in our own story, we are uncovering their history'. But our story *is* their story, it seems: 'crones are the survivors of the perpetual witchcraze of patriarchy, the survivors of the Burning Times' . The Burning Times 'is a crone-logical term which refers not only to the period of the European witchcraze but to the perpetual witchcraze which is the entire period of patriarchal rule'. A woman becomes a crone, Daly explains 'as a result of . . . having dis-covered depths of courage, strength and wisdom in her self'.[13] At this point, it becomes clear that Daly's narrative account of the Burning Times is less a presentation of external events than the story of an internal voyage, a metaphorical journey into the heart of patriarchal darkness.

In a way, this movement from history to psychology is a natural transition. For us, in the late twentieth century, all aspects of the supernatural have long since become naturalised as metaphors for inner states. We speak almost without consciousness of the metaphor of being bewitched, of diabolical difficulties, of looking hag-ridden, of being haunted by a memory or a dream. Our continuation of the internalisation process means that we are apt to interpret quite literal early modern narratives of the witch's activities as metaphors. Productions of *Macbeth* which present every supernatural incident in the play, from witches to ghosts, as figments of Macbeth's imagination or emanations of his consciousness both represent and reproduce the trend, performing their own psychoanalysis on the playtext and text of history, but unaware of their own historicity and its limitations. For Daly to speak of the hag within is to draw on what is only common sense, to us. At the same time, her retellling of witchcraft's story is also a shaman's journey to and from the land of the dead, a mystic's flight from the alone to the alone. Daly was not a student of comparative theology for nothing. What she has made of the history of witchcraft is a religious experience, an experience from which the reader emerges as a believer through empathy. For the modern feminist, reading Daly's account is above all a form of *suffering*, of learning through suffering about one's own suffering, of self-actualisation through historical narrative.[14]

In her entire narrative of the Burning Times, Daly mentions the names of only three witches. If Morgan's poem functions as a memorial, Daly's polemic functions as a blank monument, returning the focus of attention to the interior of the viewer. The one really sustained story of a particular accused woman deals with one Agnes; virtually all we are told of her by Daly are the details of her ordeal in the strappado. Daly tells us exactly what weights were used, but she is comprehensively uninterested in what Agnes said or did.[15] This silence is significant; in their incomprehensibility, their illegibility, words and stories tend to expose historical differences. Daly substitutes the single trope of the suffering body for such troublingly divisive texts. This helps to explain the very dangerous preoccupation with torture and execution in radical feminist narratives of witchcraft. Since we all have a body, and since we all fear pain and death, torture and execution create an illusion of common identity with a witch-suspect which might be shattered if Daly were to enlarge upon her life or quote her words. Like the ageing female body, the suffering female body can be used as a trope of timelessness which erases the specificity with which these experiences are mediated by social and discursive practices. Reading accounts of torture elicits empathy with the victim, but empathy differs from understanding, and even from registration of personhood, for which one may require the more difficult courage of confronting the existence of a *mind* different from one's own. One marker of cultural difference is that few of Daly's readers are likely to have experienced great pain, and fewer still will have experienced or seen pain administered in the interests of establishing truth; these lacks are bound to limit the extent to which bald accounts of who did what to whom allow us to share anything, even assuming that such sharing is desirable. Ironically, however, reducing Agnes to a tortured, voiceless body goes beyond even the interrogators in removing subjectivity from a woman, who becomes nothing but an instructive spectacle of violation and dismemberment, offering no opportunity to the reader who wants to know her.

Similarly, Elisabeth Brooke purports to be dealing with the trauma of the Burning Times by staging it as the return of a repressed or buried memory. Brooke recounts what she saw in a meditation on the Burning Times:

> I remember, how I remember, the smell of burning flesh, the hair catching alight, the awful awful agony of your feet slowly burning up. I remember the jeers of the men who watched, and the frozen dread of the women and children who were forced to watch my ending.[16]

History indeed becomes hystery when the unspeaking body is the only site which can be recollected, and when events become reduced to occasions for extended fantasies about other people's traumas. One must ask, too, what kinds of fears and fantasies are being displaced into this narrative; is there a covert pleasure in imagining the dissolution of the body, the loss of the self? Is there an anxious pleasure in the undeniable absoluteness of pain? Is there pleasure in becoming an innocent object of horror? The burning body is offered as proof positive of an oppression that might sometimes seem too subtle to confront. Yet its ontological status could not be more dubious, since it forms part of a fictional reconstruction of history in meditation. Unconsciously Brooke, like Morgan, is relying on twentieth-century respect for the discourses of testimony and personal recollection.

The myth of the Burning Times was invented at the point when the women's movement began to turn away from rights-centred public-sphere issues towards crime-centred, private-sphere issues. Domestic and sexual violence against women were foregrounded as the representative crimes of patriarchy, to the exclusion of other issues. Sexuality was to be identified as the site of women's oppression in the sense that property was for Marx the site of class oppression. Rape, sexual violence, pornography, wife-battering and (eventually) child sexual abuse became the central signifiers of patriarchy, replacing signifiers such as legal asymmetries and pay differentials. These trends were influential inside as well as outside the academy. Writers like Susan Brownmiller and Andrea Dworkin represented patriarchy's continued existence as the consequence of systematic sexualised violence against women, which in turn was the result of a fear of female sexuality. Dworkin uses both the image of the demonised witch-stepmother of fairy tales and the figure of the persecuted witch-victim of the Burning Times as figures for the suffering woman-victim of pornography and rape.[17] Similarly, Daly's witch-narrative conflates the persecution of witches with these notions of patriarchy so that the witch can become a synecdoche of female victims of sexualised violence.

Ironically, the seductiveness of the witch's place as ultimate victim is that the learned world had always sided with her against her oppressors. From Reginald Scot's alignment of witch-beliefs with ignorant peasants, to Arthur Miller's representation of the victims of House Committee for Un-American Activities via the Salem witch-trials, the witch-craze has been a synonym for pointless persecution. Far from revealing a narrative long lost by patriarchal history, radical feminists were plodding along in the footsteps of every liberal from the Romantics onwards who deplored witch-hunting as a sign of barbarity. The witch's status as victim of prejudice and superstition could be enlisted to portray feminism as enlightened. As well, the witch became crucial to the effort to make men and especially women *believe* in women's oppression, always a daunting task. 'It would be unthinkable' remarks Daly, 'for scholars to refer to Jewish pogroms or to lynchings of blacks as therapeutic'.[18] Pogroms, lynchings and above all the Holocaust do make it more difficult (though *not* impossible) to deny the very existence of racism and ethnocentrism. The Burning Times myth offers to play the same role in women's history, to authorise the need for struggle and authenticate the forms that struggle takes.

Daly lists a number of institutions responsible for the witch-craze: the Catholic church, the Inquisition; lawyers; Protestants; print culture; the professions keen to squeeze out women healers; psychiatrists; judges; but above all, male scholars and academics. Despite her own heavy reliance on male-authored secondary sources throughout her narrative, Daly argues that

> Hags are re-membering and therefore understanding not only the intent of the Sado-State – the torture, dismemberment and murder of deviant women – but also the fact that this intent is justified and shared by scholars and other professional perpetrators of the state.[19]

What becomes clear is that for Daly certain kinds of silence are the same as murder; she does not accuse male historians of ignoring witches, but of failing to attack the institutions which she sees as causing the witch-hunts. The conflation of recalcitrant male scholars with the witch-persecutors allows Daly another mode of self-referentiality: her own text can be equated with Hags and Crones, those who take on patriarchy and live to tell the tale. In this way, Daly casts herself as a witch, ensuring that anyone who disagrees with her can be cast as an inquisitor.

More importantly, however, the visceral clutch aroused by the descriptions of torture and burnings can be put to the service of accepting Daly's narrative of an ahistorical patriarchal conspiracy. Characteristically enough, Daly presents her readers with a stark choice between accepting her views and being equated with the forces of darkness. Daly irresistibly recalls the religious fundamentalists she criticises, a point made cruelly clear by Meaghan Morris's account of Daly's self-presentation, 'A-mazing Grace'.[20] In treating the Burning Times as an enabling myth, a narrative of inner discovery, Daly transforms the women's movement into a narrative of self-discovery where the point is to acquire a repertoire of knowledges which allow the believer to recognise her friends or foes. Daly's notorious intolerance of women not classed as Hags – often stigmatised by her as 'fembots' (female robots) – ironically reduplicates a rigid structure of 'acceptable' behaviour for women. Daly wants us to see her as the embodiment of the Hag, but sometimes she sounds more like Kramer and Sprenger.

Daly is able to enforce this system of discipline because of the use she makes of the myth of the Burning Times. Just as the government of Israel has been able to produce a certain kind of Holocaust memorialisation which authenticates its own militarism, so Daly is able to use figurations of the torture and execution of witches to underpin her own ideas.[21] I use this analogy advisedly, for the images and rhetoric of Holocaust history haunt Daly's text. I have already noted Daly's regret that pogroms are taken more seriously than witch-burnings; she replaces the term 'genocide' with the neologism 'gynocide', a term which at once covers over and gestures at what it replaces; she argues that gynocide provides a model for genocide because of its logic of cleansing; she refers many times to 'millions of women' as victims of witch-hunting; absurdly, she equates bad reviews for feminist books with Nazi book-burnings; and she attempts to link the murderous activities of Joseph Mengele with witch-persecutions.[22] Holocaust discourses of testimony, recollection and traumatic inarticulacy are borrowed unreflectively by Daly, Dworkin and their disciples. Attempts to inflate the number of women who died in witch-persecutions into the millions may also reflect the Holocaust paradigm, since there is little actual evidence for such figures.[23] Worryingly, this goes two million better than the Holocaust, as if a competition is afoot, and at times there does seem to be a race on to prove that women have suffered more than victims of racism or genocide (as though women have not been *among* the victims of racism and genocide). Finally, the very stress on *burning* itself seems to allude to the crematoria, although it may also point to Dresden and Hiroshima. Radical feminist witches *always* burn; they are never hanged.

What this shows is that the narrative of the Holocaust has become the paradigmatic narrative for understanding atrocity in the late twentieth century. However, in being transformed into a blueprint for comprehending large-scale violence, the Holocaust's specificity is lost, as is the specificity of whatever it is used to understand. Moreover, the Holocaust has not made the narrative of atrocity simpler. Such narratives have been shown by serious historians of the Holocaust to be deeply problematic, raising acute difficulties about who has the right to speak about what on behalf of whom, and difficulties about who can possibly be fit to listen. Writers on the Holocaust like Primo Levi, with their sensitive and exact sense of humility in the sight of the dead and of the agonising inadequacy and dire necessity of any possible representation, are light-years away from the arrogant assumption of Daly and Dworkin that they can speak for dead witches. Radical feminist history is also distant from the poststructuralist theorists' recognition of the inadequacy of any textuality in the face of such an event.[24] Moreover, the narratives of the Holocaust have proved depressingly vulnerable to the claims of those who would deny the very existence of such an event in order to serve their own racist and fascist agendas, so that even if it were ethical to steal the language, it might not be practical to do so.[25] Finally, Daly seems unaware that the Holocaust itself bore more heavily upon women, who were much less likely to be selected for work and hence survival than young men, and who were gassed automatically if pregnant or nursing an infant. In this context, Daly's wish to manufacture a Holocaust of one's own seems both morally dubious and politically naive. Not only does it elide the specificity of *both* Holocaust and witch-persecution, thus silencing those who suffered either in a new way, it also constructs a narrative which is notably unhelpful to women.

The myth of the Burning Times is not politically helpful. It might seriously be doubted whether a myth that portrays women as nothing but the helpless victims of patriarchy, and the female body as nothing but a site of torture and death is enabling, especially if these portrayals are taken to define what woman under patriarchy is, for all time. The ahistorical character of the myth of the Burning

Times is alarming: Daly wants women to be Hags, but she also wants to say that what happened to Hags once is happening to them again. Indeed, one way of recognising Hags – defining their identity – is by persecution. Another way to read the ahistoricity of the Burning Times myth, however, is to see it as an attempt to lend dignity to kinds of oppression which are usually too 'trivial' to register as problems. Likening bad reviews to book-burning or witch-burning is a plea to be taken seriously, and also a way of comforting oneself with the grandeur of fantasy, as children comfort themselves by imagining the headmistress as a fire-breathing dragon. Seeing yourself as eternally oppressed is not really liberating unless you are also presented with some inkling of a solution. Telling women that they must be Hags and also that Hags are doomed to suffer since the dawn of recorded history is not encouraging. The solutions Daly postulates are psychological and internal, rather than public and political; to become a Hag is to survive the experience of learning or reading about the Burning Times and acknowledging one's own pain and fear.

Starhawk, perhaps the best-known modern witch, makes much more explicitly political use of the Burning Times myth in her book *Dreaming the Dark*, which urges disarmament, sexual liberation and Green activism. Designed to help modern witches think about the relations between activism and ritual, it emphasises the (public) effect of ritual, drawing attention to a women's spiral dance in prison, for example. Admittedly, the book is ultimately more interested in interior tranquillity than in political nous, but the emphasis does inflect Starhawk's account of the Burning Times, though it retains much in common with Brooke's. It begins with a fictionalisation in which an (early modern) witch meditates on her likely fate:

> The thought of the church makes her shiver; she remembers her dream of the night before – the paper pinned to the church door. The proclamation of a witch-hunt? She passes her hand over her eyes. These days, the Sight is a trouble; her dreams are haunted by the faces of women in torment . . . Some have said that the Old Race still lives in the forest's hidden center. Would they shelter her? . . . And would they someday swarm out from the woods and wastes, an army of the dispossessed, to tear down the fences of the overlords, the manor houses and the churches, to reclaim their own land for freedom?[26]

The figure of recollection is dominant again; the story is told from one woman's point of view, and she is a repository of dreams of the Burning Times. However, Starhawk, who is Jewish, avoids the problematic discourse of testimony deployed so carelessly by Brooke. There is still too much emphasis on torture and pain.[27] However, there is also an unusual and enabling emphasis on a fantasy of rebellion, especially in relation to ownership of land. This trace of rebellion makes something rather different of the ahistoricity of the entire narrative in the context of Starhawk's investment in red-green and pacifist politics. An escape can be envisaged from the Burning Times, an escape into power rather than away from it; thus the repetitiousness of the Burning Times narrative, relayed through suffering women, can be ruptured. A change of direction can at least be imagined. Heartening as this is, it deals only with the problem of the Burning Times as myth. Like the other writers discussed here, Starhawk is also posing a challenge to conventional history, partly by introducing into it a self-consciously fictional reconstruction of interiority.

What of the victim of this endless cycle of patriarchal violence? In the story with which I began this chapter, she is the impossibly innocent, exceptionally knowing midwife-healer, and she derives from Barbara Eherenreich and Deirdre English's influential pamphlet on women healers.[28] Ehrenreich and English argued that the witch-craze was caused by the attempt on the part of rising male medical professionals to take over and control the regulation of women's bodies. In order to do this, doctors removed the women healers and midwives on whom the community had previously relied. These guardians of the female body therefore found themselves accused of witchcraft by those who wished to wrest control of that body from them. Using a different model of essential femininity, not as silent victim or wild Hag but as gentle, maternal, close to the earth, Ehrenreich and English added to the fantasy of the Burning Times by creating an utterly innocent victim. She was us as we should have been; she was the perfect nurturing mother that we were not, the useful woman who cared nothing for orthodox power, but who had at her disposal awesome knowledge. Above all, she is free, free of church, state, men, and the unlawful wishes for power and money which they might wickedly inspire.

Ehrenreich and English's pamphlet is light on evidence.[29] However, unlike Daly, Ehrenreich and English do not offer their work as a challenge to the patriarchal norms of history as a practice, but only to its domination by men and male agendas. They are really challenging another body of professional expertise altogether, the expertise of the medical profession, especially in relation to gender-specific issues, and some at least of their appeal rests on women's assent to the proposition that Western medicine has damaged women. Once this proposition is agreed, imagining an alternative becomes seductive. As well, the figure of the healer-witch reflects assumptions about the Middle Ages: the midwife-herbalist-healer-witch seems a spectacular collage of everything which feminist historians and others see as the opposite of medieval patriarchy, and in this way she has come to subtend a certain notion of what patriarchy is. Barbara G. Walker, for example, writes:

> The real reason for ecclesiastical hostility [to midwives] seems to have been the notion that midwives could help women control their own fate, learn secrets of sex and birth control, or procure abortions. The pagan women of antiquity had considerable knowledge of such matters, which were considered women's own business, and not subject to male authority.[30]

Here the midwife simply is the female sexual autonomy which the church cannot tolerate. There is no need to cite evidence showing that midwives were great purveyors of birth control or abortifacients to women; the myth thrives not on evidence but on a sense of likelihood deriving from *twentieth*-century political struggles. Reproductive rights, central to the myth of the healer-witch, came to the fore as a central organising principle of the women's movement in the mid-1970s, about the time when Ehrenreich and English's pamphlet was published.[31] Like Daly's work, this story is shaped by specific political realities.

Thus the healer-witch, too, is a fantasy grounded in present-day social reality; here is Starhawk's version:

> The old woman carries a basket of herbs and roots she has dug; it feels heavy as time on her arm. Her feet on the path are her mother's feet, her grandmother's, her grandmother's grandmothers'; for centuries, she has walked under these oaks and pines, culled the herbs and brought them back to dry under the eaves of her cottage on the common. Always, the people of the village have come to her; her hands are healing hands, they can turn a child in the womb; her murmuring voice can charm away pain, can croon the restless to sleep.[32]

Starhawk evokes an unchanging identity ('Her feet on the path . . .') in an unchanging world; the ideal antidote to the fragmented postmodern self. The figure of herbs and herb lore is central to this portrayal. It stands both for agriculture and for untamed nature, both of which are familiar to the old woman. It also stands for professionalism and professional knowledge, as do the woman's midwifery skills; and for domestic labour: gardening, cooking, nursing. The herbalist-witch represents a fantasy of a profession which blends into rather than conflicting with the ideology of femininity constructed for and in the domestic sphere; more simply, it expresses a fantasy in which domestic skills are valued in the community as if they were professional skills. There is more than a passing resemblance between the witch-herbalist and the fantasy superwoman heroine of the 1980s and 90s, professional women who have beautiful country gardens, bake their own bread, make their own quilts, and demonstrate sexuality at every turn. The same kind of fantasy recurs in 'The Green Woman', a short story by Meghan B. Collins:

> Sunshine coming through the open door cast a bright square on the floor planks, and dust motes quivered in falling rays like a veil of light. Tiny points of light twinkled from the shelves of crocks and jars; otherwise the room was shadowy and cool, with a tang in the air from bunches of dried plants hanging among the rafters.[33]

We might be looking at a photo in *Country Living*, but this is the cottage of the eponymous Green Woman, a healer-witch. Similarly Claire Nahmad's *Earth Magic: A Wisewoman's Guide to Herbal, Astrological and Folk Remedies* purports to be drawn from 'the ancient wisewoman's tradition, a tradition which reaches back many centuries to a time when . . . practitioners of healing and herbalism understood the earth'. This lore, the book explains, 'has been passed down in the oral tradition of womenfolk for generation after generation', despite 'the persecution of women during the witch-hunts of sixteenth-century

Europe'.[34] The guide itself, however, recalls manuals of advice on country style and decorating, as well as lifestyle publications like *The Country Diary of an Edwardian Lady*. All these texts appeal to the urban fantasy of a country life and lifestyle that is timeless, unchanging, stable and somehow 'natural'; this opposes the postmodern city.[35] The figure of the healer-witch allows this lifestyle to become the subject of pleasurable reverie, owing much to Romantic notions of the simple life. To an English eye, these discourses seem uncomfortably close to the conservative and even reactionary 'Heritage' culture of thatched cottages, country churches, and spinsters on bicycles. There is also something worryingly *Völkisch* about the insistent valorisation of the happy rural peasant at the expense of the city-dweller. The lifestyle associated with the healer-witch is increasingly subject to commercialisation, not only through the heritage industry itself, but also through the vast array of goods presented as traditional, antique, natural, or rural. Country cottages, whether inhabited by weekenders or commuters, are increasingly associated with middle-class incomes and lifestyles.[36] Regardless of the author's intention, the myth of the healer-witch meshes so easily with the traditional discourses of country life that it has become an expression of aspiration. Such figurations are problematic because they substitute often unattainable fantasy for the resolution of women's problems.

If such trends help to explain the construction of the witch as herbalist, the witch as midwife needs analysis. It is true that *Malleus Malificarum* specifically singles out midwives for attack, but otherwise there is little evidence that midwives were the prime objects of the persecutions in every country. As Stephen Greenblatt remarked tartly, we tend to see as subversive in the early modern period whatever is normative in our own, and to see early modern orthodoxy as whatever would be aberrant in the modern world.[37] Consequently, the 'subversiveness' of the midwife-witch is grounded in our belief that there is something automatically radical about a woman with control over the bodies of other women, since we equate that control with sexual knowledge and autonomy. However, the power of early modern midwives could be part of the power of church and state to *regulate* women's bodies and sexuality. The midwives who searched for witchmarks, or who determined whether a convicted woman was pregnant and might thus be granted a stay of execution, were certainly demonstrating knowledge of women's bodies, but they were doing so at the behest of state power. Church and state were not disconcerted by using this expertise. This challenges the usefulness of a myth which insists that women's knowledge of the body *automatically* subverts gender hierarchies.

How useful is the myth of the healer-witch as a feminist fantasy? While it offers nostalgic pleasures to anxious urban residents, and a way in fantasy to reconcile the conflicting demands of public and domestic spheres, this fantasy does have disadvantages. Precisely because the fantasy depends on an opposition between the modern urban world and the countryside of the past, it cannot serve as a blueprint for action. It cannot inspire ways to resolve the conflict between the domestic and the public, or offer ways for society truly to appreciate household labour. The fantasy also contains elements which reflect uncritically patriarchal notions of appropriate feminine behaviour. Starhawk's witch-herbalist is afraid of being prosecuted, but decides not to flee to the forest because 'young Jonet at the mill is near her time, and the old woman knows it will be a difficult birth'.[38] In turning the witch into a secular martyr, Starhawk reinforces the notion that women must sacrifice themselves for others. The roles of the herbalist-midwife-witch are traditional feminine roles: nursing, healing, caring for women and children. They are roles which centre on domestic space and activity, especially activities derived from women's traditional roles as homemakers, such as the provision of herbal remedies, flower-gardening and so forth. Many of these skills are represented as either innate or matrilineally inherited, as 'natural' rather than learned. The villagers say Starhawk's witch has healing hands. These figurations of innate power essentialise the witch's art, so that healing and midwifery are presented as innately feminine skills. This subtends the notion that these qualities are somehow natural to women, especially since healer-witches are never men.

The myth of the Burning Times can be traced in the writings of women who would not necessarily identify themselves as radical feminists, including some writers who predate radical feminism. While some of these are clearly based on radical feminist histories, others suggest the wider dissemination of those ideas. Some poems treat radical and other early feminist histories as 'found poems'; Anne Cameron copies out bits of Barbara G. Walker's *Women's Encyclopedia of Myths and Secrets* and arranges them as a poem called 'Witch'. She gives it 'relevance' by adding some lines about little girls being encouraged to be quiet and submissive. The juxtaposition of this observation with the lynching of the witch of Newbury is meant to suggest equivalence, but actually draws attention to the oddity of equating being made to play quietly with dolls to being beaten to death.[39] Characteristically, women writers have seen in the witch a figure of all that women could be were it not for patriarchy. In Sylvia Townsend Warner's novel *Lolly Willowes*, Lolly is a shy spinster-aunt, disregarded by the women of her family. But when she buys a cottage in the Chilterns, Lolly discovers that everyone in the village regards her as a witch, and from this comes a new, and much more powerful identity. To be recognised as a witch is to be recognised as free and independent.[40] In a much more complex and anxious way, Sara Maitland's story 'The Burning Times' dramatises the witch as a figure of all that women want to be. The story is narrated by the daughter of a woman denounced as a witch and burned, and it gradually emerges that it is the narrator herself who has given evidence against her mother. The narrator is self-oppressed. Mother of sons who disregard her and wife to a bullying husband, she dwells constantly on the image of her powerful and confident mother, who ran her own lacemaking business, while engaging in a voluptously detailed lesbian affair with another strong woman called Margaret. It is her mother's lesbian sexuality and her own unrecognised desire for Margaret that lead the narrator to denounce her mother, but plainly this daughter envies her mother at every possible level. Though the reader is encouraged to identify with the mother against the jealous daughter, the story also mobilises our fears that we may be the 'good' cowardly woman and not the confident 'witch'. Though the reader's negotiation of these categories is unstable, the categories themselves are rigidly absolute; there is nothing strong about the daughter and nothing weak about the witch-mother. The witch as martyr emerges as a signifier that resolves the conflict the story establishes by allowing the reader to absolve herself of guilt for being a wimp; we would all be strong, the story implies, were it not for the Inquisitors and fembots who dog our footsteps, making us fearful of our own sexuality.[41]

In Anne Sexton's poem, 'Her Kind', Sexton claims kinship with the witch as desirable version of the self. This was the poem which Sexton used to define her public identity as poet, beginning her readings with it: 'I have gone out, a possessed witch / haunting the black air . . . A woman like that is not a woman, quite / I have been her kind'. Sexton's witch is not fully incorporated into the social category 'woman'; she represents a kind of Kristevan negativity, a 'that's not it' and 'that's still not it'. But Sexton is also attracted by the spectacle of suffering woman; the last stanza of the poem describes the witch burning in a kind of ecstasy of death and pain: 'survivor / where your flames still bite my thigh . . . A woman like that is not ashamed to die'.[42] This association of woman with erotic burning and death also figures in Sylvia Plath's work. Though Plath chose to use the Holocaust and Hiroshima as her central myths of burning, her juvenilia contains a poem which shows her experimenting with this alternative figure of female suffering.[43] Later, however, Plath followed Sexton in writing 'Witch Burning', which dwells on the sensuousness of being burned in a manner which looks forward to 'Fever 103°': 'My ankles brighten. Brightness ascends my thighs'. For both Plath and Sexton, only fire can affirm the sexuality of the female body; being burned is a metaphor for a caress that accepts the body's responsiveness, and pain a symbol of passion.[44] The title of Plath's 'Three Women' alludes to the Weird Sisters of *Macbeth* as well as the Fates and the Furies. Like others informed by psychoanalysis, Plath uses the witch as a figure of the mother, since the poem concerns three women, a mother, woman miscarrying, and a woman giving birth but abandoning her baby.[45] Ironically, it is Ted Hughes who understands the witch in ways much closer to the ideas of Mary Daly in his poem 'Witches': 'Once was every woman the witch / To ride a weed the ragwort road / Devil to do whatever she would'. Hughes, full of touchingly *passé* tough-guy talk, makes this an occasion for near-comical male fear: 'Bitches still sulk, rosebuds blow / And we are devilled. And though these weep / Over our harms, who's to know Where their feet dance while their heads sleep?'[46] Hughes's poem makes gratifying reading for any woman who wants to see the witch as the ultimate threat to patriarchy, except that Hughes fully subscribes to the fantasy. Although the poem is terrified of what women may be doing 'while their heads sleep', it also yearns to see them at their secret rites to know what they are up to when beyond male control. This is the kind of poem one might expect from Hughes, who later brought us the full-scale Robert Graves old sow myth of material femininity in *Shakespeare and the Goddess of Complete Being*.[47] Hughes's fantasy fits perfectly with Sara Maitland's, who thinks that 'women fly when men aren't watching'. It is only that Hughes would love to watch.

Caryl Churchill's well-known play *Vinegar Tom* tells a different story. This play understands witchcraft as shaped by class as well as gender, a notion missing from the more glamorous accounts of witchcraft in a cottage. The witches are persecuted because they are old and poor, like their female persecutors.[48] The play dramatises the events surrounding one of the Matthew Hopkins trials – Vinegar Tom was the name of one of the witch's familiars – but despite the oddity of those trials in an English context, the play goes to enormous lengths to make them typify patriarchy. Churchill uses the same sources as other feminist myths of the witch, including the *Malleus Malificarum*, given prominence by the appearance of Kramer and Sprenger, a kind of music-hall double-act who chant patriarchal slogans. Churchill understands the witch as the residue or result of the witch-hunting process. Whereas for Daly and Maitland the witch is always already there, for Churchill the witch is a patriarchal construction in the sense that it is oppression that makes women rebel. As one of the accused, Alice, goes to her death, she announces 'I'm not a witch. But I wish I was . . . oh, if I could meet with the Devil now I'd give him anything if he could give me power. There's no way for us except by the Devil.' It is this construction which allows the witch to become a significant myth for the women in the audience: 'Look in the mirror tonight. Would they have hanged you then? Ask how they're stopping you now. Where have the witches gone? Who are the witches now? Ask how they're stopping you now. Here we are.' 'We' is the women in the audience; the final song makes explicit the (imagined) political usefulness of the myth of the Burning Times; it makes women's oppression visible. Now we can see what is stopping us. The identification with the witch has become total, and flattering. 'We' are the ones who would have been hanged. 'We' are not the ones who did the accusing or hanging.

Elaine Feinstein's 'Song of Power' juxtaposes the figure of the witch with two other figures of victimisation. The first is her child, bullied by other children who call her a witch, the child who 'cannot be guarded / Against enemies'; the second is the Jew, whose difference led to a different fire. The speaker's magical invocation asks that 'the strange ones' learn to 'make their own coherence / A fire their children / ay learn to bear at last and not burn in'.[49] Like other writers, Feinstein understands the figure of the witch as the difference society punishes by ostracism. Feinstein's speaker has to be a witch to find a way to speak with power for all strangers. Yet the poem also has to understand the witch-figure as 'false' to make fear of strangeness seem irrational. More than the others, this text eschews the myth of the Burning Times for straightforward liberal denuciations of mass hysteria and intolerance as found in, say, Arthur Miller's *The Crucible*. The poem wants to find a way to keep strangeness and find tolerance for it without having to risk martyrdom. The figure of the Jew, gestured at when Feinstein invokes the Jewish God approving her witch-invocation, may be what prevents the poem from investment in simplistic discourses of witches as martyrs. Rather than using the Jew as an image of women's oppression, Feinstein gestures at a range of incompatible, more or less dangerous but necessary identities which cannot simply be metaphors for one another because their organisation as simply Other is itself part of the problem.

Other writers look at the figure of the witch otherwise, focusing not on her annihilation, but on the image of the woman healer in tune with body and nature. The healer surfaces especially in images of childbirth, where the relations between body and person, and between activity and passivity, nature and culture, can seem sharpest and most important. Continuing in a tradition begun by Adrienne Rich, women writers began to revalue what Rich called 'the filthy peasant crone', the midwife, as a sister, a woman in touch with the earth and with the natural.[50] In 'Little Red Riding Hood' Olga Broumos contrasts the powers of the healer–midwife to guide the baby's head with her hand to the cruelty of forceps which 'cramp me between the temples'. The daughter goes 'straight from your hollowed basket into the midwife's skirts'.[51] In Elizabeth Baines's *The Birth Machine*, Zelda's break with acceptance and into rebellious noise during labour is understood through the image of the witch: 'she can make them flinch back, hold them off from her own magic circle'. This becomes possible for Zelda after a vision of her old schoolfriend Hilary, with whom she used to play games of witchcraft. Recovering her witch-self enables her to survive the birth and to escape the hospital with her child.[52] Sometimes the midwife-witch is found within. In Toi Derricote's poem the pain itself is a powerful goddess-witch: 'the light shines through to her goatness, her blood-thick heart that thuds like one drum in the universe emptying its stars'.[53] Plath's woman, too, becomes her own rescuer: 'a power is growing on me, an old tenacity'. 'I get high on birth stories' sighs Ger Duffy, 'the importance of it'.[54] The witch in the birthing-room aptly represents that sense of importance.

Ger Duffy's poem is also about her abortion. Sara Maitland offers an alternative vision of the healer-witch in 'Angel Maker', a rewriting of 'Hansel and Gretel' in which Gretel approaches the witch, who is also part of herself, for an abortion.[55] Likewise, Meghan Collins's Green Woman also provides abortions: 'It is true they come to me sometimes, young girls half crazy with fear, or exhausted young wives with a child in the cradle and one on the floor.'[56] The healer-witch is someone to turn to as well as an image of how to be. She is the ideal mother, the one who protects and accepts the daughter's sexuality, dissolving guilt by providing an abortion in a context of naturalness and sheltering love. But the witch-healer can also be the sign of more ambivalent feelings about motherhood. Margaret Atwood's healer-figure in 'The Healer' is self-deprecating rather than self-confident, recalling all devaluations of women's work: 'Perhaps it was only a small talent, this tinkering with the small breaks and fissures in other bodies'.[57] The healer compares her talent with the sunlight spilling out of flowers, 'unasked for and unused'. Like the small routines of childcare, the work of healing is not persecuted in Atwood's vision, but it is not much regarded either. Atwood refuses the vision of healing as a 'answer' to patriarchal disregard for femininity. Fay Weldon also invokes the figure of the close-to-nature crone in connection with pregnancy in *Puffball*. Here, however, the crone is genuinely wicked rather than benign. Liffey, the protagonist, almost bleeds to death after Mabs, the witch, has refused to take her to hospital. Weldon is openly scornful of the natural witch, representing her as backward and spiteful. In her representation of Mabs as a threat to Liffey's pregnancy, Weldon replicates the kinds of stories early modern women themselves told about witches. Her novel illustrates the diversity and the unity of the writings I have been discussing.[58] Although each woman interprets the figure of the witch differently, exploiting her plasiticity, all these writers are limited by the narrow meanings of the witch in the myth outlined here. All reproduce something of the myth, even if they do so negatively.

What does all this tell us about gender and history? The radical feminist creation of the myth of the Burning Times is difficult to analyse and discuss because it has become such a key part of many feminists' identities that to point to its limitations is bound to be painful and divisive. The myth reminds all of us that we want to find ourselves in the past, that we scan the past looking for confirmation of who we are, who we want to be. We search for something to aim for, and something to aim against. We look for stories about our own journeys, battles, passions. We search for real women, women as real as ourselves, perhaps more real than we can manage to be. Such longings may not be legitimate, but they are unavoidable; even the most boring high political history cannot escape a constricting vision of 'human nature' which points to the world of donnish infighting as much as to the world of Tudor faction government. Yet the illegitimacy of such narcissism is also painfully visible in radical feminists' attempt to make witches seem real by focusing on the essential stuff of the body in pain rather than the more difficult matter of their words. It is visible in the way the myth of the Burning Times covers over historical specificity in its eagerness to unite women, and in the coerciveness of the myth thus created. Worst of all, there are the questions of the theft of the rhetorics of atrocity this century, and their deployment to support an identity as Most Persecuted and Innocent Victim. These thefts show how far narcissism can go in clouding the past to make a mirror for the endlessly uncertain present. In thus helping ourselves, we are silencing early modern women anew. We are also denying ourselves the chance to hear historical differences which might show us just how different things could be, how fragile the assumptions which make us suffer now might seem to our descendants. If the past is different, the future can be.

NOTES

1 Recent historical restatements include Marianne Hester, *Lewd Women and Wicked Witches*, London: Routledge, 1992; Anne Llewellyn Barstow, *Witchcraze: A New History of the European Witch Hunts*, New York: HarperCollins, 1994; and Uta Ranke-Heinemann, *Eunuchs of the Kingdom of Heaven: The Catholic Church and Sexuality*, trans. Peter Heinegg, Hanmondsworth: Penguin, 1990. Recent polemical usages include Joan Smith, 'Patum Peperium' in *Misogynies*, London: Faber, 1989, pp. 55ff. I discuss literary uses below.

2 Merry E. Wiesner, *Women and Gender in Early Modern Europe*, Cambridge: Cambridge University Press, 1993; David Harley, 'Historians as demonologists: the myth of the midwife witch', *Journal of the Society for the Social History of Medicine*, 3 (1990), pp. 1–26; Richard Kieckhefer, *Magic in the Middle Ages*, Cambridge: Cambridge University Press, 1990; Gustav Henningsen, *The Witches' Advocate: Basque Witchcraft and the Spanish Inquisition, 1609–1614,* Reno: University of Nevada Press, 1980; Susanna Burghartz, 'The equation of women and witches: a case study of witchcraft trials in Lucerne and Lausanne in the fifteenth and sixteenth centuries', in *The German Underworld: Deviants and Outcasts in German History*, ed. Richard Evans, London: Routledge, 1988, pp. 57–74.

3 I use the terms radical feminism and early feminism in this chapter to denote a moment in the history of the women's liberation movement which occurred roughly in the 1970s; its hallmarks were or are the thesis that sex is the basis of women's oppression as work is the basis of the proletariat's oppression, separatism, 'difference' feminism, usually accompanied by the belief that women's values were superior to men's, an often desexualised political lesbianism, and a hard-line critique of pornography ('porn is the theory, rape is the practice'). Inevitably this is a caricature. At the same time, it is important to note that this movement influenced even those academic feminists now most eager to point to their differences from it.

4 WITCH, 'Spooking the patriarchy', in *The Politics of Women's Spirituality: Essays on the Rise of Spiritual Power within the Feminist Movement*, ed. Charlene Spretnak, New York: Doubleday, 1982, p. 76.

5 Joan Scott, 'Women's history', in *New Perspectives on Historical Writing*, ed. Peter Burke, Cambridge: Polity, 1991, pp. 42–66.

6 Michael Stanford, *A Companion to the Study of History*, Oxford: Blackwell, 1994, pp. 133–65; Geoffrey Elton, *Return to Essentials: Some Reflections on the Present State of Historical Study*, Cambridge: Cambridge University Press, 1991.

7 On identification see Keith Jenkins, *Rethinking History*, London: Routledge, 1991, pp. 39–47.

8 A difficult task in actuality, since recent research suggests that the importance of this text has been grossly overstated; see Sydney Anglo, 'Evident authority and authoritative evidence: the *Malleus Maleficarum',* in *The Damned Art: Essays in the Literature of Witchcraft*, London: Routledge & Kegan Paul, 1977.

9 'Witchcraft and women in seventeenth-century England: some northern evidence', *Continuity and Change*, 6 (1991), p. 180.

10 Robin Morgan, 'The Network of the Imaginary Mother', in *Lady of the Beasts*, cited by Mary Daly, *Gyn/Ecology*, London: Women's Press, 1979, p. 179.

11 Mary Midgeley: *Depositions from York Castle*, ed. James Raine, Surtees Society, vol. 40 (1860), pp. 8–9. Ironically, Midgeley was actually a local unwitcher. Her remedies for supernatural illnesses included placing a sickle under sick cows. On *peine forte et dure*, a punishment to force the prisoner to plead guilty or not guilty so that she or he could be tried by a jury, see John H. Langbein, *Torture and the Law of Proof: Europe and England in the Ancien Régime*, Chicago: University of Chicago Press, 1977.

12 The work of feminist historians like Lyndal Roper, Annabel Gregory and Miranda Chaytor is precisely about recovering the specificity of women's stories.
13 Daly, *Gyn/Ecology*, pp. 14–15, 16.
14 For similar emphases see E. J. Burford and Sandra Shulman, *Of Bridles and Burnings: The Punishment of Women*, London: Robert Hale, 1992; and Starhawk (Miriam Simos), *The Spiral Dance: A Rebirth of the Ancient Religion of the Great Goddess*, San Francisco: Harper, 1988, p. 20, first published 1979.
15 Daly, *Gyn/Ecology*, p. 181, and see pp. 190 and 214.
16 Elisabeth Brooke, *A Woman's Book of Shadows: Witchcraft: A Celebration*, London: Women's Press, 1993, p. 46.
17 Andrea Dworkin, *Woman-Hating*, New York: Dutton, 1974, pp. 34–46, 118–50.
18 Daly, *Gyn/Ecology*, pp. 185.
19 Daly, *Gyn/Ecology*, pp. 185.
20 Meaghan Morris, 'A-mazing Grace', in *The Pirate's Fiancée*, London: Verso, 1988.
21 On the memorialisation of the Holocaust, especially in Israel, see James E. Young, *The Texture of Memory: Holocaust Memorials and Meaning*, New Haven: Yale University Press, 1993, chs 8–10.
22 Daly, *Gyn/Ecology*, pp. 196, 208, 217, 298, 306.
23 Brooke, *A Woman's Book*, pp. 46, 50; Starhawk, *Dreaming the Dark: Magic, Sex and Politics*, London: Mandala, 1990, p. 187, first published 1982. Zsusanna Budapest goes furthest, citing the figure of thirteen million; this seems not to be based on anything at all. The first to suggest the figure of nine million was the nineteenth-century suffragist Matilda Gage. The figure currently regarded as credible by academics is 40,000 to 100,000 executions; see Wiesner, *Women and Gender*, p. 219.
24 Primo Levi, *The Drowned and the Saved*, trans. Raymond Rosenthal, London: Abacus, 1989, first published 1988; Geoffrey H. Hartman ed., *Holocaust Remembrance: The Shape of Memory*, Oxford: Blackwell, 1994; Shoshana Felman, *Testimony*, New Haven: Yale Univeristy Press, 1992.
25 Deborah Lipstadt, *Denying the Holocaust: The Growing Assault on Truth and Memory*, Harmondsworth: Penguin, 1993.
26 Starhawk, *Dreaming*, p. 184.
27 Starhawk, *Dreaming*, pp. 187–8.
28 Barbara Ehrenreich and Deidre English, *Witches, Midwives and Nurses: A History of Women Healers*, London: Writers and Readers Publishing Cooperative, 1973.
29 On midwives, see Clive Holmes, 'Popular culture? Witches, magistrates and divines in early modern England', in *Understanding Popular Culture: Europe from the Middle Ages to the Nineteenth Century*, ed. Steven Kaplan, Berlin: Houton, 1984, and 'Women, witnesses and witches', *Past and Present*, 140 (1993), pp. 45–78; Richard Horsley, 'Who were the witches? The social roles of the accused in European witch trials', *Journal of Interdisciplinary History*, 9 (1979), pp. 714–15; David Harley, 'Ignorant midwives: a persistent stereotype', *The Society for the Social History of Medicine Bulletin*, 28 (1981) pp. 6–9, and 'Historians as demonologists'; *Wiesner, Women and Gender*; J. A. Sharpe, 'Witchcraft and women in seventeenth-century England: some northern evidence', *Continuity and Change*, 6 (1991), pp. 179–99.
30 Barbara G. Walker, *The Woman's Encyclopedia of Myths and Secrets*, New York: Harper & Row, 1985, pp. 654–5. The idea that women in (say) ancient Athens had more power than modern women is especially risible.
31 See Sheila Rowbotham, *The Past is Before Us: Feminism in Action Since the 1960s*, Harmondsworth: Penguin, 1989, pp. 61–85, esp. p. 71.
32 Starhawk, *Dreaming*, p. 183.
33 Meghan B. Collins, 'The Green Woman', in *Don't Bet on the Prince: Contemporary*

Feminist Fairy Tales in North America and England, ed. Jack Zipes, Aldershot: Gower, 1986, p. 103.
34 Claire Nahmad, *Earth Magic: A Wisewoman's Guide to Herbal, Astrological, and Other Folk Remedies*, London: Rider, 1993, pp. 1–2.
35 Keith Thomas, *Man and the Natural World: Changing Attitudes in England 1500–1800*, Harmondsworth: Penguin, 1983; Patrick Wright, *On Living in an Old Country*, London: Verso, 1985, esp. chs 1 and 7.
36 Raphael Samuel, *Theatres of Memory*, vol. 1, *Past and Present in Contemporary Culture*, London: Verso, 1994, pp. 84–6, offers a wonderful account of the genesis of country kitchens.
37 Stephen Greenblatt, 'Psychoanalysis and Renaissance culture', in *Literary Theory/ Renaissance Texts*, ed. Patricia Parker and David Quint, London and Baltimore: Johns Hopkins University Press, 1986, pp. 210–24.
38 Starhawk, *Dreaming*, pp. 184–5.
39 Anne Cameron, *The Annie Poems*, Canada: Harbour, 1987, p. 85.
40 Sylvia Townsend Warner, *Lolly Willowes*, London: Virago, 1995, first published 1926.
41 Sara Maitland, 'The Burning Times', in *Women Fly When Men Aren't Watching*, London; Virago, 1993, story first published 1983.
42 Anne Sexton, *The Complete Poems*, Boston: Houghton Mifflin, 1981, p. 15.
43 'Sonnet to Satan', in Sylvia Plath, *Collected Poems*, edited by Ted Hughes, London: Faber, 1981, p. 323
44 Plath, *Collected Poems*, p. 135. See also Plath's juvenile poem 'On Looking Into the Eyes of a Demon Lover', p. 325.
45 Plath, *Collected Poems*, pp. 176–87, 272.
46 Ted Hughes, *Selected Poems 1957–1981*, London: Faber, 1982, p. 56.
47 Ted Hughes, *Shakespeare and the Goddess of Complete Being*, London: Faber, 1993.
48 Caryl Churchill, *Vinegar Tom*, in *Plays I*, London: Methuen, 1985, play first published 1978, first performed by Monstrous Regiment in 1977.
49 Elaine Feinstein, *Some Unease and Angels*, London: Hutchinson, 1977.
50 Adrienne Rich, *Of Woman Born: Motherhood as Experience and Institution*, London: Virago, 1977, p. 145.
51 Olga Broumos, 'Little Red Riding Hood', in Zipes, *Don't Bet on the Prince*, p. 119.
52 Elizabeth Baines, *The Birth Machine*, London: Women's Press, 1983, p. 72. For an illuminating discussion of childbirth narratives, see Tess Cosslet, *Women Writing Childbirth*, Manchester: Manchester University Press, 1995.
53 Derricote, 'Natural Birth' in *Cradle and All: Women Writers on Pregnancy and Birth*, ed. Laura Chester, London: Faber, 1989, p. 113.
54 Ger Duffy, 'Birth Stories', *In the Gold of Flesh: Poems of Birth and Motherhood*, ed. Rosemary Palmeira, London: Women's Press, 1990, p. 84.
55 Sara Maitland, *A Book of Spells*, London: Minerva, 1987.
56 Collins, 'The Green Woman', p. 104.
57 Margaret Atwood, 'The Healer', in *Interlunar*, London: Cape, 1988, p. 38, first published 1984.
58 Fay Weldon, *Puffball*, London: Hodder & Stoughton, 1980.

2 At play in the fields of the past

Modern witches

But remember. Make an effort to remember. Or failing that, invent.

Monique Wittig, *Les Guerillères*

Is your computer down? Is the printer misbehaving? Zsuzsanna E. Budapest has the answer:

> The computer is a device for powerful thinking, so [Laurel] uses the rune Ansuz. This is the rune of intellect, inspiration, and communication . . . Next Laurel uses the rune Sowilo . . . for regeneration, recharging, self-repair, and victory. Finally Laurel uses Elhaz, the rune of protection . . . Laurel draws these three symbols on her dark computer screen with her saliva, her essence. Visualising the symbols and the images they represent, she links them to the machine and actually endows it with a spirit she can talk to.[1]

Budapest is a modern witch, the author of a book of spells for office workers. Providing you can believe in magic, this spell offers a reversal of the most oppressive features of the job for women who work in the 'pink collar' ghettos of keyboarding, as well as anyone else intimidated by their computer. Laurel uses knowledge that goes beyond what the computer itself 'knows'. Runes cannot be typed on a normal keypad; they must be hand-drawn. This restores to Laurel control over shapes and positions. Laurel draws the runes in her own saliva, 'her essence'. This offers a tactile, bodily – even erotic – way of communicating with a machine 'normally' responsive only to disciplined movements which keep to narrow rules. Laurel's body, her 'essence', is irrelevant to these orderly transactions; her body is merely their servant. No wonder that Laurel's spell offers to 'humanise' the machine. This is a common fantasy about computers, but here it is also offered as a solution to the uncompromising blankness of malfunction.[2] Laurel draws her signs on a dark and uncommunicative screen. To adapt Donna Haraway's celebrated formulation, Laurel's notion of being a goddess is partly shaped by her experiences as a cyborg.[3] According to Margot Adler, this is by no means exceptional; computing is the most common career among modern witches.[4] Laurel's spell, however, seems to address itself less to the expertise of programmers and analysts than to those to whom computer technology is an occult mystery. Operating a machine whose inner workings are incomprehenisble leads to fantasies about the machine's malevolence and power. Laurel's spell offers to replace this 'tricky' relationship with one of affable communication. The therapeutic discourses crucial to the occult in the 1990s show up in the idea that communication with the machine will solve problems. The spell does not compel the machine to behave, but opens a way of talking to it – which comes to the same thing. As we shall see, faith in 'talking cures' is central to modern witchcraft.

It is the proximity of modern witchcraft to various authoritative discourses of the present that helps to explain its burgeoning popularity. Most academics write as if witchcraft were over and done, a marker of our difference from the past. This elides the diachronic signification of the witch, and the way that her continued meaning is the product of the present. There are people alive in the UK for whom the word 'witch' is not a reminder of an unknowable past, but a part of their living identity. It has recently been suggested that there may be as many as 150,000 Pagans in the UK today. This figure is certainly much too high, since in the US (where the movement is much larger) estimates range from 83,000 to 333,000.[5] What evidence there is suggests that Paganism is growing, and there is some reason to believe that it may be the fastest-growing religion in America, and perhaps in the UK as well. Not all Pagans use the term 'witch'. It designates a particular branch of Paganism, but one currently very popular. Some Pagans are reluctant to use the term, since they cannot control its meaning. Misinformation abounds; once people get over thinking of modern witches as Satanists slaughtering virgins by the light of the full moon like extras in a Ken Russell movie, they proceed to muddle modern witches with the New Age, a movement despised by many witches as nothing but yuppiedom with added hypocrisy. The truth can be hard to come by because modern witches are both diverse and unwilling to publicise their activities. However, one can begin to grasp the movement's refiguration of the term 'witch' for the new religion of witchcraft. Modern witchcraft is dependent on a particular reading of the history of witchcraft, one conspicuously out of line with academic wisdom on the subject.

Modern witchcraft is *not* Satanism, but an invented religion which draws syncretically on a variety of historiographically specific versions of 'ancient' Pagan religions. Some of these are themselves inventions, so that the entirety of modern witchcraft offers a unique opportunity to see a religion being made from readings and rereadings of texts and histories. No one person is in charge of the process, so modern witchcraft is not a unified set of beliefs; every interpretation is subject to reinvention by others. There are almost as many different sects and groups as there are believers, and the neophyte can easily get lost among the Gardnerians, Dianics, radical faeries, Alexandrians, hedge-witches and 'fam-trads', or family witches. Witches themselves do not see diversity as a problem, but as a sign of freedom from the constraints of organised religion. Nevertheless, these groups can be highly critical of each other, and the witches who have spoken to me often stressed the differences between groups rather than their similarities.[6] They agreed, however, that witches have important beliefs in common: all worship a Mother Goddess and her male consort (polytheism); all see the natural world as invested with spiritual significance (pantheism); all have adopted some form of 'ancient' festive calendar which marks their feasts; all emphasise ritual, though some groups deal in formal rituals and others make it up as they go along.

Feminist witches are one group within this body of worshippers. From a feminist point of view, however, all modern witches are of interest because modern witchcraft attempts to make the Goddess its principal deity. It was this aspect of modern witchcraft which attracted feminists: Starhawk, an overtly feminist witch, but not a separatist, writes:

> The rediscovery of the ancient matrifocal civilisations has given us a deep sense of pride in women's ability to create and sustain culture. It has exposed the falsehoods of patriarchal history, and given us models of female strength and authority. Once again in today's world we recognise the Goddess, ancient and primeval.[7]

While Elisabeth Brooke, a revolutionary separatist feminist witch, writes:

> behind the lesser gods was the Cosmic Mother Of All, whose breasts poured milk into the firmament and who birthed new stars, whose curved and luscious body was the very earth they trod on . . . Priestesses of the Goddess, who had many names, presided over birth and death, the blessing of fields and the building of cities.[8]

This is seductive rhetoric. It is sensuous and liquid; it celebrates the female body sidelined by the Religions of the Book (Judaeo-Christianity and Islam); it links women of power with a utopian connection between countryside and city; it offers an imaginative alternative to the patriarchal religions and their male deities. However, reviving Goddess-worship is not automatically a simple step forward for feminism. The Goddess as envisaged by modern witchcraft is not the female-authored figure she appears to be, but a male fantasy borrowed from men's writings, and women have not altogether evaded the problems this creates. Instead, the Goddess has been embraced by women who are attracted to some of her most problematic features.

Analysis of the Goddess begins with the idea that no myth is ever a single monolithic entity. Many stories already exist in several different forms, and different historical periods will privilege a particular version of a story. The methods of reading used to understand myth are constantly being revised, and these changes are often determined by political and ideological imperatives. Even the most ancient myths become caught up in contemporaneity, just as they were for their original inventors. However, both Starhawk and Brooke present the Goddess as an absolute verity recovered from a lost past. Yet both stories are marked by a particular mode of reading myth, a mode which is historically and ideologically specific, caught up in contemporaneity rather than outside it.

The problem with the Goddess is that she remains mired in the thinking of 'images of women' feminism. This thinking can be annihilatingly prescriptive, demanding that all women recognise themselves as lactating mothers, for example. Its insistence that 'positive' images of women are positive for all women in all contexts can seem cosily unaware of difficulty or diffidence. Just what might seem to constitute 'strength' and 'authority' for an exhausted working mother? Might there be times when she wants to acknowledge aspects of herself which are *not* maternal? If she is already a mother, what kind of mother goddess does she need? One who mothers her? What about cultures in which maternity has different meanings? The myth of the Goddess, with its insistence on an identity grounded in the maternal body, betrays its origins in male fantasy. Although modern witches claim to be recovering a pure matriarchal vision from the remote past, such a claim cannot really be sustained once their borrowings from more recent texts and discourses have been traced.

We must begin with Rousseau. For him, civilisation characteristically acts to corrupt the instinctual verities of 'primitive' societies. These verities can be glimpsed, and partially recovered, in the person of the Noble Savage. In a Rousseauean context, certain myths such as the myth of Prometheus so central to Romantic poetry, came to signify not merely participation in high or civilised culture, but a buried set of identities and feelings repressed by civility. As such, they appeared to possess the truth-value of any revealed source, but also the verity of that which purports to come from beyond culture, that not subject to the vicissitudes of time and change.[9] An exegetical tradition grew up which read myth as the displaced or disregarded but fundamental truth of human nature; conversely, myth could also represent a set of ideals about human nature to be restored to the degenerate consciousness of a corrupt society.

Ironically, this view found its finest and most sophisticated expression in the work of Sigmund Freud, also one of the most discerning critics of its more egregious sentimentalities. For Freud, myths are to civilisation what dreams are to consciousness: signposts to what cannot be acknowledged in rational and civilised discourse. It was Freud's one-time disciple Jung, however, who developed Freud's ideas into a more formulaic and less ambiguous method of mythic exegesis, one which insisted on reading all myths as universal human verities. Jung's theory was part of the attempt to understand myths as signifiers of hidden truths. For writers like Robert Briffault, Erich Neumann, J. J. Bachofen, Jane Harrison, Arthur Evans and, above all, the widely influential J. G. Frazer, it was not story but the secret truth which lay behind myth which was important. Indifference to context was installed at the heart of the most celebrated mythic studies.

All these thinkers believed in an originary matriarchy, located in the prehistorical ancient world, and signified by the worship of a deity called the Great Goddess or the Great Mother. The Goddess was originally discovered – or invented – by male scholars serving an agenda which was far from feminist. The myth of an originary matriarchy serves to explain and justify women's subordination through a narrative in which men wrest control from women because women are oppressive and incompetent.[10] Yet this is still the narrative promulgated by modern writers like Starhawk and Brooke. Jung and Neumann, in the meantime, saw the Great Goddess as a buried aspect of the *male* psyche, while historians and archaeologists interested themselves in unearthing – literally in the case of Arthur Evans – the figure of the Great Mother lost to male civilisation.[11] The result was to reify associations between women and the primitive, the uncivilised, the instinctual. Conversely, by insisting that such figures were the dark, repressed underside of civilisation, civilisation was reproduced as exclusively a business for men. Men alone had lost their connection with the 'dark continent' of myth and the feminine; since women were always already marginal to civilisation, they could become bearers of its repressed underside.

Given its evident debt to these mythographers, it is not surprising that modern witchcraft was invented alongside them. Despite its claims to antiquity, modern witchcraft's discursive origins can be traced back only as far as the Romantic period; as a practice, it dates from the end of the Second World War. The Rousseauean valorisation of the primitive and the Romantic faith in pantheism had an immediate impact on historians of witchcraft and creative writers. A German professor of law, Karl-Ernst Järcke, argued in 1828 that witchcraft was the ancient religion of the German people, suppressed by Christianity. Järcke was not attracted to the idea of paganism rampant, but his work encouraged the brothers Grimm and others to connect stories about the supernatural with the manly vitality of the *Volk's* religion.[12] Rousseauean ideals of primitivism are put to the service of German nationalism, foreshadowing the turn-of-the-century German scholars of the occult who pressed myths about paganism into the service of a racist creed.

Rousseauean ideas were appropriated rather differently by the revolutionary French historian Jules Michelet. For him, witchcraft was a religion of the people which originated in the lowest social levels because it was a manifestation of the democratic spirit. In Michelet's account, the peasants of the Middle Ages adapted the remains of a fertility cult into a protest against church and state. At the centre of Michelet's narrative is the figure of a woman 'with a face like Medea, a beauty born of sufferings, a deep, tragic, feverish gaze, with a torrent of black, untameable hair'.[13] This priestess, whose naked body becomes a living altar on which food is offered in a parody of the Mass, is a female figure constructed to symbolise rebellion. She recalls the female figures used to represent disorder during the Revolution, and as such she is eroticised, but her sexuality is not her own: it must act symbolically.[14] In depicting his seductive, wild sorceress, Michelet was influenced by the Silver Chamber affair of 1679, France's answer to the Overbury poisoning case, which involved Louis XIV's mistress Madame de Montespan. De Montespan had allegedly used diabolical means to rid herself of rivals, and was often depicted reclining seductively on a sofa. This scandal among the nobility typifed the decadence of absolutism, but Michelet reversed the image, making a recumbent female form the signifier of rebellion.

Michelet's work illustrates the way the centrality of a female figure does not necessarily mean that women are truly represented. Having placed a woman at the centre of his witchcraft-religion, it seemed 'natural' – or at any rate inevitable – that Michelet should decide that witchcraft was a fertility religion, with rituals meant to secure abundant crops. This involves equating the altar-body of the black-haired priestess with the earth, since both 'bear' food; this is precisely the equation made by Brooke when she describes the Goddess whose 'curved and luscious body was the very earth they [Ice Age peoples] trod on'. Such an equation, however, risks reiterating a number of gendered meanings which function to render woman passive, the prone recipient of male cultivation. The equation of woman with nature and man with culture is reconstructed. It was this idea of witchcraft as a fertility religion which caught on, reiterated by Frazer in his vastly influential study of fertility cults, *The Golden Bough*. Michelet's radicalism was unlikely to appeal to (say) T. S. Eliot, but Eliot had no difficulty in assimilating Frazer's nostalgic evocation of a lost continent of myth and ritual. What had been witchcraft's political rebellion was gradually softened into a hazy sense that witchcraft somehow offered liberation from the oppressions of the modern world in a return to a safer and more 'natural' past.

Meanwhile the Romantic poets had taken up the figure of the witch and transformed her into a muse, the object of a poetic quest fraught with danger and desire. The sexuality which came to be associated with the beautiful sorceress was still an object of fear, but also came to seem alluring because through access to the body of the woman, the poet gained access not just to wild and untrammeled nature, but also to magical control over nature. In Shelley's 'The Witch of Atlas', for example, the witch is a figure of beauty explicitly linked with a lost preindustrial past of intuition and imagination; this fits with Shelley's flirtations with a Romanticised paganism.[15] Similarly, Keats's 'La Belle Dame Sans Merci' represents the end of poetic desire, a vision of beauty that drains and depletes, but also offers the only possible satisfaction; she too is associated with a lost world of knights and legends. Medieval sorceresses played similar roles in the works of Tennyson and the Pre-Raphaelites; Dante Gabriel Rossetti's 'Sister Helen', for example, bent on magical revenge for the defection of her lover, is a frightening but also a powerful and alluring figure whose naked emotion is portrayed as more honest than the civilised hypocrisies of her opponents. Above all, such figures represent the goal of the poetic quest for wild beauty and for poetic mastery of it.

By the turn of the century, a plethora of occult societies had sprung up, all influenced by post-Romantic figurations of the primitive as a space in which the ills of industrialisation and modernity might be cured. All these groups figured the feminine as the (passive) goal of the desiring male subject's quest. Nonetheless, from spiritualism to theosophy, women played a leading part in many of these new groups; Madame Helena Blavatsky, for example, offered an account of the occult lore of ancient Egypt as an antidote to what she saw as the excessive rationalism and materialism of Western civilisation in *Isis Unveiled* (1877). Blavatsky's ideas, especially on reincarnation, were overtly racist, and they also reproduced rather than questioned the notion of woman as a space of spiritual value opposed to modernity. Yet Blavatsky was also a cross-dresser who liked to be called Jack while wearing men's clothing.[16] Such theatrical destabilisations of gender troubled confident assertions of what was essentially masculine or feminine. By contrast, the witchcraft revival, largely formulated by men, invented a fertility religion which depended on the notion of a Great Goddess who represented the biological stages of women's lives (maiden, mother, crone) as prehistorical, uncivilised.

The eventual practitioners of modern witchcraft were influenced by the writings I have been discussing, especially as transmitted through the work of Charles Leland, Margaret Murray and Robert Graves. Charles Leland was an amateur folklorist who followed in the footsteps of Järcke, Michelet and Frazer in arguing for the survival of pagan religious beliefs in Europe.[17] In *Aradia, Or The Gospel Of The Witches*, first published in 1899, Leland claimed to have become 'intimately acquainted' with an Italian woman, one of those 'who can astonish even the learned by their legends of Latin gods'.[18] This woman, Maddalena, is represented by Leland as a kind of repository of timeless paganism, and he claimed that she obtained for him another such repository: the gospel of the witches. Maddalena's book tells of Diana, Queen of the Witches, and her union with Lucifer, the sun; from this union is born a daughter, Aradia, who is to go to earth as the messiah of witches. The gospel contains the so-called Charge of the Goddess, still used today by many modern witches in a variety of adapted forms. Influenced by Michelet, Leland argued that witches constituted 'a vast development of rebels, the outcast, and all the discontented, who adopted witchcraft or sorcery for religion'.[19] Praised by feminist witches for 'an effort to regard women as the fully equal, which means superior sex', as he himself puts it, Leland merely reflects Michelet's use of goddess and witch as signifiers of what *men* lack. Moreover, the terms of Leland's statement have been suppressed; he adds that 'woman being evidently a fish who shows herself most when the waters are troubled: – "Oh, woman in our hours of ease" – the reader will remember the rest'.[20] Leland writes of the way in which the witch exemplifies woman's nature: 'it is recognised that there is something uncanny, mysterious and incomprehensible in woman, which neither she herself nor men can explain'.[21] Just as Maddalena becomes a figure of what is opposed to the present and to modernity, so the figure of woman becomes a sign of all that cannot be grasped by civilisation.

Margaret Murray's idea that the god of the witches is called Dianus owes something to Leland, but her model of witchcraft as a fertility cult centring on the worship of a horned god derives from Michelet via Frazer.[22] Despite the drubbing Murray has received from academic historians since the first publication of *The Witch-Cult in Western Europe* in 1921, she is cited as an authority in many books by modern witches.[23] Her thesis is that those prosecuted for witchcraft were actually members of a nature religion surviving from pre-Christian times which involved ritual sex with a hairy god. Murray makes few attempts to rewrite her principal male sources. She replicates Frazer's idea of a fertility cult, and also reiterates intellectual enthusiasm for goat-footed Pan, popular from Shelley to Kenneth Grahame. Murray's religion, like Maddalena's witchcraft, is transmitted intact through history: the witch-cult is pre-Christian paganism, the original religion of the British Isles. The Britons, of small stature, were driven into hiding by successive waves of invaders, Murray argues, but retained enough contact with the population to transmit their religion; again, a story of ahistorical survival, intact transmission, and the recovery of decontextualised truths.

Where Murray did depart from her predecessors was in her emphasis on the God rather than the Goddess of the witches. Though this might *seem* dubiously masculinocentric, Murray could also be seen as a mischievous turner of the tables on all those men determined to see the goal of the spiritual quest as a passive feminine muse.[24] By reinventing the chief deity as a male, Murray could install women as active worshippers and desiring subjects. Moreover, Murray herself is a winning figure. She was an ardent advocate of women's suffrage, a pioneer who took up anthropology in an era when it was not considered ladylike. She was adventurous, working on archaeological digs in Egypt in the great days of Howard-Carter and mummies' curses, and it was there that she is said to have undergone a magical ceremony designed to protect from rabies. This signals her general interest in the occult. She advanced a theory of ghosts as a kind of photographic image and announced her belief in reincarnation in her autobiography, which she began at the age of ninety.[25] Murray represents all that is best and worst in feminist representations of witchcraft as pagan Goddess-worship.

Syncretists among modern witches did not take long to conflate Leland's 'old religion' with Murray's surviving pagan cult. This became a blueprint for the reinvention of witchcraft as a practice by Gerald Gardner. Gardner had a lifelong interest in the occult; he was involved with an occult group called the Fellowship of the Crotona; he had met Aleister Crowley and knew of the Order of the Golden Dawn; he may have been a Freemason; he became a nudist early in life. In 1939, he claimed he met a woman named Dorothy Clutterbuck. 'Old Dorothy' initiated Gardner into what he later claimed was a coven of hereditary witches who had practised their rites in an unbroken line for centuries. The resemblance between Gardner's story of Old Dorothy and Leland's story of Maddalena is very striking; this resemblance suggests not only Gardner's use of Leland, but his adherence to the general notion of witchcraft as a secret buried letter, a concealed truth. Once again, the vehicle for both concealment and revelation is a woman; like Maddalena, Old Dorothy represents both mystery to be probed by the male investigator, and also disclosure of mystery. As always, femininity is associated with the secret, the precivilised, the mysterious. 'And then', wrote Gardner dramatically, 'I knew that that which I had thought burnt out hundreds of years ago still survived'.[26] The reference to burning is suggestive of Gardner's lack of historical knowledge, later to expose some of his claims as fictive.

Gardner wanted to write about his discovery, but was deterred by the witchcraft statutes, so he produced a novel, *High Magic's Aid*, in 1949. There is a special irony in this: it draws attention to the blurriness of lines between fact and fiction in the creation of modern witchcraft's truths. Starhawk cites Ursula Le Guin's magician Ged as if he were a 'real' sage, rather than a fictional creation. One of the witches I spoke to admitted (shamefacedly) to being influenced by Marion Bradley's *Mists of Avalon*. Conversely, this novel is a retelling of the Arthuriad which draws on the writings of modern witches, especially Starhawk's.[27] Such reliance on fiction feeds the modern witch's sense that she is creating her own religion, but coexists quite happily with the idea that witchcraft is also a revival of a lost or forgotten fertility cult. Both ideas are already present in Gardner's work.

In 1951, after the replacement of the witchcraft statutes with the Fraudulent Medium's Act, Gardner began publishing nonfictional works on witchcraft, and then formed his own coven, enrolling members of his nudist club.[28] The coven was soon performing rituals scripted by Gardner as well as material he claimed to have obtained from Old Dorothy. He was helped throughout by his disciple Doreen Valiente, who revealed in her autobiography that she had written some of the rituals. He never acknowledged Valiente, preferring to credit innovations to the passive muse-figure of Old Dorothy. Valiente's obscured role in the creation of Gardnerian Witchcraft is typical of the hidden place of women in scripting the witchcraft revival and in tilting its gender biases as best they could away from the idea of woman as muse and towards female fantasy. The sorceresses and muses of male fantasy were reinterpreted and inhabited by women, who were able to inhabit such an inimical space by misreading it, sometimes wilfully. One reason this became easier in the nineteenth century was the changing portrayal of women of magic in art and literature. The revival of witchcraft as a religion and the related revival of identification with the witch arose at precisely the point when *fin-de-siècle* poetry, fiction and art had begun to glamorise the witch and turn her into the much more alluring figure of the sorceress. Few women can have felt enthusiastic about inhabiting the identities of early modern crones dangling from a gibbet; this is an image difficult for anyone to recuperate by rewriting or misreading, an image singularly obdurate to the viewing eye in its figuration of all that a woman must not be. It was a different matter when witches began to look as seductive as Dante Gabriel Rossetti's *Lady Lilith*, Frederick Sandys' glowing *Morgan Le Fay*, or Edward Burne-Jones's dramatic *Sidonia Van Bork*. These images were based on texts which also glamorised the image of the beautiful sorceress, the sorceress whose wildness and unconventionality might be cognates of evil, but were also signifiers of freedom.[29] Such images were supposed to be at least partially admonitory, showing the peril of female desire while warning about female beauty as a species of inescapable and emasculating magic. However, by 'breaking the rules' of interpretation, the New Woman could appropriate at least some of the mystery and voluptuousness of such figures.[30] Painters like Evelyn de Morgan reproduced and reinterpreted the pre-Raphaelite sorceress-muse into an image of the woman artist.[31] New Women's short stories often associate the heroine's sexual appeal with occult powers, following and sweetening a tradition established by such poetic and iconographic reappraisal.[32] The women involved in founding the Golden Dawn, including Maud Gonne and the early theosophical women such as Blavatsky and Annie Besant, were both political activists and theatrical self-fashioners who used the materials of male fantasy to construct selves which resisted an easy appropriation in return.[33]

The women who entered modern witchcraft after the second wave of the women's liberation movement saw the traces of what an earlier generation of women had made: a religion that might really offer a corrective to patriarchal religious practices, a real place for female creativity and imagination. The reinvention process has continued; there have been feminist reinterpretations of all branches of Paganism, and of alchemy, astrology and the tarot.[34] Modern witchcraft allows a creative reinvention of the self, too: the witch is encouraged to identify with many attractive figures from mythology, and is allowed to choose a Craft-name for herself. This last is a hangover from the Golden Dawn initiation ritual, but it also mimics the puberty rites of some preindustrial cultures which have also been glamorised, such as the American Plains Tribes. Craft-names allude to favourite deities or concerns. Names like Starhawk, Gaia Wildewoode and Isis Eaglemoon are fairly representative. Similarly, covens are usually given a name, like Darkmoon, or Tree: Starhawk's first coven was called Compost, a joke about the grand titles witches usually choose, but also a serious reference to the problem of saving the planet. This inventiveness is well worth celebrating, however doubtful the results. By refusing to see the Goddess as the male fantasy she was, modern witches believed, they made her less of a male fantasy and transformed her into a female fantasy. But were they right? The problem for witches who want to assert creativity and control is that witchcraft remains, on the whole, tied to an historical narrative which is well-nigh inescapable as a male fantasy about what femininity should be.

Witches have recently become rather worried about their history. Despite the ongoing tension between fiction and authenticity in modern witchcraft, or perhaps because of it, many modern witches are anxious about the validity of Gardner's pronouncements, and especially about the authenticity of his *Book of Shadows*. This is the text Gardner claimed to have obtained from Old Dorothy's coven; he identified it as a sixteenth-century witch's notebook. Readers within and outside modern witchcraft have disputed this claim. Gardner's *Book of Shadows* is an implausible pastiche of Elizabethan English; it refers to witches in England being burned alive for their crimes (which never happened); it contains clear borrowings from the work of Aleister Crowley; it also contains extensive borrowings from a magazine article on an Old Sanskrit manuscript.[35] Gardner admitted to Doreen Valiente that borrowings were necessary because the Hereditary Coven's surviving rituals were fragmentary.[36] What modern witches want to know is whether Gardner had *any* contact with hereditary witches. While some witches – Aidan Kelly, Isaac Bonewits – are happy to argue that Gardner's writings represent a triumph of creative imagination, others are bothered by the proposition that the Old Religion is no older than the National Health Service. The entire dispute shows that the oldness of modern witchcraft is important to it. Even those who, like Zsuzsanna Budapest, are cavalier about Gardner claim that witchcraft is *known* to be ancient: 'I don't know whether Goddess-worship is 70,000 or 7,000 years old,' says Budapest, but 7,000 years still sounds pretty ancient, quite different from seventy years. For other witches, attempts to establish the precise age of witchcraft are somehow patriarchal: Brooke writes breezily that 'the argument as to whether our witchcraft traditions are "authentic" seems to be the usual male intellectual posturing, debating the number of angels on a pinhead'.[37] She adheres in every page of her book to the idea that witchcraft as Goddess religion is very old, and sees no need to justify this. Still others have reformulated the idea of ancient origins: 'the universal Old Religion may not have existed geographically, but it existed in the Jungian sense that people were tapping a common source'; Goddess-worship has 'an ancient universality about it' but appeared in different places at different times.[38] Another alternative is to do away with the need for objective origins by privileging the subjective: 'when you are doing a ritual and you suddenly get the feeling that you are experiencing something generations of your forebears experienced, it's probably true'.[39] Or the witch can claim an alternative, non-Gardnerian hereditary tradition: one of the witches who spoke to me told me that she has been trained by a New Forest coven who were not Gardnerians, but traditional hereditary witches. Similarly, Claire Nahmad claims that 'I was fortunate to inherit, as a child, the traditional wisdom of the Craft from my maternal grandmother'.[40] Many other writers have made this claim, not necessairly untruthfully; the point is that the age of their traditions is important to them.

Though enthusiastic about ritual, witches are resistant to its hierarchical enforcement, preferring to emphasise 'what works for you'. So some witches see the construction of historical reality in experiential terms: 'it doesn't matter whether the grandmother was a physical reality, or a figment of our imagination. One is subjective, one is objective, but we experience both'.[41] The solipsism involved, however, constitutes a substantial challenge to norms of historical or philosophical veracity. It removes the distinction between fiction and nonfiction, licensing the use of both in terms of 'what works' rather than 'what's true'. This is an exceptionally appropriate response to Gardner's apparent blurring of those boundaries. This valorisation of historical creativity rather than historical authority no doubt explains why women have been able to be so prominent in modern witchcraft; individual histories obviate the need to do battle with insititutional and social understandings of whose word goes, understandings that are invariably gendered.

Whether seen as fantasy or reality, witchcraft comes from a grandmother and not from a granddaughter.[42] The witch is a vision from the past, for only in the past can an alternative to the modern world be imagined. The sense of connection with a lost past is important to modern witches in part because they see themselves as the recoverers of the values lost to modern industrial society. Modern witches' normal understanding of their own history differs substantially from the kind of history of the movement which I have been offering. Their own history is a shaped history which constructs for them a particular kind of identity. Both Starhawk and Brooke begin their historical narratives at the end of the last Ice Age; both describe the beginning of witchcraft as a moment of pure unity between people and nature, life and death:

> Life and death were a continuous stream . . . in lowland pools, reindeer does, their bellies filled with stones that embodied the souls of deer, were submerged in the waters of the Mother's womb, so that victims of the hunt would be reborn.[43]

This passage does strongly recall M.D. Faber's theory that modern witches are seeking a return to the maternal body and the mother–child dyad. In Starhawk's text, these desires barely remain unconscious in a text which gestures so vividly at unity and flow rather than discrete differentiation, a rhetoric which recalls Cixous and Irigaray's attempts to write a feminine space radically other than Cartesian subjectivity.[44] However, Starhawk's text is really guilty of the kind of problematic assumptions of which Cixous and Irigaray were wrongly accused. Unlike their work, it does not offer itself as opaque, to-be-deciphered; instead it purports to transparency and solidity. It is not a fantasy of otherness, but a description of a lost maternal continent presumed to be actual rather than imaginary. Other witches use similarly essentialising language; Budapest draws on Arthur Evans's interpretation of Knossos to argue for a prehistoric matriarchy:

> Matriarchal women had no defence systems. They didn't even have swords, although they did use wands. All they had was superior sewage systems, elaborate baths, beautiful wall paintings, and exquisite jewellery. They were beauty-oriented, not war-obsessed, and thus were easily overrun and sacked in the cruellest sense of the word.[45]

Budapest stresses the absence of hierarchies and divisive violence. This myth of a Minoan matriarchy offers a prelapsarian utopia of originary unity which replicates the blissful mother–child dyad even as it celebrates a society with no visible differences. It also offers to appropriate some of the waning prestige of the classics for a feminocentric historical narrative. But as Stella Georgoudi points out, the entire theory rests on an odd tendency to take myth for history in a manner which paradoxically consigns femininity to a realm outside history.[46]

The modern witch's history of herself is thus a lapsarian narrative. Indeed, there is not one Fall, but many.[47] Characteristically these include the loss of Atlantis (a lost continent of the maternal indeed), the coming of Christianity to Britain, the death of Arthur, the promulgation of a Papal Bull against witches, the Burning Times, the rise of the modern industrialised world with its disregard for and despoliation of nature, the rise of Enlightenment science and medicine. Such lapses or losses are followed by attempts at recovery, in both senses of the word, in which witches are portrayed as struggling to regain what has been lost. This defines modern witches as both restorers and inventors of a lost tradition. This kind of narrative can be closely paralleled in nationalist political rhetoric, which is perhaps why some occult writings bear too-evident traces of such rhetorics, despite the general liberalism of modern witchcraft.[48] The story of idyll, decline and active recovery of a lost and more desirable past has become associated with both fascism and conservatism: it is a short step from kindly, nature-loving witches to spinsters on bicycles going to Evensong, partly because both would-be utopias embody ideas of natural order and organic wholeness in the feminine. However, most actual spinsters on bicycles would not feel very comfortable with the imaginative and creative play with the sacred and with history which is the keystone of the modern witch's sense of empowerment. When viewed as a figuration, the modern witch is only too easily understood in essentialist and heritage-industry terms; when understood as an active subject, she seems much more liberated and liberating.

Looked at from a sceptical point of view, then, the historical narrative of modern witchcraft is not problematic because it is a fantasy; it is problematic *as* a fantasy. The meanings it produces about past golden ages are a refusal of modernity which owes more to Romanticism than feminism. The myth of a lost matriarchy is disabling rather than enabling for women. To relegate female power in politics or religion to a lost past, to associate it with the absence of civilisation, technology and modernity, is to write women out of the picture. To confine female power to the marginal space of a reinvented religion which rejects any vestige of mainstream power is to reify women's exclusion from the public sphere. This explains why feminist versions of modern witchcraft are so often criticised (sometimes wrongly) for political quietism. The recovery of a precivilised space does not sort too well with mixing it in the corridors of power or even in Pagan campaigning groups.[49] Although the myths of modern witchcraft have inspired some women's activism, this has largely been confined to causes like pacifism and environmentalism, most notably in the UK at Greenham Common. While these activities are valuable, feminist witches surface as *feminist* witches less often in more narrowly feminist campaigns, such as securing equal pay or fighting for reproductive rights. Witches emerge only rarely from Pagan activities to make common cause with other women, and as long as this is so, other women will continue to misjudge them.

Modern witches' challenge to the norms of historical validity must be addressed, perhaps especially when these involve an explicit valorisation of the subjective 'what works' above the objective 'what's true'. Like most feminists of my generation, I am easily seduced by narratives which question the discipline of the masters and to historical narratives which foreground their own fictiveness. However, questioning playfulness loses its charm when the results are politically retrograde, as some occultists are – inevitably, in such a diverse community. Odinists (revivers of Norse paganism), for instance, are also in the business of questioning historical truths, but they do so in order to subtend their fantasies about fixed gender roles, clans, kinship groups and racial purity.[50] The Odinist stress on the self recalls modern witches' defences of 'what works'. If modern witches reject historical validity altogether, then how can they refute Odinism's less attractive claims, a project which some witches themselves consider extremely important? Liberating everyone to construct their own past sounds seductive, but in practice it can mean that everyone is able to avoid ever having to confront a refutation of, or even difference from, their own individual world-view. Losing sight of the otherness of the past by moulding it to fit one's personality risks becoming indifferent to the operations of ideology, which cannot in these circumstances be estranged by an encounter with a different set of assumptions or beliefs.

Moreover, modern witches' claims to be ignoring history cannot really be sustained. They are also using history, in the sense that their own historical narratives derive from an eclectic mix of historical texts, some of which were once mainstream. The process by which the nonspecialist reader makes such selections may not be to the liking of professional historians, but it does provide an intriguing instance of the impossibility of the profession controlling popular history. Ironically, this is reminiscent of the early modern period, where a village miller nicknamed Menocchio could appropriate the writings of humanists and theologians to synthesise a world-picture which they could never have intended.[51] In similar ways, modern witches have used a pot-pourri of philosophers and historians to synthesise their own world-view. Many, perhaps most, modern witches are passionate autodidacts, often bibliomaniacs whose houses are stuffed with books. Many also write: not only books, but journals, magazines, letters to mainstream and occult presses, samizdat rituals, prayers, polemics which circulate within their own covens or activist groups. They give talks, lectures and courses of instruction. Still others paint or sculpt or compose songs and music. Witches are not dutiful consumers of the truths of others, but makers of their own truths, though these by no means evade altogether the constraints of ideology. As creators, they recall Michel de Certeau's useful term 'poaching', a process of reading whereby the protocols of authorship and ownership of a text, and hence the protocols of intentionality, are discarded in favour of a mode of reading which creates by bricolage a new text.[52] Since no form of reading could be less academic, as de Certeau points out, this challenges and also reuses academic history. It brings a selection of academics into the sphere of the popular, but it also disrespectfully ignores academic protocols.

In a further twist of irony, it is the work of Carlo Ginzburg that is currently being taken up and reshaped by modern witches, displacing 'older' histories such as those of Margaret Murray.[53] One of the witches I met gave me an account of her own participation in night battles (under that name), which had, she said, been going on since the Middle Ages between white and black witches. Her own most recent encounter of that kind, she said, had been over the Twyford Down roadworks,[54] but this was a mere skirmish in comparison with the last big night battle, which had taken place during this Second World War and had resulted in a victory for the white witches which had prevented a German invasion.[55] She added that 'some book by Clineburg, I think' had described these battles. Ginzburg's narrative of what Friulian peasants thought they were doing has become a narrative of what they *really were* doing. This witch is unusual in dramatising her role as a fighter against evil; most witches choose less militaristic metaphors.[56] What is striking, however, is her use of an academic historical narrative to fashion an identity for herself as the foe of evil witches.

Self-fashioning does not, however, mean that modern witches are immune to all the effects of ideology. Rather, their choice of historical texts for validation is determined by their perception of how useful such texts will be in subtending their notion of what witchcraft is. Keith Thomas and Alan Macfarlane, the dominant voices in English witchcraft studies for over a decade, are rarely read by modern witches, and none of those I met had even heard of them.[57] Nor have I ever seen *Religion and the Decline of Magic* in an occult bookshop, perhaps because witchcraft is not mentioned in the title, perhaps because the second half of the title seems to modern witches either gloomy or simply silly. What can be poached is limited by the desires and fantasies of the reader, and by the limits set by the text concerned. While Ginzburg uncovers a hidden tradition in the depositions of peasants, following a narrative path familiar from Leland and Murray as well as Gardner, Thomas lends much less credence to the statements of accused witches, rarely quoting their words and seemingly disregarding their own beliefs about themselves. Many feminist academics might agree with witches that this has the effect of replacing a focus on women with a focus on men. Moreover, what in academic circles might seem like rigorous consideration of evidence strikes Pagans as narrow-mindedness; they would wonder why Thomas never consults materials and histories handed down orally, for instance.

These constraints also govern what can be done with the texts which have formed part of witches' self-fashioning. Despite the fact that feminist witchcraft is a rewriting of a rewriting, a poached text composed of selections from other poached texts, feminist writers have been unable or unwilling to evade the constraints imposed on them by a historiographical tradition grounded in a refusal of historicity and difference in the name of a timelessly repressed femininity which always already constitutes that which civilisation excludes. Although these historical narratives have created an opportunity for women's self-fashioning, this self-fashioning has in practice been limited by the discourses from which it draws, and also by its inability to separate itself from more general currents of discourse and ideology, especially the operative discourses of consumer capitalism. Witches do worry about occult ripoffs, mystic candles that turn out to be supermarket birthday cake candles when delivered, but they operate a 'bad apple' theory that the nature of witchcraft is divorced from capitalism and consumerism by virtue of its ancient origins. Similarly, the very notion of untrammelled creativity represented by feminist witchcraft risks obscuring the genuinely oppressive effects of ideological and material power on women's capacity to 'make' themselves into whatever they want.[58] As Rosalind Coward points out, it also risks replicating the most banal and false notion of the consumer-subject essential to late capitalism self-justification: 'do as thou wilt' is the cry of every advertisement.[59]

The same drift towards the solipsism of the consumer is equally apparent in the magic spells presented in modern witchcraft. Many so-called spells are actually narcissistic rites of self-contemplation: 'Spell to Know the Child Within'; 'Spell to Be Friends with Your Womb'. Trances and rituals too are validated as bringers of psychic health, rather than as alterations in material circumstances. It is our (always damaged) selves which need to be placated with constant offerings, and not an angry deity. Similarly, the effect of spells is said to depend on what *you* put into them: 'the quantity and quality of emotion and directed thought you put into your spell will determine its effectiveness.'[60] 'To work magic, I need a basic belief in my ability to do things and cause things to happen.'[61] 'Props may be useful, but it is the mind that works magic . . . Practical results may be far less important than psychological insights that arise during the magical working. Discovering our inner blocks and fears is the first step in overcoming them.' 'Through spells we can attain the most important power – the power to change ourselves.'[62] The discourses of self-improvement are very dominant here; the self constructed is the familiar self of late capitalism, the striving, upwardly mobile self who controls her own destiny.

At the same time, modern witches postulate the self as the origin of power:

> The oldest and wisest among us can read disorder. From dreams to the utterances of madness, the chance cracks on a tortoiseshell, the fortunate shapes of leaves of tea, the fateful arrangement of cards, we can tell things. And some of us can heal.[63]

Just how 'we' know all this is never explained because the knowledge is portrayed as instinctive, deriving from the self and its connection with 'what grows' and 'the forces of natural, healing ways'.[64] Women's closeness to 'natural forces' is celebrated; women's 'instinctive' and 'intuitive' natures are constantly asserted:

> as women we are what the patriarchy has labelled us: vessels, containers, receptacles, carriers, shrines, shelters, houses, nurturers, incubators, holders, enfolders, listeners. We are built to receive . . . Our giving takes the form of a push toward freedom for the giver, as in the act of giving birth.[65]

This is a glowing account of female altruism, and an exceedingly coercive one, precisely because it celebrates receptiveness as an innately feminine characteristic linked to the biological processes of conception, pregnancy and childbirth. It is assumed that the reader will understand and empathise with the metaphor, whether or not she is or wants to be or can be a mother. Do infertile women still count as receptacles? What if we do not want to 'receive'? I do not recognise even my experience of biological maternity in that description; it woud be truer to figure pushing a baby out as a virtually involuntary act accompanied by great fear and pain. A sanitised and sugary account of maternity hardly encourages the view that modern witchcraft will really foreground those features of the female body found problematic by other Western religions. We do not seem far from the most sentimental aspects of the cult of the Virgin Mary. One might also ask how such a notion of woman could be made to include (say) Hillary Clinton or Benazir Bhutto. The fact that such women are excluded from definitions of true femininity reifies women's exclusion from politics and society.

By contrast, one of the most interesting and positive features of modern witchcraft is one rarely hailed by witches themselves as central to the movements. This is their reconfiguration of masculinity. One of the most engagingly creative moments in *The Spiral Dance* comes when Starhawk introduces the Horned God by quoting Eliot's 'The Love Song of J. Alfred Prufrock': 'Shall I part my hair behind? / Do I dare to eat a peach? I have heard the mermaids singing, each to each / I do not think they will sing to me'. The God, Starhawk explains, is difficult to understand because he does not fit into any of the existing roles:

> If men had been created in the Horned God's image, he would be free to be wild without being cruel, angry without being violent, sexual without being coercive, spiritual without being unsexed . . . The mermaids, who are the Goddess, would sing to him.[66]

We should all be that free. There is nothing more disappointing than the realisation that the energy and creativity of modern witches has largely gone into offering men more freedoms, while telling women that they are free already. The Prufrock figure thus transformed gains additional meaning, however, if we see him as a type for the dour and anxious historian, nervously shielding his professional identity from the taint of otherness. Modern witches have a lot to offer him, a lot of charming songs to sing. Is he listening?

Modern witches' spells and rituals offer little power; that is, for the sceptic, little in the way of a heartening fantasy of power or a theatrical staging of the forbidden. Spells and rituals emphasise the self-help aspects of witchcraft, and in the case of feminist witchcraft they most often offer a magical way to act out woman's receptive and nurturing 'nature'. Brooke's spells include a blessing spell for a house, a self-blessing, a protection spell against attack or burglary, a purification spell for the home, healing spells and rites. Starhawk offers a protective filter, a spell to rid oneself of anger(!), a spell to encourage 'self-acceptance', a spell to stop feeling lonely, a safe-space spell, a spell to know the child within, and a healing image.[67] All are domestic (psychic versions of housework) or defensive (sealing the body or home against attack). Only a few spells break these patterns, and these are perhaps the most 'traditional': a love spell and a money spell. Brooke hedges her love and money spells about with cautions, and in these cautions the discourse of therapy, even the discourse of the agony aunt, swamps all else:

> Be careful . . . love spells can go horribly wrong if the object of your love really doesn't want you. If you are lonely and want a lover or partner, I suggest you concentrate on yourself. Love yourself and lovers will appear . . . you could consider the qualities you have to offer a lover – compassion, humour, warmth, and so on – and really feel your way into them.[68]

These qualities are supposed to be your unique offerings, but Brooke somehow knows what they are. This is a sad comedown from the dark and powerful rage of ancient and early modern love spells, spells which offered *genuine* therapy because they allowed the representation of rage, hate and murderous sexual energy.[69] By contrast, Brooke offers self-love of the most anodyne kind as an alternative to love of another. Don't worry about attracting boys, dear, you're far too young; get on with your hobbies and interests . . .

Brooke is similarly anxious about money spells: 'buying materialist goodies is not a good reason for a money spell, but paying for an important course of study or a trip you need to make is fine by me'.[70] Just why a course or trip is not a materialist 'goody' if you have to pay for it is unclear, but the point seems to lie elsewhere; Brooke is maintaining witchcraft's separation from the modern world and its ills. The effect is to suggest that women should not want money or 'materialist goodies', a thoroughly patriarchal notion. Starhawk, on the other hand, wants to refute the idea that magic should not be used for practical ends: 'this attitude', she writes, 'is a holdover from the world view that sees spirits and matter as separate and that identifies matter with evil and corruption'.[71] Nonetheless, she too claims that 'no matter how much hate, envy and rage we direct at tailgaters, business competitors, ex-lovers and close relations, we will not esoterically affect either their physical or their mental health, although we may affect our own'.[72] This becomes the reason for trying to eliminate such feelings, and for refusing to act on them: 'witches', Starhawk explains, 'are extremely reluctant to hex anybody', since 'what you send returns to you three times over' and 'the energy you project to another affects *you* even more strongly than the other person'.[73] Zsuzsanna Budapest too is apologetic about offering a hex: 'Let your hatred, frustration, or fear flow through you to power the spell, and then release it completely'.[74] In other words, the spell is a way to rid yourself of socially unacceptable feelings, not to validate them. Nonetheless, she recounts the disruptive effects of the spell on the lives of harassers with considerable relish. The overall effect of the gluey benignity of the spells is to replace the Wicked Witch with Glinda the Good, in an uncritical reproduction of an ideological femininity of selflessness.

This relentless repression of characteristics *traditionally considered* unfeminine in patriarchy – anger, hate, aggression, desire for sex or money – is dispiriting. This conception of benignity as 'natural' to women does not merely uphold gender hierarchy; it also offers women no way to understand or deal with situations other than pacifically, which often means passively. Within witchcraft, the passive benignity of the witch is projected backwards onto the Nature of which she is deemed to be a part. Keith Thomas has shown how fantasies of the countryside and hence nature as havens from the dangers and pressures of the city arise from urban life itself, becoming widespread only when urban life becomes the norm.[75] According to both Adler and Lurhmann, most witches are themselves urban, yet most rituals, portrayals of deities and spells draw on images of a halcyon countryside and a festive rural year. A ritual of summer solstice 20–23 June is typical:

Priestess:	Behold, the God has gone into the grain!
All:	He will feed us!
Priestess:	The sun is on the water!
All:	He will quench our thirst!
Priestess:	The God is in the corn!
All:	It will grow high![76]

No mention here of the tons of agrochemicals that have recently joined the God in the corn, the gallons of purifiers that have gone into the water. It might be possible to imagine a hymn to the God or Goddess that acknowledged such things; perhaps along the lines of Geoffrey Hill's invocation of Offa as overlord of the M5.[77] However, rituals celebrating the wheel of the year are invariably tied to images of preindustrial nature. Many of these rituals are actually performed indoors, in living rooms, partly because the requirement to be naked (or 'skyclad', as Gardner called it) makes outdoor ritual imprudent. The rhythms of urban life are almost never incorporated into invocations, rituals or spells; what is celebrated is a rural calendar which does not exist in the countryside either, and never really did. This idealised rural cycle floats free of any need to worry about drought, early frost or disease. Wheat growth may be 'natural', but so is the mildew which rots the grain; 'seasons' are not calendrically regular, but subject to disruption which can wreck food production. Those in preindustrial societies, in day-to-day contact with the capriciousness of nature, are apt to postulate more ruthless deities than comfortably fed modern witches do.

In any case, the notion of naturalness is inherently contradictory; the natural is what is desirable, but ill-health – personal or environmental – is a sign that nature has somehow been disrupted – by technology, pollution, 'stress' or a host of other villains associated with modernity. In this sense, the natural is what must be painstakingly restored – by healing rituals, for instance. So the natural is static, but at the same time vulnerable to disruption. This reflects precisely the logic of the historical narrative of witchcraft discussed earlier; the figures of the witch and the Goddess and the truths they contain are eternal, but also constantly subject to historical loss and forgetfulness, constantly requiring to be recovered. This contradiction justifies a programme of great activity and intervention mediated through a rhetoric of utter passivity, since all interventions are aimed at restoration rather than at change and adaptation.

Some at least of these interventions take forms recognisable from the field of consumer capitalism. 'You want magic? We got it!' proclaims an advertisement for The Sorcerer's Apprentice mail-order catalogue: 'athames * altar reliquary * crystals and gemstones * Temple Furniture * step-by-step Beginner's spells, plus made-to-order equipment'.[78] For those involved in more traditional witchcraft, there are 'genuine black heavy cast-iron traditional 3-legged cauldrons', available in three sizes.[79] A list of commodities like this erodes the often-asserted gap between witchcraft and mainstream society; discursively the advertisement is not distinguishable from one for Dixon's Summer Sale. As well as commodities, other services are for sale:

> Tanith: Experienced occultist and witch. Can I help you with your problems? Love, money, job, health, career . . . whatever your problem, you need not struggle alone . . . NO high fees, agreed donations only. Genuine help for all those in need.[80]

This too is recognisably therapy territory: pay now for a solution to your problems. It is difficult to argue that modern witchcraft opposes dull, workaday materialism while taking a fee (or 'agreed donation') for your occult services, or to claim that witches subvert the norms of consumer society when witchcraft can be so easily adapted to them. Why is a cauldron any different from a surplice, a washing machine or a microwave? How does paying Tanith to solve your problems differ from paying a psychiatrist to solve them? Tanith is a private, individual solution. Presumably she is not going to solve my problems by giving Britain's limp equal opportunities legislation some teeth; judging by the testimonials which adorn her advertisement, she can offer answers only to individuals (marriage, jobs, etc.). The individualistic nature of such 'answers' is apparent when I contemplate the many people I know who would not dream of joining BUPA, but do not mind using chiropractors, astrologers and natural healers. Rather like the Body Shop, whose customers have come to see the purchase of cosmetics as a positive communitarian virtue, witchcraft can work to validate the most blinkered forms of individualism, greed and self-assertion, while piously denouncing others for these very faults.

Yet other witches have plenty of political savvy. Thanks to the activism of modern Pagans, the witch is on the verge of becoming what Christopher Hill erroneously claimed for her seventeenth-century counterpart: a figure for political intransigence which refuses to equate progress with the good. Modern witches have not played much part in the politics of government, but they are deeply engaged with a different and increasingly popular political agenda of civil rights connected to environmental issues. That is, they see environmental issues *as* civil rights issues, the right to breathe clean air, and to bring up children in a green countryside rather than in a grey urban wasteland, to see animals instead of lorries. This connection has been made possible because many modern witches have cut their political teeth defending their own freedom to practise a religion of nature worship. Because most people know little of Paganism, and because the word 'witch' retains diachronically its connotations of menace to children, witches have often had problems with the police and the social services.

For example, witches told me that the press staked out the most popular Pagan bookshop in Britain, The Sorcerer's Apprentice, in the belief that it was part of a Satanic ring of child abuse, a charge utterly denied by all modern witches. After a local campaign of firebombing, graffiti and excrement by post, the owner had to close down except as a mail-order supplier.[81] Secrecy in the movement is now so strong that The Sorcerer's Apprentice now sends out its mail-order catalogue in a plain brown envelope, identifying itself only as 'SA'. Like most occult practitioners, SA are keen on freedom of speech, but also ingenious in adapting to the law. The SA's catalogue is practical but insouciant about legal disapproval. They sell a ceramic skull which they describe as having 'that just-dug-up aura' but which 'Mr Plod won't mind'. They sell a goat's head pendant which is urged on the reader thus: 'come on, all you 'orrible Satanists! Get yours while stocks last . . . Guaranteed to cause a lot of fuss'.[82] The store's owner has responded to the threat of 'Mr Plod' and society's accusations by writing a summary of child abuse and murder by clergymen and Christian fundamentalists. He has also started a society to defend Pagans' rights. This exists alongside the Pagan Federation, which is a front-door contact for European Pagans and a campaign group for the recognition of Pagan freedom of worship; they claim some success with the Home Office and the police. A Pagan called Arthur Uther Pendragon, who has achieved some media notoriety for his Craft-name and for his belief that he is the reincarnation of Arthur, has brought an individual test-case for the right to celebrate the summer solstice at Stonehenge and against the Criminal Justice Act's offence of aggravated trespass.[83] The Pagan Federation also operate a media bureau for press consultation, in an effort to combat what Pagans see as negative images of them in the press.[84]

Witches are not very prominent in any of these movements, perhaps because their separatism means that they are not interested in liberal issues like civil rights, and perhaps because society's disapproval might fall more heavily on unruly women than on nutty men. Many witches will no longer talk about their beliefs to strangers, in case the social take away their kids.[85] Many more modern witches feel that they have been driven into hiding, or back into the broom closet, as witches say. The renewal of the silencing of women in the sphere of witchcraft has unpleasant implications; perhaps there is a risk that women will be forced into the position of silent muse after all, not by their fellow Pagans, but by a society that regards difference as unforgivable in women and especially in mothers.

Witches are also perturbed about the impact of the Criminal Justice Act on their freedom of movement and worship. Directed against so-called New Age travellers, among others, the Act addresses anxieties about illicit use of the 'countryside' by people who had outrageously turned their backs on mortgage repayments and nine-to-five jobs. The accompanying rhetoric about smells, noise, unkempt children and sheer weirdness replicates all the hoary old tropes of Greenham Common; appropriately enough, since that protest too was in part an attempt to question who owned what. The Act resolves the question in favour of a simple law of property; you can only use the 'countryside' you have bought and paid for. This runs against the grain of the Pagan idea that the earth belongs to everyone. The bottom line for the right is not property or privacy *per se*, but the middle- and upper-class assumption that the undeserving and undeferential poor will stay in the cities, leaving the countryside as a refuge from them. The fact that 'New Age' travellers are often people who refuse to accept the idea that the countryside is only for their betters is disturbing, because it suggests that the middle classes may not be able to buy their way out of the urban problems they have helped to create. The effect of a heritage industry constantly pressing country kitchens, country furnishings and *The Country Diary of an Edwardian Lady* on us all should not be underestimated; of course, these items of middle-class chic were not intended to make the urban poor believe that their kids too could benefit from nature, flowers and fresh air. Ironically, the very middle-class equation of the country with an escape from the turmoil of city life, an equation which goes back to the Stuart *Book of Sports*, has ensured that the countryside is now menaced on all sides by exactly those people the middle classes left the city to evade. Travellers who do not see why their kids should grow up among concrete just because they are poor will now have it explained to them by Mr Plod.

Pagan involvement in the roadbuilding protests involves a similar clash of values. More than one witch has told me that black witches or their dupes are trying to destroy Britain's sacred sites by roadbuilding, rezoning and housing development. Daffy as this may sound, such motives may play an increasing role in motivating protests against the building of new roads, and they connect with more orthodox middle-class concerns about preserving the past. Paganism allows 'ordinary' people (i.e. not landowners) to feel that the whole of the countryside and its ancient monuments are their concern and their responsibility. The branch of the heritage industry that has grown up around Pagan interpretations of the past fosters a sense of connection with preservation for people who feel excluded from National Trust-style preservation of great houses. Unlike Blenheim, Stonehenge might have been built by or for the people. Paganism allows its adherents to feel that the past is theirs to preserve.

The same idea, a kind of green common ownership, is expressed in the Twyford Downs protests, which drew in a wide range of Pagan groups such as ELF (Earth Saboteurs for the Liberation Front) and the white witchcraft group the Tribe of Dongas. Similarly, the Oxleas Wood protests in south London, which succeeded in preventing the extension of the road system, involved the active participation of Dragon, an eco-Pagan campaigning group that brings together witches, druids and others in both campaigning and spell-casting. Some members of Dragon believe that their campaign was aided by the natural forces and earth spirits which still live in Oxleas Wood, but others were inspired by the evidence of sacred burial uncovered at Twyford. 'I saw ancient graves containing seven-foot skeletons,' said one member. But the general impetus derived from the theory is that the whole of nature is sacred, as opposed to the mainstream view that the earth is a resource to be plundered.[86] One angry Pagan remarked that nobody would put a motorway through a cathedral, so why put one through a wood?[87] The male fantasy-image of nature as a mother goddess who is not owned by anyone, though sought by many, has become an exceedingly useful political metaphor, which almost justifies its existence, and certainly would have pleased Jules Michelet.

The witches' histories, erroneous though they are, remind us of things we might otherwise forget: the excitement of recognising the strangeness and otherness of the past, the willingness to ask questions that academics cannot answer (for example, the origin of witch-beliefs), the political engagements with history, the attempt to rethink the relations between body and identity, body and spirit, the rich voluptuous imagery, the sense of fun, the reminder that the witch was in the first place the construction of popular history. Most of all, modern witches offer a new way to see history from below, history as a space that can be colonised and occupied by people who are not part of academic institutions. Because they are not constrained to interpret the witch according to the rules of evidence, modern witches have recovered the early modern possibility of appropriating her in order to tell stories about their own identities and about power and its operations. In this at least, they are right to say that they are reviving an early modern popular practice.

Modern witches' histories of witchcraft represent a much cleaner break with academic values than anything feminist historians have produced or have wished to produce. Far more than Derrida or Foucault, popular history disregards the assumptions which make Enlightenment history possible. Genuine indifference to the boundaries between memory and invention, fact and fancy, truth and fiction must alarm, and some of this alarm is perfectly justified.[88] Nonetheless, it is striking that culturally, the second of each of these pairs tends to be coded as feminine, as is the personal, the therapeutic self-inscription. Given that such coding is itself the outcome of a history in which Romanticism played a key role – given, that is, that the same factors which shaped the figure of the modern witch now oppose her to history by presenting her as 'too soft' on fact – the modern witch's identity as a figure in history and as maker of history and its rules could come to represent the irruption of 'femininity', with its semiotic uncertainties, its high affect, its lack of interest in empirical scrutiny, into the masculine space of historical empiricism. Perhaps modern witches show what feminist history might be like if it *really* abandoned empiricism altogether instead of simply calling it into question from time to time. The vision might appal: modern witchcraft can be solipsistic, mired in a self-centred present, and far too willing to ignore inconvenient truths. On the other hand, a feminist history which sought to draw on the strengths of this movement rather than simply pointing to its weaknesses might be exciting. Like modern witches, it might be speculative, unreliable, often wrong, sometimes ridiculous, politically very useful, other than authoritative, and absolutely scandalous in the academy.

None of this is surprising when we consider the long and distinguished history of women's writing of historical novels, with their championship of historical unorthodoxy, their eager interest in personality, gossip and romance, their attraction to the historical scapegraces dismissed as failures. Virginia Woolf's fantasy of Judith Shakespeare in *A Room of One's Own* is not really a very good history of early modern women writers, but it is a remarkable and moving story of an absence, a silence, a loss. What if women writing history allowed their invention to play about freely in the fields of the past, searching for fantasies that might be at least temporarily enabling or interesting, rather than (or as well as) for new ways to do empirical history? What if we were all less concerned to win the admiration of non- or antifeminist male scholars, and more eager to excite or influence other women? I am not suggesting that women are incapable of empirical history, or that empirical history is always oppressive. Sometimes an unknown truth is the most explosive thing there is, and there are appalling risks involved in parading fantasy as truth. However, this should not rule out exploiting the power of imagination or fantasy about the past. Modern witches put the project of feminist history into question more than any other group, because only they suggest that it may be less important to feminism and even to women to know the truth than to invent a good fantasy. We could try to think about how to harness the power of the imagination and the power of feeling without abandoning the project of telling the truth. We might begin seriously trying to invent ways to do history which allow for storytelling, mythmaking; ways of understanding history which allow us to see women mythmakers as historians, women's poetry or painting or fiction as history. This must involve using the poststructuralist psychoanalyses of French feminism as ways to uncover the alterity of woman's imagination at work within what might otherwise present themselves as unremittingly patriarchal discourses.

NOTES

1 Zsuzsanna E. Budapest, *The Goddess in the Office: A Personal Energy Guide for the Spiritual Warrior at Work*, San Francisco: Harper San Francisco, 1993, p. 66.

2 See Andrew Ross, *Strange Weather: Culture, Science and Technology in the Age of Limits,* London: Verso, 1991, preface.

3 Donna Haraway, 'A manifesto for cyborgs: science, technology, and socialist feminism in the 1980s', in *Coming to Terms: Feminism, Theory, Politics*, ed. Elizabeth Weed, London: Routledge, 1989, pp. 173–204, first published 1985.

4 Margot Adler, *Drawing Down the Moon: Witches, Druids, Goddess-Worshippers and other Pagans in America today*, rev. edn., Boston: Beacon, 1986, pp. 446–8, first published 1979; T. H. Luhrmann, *Persuasions of the Witch's Craft: Ritual Magic in Contemporary England*, Oxford: Blackwell, 1989, pp. 106–7.

5 Suzanne Ruthven, *Malleus Satani*, London: Ignotus, 1993, ch. 2; see also Steve Bruce, *Religion in Modern Britain*, Oxford: Oxford University Press, 1995; and, for the US, Aidan Kelly, 'An update on neopagan witchcraft in America', in *Perspectives on the New Age*, ed. James Lewis, Albany: State University of New York Press, 1993, p. 136.

6 I was fortunate enough to be able to speak to a number of practising witches about their beliefs. For reasons which will become clear in the course of this chapter, I cannot name them.

7 Starhawk (Miriam Simos), *The Spiral Dance: A Rebirth of the Ancient Religion of the Great Goddess*, rev. edn., San Francisco: HarperCollins, 1988, p. 91, first published 1979.

8 Elisabeth Brooke, *A Woman's Book of Shadows: Witchcraft: A Celebration*, London: Women's Press, 1993, p. 9.

9 Richard Jenkyns, *The Victorians and Ancient Greece*, Cambridge: Cambridge University Press, 1986.

10 Carole Pateman, *The Sexual Contract*, Cambridge: Polity, 1988. Mary Renault's historical novels are a readable representation of this view, *The King Must Die* in particular.

11 See Diane Purkiss, 'Women's rewriting of myth', in *The Feminist Companion to Mythology*, ed. Carolyne Larrington, London: Pandora, 1992, pp. 441–58.

12 Karl-Ernst Järcke, 'Ein Hexenprozess', in *Annalen der deutschen und ausländischen Kriminalrechspflege*, Berlin, 1828; Jeffrey Burton Russell, *A History of Witchcraft: Sorcerers, Heretics and Pagans*, London: Thames & Hudson, 1980, p. 133; Norman Cohn, *Europe's Inner Demons*, London: Macmillan, 1975, pp. 148–9.

13 Jules Michelet, *Satanism and Witchcraft*, trans. A. R. Allison, New York: Citadel, 1992, pp. 71ff.

14 Neil Hertz, 'Medusa's head: male hysteria under political pressure', *Repesentations*, 4 (1983), pp. 27–54; Joan Landes, *Women and the Public Sphere in the Age of the French Revolution*, Ithaca: Cornell University Press, 1988.

15 See Jenkyns, *The Victorians and Ancient Greece*, and Prudence Jones and Nigel Pennick, *A History of Pagan Europe*, London: Routledge, 1995, pp. 212–14.

16 Richard A. Hutch, 'Helene Blavatsky unveiled', *Journal of Religious History*, 2 (1980), p. 336; Alex Owen, *The Darkened Room*, London: Virago, 1989, p. 217.

17 On Leland, see Elliot Rose, *A Razor for a Goat: A Discussion of Certain Problems in the History of Witchcraft and Diabolism*, Toronto, 1962; Adler, *Drawing Down the Moon*, pp. 88–9.

18 Charles G. Leland, *Aradia: The Gospel of the Witches*, introduction by Carole Brandwood, London: Gates of Annawn, 1991, p. 2.

19 Leland, *Aradia*, p. 111.

20 Leland, *Aradia*, p. 111. In case the reader doesn't remember: 'Oh woman, in our hour of ease / Uncertain, coy and hard to please / When pain and fever wring the brow / A minstering angel thou!'

21 Leland, *Aradia*, p. 112.

22 Margaret Murray, *The Witch-Cult in Western Europe*, London: Oxford University Press, 1921.

23 For example, see Jade (Samantha River), *To Know: A Guide to Women's Magic and Spirituality*, Oak Park: Delphi, 1991, pp. 7–8; see also the supportive entry under Murray in Doreen Valiente, *An ABC of Witchcraft*, Washington: Phoenix, 1973; compare the more sceptical position of Adler, *Drawing Down the Moon*, pp. 47ff.

24 Margaret Murray, *The God of the Witches*, London: Oxford University Press, 1931.
25 On Murray, see *DNB* , and see the introduction to the OUP reprtint of her *God of the Witches*, 1985. For a modern witch's view, see Ruthven, *Malleus Satani*.
26 Gerald Gardner, *Withcraft Today*, New York: Magickal Childe, 1954, p. 39.
27 Marion Bradley, *The Mists of Avalon*, London: Fontana, 1988, first published 1983. Luhrmann, *Persuasions*, pp. 87–92; Adler, *Drawing Down the Moon*, p. 285. Mary Renault's *The King Must Die* is another crucial early influence; Renault's novel is itself heavily influenced by Frazer, Jung and Evans; see Adler, *Drawing Down the Moon*, p. 15. See also Carrol L. Fry, '"What God doth the wizard pray to?": Neopagan witchcraft and fantasy fiction', *Extrapolation: A Journal of Science Fiction and Fantasy*, 31 (1990), pp. 333–46.
28 For accounts of Gardner's career by his disciples, see J. J. Bracelin, *Gerald Gardner: Witch*, London: Octagon, 1960; Valiente, *An ABC*, pp. 152–8; Raymond Buckland's introduction to Gardner, *Witchcraft Today*. See also Luhrmann, *Persuasions*, pp. 43–9, and Adler, *Drawing Down the Moon*, pp. 78–85ff.
29 Both Susan Casteras, '*Malleus maleficarum, or the witch's hammer*: Victorian visions of female sages and sorceresses', in *Victorian Sages and Cultural Discourse: Renegotiating Gender and Power*, ed. Thais E. Morgan, New Brunswick: Rutgers University Press, 1991, and Jan Marsh, *Pre-Raphaelite Women: Images of Femininity in Pre-Raphaelite Art*, London: Weidenfeld & Nicolson, 1987, pp. 109–22 explore pre-Raphaelitism's fascination with the figure of the sorceress. Wilhelm Meinhold's melodramatic extravaganza novel *Sidonia Van Bork* was the inspiration for Burne-Jones, while Morgan came from the Arthuriad via Tennyson and Morris, and Lilith from Jewish folklore. Other influential fictions included Bulwer-Lytton's *Zanoni*, which influenced Helena Blavatsky, and William Harrison Ainsworth's *Lancashire Witches*. See Diana Basham, *The Trial of Woman: Feminism and the Occult Sciences in Victorian Literature and Society*, London: Macmillan, 1992.
30 Lynn Pearce explores the topic of women's appropriation of ambivalent and magical female figures in *Woman/Image/Text: Readings in Pre-Raphaelite Art and Literature*, Hemel Hempstead: Harvester, 1991.
31 Evelyn de Morgan's *Queen Eleanor and Fair Rosamund* (1888), oil on canvas, the de Morgan Collection, London. See Marsh, *Pre-Raphaelite Women*.
32 *Daughters of Decadence: Women Writers of the Fin-de-Siècle*, ed. Elaine Showalter, London: Virago, 1993.
33 Mary K. Greer, *Women of the Golden Dawn: Rebels and Priestesses*, Rochester: Park Street Press, 1995; Jean Overton Fuller, *Blavatsky and her Teachers*, London, 1988; and Hutch, 'Helene Blavatsky'; Anne Taylor, *Annie Besant: A Biography,*. Oxford: Oxford University Press, 1992.
34 For feminist astrology, see among others Lindsay River and Sally Gillespie, *The Knot of Time: Astrology and Female Experience*, London: Women's Press, 1987.
35 Gardner's own works, *The Meaning of Witchcraft*, New York: Magickal Childe, 1982, first published 1959, and *Witchcraft Today*. For Gardner's borrowings, see Rosemary Elizabeth Guiley, 'Witchcraft as goddess-worship', in *The Feminist Companion to Mythology*, ed. Carolyne Larrington, London: Pandora, 1992, pp. 411–24.
36 For a full discussion see Adler, *Drawing Down the Moon*, pp. 83–5.
37 Kelly, 'An update on neopagan witchcraft', p. 136; Isaac Bonewits, *Real Magic: An Introductory Treatise on the Principles of Yellow Magic*, London: Open Gate, 1972; Brooke, *A Woman's Book*, p. 59. Even Kelly still argues for an ongoing tradition, though he sees it as different from the modern witchcraft Gardner invented (p. 137).
38 Adler, *Drawing Down the Moon*, pp. 56–8.
39 Adler, *Drawing Down the Moon*, p. 59.

40 Claire Nahmad, *Earth Magic; A Wisewoman's Guide to Herbal, Astrological, and other Folk Remedies*, London: Rider, 1993, p. 5.
41 Adler, *Drawing Down the Moon*, p. 90.
42 There have been feminist utopias set in the future: Marge Piercy's *Woman on the Edge of Time*, for instance, and Monique Wittig's *Les Guerillères.*
43 Starhawk, *Spiral Dance*, p. 17; Brooke, *A Woman's Book*, pp. 40ff.
44 M.D. Faber, *Modern Witchcraft and Psychoanalysis*, Rutherford: Fairleigh Dickinson University Press, 1993. Generally, however, this is disappointingly simplistic, pre-feminist in its understanding of motherhood.
45 Zsuzsanna Budapest, *The Holy Book of Women's Mysteries*, Oakland: Wingbow, 1989, p. 284.
46 Stella Georgoudi, 'Creating a myth of matriarchy', in *A History of Women*, vol. 1, *From Ancient Goddesses to Christian Saints*, ed. Pauline Schmitt-Pantel, Harvard: Bellknap, 1992, pp. 449–63.
47 Budapest's section on the destruction of the Minoan matriarchy is actually entitled 'how we lost it'; a subsequent historical section is called 'the fall' (*Women's Mysteries*, pp. 4, 294).
48 For example, see Luhrmann, *Persuasions*, for a ritual celebrating Drake, Elizabeth I and John Dee as Arthur, Guinevere and Merlin, pp. 208–9. See also Valiente, 'Sir Francis Drake', *An ABC*, pp. 96–7.
49 Femocrats versus radicals again; on this division, see Sophie Watson, *Playing the State*, London: Verso, 1991. On critiques of New Age spirituality from within the women's movement, see Barbara Ryan, *Feminism and the Women's Movement: Dynamics Of Change in Social Movement, Ideology and Activism*, London: Routledge, 1992, p. 128.
50 Adler, *Drawing Down the Moon*, p. 277; Ed Fitch, *The Rites of Odin*, St Paul: Llewellyn, 1990.
51 Carlo Ginzburg, *The Cheese and the Worms: The Cosmos of a Sixteenth-Century Miller*, trans. John and Anne Tedeschi, London: Routledge & Kegan Paul, 1980.
52 Michel de Certeau, *The Practice of Everyday Life*, trans. Steven F. Rendall, Berkeley: University of California Press, 1984, p. 175.
53 Ginzburg is cited in a standard Pagan primer, Caitlin and John Matthews, *The Western Way: A Practical Guide to the Western Mystery Tradition*, omnibus edition, London: Penguin Arkana, 1994, first published 1985 and 1986, p. 134.
54 This witch claimed that black witches were systematically trying to destroy Britain's sacred sites so as to control society; she saw the government roadbuilding programme as a means of carrying this out, and seemed to believe that the government's power stemmed from black witchcraft.
55 See Valiente for alternative Gardnerian claims to have prevented an invasion in 1940 by raising a cone of power, *An ABC*, pp. 97, 155, and to have ended the Vietnam War, p. 330. Similar rites are said to have seen off the Spanish Armada and Napoleon.
56 This witch claimed that those 'living room witches' who did not believe in black witches were naive, or worse.
57 One witch I spoke to seemed influenced by the Thomas–Macfarlane thesis when she dismissed the myth of the Burning Times, saying that those who were burned were not witches, but 'old beggars or something'. Nonetheless, she too had never heard of either historian.
58 See Starhawk, expressing this very reservation in *Spiral Dance*, p. 206.
59 Rosalind Coward, *The Whole Truth: The Myth of Alternative Health*, London: Faber, 1989, p. 67.
60 Brooke, *A Woman's Book*, p. 141.
61 Starhawk, *Spiral Dance*, p. 125.

62 Starhawk, *Spiral Dance*, pp. 125–6.
63 Susan Griffin, *Women and Nature: The Roaring Inside Her*, London: Women's Press, 1986, p. 175.
64 Griffin, *Women and Nature*, pp. 88–9. Actually, such knowledge usually derives from books, but even books instructing the witch on (say) the use of the Tarot stress instinctive knowledge while actually providing an interpretive grid through which the cards can be interpreted: 'they are a learning, self-discovery text', writes Brooke, *A Woman's Book*, p. 197. See also Luhrmann on the constitutive effect of 'common knowledges' of tarot and astrology, *Persuasions*, pp. 144–60.
65 Charlotte Spretnak, cited by Coward, *Whole Truth*, p. 173.
66 Starhawk, *Spiral Dance*, pp. 108–9.
67 Brooke, *A Woman's Book*, pp. 141–7, Starhawk, *Spiral Dance*, chs 9–11.
68 Brooke, *A Woman's Book*, p. 146.
69 For some classical examples, see John J. Winkler, 'The constraints of desire: erotic magic spells', in *The Constraints of Desire: The Anthropology of Sex and Gender in Ancient Greece*, London and New York: Routledge, 1990, pp. 71–98, and Theocritus, Idyll 2; for early modern Italy, see Mary O'Neil, 'Magical healing, love magic and the Inquisition in late sixteenth-century Modena', in *Inquisition and Society in Early Modern Europe*, ed. and trans. S. Haliczer, London: Croom Helm, 1987, pp. 88–114, and Guido Ruggiero, *Ruling Passions: Tales of Magic, Marriage and Power at the End of the Renaissance*, Oxford and New York: Oxford University Press, 1993.
70 Brooke, *A Woman's Book*, p. 150.
71 Starhawk, *Spiral Dance*, p. 124.
72 Starhawk, *Spiral Dance*, p. 127.
73 Starhawk, *Spiral Dance*, pp. 126–7.
74 Budapest, *Office*, pp. 42–9.
75 Keith Thomas, *Man and the Natural World*, Harmondsworth: Penguin, 1983, pp. 244ff.
76 Starhawk, *Spiral Dance*, p. 190; see also Rae Beth, *Hedge-Witch: a Guide to Solitary Witchcraft*, London: Hale, 1990, Adler, *Drawing Down the Moon*, and Nahmad, *Earth Magic*.
77 Geoffrey Hill, *Mercian Hymns* (1976), no. 1, in *Collected Poems*, Harmondsworth: Penguin, 1985, p. 105.
78 Advertisement in *Prediction* magazine, August 1993, p. 4.
79 Advertisement in *Prediction* magazine, August 1993, p. 73.
80 Advertisement in *Prediction* magazine, August 1993, p. 22.
81 Ruthven, *Malleus Satani*, ch. 9.
82 The Sorcerer's Apprentice mail order catalogue, equipment list, June 1995.
83 *Independent on Sunday*, 11 June 1995. The civil rights group Liberty represent Mr Pendragon.
84 For an instance of the kind of story which worries pagans and especially witches who are parents, see 'Witchcraft row over Anglican priest in pagan sex rite', *Sunday Telegraph*, 11 June 1995, a story which makes it sound as if the vicar and the Pagans were engaging in a joint orgy. In fact, as the article admits, the 'sex rite' consisted of the insertion of a wand into a cup.
85 This is the reason that witches interviewed by me are not identified even by their Craft-names; of the three witches I spoke to at length, two were willing to be so identified, but the third was not; she was the only one with children.
86 *Independent*, 27 May 1993, cited by Raphael Samuel, *Theatres of Memory*, London: Verso, 1994. Samuel discusses Pagans as part of the heritage industry.
87 *Pagan Dawn: Journal of the Pagan Federation*, Number 115, (Beltane) 1995, p. 18.
88 Some feminists reject refutations of the myth of an originary matriarchy or of the witch-cult as patriarchal conspiracies; for a particularly spectacular example, see

Luce Irigaray, *Je, Tu, Nous: Toward a Culture of Difference*, trans. Alison Martin, London: Routledge, 1993, pp. 17, 24ff. Irigaray cites a modern witch, Merlin Stone, in support of her argument for matriarchal myths hidden within patriarchal history. I discuss this in the following chapter. Nonetheless, Irigaray is highly critical of unthinking reversions to matriarchy: see 'Divine women', in *Sexes and Genealogies*, trans. Gillian Gill, New York: Columbia University Press, 1993, p. 60.

3 The witch in the hands of historians

A tale of prejudice and fear

> They say miracles are past, and we have our philosophical persons, to make modern and familiar, things supernatural and causeless. Hence is it that we make trifles of terrors, ensconcing ourselves into seeming knowledge, when we should submit ourselves to an unknown fear.
>
> Shakespeare, *All's Well That Ends Well*

While popular historians have woven the figure of the witch into elaborate tapestries of narrative and identity, what of academic historians? What role does the witch play in academic self-fashioning? In considering this question, it is important to be clear about what kind of investigation this is. For most of the readers of this book, the review article will be a more familiar genre than the cultural studies reading of academic discourse, but it is important that the latter is not mistaken for the former. This chapter is not an overview of the contributions made by the historians of English witchcraft to its totality. There is no attempt to assess the relative merits of historians. Rather, this chapter asks what the result would be if we were willing to suspend our usual categories and analyse the works of fellow academics as if they were popular histories. What if academic histories, irrespective for the moment of their truth or falsity, could be considered as myths? What has shaped academic histories of witchcraft?

There has been some exceptionally brilliant work on witchcraft in the last ten years, work which addresses the whole question of gender and the supernatural in new and exciting ways; the field of witchcraft studies has never been more exciting or more theoretically rigorous.[1] Unfortunately, all this good work is about Continental and American witchcraft.[2] English witchcraft studies have been left in the slow lane: a gush of creativity in the early 1970s has hardened into an orthodoxy that has become difficult to dislodge or modify. This orthodoxy is almost silent about gender, though it has an unacknowledged gender subtext. Questions of gender are being addressed, but by historians overtly hostile to feminist theories and histories. Recent historians of English witchcraft are rather insular, ignoring studies of Continental witchcraft and their contributions to the theorisation of the relations between gender and popular beliefs. There is no major study of English witchcraft by a woman, and only a few minor ones.[3] The discourse of academic histories of witchcraft is still a male one, composed for the male voice.

The torpor of English witchcraft studies is inseparable from the question of why English social historians of the early modern period have been deaf to the methodological questions raised inside and outside history in the past twenty years. English witchcraft studies form an ideal site on which to demonstrate the failure of English history to come to grips with theoretical challenges, or even to defend its own practices with any kind of seriousness. Theoretical problems are raised in particularly acute form by attempts to write historically about witchcraft, not least because the witch's continued diachronic meaning makes it difficult to interpret her past. However, in the history of witchcraft in England, the question of gender in particular has been covered over, not because English historians of witchcraft are especially misogynist, but because gender is always already invisible in a methodology that cannot take account of either supernatural causation or ideology. Without apprehension of theory, academic historians of English witchcraft have created a narcissistic myth which shapes them as sceptical empiricists, confirming their academic identities. This myth heightens their reluctance to engage with theory.

To understand this myth, one might begin with a suggestive comment by a feminist historian of Continental witchcraft. Lyndal Roper writes that:

> As a profession used to addressing documents for their reliability, it is hard to know how to interpret documents which we do not believe to be factual.[4]

Roper has shrewdly identified the link between the profession of history and the epistemological problem of witchcraft 'beliefs' in this passage. But she does not explore this connection in detail, nor does she address the academic beliefs at which she gestures: in 'reliability' and its desiderata, for instance. Roper remarks that these beliefs coexist with an apparently endless fascination with the subject of witchcraft, and she explains this fascination in terms of the way it marks 'the distance which separates us from the past'.[5] This valorisation of witchcraft's utter historical difference can be seen as narcissistic rather than judicious, however. The primitivism of the witch reinforces historians' view of themselves as rational, scientific, Enlightened. Jeanne Favret-Saada claims that accounts of the cultural difference between the academic anthropologist and those who 'believe in' witchcraft function to construct the believer as the dark other of the academic.[6] The witchcraft believer is credulous, where the academic is sceptical; the believer takes words on trust, where the academic is 'used to assessing documents for their reliability'; the believer is prejudiced, where the academic is impartial; the believer is primitive, where the academic is sophisticated.[7] Those oppositions construct an identity for the believer in witchcraft which affirms the identity of the academic who recounts those beliefs.[8]

These oppositions must constantly be re-marked and rewritten in academic writings on witchcraft, not only because they constitute its hidden agenda, but because like most oppositions they are vulnerable to collapse. Beliefs in witchcraft must be recounted by the historian; the academic writer must constantly speak in the place of those who hold those beliefs in order to establish the authority of the text. There is consequently a risk that the academic may be indistinct from his or her subject-matter, a risk of 'going native', of being perceived as the other. The very process of turning the other into a spectacle may expose the historian as insufficiently different from his or her subject-matter, generating a need to re-mark the gap between the objects of study and the historian.

This fear of identification looks respectable when the object of study is a persecutory figure. If the inquisitor is an anthropologist, is the anthropologist (or the historian) also an Inquisitor?[9] However, historians are also keen to evade belief where that is the discourse of the accused, not only because it is tainted with the scent of persecution, but also because such beliefs are as alien to the empiricism of the historian as they are to any other sort of empiricism. 'History' is one of the Enlightenment discourses which gradually displaces the supernatural in the seventeenth century. Those Enlightenment discourses established their authority by staking out their own truths on terrain which had previously belonged to interpreters of the supernatural. The bodies of the possessed, of fasting women, of witches, the miraculous, all these were sites chosen by empiricism to establish its authority. It is not surprising that historians are still using the same sites, especially when historical empiricism is under attack from both poststructuralist theory and postmodern reality. Rather than trying to understand how witch-beliefs were structured for and by the believer, historians have often bent their energies towards explaining witch-beliefs *away*. Assuming witch-beliefs were an abnormality and a pathology, they sought to explain how such ideas could have arisen, rather than what those ideas were. Even now, histories of witchcraft that do not seek a global explanation of why the 'witch-craze' occurred are deemed inadequate, or read as if that is what they are offering. The only serious question to be asked about witchcraft, it seems, is still 'Why, oh why?', perhaps because only this question is distancing.

Really, the historian and the past are too far from each other, not too close. Historians should not feel menaced by the possibility that the past may engulf them, but despairing at their inability to see it at all. The 'history' of witchcraft consists of picking over fragmentary texts, almost always written down by someone other than their 'author'. So little survives. There is only one run of assize depositions in manuscript, though other manuscripts of trials in other kinds of court exist; from many cases, all that has been preserved is a tersely worded indictment, a pamphlet grinding some axe or other and subsuming the words of depositions or confessions into the author's prose, a casual reference in a letter or diary, a gaol record. Sometimes there is nothing. Nor is reading what survives uncomplicated. Lacking a shared body of interpretative popular knowledge, a knowledge or knowledges perhaps lost in the very moment when some or all of the texts were being inscribed, the texts do not 'make sense'; they cannot be read except as unreadability itself, as that incongruity between past and present we affectionately call quaintness. At times it may seem that we can only throw up our hands. Which stories sound likely? Which stories are strategic and which communicative? Which ideas are elite and which popular? Why accuse this woman and not that woman? The fragmentary narratives of witchcraft are already absurd; they are torn even where apparently most whole. It is very hard to make ourselves take early modern fears seriously enough, to imagine a world drenched in the supernatural. A barking dog, an innocent-seeming question, a domestic disaster, could be warnings of desperate importance. Feelings like this would today be called paranoid, even comical; we have to try to imagine a world in which they were as normal as the process of assessing the threat from strangers is on today's streets. Yet we cannot hope to succeed, for just as our assumptions about reliability and criminality are hardly conscious, so early modern assumptions about supernatural signs were less an articulate system than a set of half-formulated working rules. Buried beneath the surface of witch-narratives, they rarely manifest themselves even as an articulate subtext, and the historian's attempt to piece them together is itself a falsification, since it is in the nature of such beliefs that they remain unexamined. It is equally hard for us not to despise people with such beliefs and so to assume that they are all transparent and honest, forthcoming with the truth at all times, incapable of vested interests and theatrical self-fashioning. On the other hand, we may become paralysed by our own scepticism, too cynical to try any longer. Sometimes we are taking stories too seriously, sometimes not seriously enough. Can we ever know about even one story?

Given this maddening distance, the repeated rites of distantiation performed by historians are even more striking. Histories of witchcraft often set themselves up via the ritual slaughter of a rival academic who has allowed herself to become indivisible from witch-beliefs. I say 'herself' advisedly, because somehow this figure is always a woman. In the work of Alan Macfarlane, Norman Cohn and Keith Thomas, Margaret Murray plays this role. Murray saw the stories of witches and accusers as coded accounts of a surviving sect of pagans, persecuted by the intolerant church. Like all theories which read texts as a code, Murray's thesis is intrinsically improbable. It was extensively criticised when it first appeared and commands little or no allegiance within the modern academy.[10] Yet academic denunciations of her work were still being produced in the 1970s. These denunciations usually centre on asserting the 'beliefs' of historians against Murray's 'belief' in witchcraft. Macfarlane, for example, argues that 'by extracting and quoting out of context' she 'mistook what people believed to be happening for what actually did happen'.[11] Norman Cohn argues that 'her grasp of historical method was non-existent'; Murray treated 'sources' with 'manifestly fantastic and impossible features' as if they were factual.[12] Keith Thomas criticises Murray for her 'highly selective' use of evidence, and speaks of the 'deficiencies of [her] historical method'.[13] All these criticisms are perfectly justified: Murray ignores the rules of evidence when she writes of the witch-trial materials. What is surprising is not the ferocious criticisms of Murray, but the fact that this question of belief versus 'method' is the sole ground of criticism. The most logical place to begin a critique of Murray is with a refutation of her outdated and untenable reading of Frazer's *Golden Bough*. Instead, all three historians map out their criticisms in a way which emphasises the separation of 'witchcraft beliefs' and 'historical method', rather than their different anthropologies.

Dismissals of Murray are not there solely to enlighten the ignorant, but to create a historians' version of one of the most powerful myths of the Enlightenment. Read as grounding myth of identity, we might see the dismissal of Murray as the creation of a narrative in which the (male) truth of empirical history is opposed to the irrational fancies of a woman who cannot distance herself from the subject enough. The fact that Murray is a woman explains and permits her conflation with witches; she cannot be separated from them, cannot achieve critical distance from them. Enlightenment men, however, can achieve such distance; their sceptical witch-narratives acquire the force of a fantasy of masculine completion. The opposition between Murray's feminised belief and history's masculine scepticism figure the male historians as the only possible locus of truth about witchcraft. In more recent writings, the early theory of radical feminism that witches were folkhealers stamped out by the rising medical profession replaces Murray as the whipping-girl of historical method. J. A. Sharpe, for example, describes the opinion of feminists like Ehrenreich and English as 'all too predictable'; feminists are not, for him, unbiased readers of historical materials.[14] Despite the fact that more sceptical feminists like Kate McLuskie get Sharpe's approval, this reads as a casual rejection of any possibility of a feminist approach to history.[15] Theory is not raised as an issue; it seems to come as a revelation to Sharpe that feminism is not homogeneous, which does not imply a very wide acquaintance with theoretical debates about gender in the 1980s or with Continental or American feminist witchcraft studies. Instead, Sharpe contrasts the slipshod historical methods of the believing women with the sceptical objectivity necessary for true history.

This narrative casts belief in witches as the result of a kind of credulity which arises from ignorance of historical methods. This is to figure credulity as feminine, and then to conflate that figure with the figure in the text: women cannot write about women because they are women, because they cannot separate themselves from the women they write about. Enlightenment thought, on the other hand, has always offered a way to seize and clutch and penetrate the mystery of the feminine otherness that is forever excluded from wielding its powers. If academic history's myth of identity depends on the repudiation of the figure of feminine superstition in the form of believing historian or witch, the historian also constructs himself by over-identification with other figures. The figure most favoured is one who can represent the scepticism of the historian while remaining a member of the elite. Just as the figures of repudiation are always female, these figures of identification are always male, even though female sceptics did exist.[16] Wanting company in their scepticism, academics privilege certain early modern texts because those texts are seen as proleptic of the academic's own position. Continental historians have chosen for this purpose the figure of the sceptical inquisitor, one who allows them to appropriate the intellectuality of the elite without succumbing to its unattractive prejudices. English historians are similarly drawn to sceptics like Reginald Scot, Samuel Harsnett, George Gifford and John Webster.[17] Reginald Scot's *Discoverie of witchcraft* is often cited by historians as a 'source' for popular 'beliefs'. However, Scot is seen as reliable because he is distanced from the norms of his own period. This only makes sense if reliability equals distance from belief. Sydney Anglo, for example, writes that 'Scot appreciated, *as few contemporaries did*, the inconsistencies and *gross credulities* of the apologists for witch-hunting'.[18] Scot 'appreciates' the 'gross credulities' of his opponents; that is, what Scot 'knows' and what Anglo and his readers 'know' is the same thing. Scot can be congratulated for agreeing with the historian. In this context, the use of the term 'gross' is interesting; grossness is vulgarity and numerousness, while 'appreciation' is redolent of select connoisseurship. Keith Thomas, similarly, calls Scot's work 'brilliant', as if he were reviewing it for the *TLS*.[19] Praised as 'very much ahead of his time', Scot is also celebrated for his 'detective work'. While silly demonologists create unbelievable theories, Scot relies on 'a few questions asked about town' to establish 'truth' and 'commonsense'.[20] We might be in a Golden Age detective story, that pinnacle of trustful empiricism. It is not insignificant that historians, too, are often portrayed as detectives.[21]

These identifications are, in Sharpe's sense, 'predictable'; historians who see themselves as Enlightenment seekers of truth will inevitably valorise those they see as embarked on a similar quest. If you identify with Scot, his views will inflect yours, making it more difficult to identify with others, especially Scot's particular Others. These others include women, who for Scot are the repositories of unlearned and unscrutinised superstition. Though historians distinguish Scot sharply from demonologists like his opponent Jean Bodin, his argument has a lot in common with theirs. Both sceptics and demonologists created elaborate cosmological theses in order to deny that strange old women in villages had any real power. For demonologists, real power lay with the devils summoned by the witch, and by the beginning of the seventeenth century most argued that even the power to summon devils was illusory. While demonologists displaced the witch's power onto male demons or refused her even this much authority, Scot saw the witch as completely powerless, since in a providential universe divine power could brook no competition from demons or witches. Neither of these positions resemble enlightened liberalism; both rely heavily on theories of supernatural causation. Scot's scepticism and Jean Bodin's elaboration of the theory of pact witchcraft can be seen as similarly misogynistic responses to the idea that women might act as agents of supernatural causation.[22] Scot cannot bear the idea that women might be able to alter the course of Divine Providence:

> those witchmongers cannot be content, to wrest out of God's hand his almighty power, and keep it themselves, or leave it with a witch, but that, when by drift of argument they are made to lay down their bucklers, they yield them up to the devil . . . they write that the devil doth all this by God's permission only; sometimes by his license, sometimes by his appointment; so as (in effect and truth) not the devil, but the high and mighty king of kings, and Lord of hosts, even God himself, should this way be made obedient and servile to obey and perform the will and commandment of a malicious old witch, and miraculously to answer her appetite, as well in every trifling vanity, as in most horrible executions; as the revenger of a doting old woman's imagined wrongs, to the destruction of many innocent children.[23]

This is not based on 'commonsense', but on the belief that for women to alter the workings of natural law would imply usurpation of God's place in the cosmos. Like demonologists, Scot equates witchcraft with inversion and disorder, but responds by arguing that such an inversion is inconceivable in the light of Protestant providentialism.[24] Scot's contempt for women accused of witchcraft actually exceeded that of his contemporaries. This contempt is echoed in the expression 'doting old woman' which recurs in Scot's text. Scot subsequently 'explains' witchcraft as the outcome of a disordering of the witch's body and mind; in other words, as a mental illness.[25] If we must have a 'progress' narrative, we could say that with Scot begins the long process of recuperating women's supernatural power as hysteria and madness.[26]

Like Scot, George Gifford is valorised as somehow ahead of its time and also as proto-Enlightenment. Alan Macfarlane dramatises the tensions in Gifford's *Dialogue* as those of 'a mind trying to rise above the limitations and assumptions of its time, to argue its way out of a closed system'. Elsewhere he praises Gifford for 'anticipat[ing] the work of modern anthropologists'.[27] In the preface to his second dialogue he writes indignantly that 'the witches are made to believe that at their request and to pleasure them by fulfilling their wrath, their spirits do lame and kill both men and beasts'.[28] Like Scot, he dismisses the possibility that devils or witches can have any power of their own. Witchcraft is wrought by God to punish people for their sins, with demons and witches acting as God's unwitting servants.[29] Scot associates the irrationality of witchcraft with spiteful housewives; Gifford's dialogue makes great play with the 'foolish' beliefs of the 'Wife' and 'Goodwife R'. Scot is willing to blame all witchcraft involving food on bad housewifery; Gifford mocks housewives concerned with their failure to churn. The association between women and a despised, unscientific 'popular culture' is well established.[30]

Scot and Gifford's much-vaunted 'scepticism' about 'witch-beliefs' comes not from disinterestedness, but from a notion of power which explicitly excludes women. Close readings of their texts suggest that belief in witches does not correlate with misogyny; misogyny can exist perfectly well alongside scepticism, and can even subtend it. Without wishing to suggest that the same can be said of modern historians, there is some overlap between the Scot/Gifford notion of witches as 'doting old women' and the hegemonic views of Macfarlane and Thomas. The prevailing view of the English witch derived from their work sees witches as harmless old beggars who had the misfortune to be caught in a changing social system and thus to arouse the guilt of their neighbours. This kindly humanist defence of witches can also be read as patronising. It reflects uncritically the early modern humanist dislike of popular culture and its embodiment in woman. Thomas and Macfarlane's reading follows Scot and Gifford: where they deny the witch all supernatural power, modern historians deny her all *social* and *cultural* power. For Thomas and Macfarlane, those whose witch-beliefs are documented in depositions speak from the unconscious; it is their guilt that speaks, so they have no shaping power over their own narrations. The vaguely psychoanalytic origins of the term 'guilt' are important: guilt is always understood to be unconscious, and also, chronologically, infantile, hence, historically, primitive. The whole discourse (however well-intentioned) thus supports associations between the feminine and the primitive, the unspoken, the pre-historical, the material substratum of society upon which the (male) historian works. If we see the Thomas–Macfarlane witch as an enabling myth, then historical identity is grounded in the powerlessness and speechlessness of woman.[31] It also casts the historian as part of a lineage of progressive scepticism that places him firmly on the side of the future; the winning side, in fact.

As with feminist myths of witchcraft, the historians' myth too can be seen in fictional form. Umberto Eco's novel *The Name of the Rose* dramatises two investigations: the detective-friar William of Baskerville's investigation of a series of murders in a monastery, and the Inquisition's investigation of heresy among the Franciscans. Both investigations come (quite gratuitously) to involve the demonological; William's faith in the empirical methods of Roger Bacon is opposed by the monks' thesis that unnatural crimes must have supernatural causes in the workings of the powers of darkness, while the inquisitor Bernardo Gui (a 'real' historical figure) explains the bizarre events in the abbey by uncovering an innocent young peasant girl as a witch. Not at all coincidentally, the girl-victim is beautiful, sexual, practically inarticulate, completely unlearned, and utterly helpless. The Enlightenment hero cannot save her, and in the book she is duly burned.[32] Her appearance in the story guarantees the reader's sympathy with William's quest for truth by showing medieval error to be the enemy of beauty, sexuality and romance. She is symbolically aligned with the other vulnerable creation William fails to protect, the second volume of Aristotle's *Poetics*, on comedy, a book which represents the way the subversive powers of the body disrupt the sterile intellectuality of scholastic theology. Yet the book and the girl are also opposed: William's passion is to save the book (and not the girl). Alone of all the characters, William does not seize on her accusation with relief because he never believes in supernatural theories of causation; so it turns out that material girls need Enlightenment men, and not vice versa. Book and girl point to a preferable future of empirical method and republican print culture, one in which William's views are normal and Bernardo Gui's pathological. The narcissism of this myth is breathtaking, yet this book was lauded in the quality press as a true account of the Middle Ages.[33] William, whose name alludes both to Sherlock Holmes and to a typeface, is also a figure for the historian-author. It is William who is learned, who rejoices in the library, who reads several languages, who is a constructor of narratives, a teller of stories. It is William, the reconstructor of lost or buried stories, the opener of secret or hidden archives, the bespectacled polymath, who is the figure for the historian, forever returning to times which he has always already surpassed.

But, but . . . how could well-educated men who owned a lot of books have come to believe in witches?[34] The Thomas–Macfarlane hypothesis seeks to explain the origin of witch-beliefs *as* something inexplicable, and as E. P. Thompson noted some time ago, this involves a dismissal of a popular culture in which they may have made sense.[35] What this means is that Thomas and Macfarlane are taking their cue from changes in *elite* beliefs, despite their pathbreaking and painstaking examination of popular sources.[36] The exceptional richness of Thomas's sources, and the still-amazing breadth of his knowledge, obscure his emphasis on elite perspectives. The beliefs of the populace were less important than 'the witch-craze' or the 'witch-hunt', both activities of the middling and better sort. As long as witch-beliefs remain a tale told by old wives, they are not interesting enough to catch the eye of the historian. Both Thomas and Macfarlane also share a wish to get the witch out of the domestic arena and into a role in public life. It is assumed by Scot and Gifford that churning is trivial and ale-making unimportant, a view which reflects both snobbish incapacity to grasp what might matter to the poor, and the devaluation of women's work. When Macfarlane and Thomas echo this devaluation by seeking an explanation for witchcraft in the public spheres of absolutism, church doctrine and social provision, the result is to elide the specificity of witchcraft as an event which often occurs within the female-dominated spaces of the household, and to collapse women's stories about these events into a generalised and putatively ungendered body of evidence.

These narcissisms come from within history, but they also go with certain political and cultural myths of enlightenment which helped to shape the current school of social history. While providentialism is not a common belief among historians of English witchcraft, a Whiggish understanding of the Enlightenment and its benefits to history and to society will do just as well. The current gurus of the history of witchcraft and those who aspire to their places are the products of the recent revolution in historical method wrought by the rise of social history. Using methodologies developed by the postwar social sciences to examine the lives of ordinary people, social historians sought to invent history 'from below', the history of the ordinary member of society rather than the history of the exceptional leader. In the case of the history of witchcraft, this meant an exciting turn from texts written by the elite, such as literary texts and intellectual treatises, towards studies of trial documents and popular pamphlets, but it also meant that the staple repertoire of social-historical ideas were brought to bear on witch-beliefs. Witch-trials were examined in relation to the idea that human nature might not be universal. Whereas 'high' political historians still work with a single invariant model of all persons acting out of clear-eyed self-interest, like contract bridge-players, social historians proposed that motivations might differ slightly in different societies. This daring notion ironically facilitated the growth of the historical myth I have been describing. Witch-trials became an ideal site for *demonstrating* the otherness of the past, since witch-beliefs are a mark of *pre*-Enlightenment backwardness. Or rather, perhaps the desire of all to separate themselves from the witch allowed for the legitimation of otherwise heretical theories borrowed lavishly from the social sciences.

Thomas and Macfarlane produced their theories of witchcraft in the lost era of the 1950s, 1960s and pre-oil crisis 1970s, an era when it sometimes seemed that the welfare state had achieved a way of marrying democracy to capitalism without open conflict, if not without bickering, so that the middle classes, at least, had nothing to feel guilty about any more. Fuelled by an abnormal burst of prosperity, the social services and the social sciences seemed like the civilised and progressive answer to inequalities and the superstitions which regrettably lingered among those who had not had the benefit of an education. These same social sciences, unsurprisingly, could also be used to clean up history's record of dealing with the lower orders, and they could also show how progress away from the darkness of the past was an outcome of social knowledge carefully applied. Portrayed as the acme of human progress, the welfare state is half consciously figured in the histories of Thomas and Macfarlane as the way out of the superstition, brutality and conflict which characterised eras which believed in magic. The idea of beggars on the streets of London seemed incongruously Dickensian and remote in the early 1970s. In those halcyon days, however, beggars were as alien, as primitive, as witches, just as much signs of a long-gone past. It seemed much more natural to yoke them together than it does to us. To those who walk every day past the cardboard signs which read, 'Homeless and Hungry: please help', wondering if we should, the idea that such conflicts generate witch-beliefs seems enviably naive.

Notoriously, what this social-historical approach neglects is the question of gender. Just as the universalism of the Attlee welfare state obscured differences of sex and race, so Thomas and Macfarlane gave no real thought to the question of why witches were women, except to remark lamely that perhaps women were somehow less provided for than men and so more inclined to begging. What is curious is that, in England, Thomas and Macfarlane have been allowed to get away with it. As a result of feminist silence and implicit separatism, English witchcraft studies have never engaged with feminist theory or with the complexities of writing about the feminine in the past. When historians belatedly turned their attention to the question, that discussion was very nearly as empty of feminist theory as Thomas and Macfarlane's work had been twenty years ago. J.

A. Sharpe, for instance, seems not to know about the elaborate and careful theorisations of the female body across history, while Malcolm Gaskill is blankly ignorant of any feminist theorisation of motherhood or of the problematics of the maternal identity in Western culture.[37] If I were to write about (say) the Mediterranean as a region without any knowledge of Braudel, historians would rightly condemn me, but a historian can write about childbirth without any knowledge of Kristeva, or maternity without any knowledge of Klein, Chodorow or Irigaray, and no one thinks it unusual. This is not a point about political correctness; a serious theoretical *refutation* of any or all of these theories on historical grounds would be welcome. Historians' refusal to join in the debate at all suggests that they simply cannot bring themselves to take women's history and gender theory seriously.

This lack of interest in feminist and gender theory is part of a reluctance to engage with recent theoretical developments. Having created a powerful myth in which the male Enlightenment investigator is a great hero doing battle with various more or less feminine darknesses, historians have been in no great hurry to abandon their fantasy in favour of alternative theories and methodologies, and perhaps it is predictable that feminism has not received a great deal of attention. If you associate the feminine with the epitome of the silent and unenlightened, you are unlikely to go to her for Sibylline counsel on how to get through the underworld. This is not the explanation historians themselves give for the neglect of theory, however. The characteristic defence is to complain that empirical historians anticipated all of Derrida or Foucault or Hayden White anyway and are not a monolith as their critics suppose, while constructing 'theory' as a monolith of relativism which can be dismissed in a number of ways.[38] The main basis for rejecting any epistemological challenger is drably utilitarian: historians claim that they accept or reject the theories developed in other disciplines not on grounds of validity, but according to whether or not they are 'useful' for history. For a profession concerned with the austere quest for truth, they are curiously indifferent to the truth-claims of the theories they reject. This means that *no* theory can really alter what history is or should be, since this axiomatically makes it not useful; for instance, theories which assert the ultimate inaccessibility of the past can be dismissed as insufficiently useful on the grounds that they would make history impossible, and then where would we all be?[39] What, one wonders, would become of Copernican astronomy or Wittgensteinian philosophy assessed in a like manner? The fact that poststructuralism threatens to throw historians out of work does not make it untrue. Though some historinas do offer other refutations, these are usually based on fairly comprehensive misreadings of what they refute, again suggesting a certain interpretive carelessness.[40]

Joan Wallach Scott's article, characteristically entitled 'Gender: a useful category of historical analysis', makes this criterion quite plain.[41] Scott unironically dismisses Lacanian psychoanalysis in favour of object-relations theories because the latter are more useful, oblivious of the extensive literature which suggests that Lacan's readings of Freud are more incisive than those of the object-relations school, or of the literature which warns of the political dangers of both approaches. Scott's quiet canter through the edges of the poststructuralist wilderness in order to mark a trail for passing historians nevertheless brought down on her head the wrath of an older generation of historians who saw her as undermining the foundations of the discipline merely by supping with the diabolic host of theorists.[42] This response no doubt explains the hesitancy of those who hope to advance the historical debate by a few millimetres; nonetheless, the wish to maintain an agreeable consensus should not be allowed to dampen curiosity about alternative methodologies. Theories are not *tools*; they have to be refuted if they are to be rejected. The assumption that historians are free to reject anything which calls the rules of their own discipline into question makes those rules seem unreasonably confining.

Characteristically, historians move to dismiss poststructuralist approaches to texts by asserting that such approaches lead either to nihilism or relativism. Here historians have a powerful trump-card; if truth is relative, how can serious historians refute the growing band of historical 'revisionists' who wish either to deny that the Holocaust occurred or to minimise its importance?[43] The relevance of this question to the uptake of poststructuralist ideas by the intellectual community of Western Europe remains to be seen. Holocaust deniers usually couch their assertions in the most conventional possible historical rhetoric. Rather than relying on relativism, they make *absolute* truth-claims for their assertions. One of the crudest pieces of Holocaust denial in English is authored by the 'Committee for Truth in History'.[44] Historians are fond of pointing out that deconstruction's leading American exponent was a Nazi sympathiser and anti-Semite during the war, indicating the dire political consequences of deconstruction's challenge to traditional history. But in that case, traditional empirical history must also have dire implications, since most *neo*-Nazi historians adopt the most conservative possible protocols of discovery, revelation and truth-telling.

It might be equally valid to argue that notions of the indeterminacy of truth can be used against the self-proclaimed certitude of deniers. Deniers' assumption that the 'truth' about the Holocaust lies around waiting to be 'discovered' and encapsulated in a historical text forms the greatest possible contrast with the discourse of Holocaust survivors' testimonies, which affirm the impossibility of representing the ultimate 'truth' of the event. It is leading poststructuralists like Geoffrey Hartman and Shoshana Felman who have done serious work on this impossibility. Yet for no other reason than because it suits their narrow and empirical book, historians continue to argue as if poststructuralism equals or at any rate enables denial.

What poststructuralists and others have shown is that careful reading of texts and especially stories is germane to Holocaust studies. Reading in detail and with due attention to textuality need not imply a fixed or cynical scepticism; such care in reading can signify proper respect for the unique and moving humanity of stories. Many historians have stampeded themselves into rejecting a variety of illuminating methods of reading, a practice which has left many of them with no way of reading texts, as opposed to 'assessing evidence'.[45] Reading is what literary critics do. Yet as other historians know, history is nearly always an encounter with a text. Parish baptismal registers are texts, church court depositions are texts, and so are manorial accounts, the receipts for coal shipments to London, assize indictments, conduct books, ballads, pamphlets, letters, diaries, medical treatises and all the other 'sources' of social history. Even physical evidence like church architecture and archaeological strata require reading, usually in the light of some other text. Yet having decided that poststructuralist theories are not 'useful', historians have not asked themselves what method of reading *is* useful (or true), and many have not even asked themselves which method they are currently using. Most historians are still a long way from taking note of *the way in which* things are said rather than seeing this merely as a vehicle for *what* is said. Both literary critics and historians now acknowledge the importance of questions such as 'Who is speaking here? And to whom? At what time? In what kind of context?', and both also acknowledge the relevance of questions about the materiality of texts: when was this published or transcribed, by whom, and for whom? But only literary critics and a few maverick historians are yet willing to see nonliterary texts as replete with rhetorical devices: metaphors, narratives, shifts, points of view, generic conventions and so forth. While historians of ideas have recently become aware of the importance of metaphors in textuality, political historians and many social historians still carry on treating each text as a transparent window onto the mind of its writer or the *mentalité* of an entire society.

Most historians implicitly or explicitly defend these practices by arguing that interpretation arises from reading in bulk rather than reading in detail; that in order to read one single witchcraft deposition from Essex correctly, one has to have read every other document one can lay hands on from the area from which the deposition came: other court records, parish records, letters, diaries, as well as more general interpretative texts such as the writings of the elite about witchcraft, medical writings, writings on childcare, political writings and so forth. All this is indubitable, though it will come as unwelcome news to those literary critics still happily cobbling together their social histories from a few unrepresentative playtexts with reference to whichever social historian comes first to hand. However, reading a mass of material does not necessarily provide information about how to interpret it; rather an interpretative matrix is necessary in order to 'read' it in the first place. Ideally, everyone working in early modern studies would read everything early modern, in manuscript and print, including all early modern texts that do not now survive. If everyone read everything, another dream would come true of equal access to materials, and the replacement of childish territorial disputes with a republic of letters which does not privilege archives simply because they are dusty. Even if our mad dream came true, however, we would not all come up with the same narratives and explanations for early modern historical events, or the same readings of early modern texts. For one thing, such awesomely voracious readers might have dipped into different modern and postmodern texts. For another, spending our lives reading would distance us from the (illiterate?) early moderns we are trying to understand. Also we would still have to face the problem of how to read, having solved the problem of what to read. One of the few things to be said for traditional literary criticism is that it taught its practitioners to value the fine detail of individual texts because they were supposed to be Great Art. Rather than denying that value to Shakespeare and everyone else (levelling down) we could choose to extend it to everything we read, to Abiezer Coppe's *Fiery flying roll*, the Countess of Lincoln's polemic in favour of breastfeeding, Reginald Scot's *Discoverie*, the depositions of unknown women in the church courts. We could begin that celebration now, following Carolyn Porter's suggestion that we consider the discursive field as flat; that sounds a bit dull, but it might have exciting consequences.[46]

I want to illustrate the problems of neglecting how things are said with an example, so I hope I will be forgiven for singling out an ordinary competent piece of social history for criticism; it is taken from an article whose title, 'The construction and experience of maternity', suggests acquaintance with poststructuralist and sociological methods of interpretation. This does not, however, imply attentive reading.[47] A text is cited: it is entitled *The XV comforts of rash and inconsiderate marriage*, it is said to be 'done out of French', and the publication date given is 1682. The passage quoted is as follows: 'And as for her pain and peril of childbearing, I do no more wonder at it, than at the laying of a great Eg, by a Hen, or a Goose, the ordinary effect of Nature, no more, notwithstanding all their tittle-tattle'.[48] A literary critic would immediately begin to ask questions like 'Who is speaking here?', 'What genre is this?', 'Whose tittle-tattle is being refuted?'. But the historian does not pause even for a second; breathlessly, she embarks on interpretation. 'Some popular wisdom was contemptuous . . . Satirists mocked what they considered were exaggerated claims to respect for maternity'. This single text tells us what satirists thought, and that such satirists represented popular wisdom. It also 'reveals, indirectly, that the community did respect childbearing women'. The ones doing the tittle-tattle are instantly identifiable as the whole community (except for the satirists and some of the populace?). There seems no warrant for this identification in the text cited, or for that matter in the rest of the satire. Even a moderately careful reading of this passage in context makes it plain that 'they' are not the whole community, but specifically women, as the gendered phrase 'tittle-tattle' suggests, and even more specifically, 'they' are the emerging school of French feminist *précieuses*. The *précieuses* are mostly remembered now as the objects of Molière's misogyny, so it is not difficult for anyone to recognise that the anonymous pamphlet is also part of a satirical genre of misogynistic texts whose self-consciously outrageous statements are voiced through the persona of a Juvenilian misogynist; the comedy derives from the exaggeration of this masculine position and from its contrast with the supposedly exaggerated femininity of the *précieuses* and their foppish followers.[49] The self-consciousness of the appeal to common sense is implicit in the references to barnyard fowls, a trope which gestures at the common-sense pragmatism of rural tradition as against the pseudo-sophistication of urban *précieuses*; the references to hens and geese also point backwards to the medieval misogynists of the *fabliaux* tradition, misogynists who also embodied their claims in a rhetoric of citation. The trope thus makes a double appeal to tradition as opposed to innovation, a gesture which suggests that its position is addressed to an antagonist who contests rather than confirming the *status quo*. This text claims that 'the community' do *not* unequivocally support childbearing women. However, as with most misogynistic satire, it is far too self-consciously literary to allow us to decide that it represents even a strand of opinion in any unproblematic way.

Those historians who have not yet given up on the possibility of reading texts have begun to try to see historical texts as stories, as shaped narratives with particular tellers who are 'interested' in shaping the story in particular ways. Two theories have emerged which attempt to read texts in this and other ways. First, there is Quentin Skinner's theory of intentionality, where the meaning of a text is determined for the historian by what the author could be supposed to have meant by using such a word in such a context at such a time. Skinner's theory assumes that historians of ideas can reconstruct the meaning of particular terms (like, say, *virtù*) by examining their use in a variety of texts over a period of time contemporary with the text they are studying.[50] No literary critic would deny the potential usefulness of such study, which resembles the kind of lexicographical work one expects to do when annotating a text for an edition. However, its usefulness is limited, since meaning is endlessly deferred, residing in context rather than the text itself. The context is made up of other texts, however. Such a methodology depends on access to a variety of texts in similar genres by similar authors of similar social class, gender and so forth, and it *also* depends on encountering a number of texts by authors different from the author being studied in all these respects, to provide different usages.

These conditions, where they can be met at all (not, for instance, before the year AD 1000 in England) are much easier to meet for 'canonical' authors than for popular culture; one can examine all of the uses of the term 'rhetoric' in Hobbes and in other political philosophers of the seventeenth century, but the corpus of works by Hobbes is large. The corpus of works by Bennet Lane, a housewife who testified at the St Osyth witch-trial of 1582, is rather more limited, and it is much more difficult to know how to make comparisons with the 'works' of others in order to analyse her use of particular words.[51] Moreover, witchcraft deponents are not philosophers; Skinner's method is designed to elicit the Big Ideas of leading thinkers, while the historian of witchcraft may want to know something else (not what Bennet *meant by* the term 'witch', but the kind of story she could tell about them). Finally, Skinner's theory takes too little account of the lability of terms. The term 'witch' did not have a single meaning to which all writers and speakers had recourse; its meaning was a matter of contestation. 'Witch' meant differently to different speakers, illustrating gulfs in gender and education, class and beliefs, becoming a site on which other meanings could be contested, on which class and religious differences could be played out. The substratum of commonality beneath these rapid shifts in meaning from one text to another is so vague as to be useless as social history.

Recently, social historians like Natalie Zemon Davis, Robert Darnton and Annabel Gregory have begun to see popular texts as stories, reflecting on the fact that such texts may be strategic rather than transparent, self-fashioning rather than self-revelation.[52] This does not mean that such texts tell us nothing about popular beliefs; it does however complicate any simple understanding of the meanings of words. At the same time, these reformers share with Skinner a tendency to allot total control over the tale told to its teller. The model of autonomous subjectivity thus generated cannot really accommodate an analysis of the way women's trial depositions replicate the very gender asymmetries which oppressed the tellers as well as the accused. A theory of the workings of ideology in discourse is still necessary to understand those elements of stories which refuse to be rewritten, which stubbornly reappear in story after story, which determine which stories can be told and which can be believed. These elements of story fashion their teller as their teller fashions the story.

Theories of ideology are not exactly in short supply, and the position has been further complicated by the arrival of the more capacious term discourse, a word it now seems impossible to avoid and equally impossible to use precisely. In historical writings, its use owes much to the writings of Michel Foucault, and yet at the same time both historians and historical literary critics are often rightly accused of domesticating Foucault's theories, turning them from wild Nietzschean speculation into tame sociology. I do not wish to argue for a return to a pure and authentic Foucault here (an idea Foucault himself might have found laughable) but the term discourse is more useful if its meaning is somewhat restricted, and if it is not allowed to do duty for ideology as well.[53] It might be fair to say that for most theorists, discourse is the medium and ideology is the message. Discourse for Foucault is a linguistic repertoire with its own characteristic terminology and jargon spoken by a particular institution or profession; examples he cited included the discourse of psychiatry, spoken solely by psychiatrists and rich in terminology incomprehensible to a lay person. Stripped of mystification, this may seem an unremarkable insight, but the term discourse neatly encapsulates the idea of a way of speaking which acts as the principal vehicle through which power is exerted by knowledges. Taking an example from the history of witchcraft, the case of Mary Glover exemplifies what Foucault's fans have come to call a clash of discourses. Mary Glover claimed to be bewitched; on her evidence, Elizabeth Jackson was convicted of witchcraft.[54] We might read both Glover and the jury as users of discourses about and knowledges of the supernatural, discourses which encoded a body of knowledge of witchcraft and bewitchment – how to distinguish it from natural illness, how to tell who had performed a bewitchment, how to cure the victim. The fact that this knowledge is not seen as powerful or even as explanatory in the modern world does not mean that it is irrational; it embodies a notion of rationality which is no longer current. In Mary Glover's case, Glover was opposed by an alternative discourse; the physician Edward Jorden attempted to explain her symptoms as hysteria and not possession. As Michael Macdonald points out, most historians have seen Jorden as the forerunner of psychiatric explanations for possession, the creator of scientific rationality in a world of bigotry and superstition.[55] Foucaultians might see in Mary Glover's case the birth of the clinic, as the church's knowledge of the supernatural was replaced with professional medical knowledge. Matters are not so clear-cut: Jorden's medicalisation of Glover's case also draws on the supernatural, while Glover and her followers drew on medical theory to argue that she was genuinely possessed.

This does not vitiate discourse theory, though it points again to the need for careful reading; what is more problematic is its powerlessness to reveal other kinds of conflict. Analysis of discourse might show the way the Glover case was dominated by the Church of England's internal quarrels about exorcism and the fear of Counter-Reformaton conversions through the spectacular casting-out of devils. It will *not* show the Glovers' class background, what they had to eat on a Monday in Lent, and what Edward Jorden, by contrast, had for dinner. There is no point in asking discourse theory to do what it cannot do: read material circumstances. It does, however, allow the registration of at least some of the complexities and contradictions embodied in early modern texts, complexities glossed over by more traditional historical methods. For instance, most historical methods attempt to find a single unitary meaning or point of view in a text; in the Mary Glover case, Jorden can be made to 'represent' scientific empiricism, while Glover and her defenders can be read as superstitious adherents of the supernatural. Foucault was constantly pointing out the fallacy of deriving simple and single historical significances from particular texts. Nineteenth-century sermons, for example, did not for him illustrate sexual repression alone, but also an obsessive and equally oppressive wish to observe and classify every possible manifestation of desire. Similarly, Glover's defenders draw quite as much on empiricism as Jorden, though the protocols of observation and conjecture were based on a different body of knowledge. Moreover, that 'superstitious' body of knowledge was of more recent date than Jorden's medical knowledge.

Both Skinner's historicism and the narratology of Natalie Zemon Davis and Darnton assume that the historian's task is to uncover the intentions of the teller, not the meaning the text or story can produce in particular contexts. The stories told at the St Osyth trial, for instance, mean quite different things when told in the pamphlet describing the trial and in Reginald Scot's scornful allusions to them in his *Discoverie of witchcraft*. Signifiers of the supernatural become signs of superstition and popery. The protocols of testing for possession and the rites of exorcism came to mean different things to different groups within the Church of England during the Darrell controversy of the early seventeenth century. The word 'witch' itself could dwindle to a defamatory insult or leap to accusations of diabolism within the same locale within a few years, depending on the context and the listener. Often the listener could actively select from a variety of possible meanings: if called a witch, she could take mild or deep umbrage, or acknowledge the 'truth' of the label by advertising supernatural powers. Historians also assume that stories of witchcraft are based on actual events rather than on other stories, despite the high level of repetition in witch-narratives; such repetition may have made stories more rather than less believable. These historians assume that the teller is in total conscious control of her tale; neither method considers slips of the tongue, puns (intentional or unintentional), half-unacknowledged meanings which threaten to rupture a controlled surface. The meanings analysed by the anthropological methods, too, are frequently assumed to be directed outward at a large public, and the narratology of Davis and other microhistorians also assumes that strategic tale-telling is directed at persuading, or carrying conviction. Some stories also repress, manage or express conflicts social in origin but internal to the teller. Finally, applications of narratology to witch-stories share a fatal drawback with the works of those literary critics who use psychoanalysis; they cannot admit the possibility that the supernatural might actually exist, and consequently distance themselves too much from those for whom its existence was a basic assumption. The twin problems of turning the past into a spectacle of strangeness, and of the disappearance of events in martyrology and memorialisation will not go away, and are particularly visible in the historiography of the witch.

These problems resurface in more recent histories which use psychoanalysis to understand witchcraft. Freud himself mapped psychoanalysis onto possession and diabolism in his analysis of the case of the seventeenth-century painter Christoph Haizmann, who came to be possessed by the devil after selling his soul to him, and who left an account of his miraculous cure by the Virgin Mary of Mariazell at her shrine.[56] While psychoanalysis offers the richest, most rewarding and most serious ways of reading texts concerning the supernatural, it also offers ways to evade the topic altogether. This evasion occurs most often when psychobiography is allowed to displace the historical text, so that the project of 'psychology' is the inside of the person, and the historian's project is her outside, her engagment with society and culture. When that happens, the history of witchcraft exemplifies Michel de Certeau's depiction of the historical process abrogated in the history of the supernatural: 'the story provides the imaginary dimensions that we need so that the elsewhere can reiterate the very here and now. A received meaning is imposed, in a tautological organisation expressive only of the present time'.[57] An instance of this is John Demos's attempt to account for New England witchcraft.[58] Although in theory three chapters are devoted to psychoanalysis, only one chapter attempts a detailed reading of any narrative, and this looks only at one case. Given the historical myth of identity, it is no surprise to find that this is the case of a possessed woman, Elizabeth Knapp. Knapp's hidden motives and concealments become the sole object of the analysis. This displaces the unknowable strangeness of the supernatural into the otherness of woman, evading any question of Knapp's subjectivity, agency or words by treating all her acts as symptoms of a secret self which she cannot declare or know. Demos illustrates psychoanalysis's potential complicity with the most gendered features of the Enlightenment rather than its power to interrogate them.

This might be one reason that historians find it more natural to map psychoanalysis onto witchcraft than onto interwar diplomacy.[59] Why does psychoanalysis seem so natural when it comes to the supernatural in history, and what are the implications of that seeming naturalness? What kind of investments do we make in displacing the supernatural into the inner state, and what does it signify about the ways in which we are able to understand the figure of the witch? In a brilliant essay, Michel de Certeau opens the question of the relations between the historian and the supernatural. 'Historians', he writes, 'determined by their documentation, grasp sorcery only as a white space in the margins of writing and its text'. By this he means only that the 'sources' of sorcery are produced by judges and others rather than by sorcerers. In a note, he cites Foucault's comment in *Madness and Civilization* that 'history is only possible on the basis of the absence of a history'.[60] Might it be possible to go further, to say that history, as it is now understood, *must* be secular, and not only because religious belief would prevent sought-after objectivity? It is impossible for a historian to believe in supernatural causation. All modern history, and all history that modern historians are willing to count as serious history, assumes that events are either the product of natural processes or of human agency. To argue, for instance, that the New Model Army triumphed at Naseby *because* they sang psalms beforehand and were full of the spirit of the Lord would excite nothing but ridicule in military history circles, even though every military historian would instantly acknowledge that some of the soldiers themselves may have believed this. Whereas in the past history might have been written in the light of (say) the theory that all events illustrate and are informed by the intentions and providence of God, such history (the Old Testament, for instance, or Eusebius) would now scarcely count as 'history' at all. In England, Gibbon is the most familiar author of this secularisation of historical discourses, with his utter contempt for both Christianity and providentialist history as sources of distortion which bend the truth to serve an agenda.

The idea that belief in the supernatural is mistaken is taken to be necessary to histories of religion. Consequently, histories of the supernatural are written at an extreme distance from what they analyse. Historians treat believers with awe, kindliness, flippant amusement, earnest analysis. No historian of witchcraft since Montague Summers has acknowledged belief in diabolic agency, and to acknowledge such a belief would be to confess inability to write 'proper' history. Consequently, all supernatural beliefs, including witchcraft and witch-beliefs, become the repressed unconscious of history as a *discourse*; that which has to remain silent if history is to speak. The upshot is to ensure that history retains its authority over the supernatural theories of causation which it superseded. It follows that in order to exist according to its own self-definition, history must repress any hint of the supernatural as real or as capable of causing events. If I really believe in the miraculous power of a saint's relic to cure my ills, I am not only unlikely but unable to write about it in the currently fashionable, quasi-psychoanalytic and quasi-anthropolgical discourse of the history of relics. Even if I cherish such a belief, I will not find a place for it in an article in *Past and Present*.[61] Conversely, if I look at a jewelled bone with the cold eye of a historian-cum-anthropologist, a profound shift would have to take place in my point of view for me to see the relic aglow with divine radiance, or for me to believe that it had cured my influenza. Peter Brown begins his germinal study of saints with the ringing phrase, 'This book is about the joining of heaven and earth'. Really, of course, it is about no such thing. Soon Brown is explaining the 'startling behaviour' of medieval relic-hunters with reference to socio-economic pressures, and using unnecessary Latin terms to denote people's feelings about saints.[62] Brown's work was a vast improvement on the older school of history, which did not even bother to veil its contempt for the idiocies of the common people, but the underlying unease with belief which animated those studies is still detectable in his own work. This is especially odd when he deals with a form of supernatural power in which millions of people still believe: one has only to visit Lourdes or Tours to realise that whole busloads of people still find some kind of presence in relics. No doubt the structure of this belief and its place in society has changed radically since the sixth century, but it has not died out.

The result is a hollowness at the centre of historical discourse on the supernatural, which displaces the very subject it promises to address. The supernatural must be transformed into something else so that it can be discussed. For instance, the following ways to displace possession are on offer: the possessed are physically ill; they are mentally ill, in a thousand ways; they are poisoned; they are in an altered state induced by drugs; they are acting; they are taking a culturally sanctioned opportunity to express 'bad' feelings about the family, the church and sex; they are reducible to a textual sign. All these possibilities, even the last, were available to an educated early modern observer of the contorted and wildly writhing body of a victim of possession. However, most early modern observers had one more possibility in mind: that the person in question was inhabited by a demon, a demon who had moved into the body as one might invade a country or occupy a house, a demon automatically hostile to his host because at war with his whole race, a demon who had usurped the place of the soul of his victim. Alternatively, if our early modern spectator were a member of a rural village community, she might not see possession in these learned terms, but might see the possessed body as under the control of and seamless with the body of a local witch. We too might mention such a possibility. However, in order to analyse it – to move on from description, to construct a narrative – we are forced to replace the very possibility of such supernatural agency with something else. History can say nothing about angels or demons or witches until they are psychoanalytic symptoms, chemicals, illnesses, political tools, or social categories.

I do not plead for us all to become true believers; that would be impossible as well as unreasonable. However, it would be blinkered to fail to note the additional problems created for historians of the supernatural by the epistemological dubiety of the object of their researches. Military historians have no difficulty in believing in the military skill with which Oliver Cromwell fought at Naseby; they do not feel compelled to argue that this skill was an expression of his feelings about his parents, or an outcome of the consumption of benzedrine in some unknown early modern form. When confronted with Laud's ecclesiastical reforms and the objections they caused, we do not have recourse to theories of mass hysteria. When it comes to witches, however, we often invest heavily in figurations of what 'really' happened, often without first trying to think through what early modern people thought really happened. Both too strange and too close to us, the early modern witch thus constructed is not an early modern witch at all, but a mass of all that we see as romantic in its alterity. The witch is linked with drugs, with altered states, with madness and hysteria, with the disruption of language, with forbidden words, with excitingly unsayable desires. She is not linked with any small or squalid vices, like dirtiness or lying. Small wonder we then valorise her as a signifier of all the power of the outsider.

If the supernatural is the repressed unconscious of historical narrative and argument, what is its gender? In Hélène Cixous's analysis of the repression or marginalisation of the feminine in Western culture, woman is that which has been relegated to the margins of narrative. Yet narrative can only move through the agency of the feminine which becomes its repressed other, the femininity which validates male heroism. In *La Jeune Née*, Cixous analyses many such narratives, and she begins with a chapter focusing on Michelet's image of the sorceress.[63] Despite the centrality of this figure to Cixous's work, the sorceress is not discussed by feminist analyses of Cixous, or by historians of witchcraft.[64] It is as if we cannot acknowledge Cixous's ambiguous critique of a figure who has become central to our own imaginings. The powerful sorceress, for Cixous, is invented only so that her repression can serve as the driving power of a male narrative.[65] Michelet's sorceress is an instance of the wild woman who is created by man to ground the creation of a masculine narrative and a masculine civilisation.

Yet like Judith Butler, Cixous is also asking whether women can make anything of these irrevocably constructed femininities.[66] She seeks to exploit the place of Michelet's sorceress in prising open the closed space of male discourse. The psychoanalytic concept she is drawing on is the return of the repressed; Freud claimed that when that which has been repressed returns, it does so as the uncanny (*das Unheimliche*), undomestic, unsettling. Moreover, its return has the power to unsettle the realm of the canny. Uncanny also has another meaning, of course: supernatural.[67] And as Shoshana Felman shows, one source of the uncanny is female desire. When the supposed mirror of femininity reflects not masculine self-identity, but the desire of another, then the unhomely is found just where the male subject hoped to locate the homely.[68] In this sense, Michelet's sorceress, who for Michelet too metaphorises uncontainable rebellious energy, is for Cixous the excess of a female desire that threatens to disrupt the male order of the selfsame. This theorisation of Michelet can certainly help us understand the mixture of rage, puzzlement and coolness which the witch provokes in some historians.

Even though it is an account of Michelet and not of the early modern witch, Cixous's analysis contains insights into more productive ways to offer a psychoanalytic account of the witch as a figure in early modern fantasy as well as nineteenth-century fantasy. Broadly, she suggests that the figure of *la sorcière* involves a repressed desire to return to the pre-Oedipal union with the mother, and at the same time shivers with the horror evoked by that desire. For instance, the sabbat, as conceived by Michelet, is a pleasurable figuration of an alternative order, shown to us and then taken away. The sabbat is a rite of the past, a rite which itself stages a series of returns to the otherwise unsayable pre-Oedipal spaces prior to gender. It is a fantasy of this kind because (in Michelet) it involves the kind of fragmentation, or flying apart of bodily integrity under a hail of sensuous touching, which to the psyche always signifies a forbidden maternal zone. Similarly, for Cixous, even the experience of inquisitorial interrogation, which she ambiguously likens to the process of analysis, invests *la sorcière* with significance as an object of the repressed desire to return to the primal symbiosis with the mother, to the rhythms of the Imaginary. Yet these desires cannot be recognised or acted on within the symbolic:

> To break up, to touch the masculine integrity of the body image, is to return to a stage that is scarcely constituted in human development; it is to return to the disordered imaginary of before the mirror stage, of before the rigid and defensive constitution of subjective armour. It is dangerous, for the giant images then shifting along the single axis of aggressivity, that is, turned towards the exterior or the interior, are only strolling pieces endowed with a destructive power: these bits of body attack, burn, shred. An entire fantastic world, made up of bits and pieces, opens up beyond the limit, as soon as the line is crossed. For the witch (the hysteric) breaking apart can be paradise, but for another, it is hell . . . Thus the ambiguity of the witch and her daughter, the hysteric, is gradually explained.[69]

Cixous draws on Jeanne Favret-Saada's work on the connections between the body of the witch and the bodies of others which allow magic to work, and on Mary Douglas's reading of dirt and culture in terms of limits, transgressions, matter out of place.[70] These ideas help Cixous to historicise the fears and desires she discusses. These ideas are further ways of speaking about the psychic narrative of dissassociation from and abjection of the feminine, which is the mother, and the conflictual desires and fears of that abjection. It is fear of slipping back into the mother, of losing our selves, which makes us fear fragmentation, fear the return of the pre-mirror-stage self. At the same time, we also passionately desire such a return, and it is the desire which frightens us. The contingency of the witch – her scattering of her self across space, the leakage of fluids across her bodily boundaries, her transgression of the norms of such leakage, which also preoccupied early modern women and enabled her magic, makes her a symbol of that lost maternal space. The more it is desired, the more it is feared. It is this combination of psychoanalysis and anthropology, this willingness to see how fear of dirt is connected with the lost maternal body, which allows Cixous to see – with amazing accuracy, given her lack of knowledge of early modern cases – two of the principal preoccupations of the figuration of the witch in Western culture, housework and cleanness:

> In the witch's case, contagion spreads through bits of bodily waste and through odors. These signs persist throughout the hysterical tableau, occasionally with important changes; the hysteric weeps whereas the witch does not, she pours out whereas the other holds back, or vice versa. The hysteric is the remembrance of the sorceress.[71]

Cixous's theorisation of the place of the witch explains the preoccupation with dirt, filth and disorder which characterises many of the depositions against accused witches in England. Her theory also explains and illuminates the village model of the witch as one for whom boundaries have no meaning, one who flies (or as Cixous would say, *une volère*) between or over lines which are normally policed and policed especially by women.[72] All these other lines – boundaries between dirt and cleanness, between the household and the outside world, between the self and others, between the body and other bodies – are significant for women because their rupture signifies the feared, desired return to the pre-ego Imaginary unity with the mother. 'She [*la sorcière*] is mixed up in dirty things; she has no cleanliness phobia – the proper housecleaning attacks that hysterics sometimes suffer. She handles filth, manipulates waste, buries placentas, and burns the caul'.[73] These categories – dirt, cleanness, disorder, order – are *both* social and psychic.

For Cixous the concern of the sorcerous narrative with boundaries and their violation is not reducible to the symptoms of a particular individual. The figure of the sorceress is understandable only in relation to entire discourses: Michelet's, in which the feminine is as usual displaced so that a myth of male agency can be constructed, and the history of Western culture, in which the sorceress is displaced by the hysteric at the limits of femininity. Among the stories Cixous reads in her analysis of the witch is the hysteric's story, since the sorceress is figured not only as the hysteric's mother, but as the whole of that past which the hysteric cannot help re-acting and reacting against. Cixous is not alone in seeing a relation between the sorceress and the hysteric; the two have often been much more crudely aligned.[74] For Cixous, the relation between the witch and the hysteric is never altogether reducible to either sameness or the private familial realm in the form of the mother–daughter tie. It is true that the hysteric is always understood in classical psychoanalysis as the one who cannot escape the past. Her symptoms enact a return to the crises of her personal history, crises which are repeatedly traced on her body.

For Catherine Clément, however, the hysteric represents in her symptoms and discourse not merely the private realm of events, but the repressed past of patriarchy, a past which includes the moment which contained the figure of the witch. This position differs from that of the Enlightenment historian, for whom the witch represents a backward past from which society has moved away. For Clément, patriarchy is not something primitive society has left behind, but a living power structure which systematically erases the memories of its own transactions. Both witch and hysteric are comprehensible as the *limits* of revolution or dissent at their particular cultural moments. Yet at the same time the witch is also the one who articulates a cultural change that has not happened yet; the hysteric, her 'daughter' in this sense, is the mark of that change: 'She [the sorceress] transforms, she acts: the old culture will soon be the new.'[75] Arguably this is surprisingly close to Keith Thomas's understanding of the witch as the bearer of a historical change that cannot quite be accepted as yet.[76] However, although the hysteric re-enacts the moment of the sorceress, she does so with a difference. For Cixous, the hysteric is struggling not to become the witch; the witch is the hysteric inside out. 'Dora's disgust with kisses, such repulsions signify the opposite, a desire too great to find satisfaction', a desire embodied in Michelet's insatiable sorceress. The hysteric turns out to be 'a witch in reverse, turned back within herself, she has put all her eroticising into internal pain'.[77] For Clément, by contrast, the hysteric and the witch are alike in being trapped in the constructions and fantasies of an Imaginary realm which can never be articulated within patriarchy.

For Cixous, as well as for many other feminists, the hysteric is also the return of the uncanny materials which the whole of society has repressed. These materials are the dirt and bodily fragmentation or scattering that signify the lost maternal body, but these gain particular significances in particular historical contexts. For instance, the hysteric's tense concern over lower bodily strata is coupled with somatic displays of anxiety which recall the detritus of the 'filthy rites' forbidden by new codes of manners. This explains why the hysteric begins to displace the possessed woman as the locus of respectable or elite fears at the historical moment when codes of manners are changing; it may also help to explain why the witch lingered on in the countryside, where manners were slower to change. However, neither Cixous nor Clément acknowledges that witchcraft, possession and hysteria coexist as possible explanations for certain behaviours for over a century, and that all three are inflected by questions of class and education. Psychoanalysis, as a historical narrative, often seems surprisingly unable to account for ongoing conflicts without a clear winner, even though it is with these that its family dramas are largely concerned.[78] The idea that the rise of manners affected the idea of the body, turning pollution into a different kind of problem from the one before, is canvassed by Freud too, who wrote that 'many systems of civilization – or epochs of it – possibly even the whole of humanity – have become "neurotic" under the pressure of civilizing trends'.[79] Analysing this statement in detail, Norman O. Brown suggests that humanity is itself a prisoner of the past in the same sense that 'our hysterical patients are suffering from reminiscence; the bondage of all cultures to their cultural heritage is itself a neurotic and also a hysterical construction'.[80] In the sense of writing about the past, history is always already hystery, since it is always already in the act of displacing memory into a narrative enactment or theatre in which the events of the past are performed anew. In remembering the witch and reworking her, we are all hysterics.

NOTES

1 A highly personal selection of exceptionally impressive work: John J. Winkler, 'The constraints of desire: erotic magic spells', in *The Constraints of Desire: The Anthropology of Sex and Gender in Ancient Greece*, London and New York: Routledge, 1990; Luisa Accati, 'The spirit of fornication: virtue of the soul and virtue of the body in Fruili, 1600–1800', trans. Margaret A. Galucci, in *Sex and Gender in Historical Perspective*, ed. Edward Muir and Guido Ruggiero, Baltimore and London: Johns Hopkins University Press, 1990, pp. 110–40; Mary O'Neil, 'Magical healing, love magic and the Inquisition in late sixteenth-century Modena', in *Inquisition and Society in Early Modern Europe*, ed. and trans. S. Haliczer, London: Croom Helm, 1987, pp. 88–114; Guido Ruggiero, *Binding Passions: Tales of Magic, Marriage and Power at the End of the Renaissance*, New York: Oxford University Press, 1993, ch. 3; Robert Muchembled, *La Sorcière au village (XVI au XVII siècle)*, Paris, 1979, and *Sorcières, justices et société aux 16e et 17e siècles*, Paris, 1987; Lyndal Roper, *Oedipus and the Devil: Witchcraft, Sexuality and Religion in Early Modern Europe*, London: Routledge, 1994; David Sabean, *Power in the Blood: Popular Culture and Village Discourse in Early Modern Germany*, Cambridge: Cambridge University Press, 1984; and on the Americas, Ann Kibbey, 'Mutations of the supernatural: witchcraft, remarkable providences, and the power of Puritan men', *American Quarterly*, 34 (1982), pp. 125–48; and Irene Silverblatt, *Moon, Sun and Witches: Gender Ideologies and Class in Inca and Colonial Peru*, Princeton: Princeton University Press, 1987. All these works could not have been produced without the influence of feminism, and most are overtly feminist.

2 In the very different and not comparable case of Scotland, the field has been dominated by Christina Larner. I know of no separate studies of Wales or of belief in Ireland.

3 Women's studies of witchcraft in England: the only book-length study recently published is Marianne Hester's *Lewd Witches and Wicked Women* (London: Routledge, 1992); since its arguments are essentially those of Mary Daly, it has been discussed in Chapter 1. Far better are Annabel Gregory's excellent 'Witchcraft, politics and "good neighbourhood" in seventeenth-century Rye', *Past and Present*, 133 (1991), pp. 31–66; Phyllis Guskin, 'The context of witchcraft: the case of Jane Wenham, 1712', *Eighteenth Century Studies*, 15 (1981), pp. 48–71. The absence of full-length feminist work on English witchcraft necessarily means that this chapter gives women little space.

4 Lyndal Roper, 'Witchcraft and fantasy in early modern Germany', *History Workshop Journal*, 32 (1991), pp. 19–33.
5 Roper, 'Witchcraft and fantasy', p. 26.
6 Jeanne Favret-Saada, *Deadly Words: Witchcraft in the Bocage*, Cambridge: Cambridge University Press, 1980, first published in French as *Les Mots, la mort, les sorts*, 1977. See also her *Corps pour corps. Enquête sur la sorcellerie dans le Bocage*, Paris: Gallimard, 1981.
7 Keith Thomas's *Religion and the Decline of Magic* had a lesser-known working title: *Primitive Beliefs in Pre-Industrial England*. The use of the term 'primitive' also casts doubt on Thomas's relatively uncritical use of African anthropology.
8 Their existence within early modern witchcraft studies can be demonstrated to the sceptical by a brief glance at Trevor-Roper's celebrated, if dated, essay on the 'witch-craze'; the very title designates witch-beliefs as unreasoning: *The European Witch-Craze of the Sixteenth and Seventeenth Centuries*, Harmondsworth: Penguin, 1967, pp. 12, 13.
9 Carlo Ginzburg, 'The inquisitor as anthropologist', in *Myths, Emblems, Clues*, trans. John and Anne C. Tedeschi, London: Hutchinson Radius, 1990, first published in Italian 1986.
10 Some of Murray's foes point to her authorship of the *Encyclopaedia Britannica* article on witchcraft, as if academic historians routinely go about correcting or even deigning to notice popular history.
11 Alan Macfarlane, 'Murray's theory: exposition and comment', in *Witchcraft and Sorcery*, ed., Max Marwick, 2nd edn., Harmondsworth: Penguin, 1982, pp. 233–4 See also Carlo Ginzburg's reading of critiques of Murray as indicative of contempt for popular culture, in *Ecstasies: Deciphering the Witches' Sabbath*, trans. Raymond Rosenthal, London: Hutchinson, 1990, p. 4.
12 Norman Cohn, 'The non-existent society of witches', in *Witchcraft and Sorcery*, ed. Max Marwick, pp. 140.
13 Keith Thomas, *Religion and the Decline of Magic*, Harmondsworth: Penguin, 1971, p. 615, n. 77.
14 J. A. Sharpe, 'Witchcraft and women in seventeenth-century England: some northern evidence', *Continuity and Change*, 6 (1991), p. 179; see also Christina Larner, 'Was witch-hunting women-hunting?', in *Witchcraft and Religion: The Politics of Popular Belief*, Oxford: Blackwell, 1984; David Harley, 'Historians as demonologists; the myth of the midwife witch', *Journal of the society for the social history of medicine*, 3 (1990), pp. 1–26; and 'Mental illness, magical medicine, and the devil in northern England 1650–1700', in *Medical Revolution of the Seventeenth Century*, ed. Roger French and Andrew Wear, Cambridge: Cambridge University Press, 1989. The theory being denounced originated in Barbara Ehrenreich and Deidre English's work in the early 1970s, in *Witches, Midwives and Nurses: A History of Women Healers*, Old Westbury: Feminist Press, 1973.
15 Sharpe, 'Witchcraft and women', p. 180, is referring to McLuskie's discussion of radical feminists' sentimental view of witchcraft in *Renaissance Dramatists*, London: Macmillan, 1989.
16 According to her daughter, Elizabeth Cary convinced her father that an old woman about to be arraigned for witchcraft was simply replying 'yes' to every question put to her. See *The Lady Falkland Her Life: From an MS in the Imperial Archives at Lyon*, ed. R[ichard] S[impson], London: Catholic Publishing and Bookselling Company, 1861, pp. 5–6.
17 See for instance Gustav Henningsen's *The Witches' Advocate: Basque Witchcraft and the Spanish Inquisition*, Reno: University of Nevada Press, 1980; Reginald Scot, *The discoverie of witchcraft*, 1584; Samuel Harsnett, *A declaration of egregious popish*

impostures, 1603; George Gifford, *A dialogue concerning witches and witchcraft*, 1593, and *A discourse of the subtle practices of devils by witches and sorcerers*, 1587; John Webster, *The displaying of supposed witchcraft*, 1677; one might also cite Thomas Ady, *A Candle in the Dark, or a treatise concerning the nature of witches and witchcraft*, 1656.

18 Sydney Anglo, 'Scot', in *The Damned Art: Essays in the Literature of Witchcraft*, London: Routledge & Kegan Paul, 1977, p. 108, emphasis mine.

19 Thomas, *Religion*, p. 61.

20 Robert West, *Reginald Scot and Renaissance Writings on Witchcraft*, Boston, MA: Twayne, 1984, pp. 39–40, ch. 3 (title) and p. 26; Thomas, *Religion*, p. 61.

21 For two recent instances of this usage, see John Bossy, *Giordano Bruno and the Embassy Affair*, London: Vintage, 1992, review cited on back jacket; and Emmanuel Le Roy Ladurie, *Jasmin's Witch: An Investigation into Witchcraft and Magic in Southwest France during the Seventeenth Century*, trans. Brian Pearce, Harmondsworth: Penguin, 1990, publisher's blurb.

22 Jean Bodin, *De la démonomanie des sorciers*, Anvers, 1586.

23 Scot, 'Epistle to the reader', sig. B4^{r}.

24 On the demonologists' theory that devils were solely responsible for acts thought to be performed by witches, see Stuart Clark, 'The scientific status of demonology', in *Occult and Scientific Mentalities in the Renaissance*, ed. Brian Vickers, Cambridge: Cambridge University Press, 1984. Clark does not note that the effect of this theory is to take power from the witch and assign it to the male figure of the demon. On demonology and tropes of disorder and carnival inversion, see Stuart Clark, 'Inversion, misrule and the meaning of witchcraft', *Past and Present*, 87 (1980), pp. 98–127.

25 Scot also explains witchcraft as trickery, as when he says that butter does not come very well owing to witches, or rather owing to the cream having been sold the day before (I, iv), but the explanation about mental illness was the one that took hold, especially in cases of possession concerning young women.

26 On the relations between the figure of the witch and the figure of the hysteric, see Hélène Cixous and Catherine Clément. *The Newly Born Woman*, trans. Betsy Wing, Manchester: Manchester University Press, 1986, and this chapter, below.

27 Gifford's work is easily conflated with 'genuine' popular culture because he presents it in dialogue form, constructing 'typical' popular speakers to mouth his notion of what the people were benighted enough to believe. Gifford is discussed by Macfarlane, 'A Tudor anthropologist: George Gifford's discourse and dialogue', in *The Damned Art*, ed. Sydney Anglo, pp. 140, 145.

28 Gifford, A *dialogue*, sig. A2^{v}.

29 Gifford, A *dialogue*, sig. B3^{r}.

30 Tania Modleski, 'Femininity as mas(s)querade: a feminist approach to mass culture', in *High Theory/Low Culture*, ed. Colin MacCabe, Manchester: Manchester University Press, 1986.

31 J. A. Sharpe, *Witchcraft in Seventeenth-century Yorkshire: Accusations and Countermeasures*, Borthwick Institute of Historical Research, paper no. 81, (1992), p. 2. Sharpe's critique of 'the Thomas–Macfarlane witch' is especially trenchant on their lack of empathy with early modern fears.

32 The 1985 film, of course, had her rescued – but by the peasants, not by Willliam, since unlike the book it sought to portray William's reason as limited in its rejection of feeling. The destruction of the library provides a diversion which allows her to be freed, making the idea plain.

33 I have been told that it was taught in German university history courses as a portrait of the Middle Ages.

34 This is still Tanya Luhrmann's main question in *Persuasions of the Witch's Craft*,

Oxford: Blackwell, 1989, which deconstructs the opposition between books and belief by showing how books help to create belief.

35 See E. P. Thompson, 'Anthropology and the discipline of historical context', *Midland History*, 1 (1972), p. 50. See also Carlo Ginzburg's critique of the historian's continuing focus on the persecutor rather than the persecuted, *Ecstasies*, p. 2.

36 Michelet was one of the first historians to argue at length for an extant witch-cult, and his reconstruction of it made of it an organised resistance to church and state authorities. See Jules Michelet, *Satanism and Witchcraft*, trans. A. R. Allison, New York: Citadel 1992. Christopher Hill was one of the only social historians to accept the Murray thesis, in, for example, *The World Turned Upside Down*, Harmondsworth: Penguin, 1969, and *Change and Continuity in Seventeenth-Century England*, Cambridge, MA.: Harvard University Press, 1975.

37 Sharpe, 'Witchcraft and Women'; and Malcolm Gaskill, 'Witchcraft and power in early modern England: the case of Margaret Moore', in *Women, Crime and the Courts in Early Modern England*, ed. Jenny Kermode and Garthine Walker, London: UCL Press, 1994, pp. 125–45.

38 Raphael Samuel, 'Reading the signs', *History Workshop Journal* 32 (1991), pp. 88–109.

39 See, for instance, Appleby, Hunt and Jacob's assertion that 'denying the possibility of any separation of text and context (or cause and effect), postmodernist theory jeopardises all social theorising', p. 227; and '[if poststructuralism were the case] people in the past who believed themselves to be engaged in the search for truth would have to be either indulged or disabused by the historian', p. 227. Since these very eminent and able historians are trying harder than most to be fair to poststructuralist theories, these remarks are especially depressing. Joyce Appleby, Lynn Hunt and Margaret Jacob, *Telling the Truth about History*, New York: Norton, 1994.

40 See for instance Appleby, Hunt and Jacob's offering on deconstruction, which does not manage even to get the denotation of 'signified' right *Telling the Truth*, p. 214.

41 Joan Scott, 'Gender: a useful category of historical analysis', in *Gender and the Politics of History*, New York: Columbia University Press, 1988. Scott is also not too careful when summarising Lacan, offering a rather flattened account of his theories.

42 See for example, G. R. Elton, *Return to Essentials: Some Reflections on the Present State of Historical Study*, Cambridge: Cambridge University Press, 1994, p. 27.

43 In a chapter on poststructuralism, Appleby, Hunt and Jacob contrast 'those who have committed themselves to the discipine of studying evidence' with Holocaust deniers, as though the latter are not irritatingly prone to make exactly the same claims, *Telling the Truth*, p. 261. See also Deborah Lipstadt, *Denying the Holocaust: The Growing Assault on Truth and Memory*, Harmondsworth: Penguin, 1993, pp. 18–19, who writes that poststructuralism 'created an atmosphere of permissiveness toward questioning the meaning of historical events' by its 'relativistic' approach to truth. Both Appleby, Hunt and Jacob and Lipstadt know that poststructuralists themselves are not deniers (though de Man, as it turns out, was something worse), but they feel there must somehow be some link all the same.

44 See Richard Evans and Roger Eatwell, 'The Holocaust denial: a study in propaganda technique', in *Neofascism in Europe*, ed. Luciano Chles, Bonnie Ferguson and Michalina Vaughan, London: Longman, 1991, pp. 124–6.

45 Appleby, Hunt and Jacob, *Telling the Truth*.

46 'History and literature: "after the new historicism"', *New Literary History*, 21 (1989–90), pp. 253–72.

47 Patricia Crawford, 'The construction and experience of maternity', in *Women as Mothers in Preindustrial England*, ed. Valerie Fildes, London and New York: Routledge, 1990.

48 *The XV comforts of rash and inconsiderate marriage*, p. 54, cited by Crawford, p. 13.
49 See my 'Material girls: the seventeenth-century woman debate', in *Women, Texts and Histories* 1575–1760, ed. Clare Brant and Diane Purkiss, London and New York: Routledge, 1992.
50 Quentin Skinner, *Meaning and Interpretation*, Cambridge: Polity, 1988.
51 For Bennet Lane's story see Chapter 4.
52 Natalie Zemon Davis, *Fiction in the Archives: Pardon Tales and their Tellers in Sixteenth-century France*, Cambridge: Polity, 1988; Robert Darnton, *The Great Cat Massacre and Other Episodes in French Cultural History*, Harmondsworth: Penguin, 1987, first published 1984, and 'The symbolic element in history', *Journal of Modern History*, 58 (1986), pp. 218–34; and Annabel Gregory, 'Witchcraft, politics and "good neighbourhood" in seventeenth-century Rye', *Past and Present*, 133 (1991), pp. 31–66. Others could also be mentioned.
53 On discourse and ideology, see Terry Eagleton, *Ideology*, London: Verso, 1989; and on Foucault, see James Miller, *The Passion of Michel Foucault*, London: Flamingo, 1993. For feminist readings of Foucault see among numerous others Lois McNay, *Foucault and Feminism*, Cambridge: Polity, 1992, and *Feminism and Foucault: Reflections on Resistance*, ed. Irene Diamond and Lee Quinby, Boston: Northeastern University Press, 1988.
54 For Mary Glover, see the pamphlets by Edward Jorden and his opponent Stephen Bradwell in *Witchcraft and Hysteria in Elizabethan London: Edward Jorden and the Mary Glover Case*, ed. Michael Macdonald, London: Tavistock/Routledge, 1991.
55 Macdonald, *Witchcraft and Hysteria*, p. 2. Macdonald contests this assumption, arguing that Jorden was participating in the exorcism controversy.
56 Sigmund Freud, 'A seventeenth-century demonological neurosis', in *The Standard Edition of the Complete Psychological Works of Sigmund Freud*, ed. and trans. James Strachey, London: Hogarth Press, 1954, vol. 19, pp. 65–105, here p. 85.
57 'What Freud makes of history: "a seventeenth-century demonological neurosis"', in *The Writing of History*, trans Tom Conley, New York: Columbia, 1988, p. 287.
58 *Entertaining Satan: Witchcraft and the Culture of Early New England*, Oxford: Oxford University Press, 1982, chs 4 and 5.
59 Tim Ashplant, 'Psychoanalysis and historical writing', *History Workshop Journal*, 26 (1988) pp. 114–16. See also his 'Fantasy, narrative, event: psychoanalysis and history', *History Workshop Journal*, 23 (1987), pp. 165–73. Feminist literature on psychoanalsyis is vast; on the problems specifically in connection with women's history, see Sally Alexander, 'Feminist history and psychoanalysis', *History Workshop Journal*, 32 (1991), pp. 128–33.
60 'What Freud makes of History', p. 290; *Madness and Civilization*, New York: Pantheon, 1975, pp. ix, x. See also Foucault's own study of witchcraft, 'Médecins, juges et sorciers au XVII siècle', in *Médecine de France*, 200 (1969), pp. 121–8, which outlines a reading of the way demoniac experience is reductively pathologised by the emergence of medical discourse.
61 There are of course many sceptical articles about relics in *Past and Present*, including one in the 1995 volume.
62 Peter Brown, *The Cult of the Saints*, London: SCM, 1981, pp. 1ff, 87ff. I am thinking especially of Brown's use of the term *praesentia* to denote the real presence of a saint in and around a shrine, a term unknown to modern Catholics, who would simply refer to a real presence.
63 Michelet, *Satanism and Witchcraft*. For further discussion of his influence on popular history, see Chapter 2. Cixous and Clément, *The Newly Born Woman*, ch. 1, 'The Guilty One'.
64 For instance, Verena Andermett Conley, *Hélène Cixous*, Lincoln: University of

Nebraska Press, 1984; Morag Shiach, *Hélène Cixous: A Politics of Writing*, London: Routledge, 1991.

65 Cixous and Clément, *Newly Born Woman*, pp. 33, 112.

66 Judith Butler, *Gender Trouble*, London and New York: Routledge, 1989.

67 Sigmund Freud, 'The uncanny', *Standard Edition*, vol. 17, pp. 217–56, reprinted in *Art and Literature*, ed. Albert Dickson, Pelican Freud Library, vol. 14, Harmondsworth: Penguin, 1985, pp. 335–76. For Cixous's reading of this piece, see 'Fiction and its phantoms: a reading of Freud's *Das Unheimliche* (the uncanny)', *New Literary History*, 7 (1976), pp. 525–48.

68 Shoshana Felman, 'Rereading femininity', *Yale French Studies*, 62 (1982), pp. 19–44.

69 Cixous and Clément, *Newly Born Woman*, pp. 33–4.

70 Cixous and Clément, *Newly Born Woman*, pp. 34.

71 Cixous and Clément, *Newly Born Woman*, p. 35. For the prominence of housework and pollution in women's stories of witchcraft, see Chapter 4.

72 *Voler*: to fly, but also to steal, another way of infringing the boundaries of the proper, as the mother's body always does.

73 Cixous and Clément, *Newly Born Woman*, p. 36.

74 For instance, Jane Ussher, *Women's Madness: Misogyny or Mental Illness?*, New York: Harvester Wheatsheaf, 1991.

75 Cixous and Clément, *Newly Born Woman*, p. 36.

76 I am indebted to Miranda Chaytor for this reading of Thomas; personal letter, 15 August 1995.

77 Cixous *Newly Born Woman*, pp. 39, 36.

78 Lyndal Roper offers a more sustained critique of the idea of a historicised body and the history of manners in *Oedipus and the Devil*, introduction.

79 Sigmund Freud, *Civilization and its Discontents*, in *Civilization, Society and Religion*, ed. Albert Dickson, Pelican Freud Library, vol. 12, Harmondsworth: Penguin, 1985, pp. 243–340.

80 Norman O. Brown, *Life against Death: The Psychoanalytical Meaning of History*, 2nd edn, Middletown, CT: Wesleyan University Press, 1958, p. 12.

Part II

Early modern women's stories of witchcraft

4 The house, the body, the child

> The things that surround us, usually quiet, domesticated and invisible, are suddenly seen as strange . . . People, trees, animals, even objects and words have a double life.
>
> Carlo Levi, *Christ Stopped at Eboli*

Despite feminism's fascination with the figure of the witch, there have been surprisingly few attempts to read women witnesses' depositions at witch-trials as texts authored by early modern women, texts that illustrate women's ideas about witches and witchcraft. There are several reasons for this neglect. Depositions by women witnesses are often seen as unreadable, offering a tangle of signs which point only into a disorderly mass of 'primitive' superstition.[1] For example, Clive Holmes compares the depositions of the possessed and midwives to 'those who testified simply to their experience of the witch's *maleficium*'. He writes dismissively that 'this kind of testimony [i.e. to *maleficium*] is more inchoate than the other two categories; it lacks their conceptual clarity and sophistication'.[2] However, there is nothing 'simple' or 'inchoate' about such testimonies. Careful reading of them shows that they depend on a set of assumptions and tropes which make sense on their own terms, reflecting and managing the fears and desires of women.

A second objection to a reading of women's texts as women's stories is the problematic status of such texts as products of women's authorship.[3] Women's depositions were sometimes elicited by questioning from clerks or judges; they were often volunteered during a 'witch-hunt' organised by a local enthusiast or by a group of justices. As a result, feminist historians have sometimes seen women witnesses as mere mouthpieces of a patriarchal elite. It is true that elite and popular tellers of stories of witchcraft borrow from each other, absorbing new materials and views, but reinscribing and modifying them to form idiosyncratic negotiations of particular desires and fears. Some women may have tried to adopt strategically the languages and discourses of the elite in order to make their depositions persuasive. However, this is no reason to assume that women witnesses in witch trials were the dupes of patriarchy. Many of the main stories discussed here did not form part of the eventual indictment, suggesting women were not pandering sufficiently to the expectations of the JPs and the better sort. Historians have also suggested that some women's testimonies were strategic, transmuting local quarrels into stories of *maleficium*.[4] Such cases illustrate women's strategic use of witch-*discourses*, but this does not mean that they are silent about women's witch-*beliefs*. Such stories would still have had to draw on materials that made sense in order to be persuasive. Women tellers of stories about witches are making a narrative that makes sense within their world of community and household, using some very ancient materials and some recent coinages, some stories from peasant oral culture and some from print, to fashion a story that works.

A tendency to treat the stories of women witnesses as patriarchal ventriloquism may have arisen from early feminist attempts to seek a global explanation for witch-hunts in a simplistic opposition between patriarchy and femininity, or – even more simplistically – between men and women.[5] As male historians have somewhat gleefully pointed out, the theory that witch-hunting equals misogyny is embarrassed by the predominance of women witnesses against the accused.[6] However, this does not mean that gender ideology plays no part in shaping women's stories. Abandoning simple global narratives of misogyny in favour of a more detailed account of women's stories does not render the question of gender irrelevant; it poses that question in a new and pressing form. In order to read the stories produced by women deponents, feminists need to ask new questions about the role played by gender ideology in arousing women's anxieties and fears.

Another problem of authorship is that there are question marks over the 'texts' of women's depositions themselves. Women's depositions, often submitted by women who could not themselves read or write, were inscribed by a (male) clerk who may have altered them with the addition of legal jargon and in other and more substantial ways. Depositions which survive only in printed form, however, are regarded by some historians as especially dubious, since they may represent the further possible intervention of a male pamphleteer or printer.[7] The degree and kind of pamphlet 'authorship' varies greatly from one pamphlet to another. Some pamphlets claim merely to have been produced by someone in court, acting as a kind of early legal journalist; some are tissues of hearsay slung together with conspicuous zeal or haste; others were produced by people close to the action in court. Some pamphlets reproduce confessions or depositions in transcript form; others subsume these pre-texts beneath their own narrative. The St Osyth pamphlet, for instance, was produced either by Brian Darcy himself, one of the justices of the peace in the case, or by someone in his household. The writer had access to the principal depositions and confessions collected by Darcy, and there is no reason to believe that these were altered for publication.[8] Pamphleteers became more and more interventionist, less and less recorders and preface-writers, as the seventeenth century wore on.[9] But many (though by no means all) Elizabethan and early Jacobean pamphlets attempt to present assize depositions with reasonable completeness. Even late pamphets, in which trial accounts are covered with a thick layer of providential rhetoric, often represent the content of confessions with fair accuracy, though with much moralising.

Whether surviving in print or in manuscript, women's testimonies do not therefore constitute a pure or unconstrained form of female authorship. However, it is questionable whether the early modern period offers *any* texts authored 'purely' by women in this very demanding sense. Most feminists now doubt whether 'femininity' even exists in such a pure form; to be a woman is to be a hybrid, gendered, but not separate from male-dominated society. *Any text* produced by an early modern woman was prone to male intervention, in the process of composition as well as at the point of transcription or printing. Women were caught up in the discursive currents of early modern culture, whose dominant discourses were largely male constructs absorbed (albeit often critically) by early modern women. In order to tell any kind of story, women had painstakingly to insert themselves into such discourses by careful negotiation.[10]

All this implies that terms like 'witch' and 'witchcraft' were not single or fixed, but highly unstable terms, sites of conflict and contestation between diverse groups. The term 'witch' was labile, sliding across a number of different and competing discourses. It figured in, and was refigured in, the discursive self-definitions of both absolutism and antityranny, both Puritanism and Counter-Reformation Catholicism, both colonialism and resistance to colonialism. It could be appropriated by patriarchy, protofeminism, medicine, sceptical rationalism and radical religion. In villages and towns, witchcraft could become a central signifier in debates about power, employment, norms, values, property rights and land ownership. None of this implies that the supernatural aspects of witchcraft did not matter; they mattered in a variety of ways in different contexts. As the term 'witch' traversed these diverse spaces, its own meaning was revised silently or openly rewritten.[11] Women were one among many of the groups which could take up the term 'witch' and negotiate with it to satisfy private or public desires.

In what follows, I argue that some women's stories of witchcraft constituted a powerful *fantasy* which enabled women to negotiate the fears and anxieties of housekeeping and motherhood. Throughout, I am using the term fantasy in its quasi-psychoanalytic sense. In psychoanalysis, a fantasy is a story in which people both express and relieve their unconscious (and sometimes their conscious) fears, conflicts and anxieties.[12] This conception of fantasy does not imply a judgement about the truth or falsity of women's stories or their beliefs; I am not interested in determining whether supernatural events took place, still less in deciding what 'natural' events underlay them. In reading women's stories as fantasies, I do not intend to offer an explanation for all witch-beliefs, a historical account of why the 'witch-craze' arose at this particular time, or any other grand historical narrative. As a feminist literary critic, I wanted to see if anything could be gained from a close reading of various quite well-known texts. I wanted to explore the meanings which lay within their vividness, their poignancy, their tenderness, their exact and exacting metaphors. I focus on cases where the majority of witnesses were women, and look at those cases in the context of sixteenth- and seventeenth-century witchcraft depositions in general. When early modern women thought about witches and constructed their figurations of witchcraft, their fantasies reflected the need to establish or maintain a social identity within the community. Accusers and accused lived within certain definitions of female identity which were not of their making and over which they exercised little control; these women were shaped by culture even as they struggled to shape it. They moved in a world which defined a woman's role narrowly: woman was a producer of children and the one who organised and maintained the household economy. However, within this circumscribed space a rich and elaborate network of cultural meanings was assigned to productive tasks, and these meanings in turn defined female identity. Women's stories of witchcraft were caught in this network of meanings. For women, a witch was a figure who could be read against and within her own social identity as housewife and mother.

Agnes Heard was one of several women arraigned as witches at St Osyth, Essex, in 1579. The indictment reads: 'Agnes Heard, of Little Oakley, spinster . . . on 1 Jan. 1582 she bewitched to death a cow, 10 sheep and 10 lambs (£4) belonging to John Wade'.[13] This indictment, which foregrounds a male witness and plaintiff speaking about male arenas of husbandry, conceals the role that women deponents played in accusing Agnes and providing depositions giving evidence against her.[14] The women's depositions against Agnes Heard focus on a series of domestic and familial incidents, incidents in which housewifery goes awry or children sicken. One of the deponents was Bennet Lane, the wife of William Lane. Bennet tells of her encounters with Agnes: when Bennet was a widow, Agnes Heard is at her house, and she gives Agnes a pint of milk, also lending her a dish to take it home in. Agnes keeps the dish for two or three weeks, so Bennet sends Agnes's daughter home to get it, remarking tartly that 'though I gave thy mother milk to make a posset, I gave her not my dish'. Agnes duly sends the dish back, but no sooner is it returned than Bennet's spinning goes wrong:

> she could no longer spin nor make a thread to hold. Whereas she was so grieved that she could not spin, she saith, she took her spindle and went to the grindstone therewith once or twice, and ground it as smooth as she could, thinking it might be by some ruggedness of the spindle that did cause her thread to break; and so when she had ground it as well as she could, she went again to work therewith, thinking that then it would have done, but it would not do no better than it did before. Then she saith, that she remembered herself, and took her spindle and put it into the fire and made it red-hot, and then cooled it again and went to work, and then it wrought as well as ever it did at any time before.[15]

Bennet first tries the everyday method of grinding the spindle; then, having 'remembered herself', she applies a very common type of counter-magic, the heating of a bewitched object till red-hot or the application of a red-hot object to it.[16]

However, Bennet is soon in trouble again; Agnes Heard owes her tuppence, and Bennet sets out to collect it because her own church tithes are due. Rashly, she also tries to borrow some money from Agnes, who explains that she has no spare cash. Bennet tries to insist because church tithes are due that day, and Agnes agrees to borrow the money from a neighbour. She gives the borrowed money to Bennet, who says: 'Now I owe you a pint of milk, come for it when you will and you shall have it.' Agnes collects her milk and some butter the next day, but Bennet now develops serious problems in the dairy:

> the next day, she would have fleet [skimmed] her milk bowl, but it would not abide the fleeting, but would rope and roll as it were the white of an egg; also the milk being on the fire it did not so soon seethe as it would quail, burn by, and stink.[17]

At first Bennet thinks of natural causes; her animals' feeding may be the problem, or her vessels may not be clean. So as before she begins with natural remedies; she scalds all her vessels and scours them with salt, but this has no effect. Afraid of losing her entire stock of cream and milk, she recalls another counter-magical remedy: 'she took a horseshoe, and made it red-hot, and put it into the milk in her vessels, and so into her cream; and then, she saith, she could seethe her milk, fleet her cream, and make her butter in good sort as she had before'.[18]

This is only one of a series of similar confrontations between Agnes Heard and other women of her village, Little Oakley.[19] It is notable that Bennet's encounters with Agnes cannot be fitted into the Thomas–Macfarlane model of a quarrel based on a householder's refusal of alms to a suspected witch; rather, the occasion for witchcraft here is in each case an exchange or a gift whereby *both* women go out of their way to cooperate with and benefit each other. Nor does Bennet describe Agnes using any opprobrious terms or curses; there is no overt quarrel, no separable act of *maleficium* distinct from Bennet's encounters with Agnes: no transfixing looks, no mysterious or portentous speeches. What happens is that after an exchange with Agnes in which an object is transferred from one woman to another, bewitchment occurs. Significantly, these exchanges occur in women's sphere of activities, food production, and it is women's activities that go wrong afterwards. Bennet's response is in each case initially pragmatic, an assertion of household skills: regrinding the spindle, scalding the milk pans.[20] Only when these methods fail to restore order does she have recourse to counter-magic. However, the counter-magic Bennet employs to restore order is itself domestic, involving a form of cooking: she heats objects on the stove in order to unwitch them. Finally, Bennet represents herself as actuated not by godly zeal, but by the fear of losing what she must preserve: the milk and cream or 'white meats' which were vital to the early modern diet.[21] Agnes threatens to disrupt this food supply, and deprive Bennet of the food and clothing she needs. Bennet is not interested in (in the sense of involved with) the wider public issues of authority, patrilinearity, legitimacy and religion which preoccupied learned sceptics and demonologists; she represents Agnes's witchcraft as a threat to the domestic sphere.[22]

It would not be fair to describe this case as typical, but Bennet's story reveals themes that arise repeatedly in other cases. In shaping their stories of witchcraft, women focused on an encounter with the suspected woman involving either an exchange, usually of food or food-related items, or a failed exchange of food, or sometimes merely a discussion about food. Elizabeth Lord brought a drink in a cruse to John Francis, after which he sickened and died; she also gave a piece of apple-cake to Joan Roberts, a servant-girl who also fell sick after receiving the gift.[23] Elizabeth Style gave two apples to another woman; she claimed to have received one of the fruits from the devil, and it had dire effects on the recipient.[24] Apples seem to have been especially suspect: Ann Bishop also obtained one from the devil, which she gave to Agnes Vining. The devil had assured her that it would do 'Vining's wife's business'.[25] A woman who consulted Richard Napier had become 'mad and mopish' after she had accepted an apple from a suspected witch.[26] On other occasions, an exchange or failed exchange resulted in disrupted food production; when Mother Atkins was refused milk, she disrupted dairy work so that the cream burst open the top of the churn.[27] Other suspects disrupted the milk supply at the source; when Isabel Turner's request for milk was denied, she caused the household cow to give blood instead of milk, and the same fate befell the cows of Mistress Saunders after she had refused yeast to Margery Stanton.[28] Ann Wagg, on being refused milk, killed a calf.[29] Another suspect, on being refused pease, turned it rotten and uneatable, while a rich gentlewoman, passing through a village, merely divined what was in the pot on the stove, and after being called a witch for doing so, bewitched it.[30] On still other occasions, disputes arose over sales of food: when Jane Simpson sold cherries to Dorothy Hearon, Dorothy claimed that Jane had overcharged her, and Jane fell ill as a result of the quarrel.[31]

Food is therefore a constant theme in depositions on witchcraft. This can be understood in the context of the crisis in the early modern rural economy in the late sixteenth and early seventeenth centuries; as a result of certain economic and political pressures, the situation of the rural poor worsened dramatically as the sixteenth century wore on, and they became dependent on a limited diet of pulses, grain and bread, chickens, pigs and 'white meats'.[32] The last were especially crucial since they provided the only reliable ongoing sources of protein and fat, and in this context the strong association of bewitchment with the dairy is significant. Much of the pressure from this scarcity and marginality fell on the housewife, exhorted to manage frugally from every pulpit, and responsible for dairying and for the survival of herself and her household. Acute anxieties developed around the disruption of dairying; when the butter failed to churn, the result might be hunger, or at the least a cash shortage.

Women's domestic responsibilities were also invested with symbolic significance. In the case of Bennet and Agnes, we have already seen that Bennet struggles to reassert the control over spinning and dairying which has been taken from her. Housewifely authority involves the ability to transform 'natural' items into cultural items: wool is transformed into thread and milk into cream and whey. As Jill Dubisch puts it, following Mary Douglas, 'women function as transformers of natural products and processes into cultural ones', and as such they work to transform 'matter out of place' into matter in place, or cultural order. Women are responsible for preserving the boundaries of social and cultural life.[33] In early modern England, the kitchen, the dairy and the laundry are where nature and culture meet and are mediated. In cooking, churning, spinning, skimming, washing and spinning, women perform an act of culturation, turning natural materials into clean, orderly, culturally useful objects.[34] When this process is disrupted by witchcraft, the authority and identity of the housewife are put in question; she can no longer predict or control the processes of transformation required. Instead, witchcraft characteristically produces a shaming effect of utter disorder, dirt and pollution: milk behaves like white of egg, ale turns sour and smells vile, cows produce blood where they should produce milk, and pease becomes rotten, stinking and uneatable. Since domestic labour involves maintaining order by ensuring that matter does not become wrongly placed, these supernatural events threaten the housewife's self-image as authoritative and competent.

If we think of Bennet's description of the effects of Agnes's acts as her *fantasy* about what a witch was, we can see that for Bennet the witch is a kind of antihousewife, her own dark Other who causes pollution where there should be order, who disrupts food supplies which must be ordered and preserved, who wastes what is necessary. The witch is an antihousewife because she *usurps* Bennet's authority over the household in order to misuse it, to invert it. Bennet's power to order and transform is displaced and replaced by the witch's power to disorder and pollute. The witch is the identity which Bennet must suppress, define herself against, in order to fashion her own identity as a housewife. She is Bennet's dark twin, a housewife who is not a housewife, who is the dark shadow of Bennet's own existence. Whereas most historians see the witch as the church's Other, or as man's Other, I'm suggesting here that early modern women could also represent the witch as *their* Other, that female anxieties, fears and self-fashioning could also shape the notion of 'witch' at popular level. In this context, we can now begin to analyse the sudden, catastrophic, frightening loss of household power to another woman. What allows Agnes to take over?

The housewife's role involves maintaining boundaries, boundaries between nature and culture, between inside and outside, pollution and purity. Bennet has to ensure that the milk pans are clean if she is to skim successfully; skimming is itself an act of separation, as is churning. In early modern communities, one of the principal ways of representing the border of nature or culture was the boundary of the house. Within its walls, women carried out the transformative processes which sustain family life. As well, the boundaries of the house were invested with ideological significance for the woman's own identity as chaste. Moralists and writers of domestic conduct books stress that the virtuous wife must 'keep house': this means both staying home and doing housework. The relation between this model of household containment and the model of the enclosed chaste body of the virtuous woman is clear.[35] By contrast, women who were not virtuously enclosed were associated with sexual availability, economic profligacy and political disorder.[36] The physical boundaries of property become identified with the social boundaries of propriety. As well as remaining within the boundaries of the household and ordering its contents, woman was represented as guarding its resources from overflowing or escaping into the general economy. The good housewife of godly ideology therefore conserved goods for the family by keeping them within the boundaries of the home.

At the same time, witchcraft depositions reveal that the boundaries of the home were always being crossed. In the case of the dairy, milk from outside was brought in to be turned into food; in the case of brewing, grain, barm and water had to be bought, or brought from nature into culture. As well, these processes must often have involved contact with other people over whom ordering control was at best tenuous, from the servants of other householders to independent tradesmen. Moreover, the notion of the house as a closed container, with resolutely maintained boundaries presided over by the housewife, was at odds with the identity of the housewife as a member of the community. In particular, the obligation to be hospitable involved a perpetual opening of the house to the needy and to travellers, with the provision of food too.[37] Calendric festivals routinely involved the opening of the house of the farmer to the less fortunate, while more occasional celebrations such as childbirth, christenings and marriages also involved inviting people in and distributing carefully husbanded foodstuffs.[38] Exclusions from festivities could be interpreted as occasions for witchcraft: when Anne Kerke was not invited to a child's christening, she promptly bewitched the child in question, while another witch who was not invited to a sheep-shearing dinner reacted by bewitching the host's sheep.[39] In each case, the occasion for the celebration was assailed, and there is a clear parallel between these cases and the more typical encounters between suspects and housewives. House boundaries were not only broached on festival occasions, but also by the everyday exchanges of news, gossip, utensils and food. An (unwanted) visit from a neighbour, a returned domestic object, a piece of food which should have remained outside but found its way into the house, a piece of food which should have remained within but found its way out, all these could pollute by rendering permeable the boundaries of the house and thus, symbolically, the cultural boundaries it guaranteed.

This popular structure of belief was noted by the learned: John Gaule commented that witches often worked by leaving something of theirs in the victim's house, or getting something of hers into their house, and he advised that a witch loitering near the house should be warned off, lest she place an object near the threshold or in bedstraw.[40] Gaule's choice of hiding places is interesting: the threshold, as the name implies, is a liminal space, *the* boundary between inside and outside, while bedstraw is a good example of a natural material reordered and domesticated, an obvious site for anxious cleansing, since it comes into contact with the bodies of the householders. But like many modern commentators, Gaule does not notice the role that gender plays in determining this image of witchcraft. It is the association of female identity with maintaining the boundaries of and order in the house which makes the witch a fearful fantasy of what can happen when those bounds are transgressed.

Since the guarantor of order was the housewife, this polluting effect was most marked when she was already not in control of the object or person which crossed the house boundaries; in Agnes Heard's case, Bennet had to act to secure the overdue return of her milk dish, and had to beg Agnes for money to pay the church tithes. Both may be signs that Bennet had lost control of the situation and allowed Agnes to gain power over herself and her household. In Bennet's fantasy of her relations with Agnes, Agnes's witchcraft is a sign of Bennet's own (fear of) inadequacy – even as Bennet struggles to demonstrate her competence. It seems impossible to contemplate this tense and conflictual relationship without thinking of the mother–daughter bond, with all its complexities. The daughter's efforts to free herself from the controlling Mother-Other lay bare her weaknesses even when she asserts her strengths.

The same themes recur in another range of female fantasies of witchcraft which overlap with the one sketched above. These are cases in which the identity of the deponent (and often the witch) as mother is central to understanding the stories that are told; like the cases involving housewifery, food is a central issue. The role of mother and the role of food provider are crucially linked even today, and this linkage was even more central to early modern notions of maternal identity.[41] The mother's body provides the child with its first food needs, in the womb and at the breast, and the mother as housewife is responsible for producing and providing food for the household.[42] Children were the principal economic and social products of women's labour; while richer parents might value children as a source of continuity in an inheritance system, poorer parents needed their labour.[43] Different as these modes of valuation might appear, both saw women's childrearing labour as crucial. Food supplies had to be produced and maintained in order to raise children.

Like the house, the body has boundaries. As Mary Douglas and others have noted, the bodies of women are more 'leaky', permeable and problematic than the bodies of men. This is partly because of maternity, in which the boundaries of a woman's body are broached and the body itself distended and ambiguous during pregnancy, representing an uncertain number of bodies. In breastfeeding too, the body exudes matter, and the line between the maternal body and that of the suckling child becomes impossible to draw. The maternal body, though venerated, is also a problematic source of pollution. Consequently, childbirth itself was surrounded by rituals in which women were again the prime movers in organising and maintaining boundaries. After childbirth the maternal body was safeguarded by the lengthy lying-in process, but during that time the mother was liminal, and therefore vulnerable. Breastfeeding, too, was an anxious period of vulnerability. Breastfeeding was followed by a longer period of maternity in which the maternal role of food provision coalesced with the role of housewife. Women's depositions in witchcraft cases involving children or mothers often reflect the anxieties produced by all stages of the maternal life.

Although most cases of child bewitchment involve older children, I want to look first at a number of cases involving the bewitchment of children in the womb. Pregnancy was often an anxious time for early modern women, especially if the child was greatly desired.[44] It was usually understood as a time of illness, and early modern medical texts focus on the problem of how to prevent miscarriage. Some at least of the remedies offered were quasi-magical, like the nourishing caudle recommended by the Duchess of Buckingham to her niece Lady Cartwright, which closely resembled the caudle drunk during labour, and the girdles modelled on the girdle of the Virgin which were passed on from mother to daughter.[45] In this highly charged context of female connections, it is not surprising that some women came to believe that other women could cause miscarriage. Jennet Hargraves, for example, was said to have caused the death of a child in the womb, while Doll Barthram confessed that her familiar had 'nipped out the brains of an unborn child'.[46] Some of Richard Napier's female patients also believed that witches had caused their miscarriages or stillbirths: Mistress Underhill was said by Napier to 'fear ill means' when she miscarried in March 1627, while Mistress Mason lost her baby, pined, and was consumed after a suspected witch threatened her for buying a hare. Mistress Woodward also suspected witchcraft when she had a succession of stillbirths after a property dispute with Alice Coleman.[47] These events are more explicable in the light of what we have already learned about the image of the witch as usurper of the authority of other women over the domestic realm. Medical and popular knowledge alike affirmed the power of the mother's thoughts and feelings to shape the child *in utero*; by usurping her place, the witch or her familiar could do the same.[48] These thoughts and feelings are ideologically overdetermined: the mother must *avoid* unfeminine feelings of rage, frustration and fury if she is to avoid miscarriage. These feelings characterise the witch as the opposite of what the early modern woman should be. Again, the witch is the dark other of the early modern woman, expressing and acting on desires that other women must repress to construct their identities as mothers.

The notion of the witch as antimother plays an even more obvious role in cases involving childbirth and lying-in. In order to understand the ways in which fantasies of witchcraft could develop around these events, it is necessary to understand the way the events themselves were organised. As Adrian Wilson has recently demonstrated, childbirth was a female ceremony and festival for the early modern woman. When labour began, the mother's husband would summon to the birth not just the midwife, but a group of other women who assembled in the expectant mother's chamber. These women, known as 'gossips', from godsib, were selected for attendance by the expectant mother, and might include her own mother and also her closest female friends. As Wilson explains, the space of the birth was a collective female space, constituted by the presence of gossips and midwife and the absence of men. The gossips were responsible for physically and symbolically enclosing the birthing-room, by blocking keyholes and hanging up heavy curtains. They also prepared the mother's caudle, a hot drink containing warmed ale or wine with sugar and spices; this was the mother's drink throughout labour, and the gossips symbolically mothered her by supplying her with this special food. Its specialness, like the enclosure of the room, marked the mother's separation from normal household affairs and from the outside world.[49]

The key figure in preventing harm was the midwife, who guaranteed and subtended the order threatened by the witch.[50] In doing this she often had recourse to magical and counter-magical forms and formulae, showing how birth was heavily invested with magical significance. Many of her remedies involve symbols of binding, opening and closing. The use of girdles, with or without the blessings of St Margaret, and the opening of chests and doors suggest (very ancient) concerns about the opening and closing of the woman's violently labouring body, and reflect the preoccupations which govern the entire birthing ritual.[51] An event so surrounded by the careful policing of geographical and bodily boundaries is an event which can be viewed as potentially disruptive and polluting, and also an event which renders its immediate participants acutely vulnerable.

Early modern childbirth was a festival in the feminine sphere, and as with other festivals, exclusion from it could become a signifier of witchcraft. No fewer than five of Richard Napier's female patients reported that they believed themselves to have been bewitched by women who had not been invited to be gossips.[52] One of them, Mistress Style, approached Napier after her child was stillborn; she suspected Margaret Wilbe, who had not been called to the labour.[53] Though the birth itself was crucial for constituting a community of women and an enclosed space, these processes created a category of harmful outsiders who might act against the controls which they had not helped to set up. The witch appears again as the alien alternative to the strictly organised control of nature and pollution on which the birthing ritual centres.

In women's fantasies, then, the witch used the childbirth ceremony to harm the vulnerable woman. A case in point comes from the confession of Ellen Greene, of Stathern in Leicester. Greene claimed that Joan Willimot, another witch-suspect who was also on trial, had ordered her to harm Mistress Patchett after Joan had quarrelled with her. Ellen duly carried out her commission:

> she then said Willimot called her (this examinate) to go and touch the said John Patchett's wife and her child, which she did, touching the said John Patchett's wife in her bed and the child in the grace-wife's [midwife's] arms.

> And then she sent her said spirits to bewitch them to death, which they did, and so the woman lay languishing by the space of a month and more, for then she died; the child died the next day after she touched it.[54]

Ellen called either during the childbirth ceremony itself, or shortly afterward, since the child was still being held by the midwife when she touched it. Ellen may be implying that Joan Willimot approached her because Ellen would be invited to the ceremony and would have access to mother and child.

The process of attempting to safeguard the woman and child continued after the birth. During lying-in, the birthing-room retained its closed aspect; at first, the mother was confined to her bed for a period that varied from three days to a fortnight, and throughout this time the bedlinen remained unchanged.[55] At this stage only women could visit the mother, possibly only those who had been present at the birth itself. The linen was changed for the next stage, when the woman was allowed to sit up, and for another week to ten days the mother remained in her room. This was often accompanied by a women's feast in the lying-in chamber, and also by further visits from women in the community, who would drink the caudle which had sustained the mother during childbirth, symbolically uniting themselves to her by one form of commensality or another. In the third and final stage, the mother could move about the house, but did not venture out of doors; this stage too lasted for a week to ten days, and at this point the restriction on male visitors was relaxed. The whole process took about a month, and was followed by a resumption of household duties by the new mother and a rejoining of the community, often symbolised by the mother's churching or purification. The mother to be churched went to church wearing a heavy veil, with her head bent, and only after the ceremony did she look at the sun, the sky and her neighbours, as well as resuming sexual relations with her husband.[56] The lying-in period is a series of carefully marked stages through which mother and baby pass. It is characterised by a mixture of anxiety about closure and an unexpected openness; the woman remains in the closed-off room, but the house becomes progressively more and more open to visitors who partake of food shared by the mother. In the light of what has gone before, this combination of openness and anxiety about boundaries sets the scene for witchcraft fears and stories to develop around the mother's lying-in. As Lyndal Roper shows, during lying-in the mother's authority over the household is suspended; she is no longer up and about, patrolling its boundaries.[57] As we have seen, witchcraft occurs when women lose control of the processes of housewifery to another woman, so it is not surprising that a woman who has already renounced household control might seem especially vulnerable.

One case from near Doncaster involves the importance of the ceremony of childbirth and the lying-in period to women's fears of and fantasies about witchcraft. Joan Jurdie was presented twice for witchcraft. The second presentation involved depositions from women about a series of events during the childbed and lying-in of Janet Murfin, who was dead by the time of the trial. Allegedly her death was due to Jurdie's malice. Anne Judd deposed that:

> Joan Jurdie, wife of Leonard Jurdie of Rossington, being bidden to the labour of Peter Murfin's wife, of Rossington, did not come of three or four days after she was delivered, and when she came she would neither eat nor drink with the said Murfin's wife, and because the said Peter Murfin did not come into the house to drink with her, and this examinate going home with her unto her own house, she said to this examinate that Peter Murfin would not come in and drink with her, but tell him that I say he had as good have come. And the day following this examinate, having occasion to go to the said Joan Jurdie's house, Jane Througheare, servant to the said Jurdie, asked this examinate how her sister and child did, this examinate made answer again, very weakly, whereupon the said Joan Jurdie made answer again, abide her, she is not at the worst, she will be worse yet.[58]

Anne Judd and Joan Jurdie are both on the move, entering and leaving the houses of others. Joan has been invited to attend the birth, probably as a gossip, but does not put in an appearance till after delivery, during the first week of lying-in. Joan has not involved herself in the community of women around birth, and she rejects the symbolic involvement in that community figured by eating and drinking with the new mother. Jurdie marks her separateness from Janet's person and household by refusing her gestures of inclusion. The grounds for her refusal also imply a disorderly carelessness about rules; usually men were excluded from the ceremonies of childbed, and even from the lying-in room in the early stages. Presumably these rules explain Peter Murfin's refusal to come in and drink with Jurdie. It is not surprising that when Janet began to feel ill her thoughts turned to Jurdie's visit. 'Woe worth her', she remarked to Anne Judd, 'for I did well till Joan Jurdie wife came.' Katherine Dolfin, another deponent, reported that she too called on Janet during the lying-in period, when Janet told her 'I was never well since Saturday that Jurdie wife was here'. Jurdie had refused to share food with Janet, and now Janet cannot eat at all: 'I could never eat any meat but supping-meat [since Saturday].' She cannot eat, and she cannot provide food: Peter Murfin, the sole male deponent in this case, remarked that his wife's milk had turned to blood before she died.

As in the case of Agnes Heard, Joan Jurdie was constructed as a witch by Janet Murfin and other women in Rossington because she evaded housewifely control. She refused the hospitality which symbolised those rules and controls, but she had nevertheless crossed the boundaries of the household at a time when its inhabitants were especially anxious about pollution and when Janet's own authority was particularly weak. Since Jurdie had refused to help safeguard Janet's childbirth and to acknowledge her role as food provider, it's not surprising that the effect of her malevolence was to pollute Janet's body as a source of food for her infant; the turning of Janet's milk to blood symbolises the witch's transformation of the woman from mother into antimother, from giver of life to giver of death. At the same time, Janet came to resemble Joan in this; Joan refused symbolic oneness with Janet as mother, thus casting herself as an antimother who then also transforms Janet into an antimother. Janet is under Jurdie's control; she comes to resemble Jurdie in an inverted form of the customs which Jurdie refuses and which would symbolically unite her to the mother. Again, the twin figures of mother and daughter surface in the mind; Jurdie is the bad mother who will not authenticate her daughter's maturity/maternity.

Another story involving childbed and lying-in was told in the St Osyth trials of 1579. A servant named Grace Thurlow deposed that a woman named Ursula Kempe had killed her child in the cradle by witchcraft.[59] As Grace told it, events were as follows:

> about three-quarters of a year ago she was delivered of a woman child, and saith, that shortly after the birth thereof, the said Ursula fell out with her, for that she would not suffer her to have the nursing of that child . . . she the said Grace nursing the said child, within a short time after the falling out, the child laying in the cradle, and not above a quarter old, fell out of the cradle and brake her neck and died. The which the said Ursula hearing to have happened, made answer, 'It maketh no matter, for she might have suffered me to have the keeping and nursing of it'.[60]

Both Grace and her child were in a liminal space following the birth. Ursula, excluded from that space and denied a role in the infant's nurturance and feeding, becomes an invader and destroyer, an antimother instead of a mother-analogue. The dubious line between mother and child allows Ursula to act again, against Grace this time; Grace is still in the vulnerable lying-in period when Ursula comes to see her:

> And the said Grace saith, that when she lay in the said Ursula came unto her, and seemed to be very angry for that she had not the keeping in of the said Grace, and for that she answered unto her that she was provided.[61]

Ursula had asked to be the hired nurse or lying-in-maid who superintends the household while the mother rests during lying-in. She had already asked to be the wetnurse, and in many small households the two roles may have overlapped.[62] Ursula has asked therefore to replace Grace in the household, to take control of it and also to take over Grace's maternal role in caring for the baby.[63] Since it is apparent from the following dialogue that Grace already suspected Ursula of witchcraft, her refusal is not surprising. Ursula seems to have acted suspiciously by taking too much interest in taking on Grace's role. Since a witch was someone who usurped household authority, this interest in taking up that position was in itself dangerous.

The two women discuss their differences during Ursula's visit, and eventually Grace confronts Ursula:

> the said Grace saying that if she should continue lame as she had done before she would find the means to know how it came, and that she would creep upon her knees to complain of them . . . And to that the said Ursula answered, 'It were a good turn'.[64]

Neither woman is speaking plainly. Grace hints that she will take action if she becomes ill again, implicitly acknowledging her suspicions of Ursula by threatening her, and Ursula refuses to acknowledge Grace's hints, representing herself as innocent by agreeing that prosecuting the one who hurts you is a good thing. Grace takes this as a denial, and warns Ursula more explicitly, saying 'Take heed, Ursula, thou hast a naughty name'. Ursula responds assertively that 'though she could unwitch, yet she could not witch':

> and so promised the said Grace that if she did send for her privily, and send her keeper away, that she would show the said Grace how she should unwitch herself today or at any other time.[65]

Ursula is still trying to be Grace's keeper, and is offering her special unwitching skills in exchange for the role. To Ursula, this may still seem a dispute about a job; to Grace, Ursula is still taking too much interest in taking over Grace's household. Grace is not about to allow a woman she already suspects of too much interest in her household to take up a power position in it. At the same time, she cannot prevent Ursula from taking up a role as antimother. Instead of nourishing Grace and her baby, Ursula assails them; refused authority by Grace, Ursula takes it anyway.

As Grace's fantasy of what a witch 'was', Ursula represents an antigossip, an antiwetnurse, an antikeeper or lying-in-maid. She usurps Grace's domestic and maternal authority for disorder rather than order, exactly what Grace feared when she refused Ursula the jobs of nurse and keeper. Ursula is Grace's antithesis, active where Grace is reduced to passivity, mobile where Grace is confined, in control where Grace's household authority is in abeyance, an outsider where Grace is held inside, malevolent where Grace seeks to be protective. Ursula also represents Grace's anxieties about the opening of the house to the community; the walls of the lying-in room are maintained against light and air, but it is also problematically open – as are Grace and her baby – to the scrutiny and agency of other women.

Another St Osyth case involves the moment when the lying-in period ended and mother and child were welcomed back into the everyday life of the community. Joan Smith deposed that she was met at the door of her house by a group of women; the occasion was that of her first church-going after the birth of her child.[66] The women were at the door ready to draw the latch; this account may point to a ceremonious reception of the new mother and child after the lying-in period ended. The presence of Joan's mother, previously informed that she is going to church and ready to draw the latch, suggests that this was a women's custom:

> Joan saith, that one holy day in the afternoon since Michaelmas last, she had made herself ready to go to church, and took in her arms her young child, and opening her door, her mother (grandmother to the child), one Redworth's wife, and Sellis his wife were at the said door ready to draw the latch, she this

> examinate telling her mother she was coming out of doors to churchward. Whereat the grandmother to the child took it by the hand and shook it, saying, 'Ah, Mother Pugs, art thou coming to church?' And Redworth's wife looking on it said 'Here is a jolly and likely child, God bless it'. After which speech Sellis his wife said 'She hath never the more children for that, but a little babe to play withal for a time'.[67]

Joan saw Cicely Sellis's words as sinister; she shows too much knowledge of and interest in Joan's household in general, and the child in particular.[68] Joan deposed that within a short time after that her child sickened and died, but she added an unusual disclaimer, saying that her conscience would not allow her to charge Cicely with the death of the child.[69] Excessive knowledge of and interest in a child are characteristic signs of maleficence. Though the story foregrounds Sellis as especially guilty, Joan Smith's reluctance to blame her may stem from her feeling that the other women's lavish praise of the child was generally unlucky; this was a powerful folk-belief, connected with the evil eye, as late as the nineteenth century, when a Herefordshire mother comments on her dead daughter: 'folks would allus be admiring her so. I was afeard summat 'ud happen to her'. Ruth Tongue also reports that Somerset people believed that one should 'never praise [a child] to its face or you will be thought to ill-wish it'.[70] It's significant that the encounter happens on the doorstep, the very threshold of the house and the community, a threshold which Joan and her child were just about to cross for the first time to seek the protection of church. Their liminal location symbolises their liminal status and vulnerability to witchcraft.

Other cases also illustrate the vulnerability of the unsocialised infant. Socialisation was often identified with the moment of weaning, the moment when the infant ceased to be dependent on the body of a woman. Like the labouring and lying-in mother, the unweaned infant was liminal, vulnerable to witches. Goody Smith of Suffolk, for example, confessed, after being 'watched' for three nights, that 'being disconted [discovered] that it [the child] was not weaned she went and touched the child in the cradle and immediately it sprung up in the cradle and being taken with strange fits and immediately died'.[71] Agnes Staunton also assailed a child in the cradle. Requiring yeast of the wife of Richard Saunder, she 'went away murmuring' after being denied. After her departure

> her young child in the cradle was taken vehemently sick, in a marvellous strange manner, whereupon the mother of the child took it up in her arms to comfort it, which being done, the cradle rocked of itself six or seven times, in the presence of one of the Earl of Surrey's gentlemen, who seeing it, stabbed his dagger three or four times into the cradle ere it stayed, merrily jesting that he would kill the devil if he would be rocked there.[72]

While the woman reacts with affection, offering the child her body as protection and comfort, the gentleman reacts with violence and bravado, mingled with jokey scepticism. Class conflict over the interpretation of supernatural acts, very visible here, is also gender conflict. The mother cuddles; the gentleman stabs. The story may reflect the very durable folk-belief that making or mending a cradle with elder wood gave a witch the power of rocking it from afar, so violently that any baby in it would be hurt or thrown out.[73] Cradles and clothing could also be synecdoches of the witch's effect on the child's body, demonstrating the turmoil within by visibly untoward movement. Forensically, what the gentleman does may be right, but there is something shocking about stabbing into a baby's cradle, even when it is empty, in a world of sympathetic magic. One cannot imagine the mother doing it. Is the gentleman there to act in ways not permitted to mothers? As the witch is? As part of the mother's fantasy? The good mother asserts control over the child by picking it up and holding it (still?), using affection and the body, the gentleman tries to assert control over the evil agent, using a weapon. This offers a very clear instance of two actors with different, socially determined understandings of events.

More often, witchcraft assailed older children. This was tragic because older children were often more greatly loved, having become individuals to their parents and passed safely through the notoriously chancy period of infancy.[74] Cases of witchcraft involving children occurred so frequently that even the learned noticed.[75] They involved the mother and sometimes both parents in an increasingly frantic chase for some way to halt the progress of a child's illness.[76] As with adults, many cases involving the bewitchment of a child centred on a gift of food from witch to child. Margery Adyn, a Dorchester suspect in 1634, gave a cake to her neighbour's daughter; the girl's mother deposed that 'she was never well since'.[77] Jane Brooks gave an apple to a small boy, stroked his right side and shook him by the hand; her touch alone sent him into a violent convulsion, but he became much worse when he unwisely ate the apple she had given him.[78] Anne Ellis, a Welsh suspect, was said to have caused the illness of two children who ate her bread.[79] Margaret Morton gave the four-year-old son of John Booth a piece of bread, after which he became violently ill, while Goody Smith gave two children apples, 'wishing that they might do them hurt'; her wishes were fulfilled when both children died.[80] Another suspect gave gifts of an apple and a piece of bread and butter to children, who also suffered as a result.[81] Alice Wade, confessing to bewitching a daughter of gentry family named Elizabeth Mallory, was pressed to recall whether the Mallory family had ever received food from her; eventually she recalled offering them a dish of nuts when they visited her. When Jane Watson brought an apple to the child of Jonas Cudworth, the child reported that 'she was very earnest [for me to] have it'.[82] These suspects used a gift of food to take control of a child's body in a manner resembling that of Snow White's wicked stepmother. The stepmother figure is not irrelevant to the discussion, since early modern women saw witches as inverted mothers, and since in some cases the death of the mother was the result of the witch's usurpation.

Another way to understand these cases is offered by the following unusually detailed deposition from Yorkshire, which offers a reading of the meaning of food in the context of witchcraft. The deponent is Mary Moor, who said that:

> she heard Susan the wife of Joseph Hinchcliffe, and Ann the wife of Thomas Shillitoe, both of Denbigh, discoursing thus together. The said Susan said to Anne 'If thou canst but get young Thomas Haigh to buy thee threepenny-worth of indigo, and look him in the face when he gives it thee, and touch his locks, we shall have power enough to take his life . . . and if thou canst but bring nine bits of bread away, and nine bits of butter in thy mouth, we shall have power enough to take the life of their goods.[83]

This deposition explains why other Yorkshire villagers became suspicious when Mary Wade demanded a piece of bread from Elizabeth Mallory, and was insistent upon having it 'though she was not in want'. The deponent was explicitly asked 'whether she conceived the said Mary Wade was so importunate for the piece of bread for want or no', to which she replied that 'for diverse years by past she had been their [the Wades'] neighbour, but she could not perceive but that their house was furnished with bread and good bread'.[84] The exchange of an object, a look, a touch, gives the witches power over a child's life; taking away food in the mouth, bringing it into contact with the witch's body, gives power over goods, over the household economy and wealth. This deponent interprets the witch as one point in a moving current of objects which can connect her body with those of other people and give her power over them. A gift of food breaches the boundaries of the body; it is taken in, by witch or victim. In the victim, it is an invader, the representative of a hostile power. Apples, cakes, bread, drinks can all be innocent-seeming Trojan horses through which the power of the witch can enter the defended citadel of the body. In the witch, the piece of bread is held, confined within her mouth; it embodies the victim who will be engulfed. A gift of food to a witch can turn traitor and become the instrument of her power over the giver.

Food has significance for women because it is a means of nourishing, sustaining and protecting – and therefore controlling – the bodies into which it is instilled. The witch's food reverses this positive charge; instead of sustaining, it destroys. The witch's gift of food to a *child* puts her in the place of the mother. The mother is responsible for feeding and maintaining the child, overseeing it, stroking and caressing it. It is the mother who knows the child's foibles, whose identity is mixed with the child's. Witches adopt these protocols, behaving as if they were the mothers of the children they bewitch; they feed them, stroke them, take too much interest in them, know too much about them. A Northern witch simply remarks twice 'here's a fine child' to Jane Carr's infant, after which the child is taken 'a-shrieking'.[85] This woman may have showed too much interest in the child or praised it too much on purpose, a pattern visible in the story of Cicely Sellis discussed earlier.[86] Sometimes it was enough for a witch simply to meet with a child for it to sicken; Anne Kerke, alleged to have disposed of numerous children, encountered the offspring of a neighbour with whom she had fallen out that day, and as a result both sickened.[87] On other occasions, a household encounter would cause the bewitchment of a child rather than livestock or housewifery. When Ann Wagg was refused whey, a child became ill, and it died when she made a return visit to ask for butter.[88] Alice Stokes and her daughter bewitched the child of a woman who had accidentally thrown water on the younger girl.[89] In women's fantasies of bewitched children, the witch represents the threat of losing authority over the child. The resulting chaos of the child's body mimics the disordering of housework when the housewife loses control of it to a witch. Bewitched children exhibited symptoms of horrifying vehemence: extravagant and uncontrollably violent convulsions and rigours, the body thrown about as if by unseen hands, twisted and trembling. 'Strangely handled' is the early modern phrase for this, and the phrase implies that the child is being unnaturally controlled by someone else; not, as might be appropriate, a parent, but a usurping figure who cannot be seen by the parents.[90] This usurpation is made especially clear in a Wiltshire deposition: Margaret Fowler describes the way a suspect named Joan Meriwether 'tooke the said child into her armes and kissed the child'. When Joan leaves, the child 'did fall into a very great distemper, as if it had been ready to have flowne out of this informants armes after the said Joane'.[91] As if Joan were its mother, but a mother who wants to hurt her child; as if Joan represented Margaret's worst fears about herself, her worst fears about the steadfastness of her child's love for her, as if Margaret's arms were no longer a safe harbour for the child? This mixture of love and terror is painfully dramatised in such stories. The witch also acts as a metaphor for the experience of watching a child's illness and being able to do nothing as it suffers, an agonisingly common experience for early modern families. The body whose suffering one can normally relieve struggles against an unseen force, seemingly alone, beyond help, beyond love. And yet . . . are these tormented bodies really as divorced as they seem from the mother's vulnerable (and infantile) core? Maternity and regression coexist in stories where the witch is also the bad mother of the mother, too controlling, too close.

The bizarre vomiting associated with possession signifies the child's removal from the family community of commensality and also the rejection of maternal nurturance; bewitched children vomit household objects, women's tools, such as pins and needles, as if they were physically signifying their violent rejection of their mothers.[92] Often there are signs that the bewitched child is no longer socialised; the child may lose the power of speech, may make strange animal cries, utter curses, be unable to join family prayers, refuse food.[93] The socialisation of children is the mother's responsibility, and the lapsing of bewitched children into the presocial signifies the failure of her power over them and their outright rejection of that power. (What does it signify to the children, thus enabled to reject the maternal?) Stories of child bewitchment express and manage mothers' fears that their children will not love them or will reject them. They also reveal deeper fears of children themselves and of the infant within: fear of children's uncontrolled animality, voracity, violence. The witch could become the bearer or carrier of the fear and violence that could not be acknowledged within early modern ideals of maternity, helping to define those ideals. At the same time, *and for the same woman, in the same story*, the witch could represent the mother's passionate wish to shelter her helpless and needy child from harm.

In women's stories, the witch was a woman who sought to enter into an inappropriately close or quasi-maternal kind of relation with the housewife as well as with her children, rather than remaining an egalitarian neighbour. The fear of a too-close relation with the mother is not confined to men.[94] French feminist critics of psychoanalysis have stressed the importance of unresolved conflicts around the inability of the girl-child to separate herself fully from the mother.[95] The witch, like the smother-mother, denies the housewife any adult, open role as neighbour and tries instead to draw her (back) into a problematically close mother–child bond. Women's stories about witches might express and offer fantasy resolutions for the daughter's fear of the mother, as well as the mother's fears for and of the child. The witch's actions replicate those of the 'real' mother, pointing to the ambiguity of maternal behaviour as a signifier of feelings or intentions. What seems like love can destroy.

But if women's stories about witches were determined by constants like their association with food preparation, household boundaries and maternity, why did women stop telling such stories? Another witch-story told by a country woman, a Mrs Falconer of Leafield, Oxfordshire, is suggestive:

> When I was a little girl, my mother had a new baby, and of course I was in the bedroom when this old lady came up in the bedroom, and was talking to my mother, and then the dog belonging to her began to howl. My mother was very concerned, and she said, 'Oh! do make that dog stop his noise. I hate to hear a dog howl'. Then this old lady says, 'Let 'en howl, let 'en 'owl. 'E's 'owling arter that child.' And 'er said, 'Is anything the matter with that child?' 'No, not that I know, except that it's going to die.' And my mother was very concerned about it, and main frightened, and she wouldn't let anyone go anywhere near for days, for fear they'd tell her something to hurt this baby what was the matter. They went to Charlbury . . . to fetch the doctor, to see if there was anything the matter, and he said, 'No, there's nothing the matter with it. No earthly reason why it should die.' But it did die, and that's all I can tell you.[96]

The strange woman invades the bedchamber, inspects the newborn unbaptised or chrism child, shows too much knowledge of it, and makes a remark predicting its death. Of course she turns out to be a witch. What makes this story distinctive is not its content. It is the date on which it was recorded: 18 August 1962, from an octogenarian village woman who remembered its events from childhood. Nor is this story unique. Nineteenth- and twentieth-century folklorists record numerous stories and beliefs about witches which exactly parallel the tropes, narratives and ideas found in early modern women's depositions. Both food and babies remained especially vulnerable. Stories of bewitching the churn continue into the post-First World War era, as does the remedy Bennet Lane used to restore its function.[97] The kind of anxiety expressed in Mrs Falconer's story, and in the depositions of early modern women, also remained apparent in women's stories until relatively recently. Belief in the power of looking, in the fearful significance of too much interest in and knowledge of the household, in the especial vulnerability of babies, in the baneful influence of too much praise of a child, and in the sinister effect of disrupting the lying-in process and the riskiness of venturing out too quickly, continued into the twentieth century among village women, and some village men.[98] There is ample evidence of the continuity of the kind of stories I have been discussing among rural communities up to this century. Though this evidence is not without its own problems, its sheer abundance suggests that feminist historians of witchcraft should consider looking for the reason for the decline of women's stories about witches in this century rather than in the seventeenth- and eighteenth-century texts which document the declining belief of the elite.[99] It also supports the theory that the rural people did not stop telling witch-stories; courts stopped listening.[100] The 'witch-persecutions' have been studied as a strictly legal phenomenon, and this has been falsely equated with witch-belief; it is as if all of us, academic and popular historians, are interested only in the question of why learned persons believed in witchcraft and how it could fit into the legal system. Once the scandal of an impossible crime is abolished, we lose interest in the stories. The popular beatings and lynchings of women for witchcraft, which continued into the late nineteenth century in the teeth of elite disapproval, do not count as a 'witch-craze'. Lynchings remain unexamined, even though they may have claimed many lives. Yet they are the product of the continued circulation of stories about witches, stories which flow along lines of folktale, gossip, neighbourly communication and rumour, without ever catching the eye of court recorders.

Not only are such stories durable, resurfacing even in well-known folktales like 'Hansel and Gretel' and 'Snow White'; they are also not confined to England. Much has been made, and rightly, of the difference between English witchcraft trials and those on the Continent. However, in pointing to the different regional and geographical figurations of the witch in learned and legal discourse, it is possible tacitly to assume that there is also a yawning cultural gap at the popular level, and this may be rather less true. Though there are significant differences between the Essex witches of the St Osyth case and Lyndal Roper's witches of Augsburg, there is also a significant degree of overlap; concerns about the maternal body and its vulnerability, and about the role of the keeper or lying-in-maid surface in both sets of stories, along with deeper and less articulate assumptions about the role of neighbours in social-identity formation and the place of gender in deciding the boundaries of the self. Though differently inflected by different social and even geographical contexts, similar concerns and even tropes surface. In the next chapters, we will see that England also witnessed witch-stories containing discursive traces of much older supernatural beliefs, just as Italy did; that England, like the Norman Bocage in the 1960s, had official unwitchers who stood outside the normal geographical boundaries of the neighbourhood and therefore were able to act against one of its members; that England, like its North American colonies, saw combinations of magic and the sacred which regularly shocked the elite while seeming normal to the community. These overlaps are the result of continuities in the way village communities consitutute themselves, but also because of ongoing figurations of gendered responsibilities and the gendered body.

NOTES

1 See Jeanne Favret-Saada, *Deadly Words: Witchcraft in the Bocage*, Cambridge: Cambridge University Press, 1980.

2 Clive Holmes, 'Women, witnesses and witches', *Past and Present*, 140 (1993), p. 46. For a dismissive approach to women deponents from a feminist historian, see Christina Larner, 'Was witch-hunting really women-hunting?', in *Witchcraft and Religion: The Politics of Popular Belief,* Oxford: Blackwell, 1984, p. 86.

3 J. A. Sharpe, 'Women, witchcraft and the legal process', in *Women, Crime and the Courts in Early Modern England,* ed. Jenny Kermode and Garthine Walker, London: UCL Press, 1994, pp. 106–24; Holmes, 'Witnesses', pp. 47–50.

4 Annabel Gregory, 'Witchcraft, politics and "good neighbourhood" in seventeenth-century Rye', *Past and Present*, 133 (1991), pp. 31–66.

5 Recent 'historical' recapitulations of this thesis include Marianne Hester, *Lewd Women and Wicked Witches: A Study of the Dynamics of Male Domination*, London: Routledge, 1992, and Anne Llewelyn Barstow, *Witchcraze: A New History of the European Witch Hunts*, New York: HarperCollins, 1994. Feminst historians have generally moved away from this conclusion.

6 J. A. Sharpe, 'Witchcraft and women in seventeenth-century England: some northern evidence', *Continuity and Change*, 6 (1991), pp. 179–99, and 'Witchcraft in seventeenth-century Yorkshire: Accusations and Countermeasures', Borthwick Institute of Historical Research, paper no. 81 (1992); Holmes, 'Witnesses', pp. 46–7; David Harley, 'Historians as demonologists: the myth of the midwife witch', *Journal of the Society for the Social History of Medicine*, 3 (1990), pp. 1–26, and 'Mental illness, magical medicine, and the devil in northern England 1650–1700', in *Medical Revolution of the Seventeenth Century,* ed. Roger French and Andrew Wear, Cambridge: Cambridge University Press, 1989.

7 There is only one (incomplete) run of assize depositions available in manuscript, for the Northern Circuit from the mid-seventeenth century (PRO, ASSI 45) though of course there are manuscript sources for quarter sessions cases and other minor courts.

8 *A true and just record, of the information, examination and confession of all the witches taken at St Oses in the countie of Essex, . . . by W. W.*, 1582, printed in Barbara Rosen, *Witchcraft in England 1558–1618*, Amherst: University of Massachusetts Press, 1991. Hereafter *TJR*.

9 See Rosen, *Witchcraft*, p. 333.

10 Clare Brant and Diane Purkiss, 'Introduction: Minding the Story', in *Women, Texts and Histories 1575–1760,* London: Routledge, 1992, pp. 1–12.

11 Philip Tyler examines the instability of 'witchcraft' in 'Church courts at York and witchcraft prosecutions 1567–1640', *Northern History*, 4 (1969), pp. 83–5.

12 Louis Montrose, '"Shaping fantasies": figurations of gender and power in Elizabethan culture', *Representations*, 2 (1983), pp. 61–94; see Lyndal Roper, 'Witchcraft and fantasy in early modern Germany', *History Workshop Journal*, 32 (1991), pp. 19–33.
13 Agnes Heard was indicted on the lesser charge of witchcraft, rather than murder by witchcraft like many of the other women involved in the 1582 prosecutions: James Cockburn, *Calendar of Assize Records: Essex Presentments: Elizabeth I*, London: HMSO, 1978, p. 225, transcribed from PRO, ASSI 35 24/1. Heard was found not guilty and released. On the problems of using assize records see Cockburn, 'Assize records as historical evidence', *Journal of the Society of Archivists*, 5 (1972), pp. 215–31.
14 The depositions are printed in *TJR*. This pamphlet uses depositions from witnesses not mentioned in indictments, but evidently collected in an attempt to build up cases against the accused. On the process of constructing an indictment, see Cynthia Herrup, *The Common Peace: Participation and the Criminal Law in Seventeenth-Century England*, Cambridge: Cambridge University Press, 1987, pp. 93–101.
15 *TJR*, p. 147. On the importance of spinning to the household economy, see Sue Wright, '"Churmaids, huswyfes and hucksters": the employment of women in Tudor and Stuart Salisbury', in *Women and Work in Pre-Industrial England*, ed. Lindsey Charles and Lorna Duffin, London: Croom Helm, 1985, pp. 109–10.
16 For similar instances, see the remedy of burning thatch from a witch's house; C. L'Estrange Ewen, *Witchcraft and Demonianism*, 1933, p. 165 (hereafter Ewen, *WD*), and the discussion in Chapter 5 below.
17 *TJR*, p. 148.
18 *TJR*, p. 148.
19 Andrew and Anne West depose that after a dispute about the destination of a farrow of pigs, their pigs fell sick; after another encounter with Agnes, Anne finds she cannot make ale, as does Godlife Osborne, another Little Oakley housewife who exchanges objects with Agnes. *TJR*, pp. 149–50.
20 Sceptics were likely to see Bennet's interpretation of the bizarre disruption of houswifery as a cover for her own sluttish household disorder; this 'explanation' is for instance advanced by Reginald Scot, *The discoverie of witchcraft*, 1584, XII, xxi.
21 J. C. Drummond and Anne Wilbrahim, *The Englishman's Food: A History of Five Centuries of the Englishman's Diet*, revised by Dorothy Hollingsworth, London: Pimlico, 1932, pp. 55–7. For other cases of witchcraft centring on the dairy, see J. Strype, *The Life of Sir Thomas Smith*, 1698, pp. 129–30; the case of Margaret Morton, in *Depositions from York Castle*, ed. James Raine, Surtees Society, vol. 40 (1860), p. 38, hereafter *YD*; both cases also feature women deponents. See also Scot, *Discoverie*, XII, xxi, and George Gifford, *A Dialogue concerning witches and witchcrafts*, 1593, sig. G^{v}. See also George Lyman Kittredge, *Witchcraft in Old and New England*, New York: Russell & Russell, 1929, pp. 163–73.
22 For similar cases of witches disrupting food production, see below, and also Hester France, who curses a servingmaid by praying that she should never bake again, *YD*, pp. 51–2. For a Continental case where food is central in a different way, see David Warren Sabean, *Power in the Blood: Popular Culture and Village Discourse in Early Modern Germany*, Cambridge: Cambridge University Press, 1984, pp. 109–10.
23 *A detection of damnable driftes, practized by three witches arraigned at Chelmisforde in Essex*, 1579, in Rosen, *Witchcraft*, pp. 93–4.
24 Joseph Glanvill, *Saducismus Triumphatus*, 1681, p. 133.
25 Glanvill, *Saducismus*, p. 298.
26 July 1619: Ronald Sawyer, '"Strangely handled in all her lyms": witchcraft and healing in Jacobean England', *Journal of Social History*, 22 (1989), p. 477. Napier's accounts are especially valuable because many women consulted him about suspected

bewitchments which never came to court. For a striking set of parallels involving witches who gave gifts of food in order to bewitch, see Roper, 'Witchraft and fantasy', p. 28.

27 Ewen, *WD*, p. 173.

28 Ewen, *WD*, p. 39; C. L'Estrange Ewen, *Witch Hunting and Witch Trials*, 1929, p. 82, hereafter Ewen, *WH*; Ewen, *WD*, pp. 150–1.

29 Ewen, *WD*, pp. 319–20.

30 Ewen, *WD*, p. 453.

31 *YD*, 124–5; Joseph Glanvill noted that gifts of food from a witch were dangerous, especially apples: *Saducismus*, p. 25.

32 On the economic crisis in rural areas see *The Agrarian History of England and Wales*, vol. IV, ed. Joan Thirsk, Cambridge: Cambridge University Press, 1967, especially pp. 399–465; and for the creation of a class of settled poor and an underclass of beggars, see Keith Wrightson, *English Society 1580–1680*, London: Hutchinson, 1982, pp. 140–2; on diet see Drummond and Wilbrahim, *Englishman's Food*, and Stephen Mennell, *All Manners of Food: Eating and Taste in England and France from the Middle Ages to the Present*, Oxford: Blackwell, 1985, pp. 41–6.

33 Jill Dubisch, 'Culture enters through the kitchen; women, food and social boundaries in rural Greece', in *Gender and Power in Rural Greece*, ed. Jill Dubisch, Princeton: Princeton University Press, 1984, pp. 195–6; Mary Douglas, *Purity and Danger: An Analysis of the Concepts of Pollution and Taboo*, London: Ark, 1966.

34 For the emerging printed discourses defining the duties of the early modern housewife, see Thomas Dawson, *The good housewife's jewel*, 1585, and Gervase Markham, *Countrey contentments . . . the english hus-wife*, 1615. Like Thomas Tusser's *Five Hundred Points of Good Husbandry* 1573, these books combine recipes with medical matters, remedies, dairying procedures and brewing guides.

35 Philip Stubbes, *A christal glasse for Christian women,* 1618, sig. A3^{r}.

36 Lisa Jardine, *Still Harping on Daughters: Women and Drama in the Age of Shakespeare*, Brighton: Harvester, 1983, ch. 4.

37 Felicity Heal, *Hospitality in Early Modern England*, Oxford: Clarendon, 1990.

38 Heal, *Hospitality*, ch. 9.

39 Ewen *WD*, pp. 189–90; Keith Thomas, *Religion and the Decline of Magic*, London: Penguin, 1971, p. 664.

40 John Gaule, *Select cases of conscience touching witches and witchcraft*, 1646, pp. 129, 144. Gaule also notes that witches ungratefully work 'by occasion of good turns', p. 129. A Continental instance of this belief occurs in Nicholas Rémy, *Demonolatry*, reprinted London: 1930, p. 143, where Rémy claims that the country people believe that they can get relief from witchcraft by stealing food or drink from the house of the witch.

41 Nickie Charles and Marion Kerr, *Women, Food and Families*, Manchester: Manchester University Press, 1988.

42 See Tusser, *Good Husbandry*, and Markham, *Countrey Contentments*; and Kate Mertes, *The English Noble Household*, Oxford: Blackwell, 1988.

43 On the high economic and emotional value of children in early modern England, see Linda Pollock, *Forgotten Children: Parent–Child Relations from 1500 to 1900*, Cambridge: Cambridge University Press, 1983; Margaret Pelling, 'Child health as a social value in early modern England' *Journal of the Society for the History of Medicine*, 7 (1988), pp. 135–64.

44 Linda Pollock, 'Embarking on a rough passage: the experience of pregnancy in early modern society', in *Women as Mothers in Pre-Industrial England*, ed. Valerie Fildes, London: Routledge, 1990, pp. 39–67, and Patricia Crawford, 'The construction and experience of maternity in seventeenth-century England', in Fildes, pp. 3–38.

45 For these and other remedies to prevent miscarriage in the early modern period, see Angus McLaren, *Reproductive Rituals: The Perception of Fertility in England from the Sixteenth to the Nineteenth Century*, London and New York: Methuen, 1984, pp. 46–9.

46 Ewen, *WD*, p. 246; *The triall of Master Dorrell*, 1597; not a reliable source – the familiar confesses to the crime himself – but testimony to the preoccupation, since Darrell excelled in exploiting popular fears; by contrast Ewen also records a case in which it was argued that witches had no power to hurt babies in the womb: Ewen, *WD*, p. 317.

47 Sawyer, 'Strangely handled', pp. 476–8. Other witches could cause false pregnancy; Agnes Staunton made one of her woman victims swell up as if she was with child; see *A detection of damnable drifts*, p. 97.

48 See McLaren, *Reproductive Rituals*, pp. 49–50, especially the belief that frustration and anger in particular could cause miscarriage.

49 Adrian Wilson, 'The ceremony of childbirth and its interpretation' in *Women as Mothers in Pre-Industrial England*, ed. Valerie Fildes, pp. 68–107; see also his 'Participant or patient? Seventeenth-century childbirth from the mother's point of view', in *Patients and Practitioners: Lay Perceptions of Medicine in Preindustrial society*, Cambridge: Cambridge University Press, 1985, and Roper, 'Witchcraft and fantasy', pp. 27–9. Like churching, the childbirth ceremony could be controversial; Heal, *Hospitality*, pp. 335–7.

50 The association between midwifery and witchcraft accusations has recently been questioned by Harley, 'Historians as demonologists'; though many midwifery ordinances contain insistent denunciations of midwives who use magic (see McLaren, *Reproductive Rituals*, pp. 46–53), these refer to what villagers would have considered 'white magic' charms to save the lives of mother and baby. For the case of a northern midwife accused of charming using babies, see Chapter 5.

51 For these charms see McLaren, *Reproductive Rituals*, pp. 50–2; Kittredge, *Witchcraft*, p. 115; Thomas, *Religion*, p. 222.

52 Michael Macdonald, *Mystical Bedlam: Madness, Anxiety and Healing in Seventeenth-Century England*, Cambridge: Cambridge University Press, 1981, p. 109.

53 Sawyer, 'Strangely handled', p. 478. Although there is no trace of the continental belief that unbaptised children were stolen by witches to make flying-ointment in English witch-stories, a midwife's ordinance does insist that stillborn children be lawfully buried and not cast into a ditch; Bodleian MSS, Oxford Archdeaconry Papers, Berks C. 162, fo. 82[r], cited by Clare Gittings, *Death, Burial and the Individual in Early Modern England*, London and New York: Routledge, 1988, p. 83.

54 *The wonderful discoverie of the witchcrafts of Margaret and Philippa Flower*, 1619, in Rosen, *Witchcraft*, p. 379. This pamphlet is at best a mere summary of women's depositions and confessions. It has an agenda about the violation of class boundaries and the power of devils. For another case of this kind, see *The witches of Huntingdon*, 1646, p. 6.

55 This account is heavily reliant on Wilson's work, though some interpretations are my own. There are obvious parallels, too, with the situation Roper and Sabean describe in Germany.

56 On churching see Thomas, *Religion*, pp. 42–3, 68–9, and Kittredge, *Witchcraft*, p. 145.

57 Roper, 'Witchcraft and fantasy', pp. 21–2. Roper's sources are German, but her case studies provide intriguing parallels with the English stories discussed here.

58 Charles Jackson, 'Alleged witchcraft at Rossington, near Doncaster, 1605', *Gentleman's Magazine*, 202 (1857), pp. 593–5.

59 Ursula Kempe, also known as Grey, was gaoled at the same time as Agnes Heard (29 March 1582) and was tried with a group of other women who were also accused of

murder by witchcraft. Her indictment specifically cites Grace's evidence, but does not mention Grace by name: 'On 3 Oct 1581 at St Osyth they [Kemp and Alice Newman, another accused witch] bewitched Joan daughter of John Thurlowe so that she died on 6 Oct.' Cockburn, *Calendar of Assize Records*, p. 223.

60 *TJR*, p. 107.

61 *TJR*, pp. 107–8.

62 Wilson, 'Ceremony', pp. 76–7.

63 Since Grace was a servant, she may not have had a separate household; it might be more accurate to speak of Ursula's superintendence of her living-space.

64 *TJR*, p. 108.

65 *TJR*, p. 108.

66 This may have been for churching; see Kittredge, *Witchcraft*, p. 145, who reports that in Wales at the end of the seventeenth century 'the ordinary women are hardly brought to look upon churching otherwise than as a charm to prevent witchcraft'. Similarly, the *Denham Tracts* report that it was believed that the mother should not go out of the house until she goes to church (1892–5, p. 113).

67 'Mother Pugs' is an endearment; *TJR*, p. 134. Cicely Sellis (or Sylls, Silles) was indicted at Chelmsford assizes on 29 March 1582: the indictment reads: 'On 1 Sept. 1581 at Little Clacton they [i.e. Sellis and Alice Manfield] burnt a granary (100 marks) belonging to Richard Rose. On 4 June 1581 at Great Clacton, Silles bewitched John son of Thomas Death so that he died the same day' (Cockburn, *Calendar of Assize Records*, n. 1302). Sellis was acquitted of arson but convicted of witchcraft. Joan Smith's deposition did not form part of the indictment.

68 See John Aubrey on the evil eye in 'Remaines of Gentilisme and Judaisme', and in 'Miscellany', *Three Prose Works*, ed. John Buchanan Browne, New York: Centaur, 1972, pp. 227, 109–10; Aubrey also notes the susceptibility of children to the evil eye (p. 109).

69 *TJR*, pp. 134–5. For the special religious status of the chrism child, see Gittings, *Death*, pp. 83–5.

70 See Ella Mary Leather, *The Folklore of Herefordshire,* 1912, p. 53; Ruth Tongue, *Somerset Folklore*, ed. K. M. Briggs, London: Folklore Society, 1965, p. 135.

71 Ewen, *WH*, p. 293. 'Watched' could mean that the witch was guarded by supervisors who waited for her familiars to appear.

72 *A detection of damnable driftes*, p. 96. The pamphlet does not record the identity of the deponent, but it must be either Richard Saunder deposing for his wife, or Mistress Saunder; it is unlikely to be the violent 'gentleman', since he is unidentified.

73 Christina Hole reports this belief as an aspect of mid-nineteenth century Cheshire folklore, in *Cheshire Folktales*, London: Macmillan, 1967, p. 120.

74 Gittings compares Evelyn's comments on the loss of his five-year-old son with his terser record of the death of his seven-week-old baby son (*Death*, pp. 82–3); the same pattern of feeling may not necessarily apply to women. For women writers' grief for babies and children's deaths, see Kate Lilley, 'True state within: women's elegy 1640–1740', in *Women, Writing, History*, ed. Isobel Grundy and Susan Wiseman, London: Batsford, 1992, pp. 72–92.

75 Gaule, *Select cases of conscience*, p. 134. There are signs that printers of witchcraft pamphlets recognised popular anxiety about this phenomenon; one of the few Continental pamphlets translated and reprinted in England before 1660 was entitled: *A strange report of sixe of the most notorious witches, who by their divelish practises murdered above the number of foure hundred small children*, 1601.

76 Sharpe, 'Accusations and countermeasures', gives a good account of the struggle to find a remedy, but one which takes little interest in the question of gender. Sharpe does discuss women's agency in seeking remedies briefly in 'Witchcraft and women', pp. 189–92.

77 *The Municipal Records of the Borough of Dorchester, Dorset*, ed. C. H. Mayo, 1908, pp. 664–5, B/2/8/1, cited in David Underdown, *Fire From Heaven: Life in an English Town in the Seventeenth Century*, London: Fontana, 1993, p. 79.
78 Glanvill, *Saducismus*, p. 118, based on an account by Robert Hunt, one of the JPs in the case. Glanvill records that Brooks was executed on 26 March 1658.
79 Ewen, *WD*, pp. 332–4. Anne Ellis made a successful prison break during her period of detention before trial, and was in any case found not guilty.
80 Morton: *YD*, p. 38, and Ewen, *WD*, pp. 395–6; Smith; Ewen, *WH*, p. 293.
81 Thomas Ady, *A candle in the dark, or a treatise concerning the nature of witches and witchcraft*, 1656, p. 79.
82 Alice Wade: *YD*, pp. 75–8, Ewen, *WD*, p. 398; Jane Watson: *YD*, p. 92.
83 *YD*, p. 209.
84 *YD*, pp. 75, 77.
85 Ewen, *WD*, p. 323. For another German parallel, see Roper, 'Witchcraft and fantasy', p. 29.
86 Taking too much interest in one's neighbours and their property is one sign of the evil eye in modern Greece; see Michael Herzfeld, *Anthropology through the Looking-Glass: Critical Ethnography in the Margins of Europe*, Cambridge: Cambridge University Press, 1987, p. 173.
87 Ewen, *WD*, p. 189.
88 Ewen, *WD*, pp. 319–20.
89 Margery Stanton: Ewen, *WD*, pp. 150–1; Alice Stokes: Ewen, *WD*, pp. 200–1, and *The most cruell and bloody murther committed on the bodie of a child . . . with the several witchcrafts and most damnable practises of one Johane Harrison*, in Rosen, pp. 323–6. Rosen suggests that the pamphlet records the story of Alice and Christina Stokes (who appear in trial records) under different names, p. 323.
90 Sawyer, 'Strangely handled', p. 462.
91 B. N. Cunnington, *Records of the County of Wilts*, Devizes: 1932, p. 242. The deposition is dated 14 August 1665. The child dies.
92 For cases of vomiting linked with bewitchment and possession see Ewen, *WD*, pp. 230ff, 398; *YD* pp. 75–8.
93 See *YD*, pp. 75–8, and Stephen Bradwell, *Mary Glovers late woefull case, together with her joyful deliverance*, BL MSS Sloane 831, repr. in *Witchcraft and Hysteria in Elizabethan London: Edward Jorden and the Mary Glover Case*, ed. Michael Macdonald, London: Tavistock/Routledge, 1991.
94 Klaus Theweleit' s study of the fear of the mother in men of the *Freikorps* brilliantly demonstrates this fear among men and its violent consequences: *Male Fantasies*, vol. I: *Women, Bodies, Floods, History*, trans. Stephen Conway with Erica Carter and Chris Turner, Cambridge: Polity, 1987.
95 Luce Irigaray, 'And the one doesn't stir without the other', *Signs*, 7 (1981), pp. 60–7.
96 Katherine Briggs and Ruth Tongue, *Folktales of England,* London: Routledge & Kegan Paul, London, 1965, pp. 58–9.
97 See William Henderson, *Notes on the Folklore of the Northern Counties of England and the Borders*, 1866, p. 146 (story from 1866); Ruth Tongue, *Somerset Folklore*, p. 77 (story from 1935); John Harland and T. T. Wilkinson, *Lancashire Legends*, 1873, pp. 243–4; Sidney Oldall Addy, *Household Tales with Other Traditional Remains*, 1895, p. 36, where the witch disrupts churning after being refused milk, and J. C. Atkinson, *Forty Years in a Moorland Parish*, 1891, p. 99 for the remedy of the hot poker; for this remedy see also T. F. Thistleton-Dyer, *Domestic Folk-Lore* (1891), p. 170 (nineteenth-century story). See also Katherine Briggs, *A Dictionary of British Folktales*, 4 vols, London: Routledge & Kegan Paul, 1970–1, pp. 614, 695–6.

98 See Richard Blakeborough, *Wit, Character, Folklore and Customs of the North Riding of Yorkshire*, 1898, pp. 176–7; Henderson, *Notes on Folklore*, pp. 143–4, 151; Mary Williams, *Witches in Old North Yorkshire*, Halifax: Hutton Press, 1987, p. 17; Ella Mary Leather, *Folklore of Herefordshire*, 1912, pp. 51ff, and on not going out until you go to church (a relic of churching?), p. 113.

99 For a summary of the problems of authenticity and nineteenth-century folklorists, see Neil Philip, 'Introduction', *The Penguin Book of English Folktales*, London: Penguin, 1992.

100 For a recent restatement of this theory, see C. Unsworth, 'Witchcraft beliefs and criminal procedure', in *Legal Record and Historical Reality*, ed. T. G. Watkin, London: Routledge, 1989, pp. 71–89.

5 No limit

The body of the witch

> Jack told me that they both think that after I put them to bed and kiss them goodnight, I go out of the room and remove my mask and clothes, and reveal myself to be a witch. I was a bit taken aback but at the same time it felt that because they could say it we could all know I wasn't really a witch. Sometimes I do feel a witch!
>
> Mother of two sons, aged five and seven, cited by Rozsika Parker in *Torn In Two: The Experience of Maternal Ambivalence*

The last chapter showed that the witch could represent women's fantasies, desires and fears, especially about maternity and the household. In this chapter, the figuration of witchcraft itself – the witch's power over people and things – is shown to have reflected and reproduced a very specific fantasy about the female body in general and the maternal body in particular. When understood in terms of the magic she performs and the power she exerts, the witch is a fantasy-image of the huge, controlling, scattered, polluted, leaky fantasy of the maternal body of the Imaginary.[1] However, this body and the acute terror and longing it evokes can only be understood in relation to specific cultural circumstances. In the early modern town or village, there were two specific ways in which that image of the body was socially mediated: first, it represented everything that it was the housewife's job to exclude from the household, and secondly, it represented the diseased body of early modern medicine. Through that medical system, too, it pointed back to the normal body, always prone to fall into greater abnormality if female. The body in both elite and popular early modern thought was flowing with humours or liquids, resembling a bag full of potentially polluting substances. This idea of the body was shaped by fears that bodies may not be fully confined and kept separate from one another, resulting in problematic contacts and impingements. To the early modern villager or town-dweller, one way to understand those impingements was as witchcraft. Witchcraft was, among other things, a form of power which involved exchanges between bodies, and the counter-magic used to defeat it reflects this understanding.

Although counter-magic came to seem morally indistinguishable from witchcraft to the godly, many people made sharp distinctions between helpful and harmful magic. At first, glance, one basis for such a distinction is spatial; whereas the witch almost always came from the same village as her victims, unwitchers or cunning folk usually came from another nearby community.[2] However, this spatial distinction was apt to break down: counter-magic could be located by its users either deep within the household or outside the boundaries of the community. Magic is about degrees of closeness, when closeness becomes unwelcome invasion. It is about setting and controlling limits: geographical, familial, local. Such concerns are the housewife's, and counter-magical remedies bear a strong resemblance to recipes, or to guides to household care of the kind which proliferated in the late sixteenth and early seventeenth centuries.[3] This points back towards the body of the witch: the figure of the house and the figure of the body were interchangeable as metaphors for each other in the early modern period, and both household and body were common metaphors for the community and the polity.[4] All three had to be well ordered, that is, hierarchically; all three had to have secure boundaries which marked them off as discrete entities.

Magic and its remedies deal with borders, markers, distinctions, insides and outsides, the limits of bodies, and also that which breaches those boundaries; bodily fluids, exchanges of objects through bodies and across thresholds, words that pass through the guard of the ear and enter the mind of the hearer. Women's bodies, by virtue of their reproductive capacities, are seen as more open, more grotesque, less autonomous. The identification of the embarrassing and boundless body with the feminine may be one of the constants of Western culture. As Elizabeth Grosz writes, drawing on both Cixous and Irigaray:

> Can it be that in the West . . . the female body has been constructed not only as a lack or absence, but with more complexity, as a leaking, uncontrollable, seeping liquid; as formless flow; as viscosity, entrapping, secreting; as lacking not so much or simply the phallus but self-containment – not a cracked or porous vessel, like a leaking ship, but a formlessness that engulfs all form, a disorder that threatens all order?[5]

For Grosz, this image of femininity is a cultural construction which might be strategically exploited by modern feminists to unsettle the solidity of the masculine Cartesian body. This underestimates the threatening power of formless or boundless female bodiliness. The female body as formless spillage is a product of the infant's perception of the maternal body as coextensive with its own. In order to be a Cartesian subject, culture insists, the infant must acknowledge its own separation from the maternal; at the same time, separation is always a precarious achievement, and the adult retains a trace of fear at being re-engulfed by the endless body of the fantasy-mother. In classical psychoanalysis, the little girl fears re-engulfment by the fantasy-mother more than the boy, because her separation from the mother is less complete. Julia Kristeva's work on the need to expel the fantasy-mother in order to achieve a whole, 'clean', ordered self and to maintain it shows how pollution can directly threaten that self.[6] The terror and desire evoked by the maternal body are echoed in responses to the fluids which proceed from the female body. Having abjected and repressed the giant and fluid fantasy-mother, the infant fears her return in the form of liquids, engulfing bodily closeness, pollution. Hence, as Klaus Theweleit has shown, that maternal body can also be made to represent other forms of matter out of place which evoke reactions of shame and disgust, including the excremental and also the dead.[7]

Such links are neither natural nor inevitable. It is not inevitable that a woman should feel threatened in this particular way by another woman entering her home or saying certain words to her. They are produced by a confluence of medical discourses and social factors. In early modern England, elite medical theory borrowed from classical medicine in understanding women as moister, and more polluted and flowing as a result, thus more prone to impinge leakily on someone else's space. Early modern medicine, which in garbled form did influence the practices of cunning folk as well as the counter-magical activities of villagers and townsfolk, understood all bodies as flowing with substances which threatened to get out of hand. For Aristotle, to be formless and female was to be *ateles*, lacking an ending, literally endless. Women's bodies, in particular, were inferior, and therefore more prone to become unbalanced; inferior because moister, colder, wetter than the masculine.[8] Because it was seen as wet, the female body was seen as messier and leakier than the male body. Its coldness meant that it was more formless, since it was thought that it was heat which allowed matter to solidify. The female's runniness was seen as an outcome of her chilliness. In Aristotle's *On the Generation of Animals*, still a standard guide to biology in the early modern period, though not an uncontested one, Aristotle explicitly states that 'the action of the semen in the male in "setting" the female's secretions in the uterus is similar to that of rennet upon milk'. This setting was the first necessary step in conception, and it was performed by the heat of the semen.[9] Women's venereal desires, and in particular their feared sexual insatiability, also derived from this coldness; for Aristotle, women sought heat in copulation to prevent themselves from collapsing into formlessness. These medical understandings of woman as chilly molten goo were reinforced by social factors. The association between women and childcare, the maintenance of household order, the dispersal of dirt and pollution, cultural notions of what constitutes matter in and out of place, ideas about where boundaries should be, all suggested the rightness of disgust with female boundlessness and its equation with fear and pollution.

In this cultural context, it is not surprising that the witch's body is figured as plurally coextensive with or diffused through a variety of objects. We can see how the boundlessness of the witch's body was understood by turning back to a very simple, very common and very persistent counter-magical remedy that we have already seen in action. When Bennet Lane could not skim her cream, she applied the magical remedy of heat to unwitch her milk vessels. Bennet was using a particular version of a counter-magical remedy which took many different forms: applying heat to the bewitched object in order to gain power over the witch. Everyone knew that the witch could be driven out of the churn by heating a red-hot poker which would then be put in it; sometimes this was believed to burn the witch herself. This method of removing the witch from the household survived until the twentieth century in the north of England.[10] In another form, the remedy of heat turns up in connection with the witch's house: a common method to break bewitchment was either to burn a piece of thatch taken from the witch's house, or to heat a tile from her roof; this would either have a curative effect, or more commonly bring the witch to the spot. When Sarah Cooke's child became inexplicably ill, a passing traveller suggested a remedy; she stole a tile from the roof of Joan Cason, whom she suspected of witchcraft, and heated it until it was red-hot on the stove. The traveller explained that if the child were bewitched the tile 'will sparkle and fly round about the cradle'. Shortly after the tile had sparkled, Joan Cason appeared.[11] The burning of the witch's hair to cure the victim and the execution of the witch were also believed to have a curative effect. Often the witch's body was thought to be coextensive with that of her familiar; if the latter was hurt, the former suffered. A family bewitched by Ellen Smith saw a rat going up a chimney; they are surprised when it comes down as a toad, but they draw the right conclusion, and

> taking it up with the tongs, they thrust it into the fire and so held it forcibly. It made the fire burn as blue as azure, and the fire was almost out; and at the burning thereof the said Ellen Smith was in great pain and out of quiet.[12]

Similarly, a cunning man advises Dorothy Dunent to defeat Amy Duny's assaults on her child by hanging the child's blanket in the chimney corner all day, and at night throwing anything found in it into the fire. A toad was found in the blanket, and being held in the fire by the tongs, 'made a great and horrible noise, and after a space, there was a flashing in the fire like gun-powder, making a noise like the discharging of a pistol, and thereupon the toad was no more seen'. The child recovered, but Amy Duny was found with face, legs and thighs 'much scorched and burned'.[13]

These remedies depend on 'sympathetic' magic, the idea that whatever has been in contact with a person carries some of their aura and can be used to gain power over them. In the early modern period, sympathetic magic became a way to fantasise about gender through stories of bewitchment and counter-magic. The witch, usually a woman, had the power of extending herself into and thus overpowering the controls governing the households and bodies of others. Her magic itself represented her as formless, able to go through what was supposed to be marked off or contained. Yet it was this formlessness which allowed her victims to fight back. In entering the churn, the witch made herself vulnerable to counter-attack within the churn. The witch's house is an extension of her body; when it is burned, the witch is hurt.

All bodies could be understood as boundless in the world of magic. Another and more startling form of counter-magic used by several cunning women rather than by laywomen illustrates the connectedness of bodies in a different way; it focuses on the circulation of breath and on the mouth as an opening in the body's boundaries. A Northumbrian woman called Margaret Stothard was summoned when Jane Carr's child was suffering from a terrible illness believed to be caused by witchcraft. Stothard cured the child by putting her mouth to the child's mouth, whereupon 'she made much chirping and sucking'. After this magical mouth-to-mouth resuscitation, she said she 'would warrant the child would do well enough'.[14] In a variation on this theme, a midwife called Mistress Pepper healed sick people using the bodies of infants. When Robert Pyle fell ill, he sent for Pepper, and his wife Margaret described her remedy as follows; she 'took this informer's child, and another sucking child, and laid them to his mouth'. Margaret asked Pepper why she did this, and Pepper explained that the breath of the children would suck the spirits out of him.[15] One of the children is unweaned: a vulnerable time, as we have already seen, but also a time when the infant's body routinely blends with the body of another in suckling, and at the mouth. Here, the bodies of these infants provide a clear space into which evil spirits can be drawn. Even more bizarre is the remedy of Anne Nevelson and Katherine Thompson, two northern cunning women who applied a white duck to the mouths of the sick, while reciting a charm.[16] In all these cases, the central notion is that illness or *maleficium* can be drawn out of one body by another. The mouth is a bodily opening through which pollutants enter because nourishment is constantly passing through it, and is also the place through which the malignant force may be extracted from its warm home. The idea that illness could be transferred from body to body where boundaries are permeable suggests that the model of the body being used here is that of the body in a circuit of contact with other bodies. Yet this circulation and exchange between bodies was also precisely how the witchcraft came about in the first place. Unwitchers like Margaret Stothard reversed the procedures of the witch; like her, they breached the limits of the victim's body, opening it up to their control; like the witch they made problematically intimate contact with another person, either *in propria persona* or through another body.

Another, related way of unwitching also reveals the interconnectedness of bodies in witchcraft. Joan Guppy was expert in curing those bewitched or taken with the 'black fairy', 'but where she bestoweth it [the disease] the Lord knoweth, but she quickly freeth herself from it again, and layeth it as it is supposed upon some beast, fowl, or worm, if not upon a Christ creature'.[17] A nameless woman who entered the sick-room of the Earl of Derby relieved his (bewitched) condition, but only by becoming very ill herself.[18] When Margaret Stothard had cured Jane Carr's child, Jane noticed that a calf immediately afterwards went mad, and had to be killed.[19] Jane Watson, said to be a 'medicer', cured the sickness of Elizabeth Richardson, but immediately after a dog mysteriously died.[20] The learned controversialist Richard Bovet noted the power to transfer illness or a curse from one person to another.[21] In all these cases the witch or unwitcher was believed to have transferred the illness or witchcraft from the sick person to another body, either her own or that of a third party. Illness could be unwitched into nature instead of into a creature. When the mother of a sick child approached Jenkyn Pereson for a cure, Pereson said that the child was suffering from the fairy, and offered an elaborate remedy:

> She bade her send two for south-running water, and these two shall not speak by the way, and the child should be washed in that water, and dip the shirt in the water, and so hang it upon a hedge all that night, and that on the morrow the shirt should be gone and the child should recover health.[22]

This is a double displacement ritual; the idea that illness could be transferred to running water is very old, and it may also be transferred to the child's shirt, hence the prediction that this would vanish.[23] The disease of 'the fairy' was thought to come from wild nature, and the ritual aims to reverse its proceedings by returning it to its point of origin.

Other forms of counter-magic involving a notion of the connections between bodies are also recorded. When the father of a sick child consulted Mother Gillam, she advised 'cutting a piece of the witch's coat and burning it together with the child's underclothes'; this brought about the child's recovery.[24] This remedy too reversed the witch's activities; the story of Bennet Lane's milk dish revealed how a witch could gain power over a household by obtaining some object from it, while rural communities retained a fear of giving anything to a witch, especially a piece of silver, lest it give her power over the family.[25] The Flower women killed the young Earl of Rutland by burying his glove.[26] Cunning folk as late as the nineteenth century were still giving the same advice: a man whose horses were bewitched was advised by a stranger to 'go to the old woman's cottage, and either beg, borrow, or steal something'. The object would give him power over its owner.[27] Anne Bodenham claimed that she could gain power over two potentially murderous women if she could get 'the tails of their coats, or of their smocks, and if she had that she could make the house fall about their ears, and could do more than Master Lilly or any one whatsoever'.[28]

The so-called 'witch-cake' prepared by a cunning man for Elizabeth Hancocke, bewitched by Mary Smith after she had accused Mary of stealing chickens is similar. The 'recipe' combines medical practice with counter-magical procedures:

> flour to be mixed with the patient's own waters, and baked on the hearth, one half to be applied in the region of the heart, the other half to the back. The cake to be first spread with an ointment like treacle, a powder to be cast upon it, and certain words to be written in a paper.[29]

Analysis of urine was crucial for early modern diagnosis, but though the importance of urine is borrowed from those professional discourses, it plays a different role here. Another typical remedy was the magical bottle or bellarmine, which closed off the witch's own waters when it was sealed. In the bottle were placed the witch's hair or a piece of her clothing, and ideally her urine. The bottle was then sealed. The bellarmine was supposed to seal the witch's body, making her unable to urinate. Symbolically, however, its significance lies in its constriction of the witch's body. Unable to expand and pollute, she is rendered harmless.

The formlessness of the witch's body is also attested by her ability to transform herself into other bodies, to shift shape. In women's depositions the witch was often represented as an antimother; contemporaries could also see the witch as an anti-infant in stories of witches who transformed themselves into animals in order to suckle the milk of pigs or cows.[30] Anne Bodenham was said to be able to 'transform herself into any shape whatsoever, *viz*, a mastiff dog, a black lion, a white bear, a wolf, a monkey, a horse, a bull, and a calf'. Similarly 'Ann Baites hath been several times in the shape of a cat and a hare, and in the shape of a greyhound and a bee, letting the devil see how many shapes she could turn herself into'.[31] Just as the witch could extend her bodily identity into houses and rummage among children's clothes, so she could unfix the limits of her own body by shifting shape. This Protean fluidity was frightening because it meant that there was perpetual uncertainty about the witch's 'true' identity, and because the witch's boundlessness recalls the fantasy-mother, engulfing, literally swallowing up the household and its riches.

The image of the witch that emerges from these stories of magic is of a body involved with rather than excluded from the society of other bodies. In each case, the countermeasure involves breaching the boundary of a body or household either by violence or by bringing it into contact with another body, symbolically or actually. Exchanges of breath, blood, urine, clothing or food characterise the counter-magical remedies. As suggested above, this implies that the remedies are reversals of bewitchment, acts of *un*witching which restore power to the proper authorities by duplicating and undoing a previous transgression. The image of the witch thus emerges in yet another inversion of the housewife and mother. Just as the housewife is involved in the circulation and exchange of goods and gifts with her neighbours, so the witch is involved in similar networks of bodily exchange and transfer of power. Just as the boundaries of the mother's body blur and blend with that of her child, so the witch breaches the protective space around the body with a look, a gift, a touch, a word or a visit. Unwitching involves reversing that contact by mirroring it precisely, bringing together (say) pieces of a witch's garment and pieces of a child's shirt. From unwitching, we get a clearer picture of what constituted bewitching, but we also see how deeply feminised the notion of the witch was, how close to normal or normative ideas about woman, and how that image was shaped by the anxieties and contradictions inscribed in those ideas.

If the witch in these encounters seems formless, too soft or liquid, she could also be understood as unnaturally hard and dry, especially for a woman. This fitted with the humoral theory that age withered women. The trial of Anne Kerke, for instance, involved an attempt to test the idea that a witch's hair could not be cut.

A justice produced ten or twelve of her hairs to refute this notion. But 'upon a serjeant attempting to cut them [her hairs] with a pair of barber's scissors, they turned round in his hand, and the edges were so battered, turned and spoiled, that they would not cut anything'. When an attempt was made to burn the hair, the fire flew from it.[32] This hardness was a sign of the witch's power, for while it prevailed, counter-magic was impossible. Even the remedy of scratching, discussed in detail below for its attempt to control the witch by breaking her body open and forcing it to give up a secretion, might fail if the witch were impermeable. A Northampton case illustrates this fear. A deponent reported that

> John Walker being stricken very lame in all his limbs, and suspecting Alice Harrys desired to scratch her, but being brought to her could not a long time draw any blood from her hands or face yet at length with much ado got a little and so recovered instantly and threw away his crutches.[33]

Even more striking was the story of the immunity of the witch of Newbury to the violence of a group of Parliamentarian soldiers.

> One set his carbine close unto her breast, where discharging, the bullet back rebounded like a ball, and narrowly he missed it in his face that was the shooter; this so enraged the gentlemen, that one drew out his sword and manfully run at her with all the force his strength had power to make, but it prevailed no more than did the shot, the woman still though speechless, yet in a most contemptible way of scorn, still laughing at them which did the more exhaust their fury against her life, yet one among the rest had learned that piercing or drawing blood forth from the veins that cross the temples of the head, it would prevail against the strongest sorcery, and quell the force of witchcraft, which was allowed for trial; the woman hearing this, knew then the devil had left her and her power was gone, wherefore she began aloud to cry, and roar, tearing her hair and making piteous moan, which in these words expressed were 'And is it come to pass that I must die indeed? Why then his excellency the Earl of Essex shall be fortunate and win the field'.[34]

With this highly gratifying disclosure, the witch proves that Satan is on the king's side, since Essex was the leading Parliamentarian general. This political tilt does not prevent the story from absorbing a number of ideas from popular culture, even though some are inflected by more educated pre-texts like the story of Achilles' invulnerability and of Talos' ichor. At root, however, it is still a story of a village witch. Since her specious magical armour has been unlocked by the act of piercing her at a particular spot, her body is no longer invulnerable. So she is shot and sinks to the bottom of the river. Her initial invulnerability and subsequent collapse can be allegorised as a story of the decline of Royalist military fortunes, and it partakes in particular of the logic of siege. Both cities and castles under siege are often compared to the female body, just as Petrarchan poetry borrowed the language of war to describe seduction.[35] Here, after artillery has failed, a sneak attack on the body's weak point causes its defences to collapse.

This military imagery illustrates the way masculine military power constructs itself in opposition to femininity, so that, as Theweleit noted, misogyny is the outcome of the identities produced among bands of soldiers threatened on all sides by the extreme pollutions of death and corpses. These arouse terror of the maternal body and a need repeatedly to abject it or destroy it.[36] The proliferation of witch-hunters during the Civil War suggests a possible connection between military activity and fear of witches; once the war is over fear of witches begins to ebb. In the case at Newbury, too, the attack on the witch is both a representation of warfare as usual, and an outlet for its stresses and strains. This shows how the witch's hardness could be understood – and resented – as willed resistance to law, force, or simply to male violence, and hence as provocative. If the formless body of the witch, into everything, was a source of terror, the 'hard' witch also frightened. Her resistance to the violence of her assailants represents her supernatural power, but also makes her a problem in terms of gender; she is not supposed to be as hard as a hero.

The elite idea that witches were mostly identified by the populace by their ugliness reflects the idea of the hard witch, for ugliness is apotropaic, turning away the would-be phallic gaze.[37] The ugly old witch with warts and a beard is a figure who refuses to be controlled or managed as a soft or yielding object of desire, just as the witch of Newbury refuses to be 'penetrated' by shot. A related popular superstition sees ugliness is a sign of supernatural strength.[38] Ugliness is another way of being too hard and dry. The hard-bodied witch recalls the bad mother, who refuses to yield to the infant's needs and to be pliant to his wishes. She is beyond maternity, partly because her hardness and dryness are the results of age, and partly because they are the antithesis of the desired maternal body, flowing with clean nourishment. The witch's resistance to the soldiers provokes more and more violent responses, as if something were driving them on. In the logic of the story this is a way of demonstrating the fact of the woman's identity as a witch, but in psychic logic the witch's invulnerability works to license violence against her, violence tinged with the terror of the maternal. Her hard body is a pre-text for violence against her invasive magical power, itself an extension of her body. The witch's body must be hard *because* it is edgeless and polluting.

Consequently, women who feared bewitchment were also paradoxically enabled, and in some ways psychically impelled, to take action against the witch, action which might involve behaviours at variance with the range of feminine ideals available to women in the early modern period. The witch was pollution, especially when in places that had to be kept clean, like the churn. She had to be cleaned away. Unwitching practices give us useful insights into women's agency and resources in combating witchcraft. The housewife had other resources available besides formal counter-magic, though many of these are tinged with the colours of ritual. She could seek a public or private reconciliation with the woman she suspected of witchcraft. The wife of Thomas Rennard enacted an especially public and theatrical rite of apology. When her child was sick, she remarked to Thomas 'I fear this wife has wronged my child':

and then, not long after, his wife meeting the said Elizabeth at her own door, she did fall down on her knees and asked her forgiveness, and the child did soon after recover.[39]

Witchcraft often took place on the boundaries of the victim's household; reconciliation takes place in or near the witch's house, in the liminal space of the doorway. This was also a relatively public space; in all local disputes, it was often important to be seen to be reconciled, to make a public act of forgiveness. Mistress Rennard was also acting out her gender role here, eschewing proscribed violence and doing 'women's work' in recreating social harmony.

However, there were alternatives to self-abasement. When Mary Midgely was suspected of bewitching the cows of the Wood family, Mistress Wood took an altogether firmer line. She confronted Mary, and 'told her that she had made the fault, and desired her to remedy it if she could'. Mary was understandably reluctant to confess, but after accepting sixpence from Mistress Wood she explained that the cows would recover if a handful of salt and a sickle were placed under each of them. When Richard Wood met Mary subsequently, it was Mary who sought reconciliation, giving him an apple as a gesture of amity and apologising for her wrongdoing.[40] Other accounts record the success of confrontational methods. When the mother of another sick child confronted Goody Cross, Cross admitted bewitching the child and agreed to reverse the harm; she visited the infant and simply uttered the words 'God bless thee!', after which it recovered. Anne Ellis was persuaded to admit and undo her *maleficium* with a blessing by the mother of another sick child. For four days she refused to do so, presumably involving the mother in a long campaign of importunings, but as soon as she said 'God bless thee', it recovered.[41] When Joan Booth suspected that Margaret Morton had bewitched her four-year-old son with a piece of bread, she 'mistrusting that the said Margaret Morton had bewitched her child, did send for her, who asked the child forgiveness three times'. The ritual character of the apology is notable.

Presumably, this did not work. Joan proceeded to ritual violence, which proved more effective 'and then this informant drew blood from her with a pin and immediately after the child amended'.[42] These cases indicate that the formal and public procedures of an assize or quarter sessions investigation might be preceded by a more informal local process which followed the same pattern: an attempt to get the suspect to confess and to make reparation. Other women, men and children adopted more cautious strategies; Elizabeth Crosley's case is an instance. As we have seen, it was sinister to take too much interest in an illness or calamity, or to know too much about it. When the two-year-old John Shackleton was taken with terrible pains and convulsions, a minister named William Whaley visited, and mysteriously told the maidservant attending the sick boy that if they were to meet anyone on the way home they would long 'to mawl them on the heads'. After this advice, they set out, and met Elizabeth Crosley:

> and the maid perceiving it to be her shunned the way; notwithstanding, the said Elizabeth asked how the child did, but this informer suspecting her to be a witch did not tell her how ill it was, but said it was indifferent well, at which she seemed very angry.[43]

The maid was reluctant to encounter Crosley, and her companion was reluctant to speak with her, or offer any information on the child's illness. It was especially deadly to allow a witch the last word. Encounters, words and information are all occasions for power. Here the guardians of the bewitched child adopt a cautious, low-risk strategy.[44]

In Jeanne Favret-Saada's work on modern Bocage beliefs in witches, she stresses that in several cases a victim of witchcraft fails to confront the witch-suspect with sufficient power and authority, with the result that the witch's hold over the subject is strengthened by further encounters.[45] There were risks in a cautious policy of avoidance when dealing with witches, as another story shows. The deponent is a child, Hugh Lucas:

> who looking stark on Jone Lucas at the church, she asked him whether he would outface her, but the boy being afraid, replied not, but went home, and being on a wall, fell into a trance, and so continued twelve hours, and in his fit he saw Jone Lucas come to his bedside four times; but the next day he met with her, tripped up her heels, beat her, and so had never any more fits.[46]

When Hugh attempts a direct confrontation, but withdraws on being challenged, the witch gains power over him. When he exerts himself to confront Lucas and exercise violent control over her body, he regains control of his own. In another story, a boy searching for a lost cow surprised an old woman, who said 'Boh' to him; he immediately became speechless. Later, seeing the old woman supping with other people, the boy knew what to do: he 'ran furiously upon her and threw her pottage into her face and offered some other violence to her'. Everyone present grasps the meaning of his actions. They suspect that the woman 'has done some hurt' to the boy, and hurry her off to gaol, where the gaoler takes it upon himself to blackmail her into removing her curse. At that very moment, the boy later deposes, the woman appeared in his window, grinning, 'until he took up a form leg and therewith gave her two good bangs on the arse'. The marks of the blows are discovered later on the witch's body.[47] These boys become violent as a way of combatting the 'hardness' of the witch.

Violence could break through the witch's hardness, or contain her formlessness. Like the maternal body, the witch's body is locked into a controlling, dominating relation with the bodies of others; it is the seat of her power, and it can be located wherever her power is.[48] This helps to explain the most common form of counter-magic in the early modern period, which was to scratch the suspected witch in order to make her bleed.[49] Joan Guppy was scratched; Hester France was scratched by two of her victims, as were Anne Kerke, Jane Brooks, Ann Wagg and Elizabeth Stile – to name but a few.[50] When a cunning man advised that a victim scratch Elizabeth Stile, he specified that it must be done 'so that you draw blood of her'.[51] Such confrontations could escalate to a point where scratching the witch provided an occasion for real violence. Some members of the gentry solve the problem of witchcraft by attacking a suspected witch, pricking her (perhaps to draw her blood) and then stabbing her in the face with a knife. When Andrew Camp thought that Mistress Bailey had bewitched his children, he dragged her into the street and wrestled her to the ground. His wife clawed Bailey in the face, 'and said she would claw the eyes out of her head, and her tongue out of her mouth'.[52] The courts were not always complacently approving in such cases. Henry Thompson was indicted for murder after he had 'very violently' fallen upon, and beaten Margaret Hill, 'a poor old widow'. Thompson called Hill a witch, and accused her in particular of bewitching his mother. Eventually he was persuaded to desist when he 'made [her] kneel down of her knees, and ask him forgiveness'. The informant in this case, Anne Ashmore, cowered in bed, terrified that Thompson would turn on her too if she intervened. Hill died of her injuries three weeks later.[53] When Anne Warberton's house was invaded by those who suspected her of witchcraft, her child was severely injured in the ensuing fracas, and later died.[54] As late as 1875, a woman named Anne Turner was murdered in the Warwickshire village of Long Compton by one James Heywood, who believed that she had bewitched him and that he had to undo her spells by spilling her blood. He was convicted, but only of manslaughter.[55] Such violence might seem explicable in the light of the witch's power, but it also seems excessive when offered to the frail body of an old woman by one or more large men. That excess is what arises from the way the fear of the witch is not only a fear of a perfectly real hazard to family and self, but also a terror of losing the self altogether to the malign and unseen power of another. In comparison with the infinitely extendable body of the witch and her equally formidable hardness, grappling with a real and tangible body that could be assailed may have been a relief.

Questions of agency, violence and the formless and hard bodies of the witch come together with the theme of problematic motherhood around the figure of the witch suckling her familiar. The familiar is a collaborative construction, the result of negotiation and compromise between elite and populace, accuser and accused, men and women. The elite expected pact witchcraft, witches involved with devils. Popular conceptions of the witch, however, saw her power as an emanation of her quasi-maternal body. A compromise which eventually hardened into orthodoxy, and can actually be seen doing so in some confessions, was to invent the familiar, the demon who rendered the witch a perverse kind of mother, and to substitute the demon's habit of sucking the witch's blood for the sexual acts common to demonological fantasy. Just as the witchmark is the conduit between the witch's body and her familiars, so the *idea* of the witchmark is a conduit between demonological explanations of witchcraft as the power of demons and rural understandings of the witch herself as the bearer of power. The English witchmark was not a spell or seal, but a polluted organ out of place, a teat or nipple inappropriately displaced into a part of the body associated with pollution.[56]

Early modern medical writers believed that breast-milk was the blood which has been nourishing the foetus in the womb, drawn up to the breasts via a large vein, and purified into milk. Clean, nourishing blood was separated from the impure blood which continued to be shed from the womb as lochia. Aristotle thought that when a child was born the residue that was no longer needed to feed it in the womb was bound to collect in the empty spaces of the breasts. Isidore writes that 'whatever blood has not yet been spent in the nourishing of the womb flows by natural passage to the breasts, and whitening by their virtue, receives the quantity of milk'.[57] 'The milk', wrote Guillimeau, 'is nothing else but blood whitened, being new brought to perfection and maturity'. He compares refusal to breastfeed with abortion, refusal to nourish with blood.[58] Even when anatomical studies made it obvious that no vein ran from womb to heart or breast, medical writers clung to the idea of milk from blood: Helkiah Crooke wrote enthusiastically that the breasts were uniquely well placed to change blood into milk because of their proximity to the heart.[59]

In Erasmus's colloquy 'The New Mother', Eutrapelus visits Fabulla to congratulate her on the birth of her son, and to give her a lecture on infant-feeding. Fabulla stands up to him well on labour and birth, but the pedant becomes inspired when it comes to the breast. Horrified to find her using a wetnurse, he explodes: 'Do you suppose it makes no difference whether a delicate infant drinks in congenial and familiar nourishment and is cherished by the now-familiar warmth or is forced to get used to somebody else's?' Erasmus's suddenly articulate man makes it clear that there was a connection between the anatomy of blood vessels leading from the womb through the heart to the breast, and the ideology of motherhood and mother-love, expressed through mother-blood.[60] The breast was a redeemed part of the open, dirty body of the childbearing woman, a part where her polluted blood was purified by the fires of maternal love so that it could become an expression of that love.

However, the blood or milk was still linked with the womb and genitals from which the foetus emerged. Almost anything could corrupt the milk if it (re)established a link between breast and lower body. Guides to choosing a nurse stressed that she must have given birth at least a month ago so that the milk is well purified; nor must her child be more than eight months old, in case the milk is too old. Milk could be corrupted by copulation: John Jones in *The art of preserving body and soul* argued that concupiscence could poison the milk by contaminating it with foul humours, while others such as A. M. argued that copulation would attract blood away from the breasts and diminish the milk supply.[61] Colostrum, the rich creamy pre-milk made during pregnancy was taboo. Significantly, it was known as witch's milk. These ideas acted as curbs for female bodily activity; they also pointed to an anxiety about the invisibility of the breast-milk swallowed by the infant. Once inside, milk could not be checked for impurities or subjected to any other kind of scrutiny. The mother–child dyad that results cannot be scrutinised, checked or inspected by the eyes of science or the church. Flowing from mother to child, breast-milk integrates the child's sucking mouth into the tidal and alarming flows and ebbs of the maternal body. The vulnerable newborn is fed with a substance whose provenance must be doubtful: the poison bag of the female body.

To this medical ambivalence was added social anxiety. Early modern husbands seem to have been much less enthusiastic than medical writers about maternal breastfeeding. Damage to the breasts by the infant or by infection may have been a greater problem. Diaries refer to the abscesses and engorgement inevitable in the days before antibiotics: Nehemiah Wallington, for instance, notes that his wife 'began to have sore breasts so that the child did not suck for three days together that we were fain to put it forth to nurse in the country for wife was in such pain with her breasts'. Alice Thornton similarly reports that her son Kitt 'did so nip the head [of the breast] that I was in fear of a gangrene. And the extreme pain cast me into a fever . . . so that I could neither stand nor go for four months'.[62] In an era when mastitis and abcesses ('milk fever') were common and life-threatening, there was a link between lactation, pain and pollution. Because the openness of their bodies was a conduit for infection, it was more difficult for early modern women to lie back and experience the *jouissance* of a flowing body.

There were other, deeper, less articulate fears.[63] Early modern anxieties about wet-nurses, shared by intellectuals and mothers, were the product of the ambivalent status of the breast as an agent of infant-feeding. The metaphor of the infant said to be 'changed at nurse' represents the belief that the nurse, by nourishing the infant with her purified blood as milk, was at the same time subtly diluting his lineal identity and substituting her own for it. This was literalised in stories of nurses who changed their babies with the babies of the gentry whom they were paid to feed, to give their children every advantage: Guillimeau writes that 'the milk (wherewith the child is nourished two years together) hath as much power to make the children like the nurse, both in body and mind, as the seed of the parents hath to make the children like them . . .'[64] The lasciviousness of Juliet's nurse would have made her a dubious choice by any parent. To an early modern audience it might have explained Juliet's tearaway sexuality and flagrant disobedience; she may have sucked more than wisdom from the teat. These anxieties metaphorised fears of servants' influence, and still deeper worries about the role of the mother in determining the child's identity. On the face of it, medical writers approved of maternal nurturance as a way of keeping the child's identity in the hands of the family: 'If she nurse him,' writes Guillimeau,

> he sucks and draws her own blood whereupon grows a familiar inwardness, and the child (when he comes to years of discretion) finds himself bound to his mother, for many benefits; both in that she hath born him nine months in her womb, and also because she has nursed him, watched him, and often

made him clean. In recompense whereof he endeavours to show her a thousand delights . . .

This idyllic scene of gratitude and respect is counterposed by the disorderly spectacle of a baby whose nurse has become the object of his love: 'if one offers to take him out of the nurse's arms, he will fly in their faces, and if it were possible he would even pull out their heart; and all this proceeds from that inward affection of the child, to which no love can be compared'. These metaphors of animal fierceness symbolise the child's loss of parental identity, but also paternal identity; his conquest by the animality and bodiliness of the nurse is a conquest by the feminine. The wet-nurse symbolises the power of the feminine to obliterate male self-replication, an anxiety which also haunted the processes of conception and pregnancy.[65]

As well as worries about the polluting female body, class anxieties and anxieties about patrilinearity, there were also anxieties about the boundary between humans and animals. Early modern writers drew on the ancients, who distinguished human lactation from animal feeding. Aristotle pointed out that the breasts of animals being underneath, did not interfere with their mobility. In humans, however, they developed on the chest to cover the heart. This became a sign of man's uniqueness: Albertus Magnus enthused that human beings were fed from the area near the heart and not from a place near the shameful organs of women.[66] Although early modern women often used an animal to draw off overfull breasts, they were much more anxious than we are about feeding a child animal milk. Guillimeau writes that 'a certain child was nourished with the milk of a Bitch, but he would rise in the night and howl with other dogs'. Early modern parents were reluctant to give their infants cows' milk, lest it transmit animal qualities.[67]

Despite the struggle to maintain lactation as a pure event in the dubious terrain of the female body, these distinctions had to be maintained rigorously in discourse and in practice because that body was such a doubtful space. As Iris Young points out, 'once we cease to see the breast in terms of the male gaze which gives it solidity as an object and begin to talk of the breast from the woman's point of view, the breast becomes blurry, mushy, indefinite, multiple, and without clear identity . . . Irigaray suggests that a metaphysics generated from feminine desire might conceptualise being as fluid rather than as solid substances'.[68] This is the formless maternal body. Psychoanalysis reminds us of the infantile fears and anxieties which go with the breast; as Joyce McDougall writes, the baby who is hungry is experiencing what Klein called envy, that is, the trauma of otherness, the dependence on attributes of the other that one does not possess and control. Need-objects become objects of hate as well as love for the baby; the breast, as a bad and hated object, awakens the anguished fear that one might destroy this source of life. Babies that have to wait for a feed grow so full of hate that they refuse the breast even when it is offered. The mother must represent all the valuable qualities of the breast-universe – food, warmth, tenderness, and so on. She must also help her infant get rid of the persecuting and hated breast that the baby cannot eject alone without damage.[69] This is reminiscent of the early modern breast as described by anatomists, a place where the bad is purified and transformed. In and through the breast, anxieties about and longing for the maternal body are expressed.

Some of these fears and desires were projected onto the figure of the witch, who acted to mark all appropriate boundaries by transgressing them. As with all fantasies about the witch and her body, violent fear or desire is abjected into the witch, who signifies both men's and women's idea of the bad lactating mother. These worries translate into the elaborate fantasy of the witch and her suckling familiar. The witch gives blood instead of milk; the purified blood that is milk, and hence the narrative of the female body as a source of nourishment rather than poison, does not exist as far as she is concerned. Her body is all poison. Her refusal or inability to purify blood into milk is also connected with her lack of milk; witches are often accused of diverting milk supplies to their own ends, of demanding milk from householders, of stealing the breast-milk of women or animals, and (most significantly of all) of turning milk into blood, that is, turning it back into pollution. This means the witch transgressed the horizontal division which marked the pure female body from the impure female body: polluted blood sinks, while pure blood rises to the breasts. Witches fed their familiars on impure blood. Most 'teats' or 'witchmarks were located on the genitals or near the anus. Finally, witches' suckling of familiars in the guise of animals blurred the boundaries between humans and animals.

An especially vivid description of a witch's teat is given in the case of Alice Samuel, whose body was examined by the gaoler after death:

> he found upon the body of the old woman Alice Samuel a little lump of flesh, in manner sticking out as if it had been a teat, to the length of half an inch; which both he and his wife perceiving, at the first sight thereof meant not to disclose because it was adjoining so secret a place which was not decent to be seen. Yet in the end, not willing to conceal so strange a matter, and decently covering that privy place a little above which it grew, they made open show thereof unto diverse that stood by. After this the jailer's wife took the same teat in her hand, and seeming to strain it, there issued out at the first as if it had been leesenings[70] (to use the jailer's word) which is a mixture of yellow milk and water; at the second turn there came out in similitude as clear milk, and in the end very blood itself.[71]

Prodigies such as monstrous births were often displayed to the gaze of the populace.[72] This display gives the people symbolic power over what is 'strange' by opening it to their examination: so it is here. The centrality of the jailer's wife to the process of display, which parallels the centrality of the midwife to the discovery of the witchmark, makes it impossible to locate the anxieties of the mark in gender difference *alone*.[73] What is nervously described here is the maternal body feared by *both* men and women. The ideal mother purifies her own pollution in order to create breast-milk; the witch-mother produces polluted, creamy milk from near 'that privy place'. The maternal and bodily disorder symbolised by the witch's teat harmonises with the fantasy of the witch as the dark other of the mother and housewife. The witch usurps maternal and housewifely control for the purpose of inverting its ordering functions; the witch's body represents a maternity that has become a sign of dirt. The teat's location and its morphology symbolise the 'matter out of place' that shows witchcraft has occurred. There is an uncanny homology between the witch's body and the bodies of the bewitched; bewitched women and animals give blood instead of milk, and the witch's teat dispenses blood.

What of the witch's own investment in the notion of the suckling familiar? The witch's teat was believed to feed her familiars, understood as small demons, but upon analytic pressure dispersing into a horde of diverse creatures. The multiplicity of identities hidden away under the single name 'familiar' can be glimpsed by an examination of their names. There are names which point backward to fairies and folk-spirits: Robin, Dick, Piggin (reminiscent of Drayton's Pigwiggin), Liard, Hob, Rutterkin, Puckle. There are folktale hero names like Jack and Tom. There are literal figurations of the familiar's role (Suckin). There are the names of animals (Puss, Great Tom Twit and Little Tom Twit). There are names suggestive of Puritan ideas of magic (Blackfast, Hardname), names redolent of recusancy, such as saints' names (Antony). A few have pet's names (Bid) and others plain ordinary personal names (Will).[74] At times, deponents seem to conflate wax images with familiars, calling familiars poppets, puppets or mammets.[75] There is no way to know how many of these names were assigned by the witch, how many by her examiners, how many by the pamphleteers, but their plainness and in some cases their relation to fairy lore point to popular origins. Perhaps their diversity points to multiple investments in the idea of the familiar. All these names are alike in figuring the familiar as small, and all have a certain affectionate sound, connoting the relations between master and servant, owner and pet, parent and child. Some at least are blatant baby names. Since such a display of affection and tenderness towards what the court was bound to see as a demon must have been impolitic, one can only suppose that these affectionate relations formed a central part of women's own fantasies about the familiar.

As the names indicate, the relation between witch and familiar was often represented in the witch's own confession as an elaborate maternal or quasi-maternal interchange. Just as some women prophets represented themselves as both mothers and infants, nourishing and nourished by God, so witches represented themselves both as the mothers of suckling infant-familiars and as children nurtured by their care.[76] The popular notion of a blood pact between a familiar and a witch could be reshaped into a model of deformed maternity. Although familiars mostly resembled animals, one account does mention a familiar 'like a child'.[77] As in women's depositions, food is central to the witches' statements. Contemporaries understood the witchmark as a conduit which opened the witch's body and made it a source of food for familiars, and witches often confess that familiars drink their blood. This was the most usual way to understand the familiar, but it was also not incompatible with seeing it as sexual partner, mother, friend, enemy, foe of living or dead children already belonging to the witch.

In some narratives, the familiar is a kind of psychic resource, providing a way of coping with otherwise unbearable conflicts or ambivalences towards children. Malcolm Gaskill has recently unearthed a case of a woman for whom the relationship with the familiar was a substitute for the agonising absence of dead children. 'She heard a voice calling to her after this manner, "Mother, Mother" to which the said Margaret answered "Sweet children, where are you? What would you have with me?"'[78] Margaret Moor's case is more complex than the mere adoption of a fantasy of a familiar-child might suggest. The familiar is also the enemy of her one surviving child, and it is because she threatens the life of this child that Moor is obliged to help her: '[she] demanded of her her soul, otherwise she would take away the life of her fourth child which was the only child she had left'.[79]

Moor's familiar represents her dead child, or more accurately represents himself as that child. However, its role is more ambiguous than Gaskill implies. Its voice also articulates Moore's own illicit desire to harm her children. Her case was by no means unique; familiars often voiced the wish to harm children as well as the need to protect them, desires which could only be acknowledged as the promptings of temptation. Susanna Smith confessed that the devil tempted her to kill her children, but 'she strove with him 24 hours before he went from her but she would not kill them, but being desired to relate further of her witchcraft there rise two swellings in her throat so that she could not speak . . . ' Smith's wishes are literally unspeakable; in this account her attempt to articulate her desires even at one remove produces only silence. Priscilla Collit was also tempted 'to make away with her children, or else she should always continue poor'.[80] Similarly, Elizabeth Frauncis believed herself to be pregnant after a liaison with a neighbour set up by her familiar, 'she, doubting herself with child, willed Satan to destroy it, and he bade her take a certain herb and drink it, which she did, and destroyed the child forthwith'.[81] In these cases, the familiar is not only a covert representation of a maternal wish to harm a child, but also the child's competitor, offering a better future than the child can, and voicing on behalf of the woman a sense of entitlement she cannot articulate. These stories recall 'Hansel and Gretel'; before the Grimms' pious intervention, it was the children's own mother who wished to expose them because of the family's poverty.[82]

At the end of such folktales, the abandoned child frequently returns laden with the food or wealth the family lacks. In trial depositions, the familiar could play the part of the returning child, offering to act as a substitute for the child in its role as that which works to sustain the parents, elevating them into a better future, mothering them. Elizabeth Stile's familiar, a rat, 'had provided for her both milk and cream against her coming home'.[83] In the few English confessions involving accounts of the sabbath, food is much more central to events than sex; Anne Whittle, one of the Lancashire witches, claimed that when meeting a familiar with another witch, Elizabeth Southern:

> there was victuals, viz. flesh, butter, cheese, bread and drink, and [he] bid them eat enough. And after their eating the devil called Fancy and the other spirit . . . took the remnant away.[84]

However, the devils' feast is duplicitous, since 'they were never the fuller or better for the same'.[85] These pleasures rest firmly on Whittle's self-representation as a needy, undernourished child; Elizabeth Stile, too, stresses the contrast between her familiar's generous provision of milk and cream and the stinginess of her neighbours' refusal of it. Representing her familiar's care as both maternal and neighbourly, she shows how the fantasies of abundant diabolic feasts also represented a nurturance absent from the witch's environment.

This appealed to the rural poor, chronically short of food. It was the sabbath viands which the young Edmund Robinson remembered from the Lancashire case of 1613, and reproduced in his own testimony, as did Anne Armstrong. In these stories, the devil is not the object of desire, but a nurturant host who provides for his guests. Sabbaths are imbued with the symbolic significance of commensality: the witches constitute a counter-community with its own idyllic commensality, a commensality which unites the participants.[86] Anne Whittle's statement that this demonic food did not really nourish the recipients contrasts with the image of nurturance, but harmonises with the many folktales in which fairy gifts turn out to be illusory, and may have been intended as a strategic sop to those eager to argue that no one ever did well out of a bargain with the devil.[87] It suggests an awareness of the gulf between a fantasy of abundance and the struggles of mundane reality. Whittle acknowledges the pleasures of the fantasy while pointing to its evanescence.[88]

The witch could therefore both mother her familiars and be mothered by them. This chiasmus can also be seen in texts which stress the openness of the witch's body to her familiars. Like the relocated witch-teat, these figurations of the witch's body stress its boundlessness. Alice Samuel confessed that her familiar, which took the form of a dun chicken, had ceased to plague the Throckmorton children because:

> the said dun chicken with the rest are now come into her, and are now in the bottom of her belly, and make her so full she is like to burst, and this morning they caused her to be so full she could scant lace her coat, and that on the way as she came, they weighed so heavy that the horse she rode on did fall down and was not able to carry her.[89]

Elements of merry jest and *fabliaux* creep into this story, genres in which Alice Samuel's body bulging with chickens might figure comic abundance rather than threat. This is the paradox of the familiar, nurturative in dearth but threatening to sufficiency, like the grotesque or carnivalesque itself. Goody Smith confessed that 'her imps hang in her secret parts in a bag and her husband saw it . . . and that these imps sucked on her'.[90] Familiars traversing the boundaries of the witch's body also figure in the Flower case. Margaret Flower confessed that:

> she hath two familiar spirits sucking on her, the one white, the other black-spotted; the white sucked under her left breast, and the black-spotted within the inward parts of her secrets.[91]

Although this motif can be explained in relation to the figuration of the witch as grotesque antimother, it seems worth pointing out that both the Flower and the Samuel cases involved the bewitchment of young members of gentry or noble families. Cases involving the better sort tend to re-present witchcraft as a threat to patrilinearity rather than maternal authority; this tendency is marked in the Flower case, where the witches are a threat to the family line. In this context, the disorderliness of the witch's maternal body has been appropriated to represent a threat to the order of generation and class. This reinscription of a female anxiety as a misogynist trope of woman-as-other is characteristic of elite responses to the witch.

The witch's familiars could be represented entering into an exchange relationship with the witch that uneasily parallels her relations with neighbours. Like neighbours, and also like children, familiars could be unduly demanding and unpleasant. Ursula Kempe confessed that her familiars had been sent to her to drink her milk after she had refused milk to Mother Turner. The same spirits were appropriated by Elizabeth Bennet, unluckily for her as it turned out, 'for that she denied the said Mother Turner of milk, they many times drank from her milk bowl'.[92] These spirits were not servant-demons, but malevolent fairies. Joan Upney's familiars proved equally unsatisfactory: her mole pined away and died, and her replacement toads kept abandoning her for other people.[93] None of these women were talking about familiars as the demonologists understood them; in their depositions we can see the entire compromise of English witch-discourse breaking up along the seam of the familiar, here threatening to dissolve into its discursive parent, the fairy. Yet there is also an underlying cogency. Greedy and neglectful familiars mirror maternal fears of child misbehaviour; there was no place in early modern ideology for mothers to express feelings of hostility to children, but the witches' fantasies about their familiars may be a coded representation of their unspeakable fears and loathings; the more so since many witch-suspects, including Ursula Kempe, were convicted in part on the evidence of their children.[94]

Some familiars could be night-terrors. Joan Cason spoke about her 'familiar' as an unwelcome ghost that 'did divers years since (but not lately) haunt her house, and many other houses in the town'. She hears it crying out 'Go to, go to'.[95] Familiars could be aggressive, and when suckling could behave less like children and more like blood-drinking animals: Margaret Bates found that 'when she was at work, she felt a thing come upon her legs and go into her secret places and nipped her in her secret parts where her marks were found'. Anne Usher found that 'a thing like a small cat came over her legs once or twice and that it scratched her mightily'. The cat, however, seems to have made Usher pregnant, since next 'she felt two things like butterflies in her secret places'; Usher responds with some violence to their movements 'with witchings, dancings and sucking and she felt them with her hands and rubbed them and killed them'. Others were disappointments: Usher had another diabolic encounter when 'another time when she sat a-spinning, a polecat skipped into her lap and spake to her and said if she would deny Ch. god and C. he would bring her vittles which she after consented but he never brought her anything after'.[96]

These disappointments reflect poor women's fatalistic sense that there was no escape for them from misery, that family and friends would not value them enough to take care of them in old age, that children would not piously show gratitude for their upbringing, that promises from the powerful could not be relied on. These women made familiars in the image of the grim world in which they found themselves. If they saw themselves as mothers of their suckling demons, it was as neglected mothers, sometimes as angry mothers. In this, their fantasies about demons replicate the pattern of village women's fantasies about witches. This is not surprising: fear of and desire for the mother is easily translated into fear of and desire for the child. In stories about witchcraft, the witch's boundless body is troubling because it does not obey the rules of cleanliness and propriety which protect identity from maternal reabsorption, so that it becomes a source of pollution which blocks clean nourishment. The witch's teat and her practice of suckling her familiars is the visible sign of this pollution and its concomitant power to disturb other categories and identities. The witch's resistance to order must be overcome, often by violence; this means that the witch becomes an occasion for machismo, and for acting out anxieties about the mother. In witches' fantasies about themselves, the witch plays the role of mother to familiars who she hopes will mother her, but who often turn out to be mischievous and irresponsible children, incapable of assuaging her terrible loneliness.

NOTES

1 For the relation between this psychoanalytic idea and the figure of the witch, see Chapter 3.

2 See, for instance, the St Osyth cases; Ursula Kempe seeks out a cunning woman in a nearby villlage, but Ursula's victims come from her own community. I discuss this further in Chapter 6, below. In the Bocage, according to Jeanne Favret-Saada, they still look for an unwitcher outside the village boundaries (*Deadly Words: Witchcraft in the Bocage*, Cambridge: Cambridge University Press, 1980, p. 43).

3 Kieckhefer cites a fifteenth-century book of housewifery which also contains numerous magical and counter-magical procedures (*Magic in the Middle Ages*, Cambridge: Cambridge University Press, 1990, p. 3), while Brian Levack has recently commented on the fact that witchcraft often involves the female realms of cooking

and healing, *The Witch-Hunt in Early Modern Europe*, London and New York: Longman, 1987, p. 126.

4 On house and body, see Jonathan Sawday, *The Body Emblazoned: Dissection and the Human Body in Renaissance Culture*, London: Routledge, 1995, pp. 161–3; the body as a political metaphor finds a well-known and conservative expression in the Fable of the Belly in *Coriolanus*.

5 *Volatile Bodies*, Bloomington: Indiana University Press, p. 203.

6 *Powers of Horror*, trans. Leon S. Roudiez, New York: Columbia University Press, 1982, esp. p. 71.

7 *Male Fantasies, vol. I, Women, Bodies, Floods, History*, trans. Stephen Conway with Erica Carter and Chris Turner, Cambridge: Polity, 1987.

8 On women's increased coldness and wetness and their failure to attain human perfection, see Aristotle, *On the Generation of Animals*, 728A 19–22. Debates among the ancients about this point were not resolved in the early modern period, but what one might term popularised medical discourses, such as that found in manuals of midwifery and in other lay people's books, ovelooked these learned disagreements in favour of bald assertion. See Ian Maclean, *The Renaissance Notion of Woman*, Oxford: Oxford University Press, 1980, for a summary.

9 Book 2, ch. 4.

10 Sidney Oldall Addy, *Household Tales with Other Traditional Remains*, 1895, p. 170.

11 Ralph Holinshead, *Chronicles of England, Scotland and Ireland*, 1587, vol. III, p. 1560, in Barbara Rosen, *Witchcraft in England 1558–1618*, Amherst; University of Massachusetts Press, 1991, p. 164. C. L'Estrange Ewen, *Witchcraft and Demonianism*, 1933, p. 166, hereafter *WD*. This is the well-known case in which the jury acquitted Cason of *maleficium* but convicted her of trafficking with spirits, believing that she would escape the death penalty, until a lawyer in the gallery pointed out that conjuring was a felony under the very statute under which she had been arraigned. She was duly hanged. The burning-roof counter-magic was also tried in Elizabeth Sawyer's case, dramatised by Dekker, Ford and Rowley, though this method was scorned by Henry Goodcole her confessor and memorialist, and by the urban and sophisticated dramatists. Henry Goodcole, *The wonderful discovery of Elizabeth Sawyer, a witch*, 1621, and Ewen, *WD*, pp. 257–9.

12 *A detection of damnable driftes*, 1579, in Rosen, *Witchcraft*, p. 95.

13 *A trial of witches at the assizes held at Bury St Edmunds for the County of Suffolk on the tenth day of March 1664*, 1682, rept. in Ewen, *WD*, p. 352.

14 Ewen, *WD*, p. 323; this is the child who fell ill after a woman had simply said 'here's a fine child'.

15 *Depositions from York Castle*, ed. James Raine, Surtees Society, vol. 40 (1860), p. 127, hereafter *YD*, a partial transcription of PRO ASSI 45 7/2/62, 103. Pepper also used holy water and a silver crucifix. Harley thinks that Pepper's status as midwife is irrelevant to her prosecution for charming, but plainly its relevance lies in the second sucking infant she produces (from where?) to use in the remedy. He also discusses Pepper's case in 'Mental illness, magical medicine, and the devil in northern England 1650–1700', in *Medical Revolution of the Seventeenth Century*, ed. Roger French and Andrew Wear, Cambridge: Cambridge University Press, 1989, p. 131.

16 *YD*, p. 127; Peter Rushton, 'Women, witchcraft and slander in early modern England: cases from the church courts at Durham, 1560–1675', *Northern History*, 18 (1982), pp. 116–32, here p. 120. This idea of mouth-to-mouth transmission also surfaces in a form rewritten as demonology in the confession of Joan Willimot, who claimed that William Berry promised to give her a fairy which would do her good, and blew it into her mouth. *The wonderful discoverie of the witchcrafts of Margaret and Phillippa Flower*, 1619, in Rosen, *Witchcraft*, p. 377.

17 Deposition of Mistress Abingdon in defence of Judith Gibbes, against whom Guppy brought a Star Chamber action for assault; I return to this case later. C. L'Estrange Ewen, *Witchcraft in the Star Chamber*, 1938, p. 26. The godly discourse spoken here suggests that among the issues at stake may be a dispute between Puritans and others.

18 John Stow, *Annals of England*, London, 1600, pp. 1275–7, reproduced in full in Rosen, *Witchcraft*, pp. 308–9.

19 Ewen, *WD*, p. 323.

20 *YD*, pp. 92–3; Ewen, *WD*, pp. 400–1.

21 Richard Bovet, *Pandaemonium, or the devil's cloyster*, 1684, p. 231. These stories may have been shaped by the Bible's most famous exorcism, the episode of the Gadarene swine. These beliefs persisted into the nineteenth century; see for instance Robert Hunt, *Popular Romances of the West of England*, London, 1865, 3rd edn, 1881, p. 78.

22 *Depositions and other Ecclesiastical Proceedings from the courts of Durham*, ed. James Raine, Surtees Society, vol. 21 (1845), p. 100.

23 For a medieval charm to displace illness onto running water, see Kieckhefer, *Magic*, p. 65.

24 *The triall of Master Dorrell*, 1597, pp. 99–103.

25 Addy, *Household Tales*, p. 71.

26 Edmond Bower, *Dr Lambe Revived, or witchcraft condemned in Anne Bodenham, a servant of his*, 1653, p. 8.

27 J. C. Atkinson, *Forty Years in a Moorland Parish*, 1891, pp. 45–6.

28 *Dr Lambe revived*, p. 8.

29 *A true narration of some of those witchcrafts which Mary, wife of Henry Smith, glover, did practice*, 1616, in Ewen, *WD*, pp. 230. For contemporary collections of recipes, see Thomas Dawson, *The good housewife's jewel*, 1585, and Gervase Markham, *The English hus-wife*, 1615. For spells involving urine, see Ewen, *WD*, pp. 230, 363, 364, 386, 390.

30 C. L'Estrange Ewen, *Witch Hunting and Witch Trials*, 1929, p. 295.

31 *Dr Lambe's darling*, p. 6; *YD* p. 191.

32 *The triall of Master Dorrell*, pp. 102–3.

33 BL, MSS Sloane 973, fo. 7, a Northampton case of 1612, transcription in Ewen, *WD*, p. 211.

34 *A most certain, strange and true discovery of a witch, being taken by some of the Parliaments forces*, 1643.

35 Peter Stallybrass and Ann Rosalind Jones, 'The politics of *Astrophil and Stella'*, *Studies in English Literature*, 24 (1984), pp. 53–68.

36 Theweleit, *Male Fantasies*.

37 The notion is mentioned by Reginald Scot and George Gifford, but not by any deponents I have encountered.

38 Ruth L. Tongue, *Somerset Folklore*, ed. K. M. Briggs, London: Folklore Society, 1965, p. 144.

39 *YD*, p. 58. It is ambiguous in this deposition whether Rennard apologises or the witch; in either case, the act is the outcome of Mistress Rennard's agency in going to visit the troublemaker.

40 *YD*, pp. 8–9.

41 Goody Cross: Bodleian MSS Ashmole 1730, fo. 164^{v}; Anne Ellis: Ewen, *WD*, 332–3.

42 *YD*, p. 38.

43 *YD*, p. 8. In societies in modern Europe which still believe in 'the eye' and other forms of supernatural malevolence, people are reluctant to talk about such matters or even to name them for fear of increasing their power over them, and also from a structural dislike of sharing their views with others; see Michael Herzfeld,

Anthropology through the Looking-Glass: Critical Ethnography in the Margins of Europe, Cambridge: Cambridge University Press, 1987.

44 All this pertains to the populace; the gentry had other forms of agency and prevention available. Often markedly more reluctant to believe that witchcraft had occurred, they could consult a wide range of professionals including doctors and clergy, as well as seeking advice from cunning folk. Characteristically, this took power and initiative from women and put it in the hands of *paterfamilias*, the doctor and the minister. Sometimes the women of gentry families are evidently the ones who suggest popular remedies where doctors and prayers had failed; see for example *The witches of Warboys* 1593, in Rosen, *Witchcraft*, pp. 240ff, Ewen, *WD*, p. 173.

45 Favret-Saada, *Deadly Words*, pp. 70–3, 103–4.

46 'A brief abstract of the arraignment of nine witches at Northampton', 1612, BL, MSS Sloane 972, fo. 7, transcribed in Ewen, *WD*, p. 211.

47 *A collection of modern relations of matter of fact concerning witches and witchcraft upon the persons of people*, 1693, pp. 50–1.

48 For a fascinating reading of the problematic and gendered grotesqueness of the witch's body in Friuli which suggests parallels as well as differences with the English idea of the witch, see Luisa Accati, 'The spirit of fornication: virtue of the soul and virtue of the body in Fruili, 1600–1800', trans. Margaret A. Galucci, in *Sex and Gender in Historical Perspective*, ed. Edward Muir and Guido Ruggiero, Baltimore and London: Johns Hopkins University Press, 1990, pp. 110–40.

49 This too was still going in the nineteenth century: Addy, *Household Tales*, p. 171.

50 Kerke: Ewen, *WD*, p. 191; Guppy: Ewen, *Star Chamber* p. 26, France: *YD* pp. 51–2; Atkins: Ewen, *WD*, p. 174; Stranger: *YD*, p. 113; Wagg: Ewen, *WD* p. 319; Brooks: Ewen, *WD*, pp. 336–7; Style, *A rehearsal both straung and true, of hainous and horrible actes comitted by Elizabeth Stile, alias, Rockingham, Mother Dutten, Mother Devell, Mother Margaret, fower notorious witches, apprehended at winsore*, 1579, in Rosen, *Witchcraft*, p. 89.

51 *A rehearsal*, in Rosen, *Witchcraft*, p. 89.

52 *Hertford County Records*, vol. I, ed. W. J. Hardy, 1905, p. 137.

53 *YD*, pp. 96–7.

54 *Records of the County of Wilts*, ed. B. H. Cunnington, Devizes, 1932, pp. 155–6.

55 J. A. Brooks, *Ghosts and Witches of the Cotswolds*, Norwich: Jarrold, 1981, p. 16.

56 On the English witchmark and its peculiarities, see Keith Thomas, *Religion and the Decline of Magic*, Harmondsworth: Penguin, 1971, pp. 530–1; the witchmark was given official status in the Act of 1604, which made it a felony to entertain or feed spirits. See also Clive Holmes, 'Women: witnesses and witches', *Past and Present*, 140 (1993) pp. 67–9, and see Chapter 9.

57 *Generation of Animals*, 4.8; see also Galen, *De usu partium*, 2.639, and Hippocrates, *Aphorisms*, 5.37, 52; Isidore of Seville, *Etymologiarum*, 11. 1. 77; Bartholomaeus, *Properties of Things*, 5.34.

58 Jacques Guillimeau, *Child-birth*, 1612. Guillimeau was a pupil of Ambroise Paré, and his book was popular; see Samuel Radbill, 'Pediatrics', in *Medicine in Seventeenth-Century England*, ed. Allen G. Debos, Berkeley: University of California Press, 1972, p. 239. See also Laurent Joubert, *Erreurs populaires*, Bordeaux, 1579, p. 451.

59 Helkiah Crooke, *Microcosmographia*, 1615, 3.20.

60 Desiderius Erasmus, *The Colloquies of Erasmus*, ed. and trans. Craig R. Thompson, Chicago: University of Chicago Press, 1965, p. 273; Luther also believed in breastfeeding as a maternal duty, 'The estate of marriage', in *Works*, vol. 45, p. 40.

61 Guillimeau, *Child-birth*, p. 5; John Jones, *The art of preserving bodie and soule*; A. M., *A rich closet of physical secrets*, 1652.

62 Wallington, cited in Linda Pollock, *Forgotten Children: Parent–Child Relations from*

1500 to 1900, Cambridge: Cambridge University Press, 1983. Alice Thornton in *Her own life: Autobiographical Writings of Seventeenth-Century Englishwomen*, ed. Elspeth Graham *et al.*, London: Routledge, 1989, p. 157.

63 The fear expressed most often was that breastfeeding had a contraceptive effect; this was a worry primarily for the upper classes, however.

64 Guillimeau, *Child-birth*, p. 7. See Christine Klapisch-Zuber, *Women, Family and Ritual in Renaissance Italy*, trans. Lydia G. Cochrane, Chicago: Chicago University Press, 1985, ch. 7.

65 Klapisch-Zuber, *Women, Family and Ritual*, p. 161. On maternal power to shape the body, see my D. Phil thesis, 'Gender, power and the body: some figurations of femininity in Milton and seventeenth-century women's writing', Oxford, 1991, section 2, on monsters.

66 Aristotle, *The Parts of Animals*, 4.10; Albertus Magnus, *Quaestiones*, 2.13–6.

67 Guillimeau, *Child-birth*, p. 13; Radbill, 'Pediatrics', p. 251.

68 Iris Marion Young, 'Breasted Experience: The look and the feeling', in *Throwing Like a Girl and Other Essays*, Ithaca and London: Cornell University Press, 1992, pp. 189–209.

69 Joyce McDougall, *Theatres of the Mind: Illusion and Truth on the Psychoanalytic Stage*, London: Free Association Books, 1986, p. 184.

70 Leesenings: either loosenings, or lees (dregs). This is the jailer's word, and may refer to a midwifery term for kinds of breast secretion. The fact that the author of the pamphlet does not know its meaning suggests that his account is based very closely on the jailer's description.

71 *A true and particular observation of a notable piece of witchcraft practised by John Samuel the father, Alice Samuel the mother, and Agnes Samuel the daughter, of Warboys in the county of Huntingdon*, 1589, in Rosen, *Witchcraft*, pp. 296–7.

72 On monsters and display, see Purkiss, 'Gender, power and the body', section 2, ch. 4.

73 In England, midwives' main involvement with witchcraft cases was in searching for the witchmark at which the familiar was thought to suckle. Matthew Hopkins travelled with a female midwife and witchfinder. For a case where this role was taken over by the nascent male medical establishment – resulting in the announcement that the women involved were innocent – see Ch 9.

74 Rosen has a useful index of familiars' names, which allows the reader to see a full conspectus at a glance, *Witchcraft*, p. 396. On fairy names, see Katherine Briggs, *The Anatomy of Puck*, London: Routledge and Kegan Paul, 1959, and *A Dictionary of Fairies*, Hammondsworth: Penguin, 1976.

75 Alice Manfield confessed to having a familiar called Puppet, also known as Mommet, while Joan Pechey 'denieth that she hath or ever had any puppets, spirits or mommets, or that she had any spirits which she bought', *A true and just record . . . taken at St Ores*, in Rosen, *Witchcraft*, p. 129, hereafter *TJR*.

76 On women prophets as mothers and infants, see my 'Producing the voice, consuming the body; women prophets in the seventeenth century, in *Women, Writing, History*, ed. Isobel Grundy and Susan Wiseman, London: Batsford, 1992, pp. 139–58, esp. pp. 146–7.

77 Ewen, *WH*, p. 295.

78 Malcolm Gaskill, 'Witchcraft and power in early modern England: the case of Margaret Moore', in *Women, Crime and the Courts in Early Modern England*, ed. Jenny Kermode and Garthine Walker, London: UCL Press, 1994, pp. 125–45.

79 The case is transcribed in *East Anglian Notes and Queries*, 13 (1909), pp. 277–8.

80 BL, MSS Add 27402, in Ewen, *WH*, pp. 296, 299.

81 Rosen, *Witchcraft*, p. 74; this is a story which cannot help but recall the myth of the midwife-witch-cum-abortionist, but here the point is that Elizabeth Francis has clearly understood her own efforts to procure an abortion for herself in 'moral' terms.

82 See Jack Zipes, *The Brothers Grimm: From Enchanted Forests to the Modern World*, London: Routledge, 1988, pp. 75, 120.
83 *A rehearsal*, in Rosen, *Witchcraft*, p. 88.
84 *The wonderful discoverie . . . in Lancaster*, in Rosen, *Witchcraft*, pp. 362–3.
85 *The wonderful discoverie*, p. 363.
86 For a brilliant analysis of the centrality of commensality to community, see Elias Canetti, *Crowds and Power*, trans. Carol Stewart, Harmondsworth: Penguin, 1973.
87 For an especially clear and grim instance, see 'Yallery Brown', in 'Legends of the Lincolnshire Cars', *Folklore* 11 (1891).
88 See Thomas, *Religion*, pp. 620–3. In one case, the familiar is a different kind of protector, a husband: One witch deposed that she was married to the devil, for instance: 'the devil appeared to her like a man and that she was married to him in another parish and that he lived with her 3 years and that she had 2 children by him in that time which were changelings . . . it were 60 years since the devil wooed her to marry him . . . he had that carnal use of her but was cold and enjoined her before marriage to deny God and Christ (Ewen, *WD*, pp. 303–4).
89 *A true and particular observation*, in Rosen, *Witchcraft*, p. 280.
90 BL, MSS Add. 27402, fos. 104–21, in Ewen, *WH* p. 293, Suffolk 1645.
91 *The wonderful discovery*, in Rosen, *Witchcraft*, p. 381.
92 *TJR*, p. 125.
93 *TJR*, p. 125; Joan Upney, *The apprehension and confession of three notorious witches*, 1589, in Rosen, *Witchcraft*, p. 186.
94 Lyndal Roper, 'Witchcraft and fantasy in early modern Germany', *History Workshop Journal*, 32 (1991), p. 21.
95 Holinshead, *Chronicles* in Rosen, *Witchcraft*, p. 165.
96 Ewen, *WH*, pp. 304, 306.

6 Self-fashioning by women

Choosing to be a witch

> World is crazier and more of it than we think
> Incorrigibly plural.
>
> Louis MacNeice, 'Snow'

We rarely think of witches in connection with agency. Agency is the power to shape one's own life and story. Being accused of witchcraft is thought to remove your identity and replace it with one that is not of your choosing. Having a reputation for witchcraft is seen as something which is done to women, not something they do. Anyone who participates in such labelling is seen as the mouthpiece of a patriarchal ideology of submission. The agency of witches in shaping their lives, reputations and confessions is thereby erased. Women involved with witchcraft entered vigorously into a struggle to control the meaning of their own lives. Usually, we know about their activities because they eventually lost the fight to determine how they were seen and what stories could be told about them. This should not lead us to underrate their energy and ability, even if the version of that story which has come down to us was written by others. Some women actively sought a social identity as magic-users, though not necessarily as witches. Others accepted and reinterpreted the identity of witch when it was suggested to them by others. Still others showed a different kind of agency: they created stories about themselves using cultural materials which had become devalued by the elite. Finally, women's confessions show women accused of witchcraft shaping their own stories.

Female agency is most visible as a struggle between different ways of interpreting the world; cracks in apparently seamless pamphlets or confessions often signify broader faultlines in early modern society as a whole. The denunciation of Anne Bodenham and Anne Jefferies as users of evil magic pointed to their adherence to older, Royalist, traditions disliked by the godly. Their opponents were not necessarily using the term 'witch' disingenuously to get rid of opponents; they may genuinely have interpreted ungodliness as tantamount to a pact with Satan. On the other hand, when the term 'witch' was used of Joan Upney, a different kind of discursive fissure is revealed. There was no longer any place in discourse for someone with her beliefs. 'Witchcraft' became a dumpster for ideas of the supernatural which the better-educated had begun to discard. In one sense, it is difficult to make claims for the agency of poor baffled Joan Upney, whose statements in court reveal inability to grasp the nature of the charges laid against her. However, Joan's adherence to a world-view and a notion of the supernatural profoundly alien to the authoritative discourses enshrined in the witchcraft statutes also demonstrate her relative independence of the very ideologies that the godly were trying to inculcate in the people. Her ignorance of them made her vulnerable when they were mapped awkwardly onto her as part of a witch-hunt, but she had been free of them previously in the sense that she had never troubled her head about them until some neighbours acccused her of being a witch.[1]

Just how did women become witches – to their neighbours, to themselves? Given the centrality of maternity and of the maternal body to understandings of the witch, we might be tempted to analyse the idea that witchcraft runs in families in bodily terms. One of the most common ways of identifying a witch was to spot a member of a family known to contain witches. Daughters and even sons of accused or convicted witches were very often accused themselves, usually later in life. Instances are almost too numerous to cite. They include Alice Chaundler, hanged at Malvern in 1572, whose daughter Ellen Smith was accused in 1579, and the witches of the Lancashire trial of 1612/13.[2] Margaret Morton was bluntly said to be suspect because 'her mother and sister, who are now both dead, were suspected to be the like'.[3] Early modern culture lacked a theory of genetics. In godly circles at least, congenital causes were not simply biological, but could also be understood morally. Offspring were thought to reflect the moral state of their parents. Incest could result in the birth of a monstrous child, for example, which therefore testified to the sin of its parents. Race, to us a matter of genetics, was a mystery to early modern people.[4]

Despite these ideas about inheritance, however, early modern writers – even the learned – rarely suggest that witchcraft is inscribed in the body by the parents. Instead, for villagers and townsfolk, witchcraft runs in families in the same way that shoemaking and brewing do. It is a trade, and trades in early modern society are very often family affairs. People expected to hand on both skill and business to their children. Housewifery, too, with its close connections with witchcraft, was handed down as an economic skill from mother to daughter.[5] Consequently, it's not surprising to learn that Elizabeth Frauncis's grandmother, Mother Eve, is said to have *taught* her witchcraft. Frauncis 'learned this art of witchcraft at the age of 12 years, of her grandmother, whose name was Mother Eve of Hatfield Peveral, deceased'.[6] Her grandmother also taught her how to enter into a pact with Satan, or 'to renounce God and his word', in a parody of the baptismal service in which the godparents are asked 'Do you renounce Satan and all his works?' At the Lancashire trial of 1613, the nine-year-old Jennet Device describes learning a charm from her mother, as other children might learn prayers or recipes. Mother Sutton had her daughter resident with her 'as some say, to make her a scholar unto the devil himself'.[7] Eventually, spells and familiars circulate around the village or town almost as commodities, almost like the household items and small sums of money which could be the occasions of witchcraft. Witchcraft itself is caught up in the currents which flow between households and individuals, and whose maintenance and regulation is itself a household task. For instance, Elizabeth Frauncis is taught witchcraft by her grandmother, but she is soon instructing a friend rather than a relative, Agnes Waterhouse. By giving Agnes Waterhouse her cat familiar, Frauncis repeats the initiation performed on her, 'and taught her as she was instructed before by her grandmother Eve'.[8]

It was a short step from there to seeing witchcraft as analogous to a family business or minor profession. Both Ursula Kempe, whom we have already met, and Anne Bodenham presented themselves as offering services to their communities as cunning women or unwitchers. In Ursula's case, these skills had been acquired by her contact with a cunning woman from a distant village, who taught her a charm. Ursula then offered that charm (unwitching) to her acquaintances, acquiring a reputation for skill. This acquisition of skill from a professional 'master' is even more important in Anne Bodenham's case. She was employed as a servant by the notorious Dr Lambe, 'Buckingham's wizard', a cunning man and prognosticator who eventually met his death at the hands of an angry London mob. Fascinated by his predictions, she asked him to employ her and to teach her his trade – or so she claimed. For some years after, she applied his methods, discovering stolen objects, predicting lucky and unlucky days, and raising spirits by 'reading in some of his books'.[9] Dr Lambe was one of the best-known cunning men in the country; if Bodenham wished to advertise (or fantasise) an origin for her magical 'arts', she could have lighted upon him as her teacher, one able to lend her a certain notoriety, if not legitimacy.[10] The narrative Bodenham offers is typical of the normal process by which women eventually set themselves up in business. Women often inherited a business or trade from a husband, father or master; there are instances of this in brewing, clothmaking and printing.[11] This may point to the simple truth of Bodenham's story, but it may also show her reuse of cultural materials and stories to fashion her own identity as a witch. At the same time, the role of master was close to that of husband or father, close enough, at any rate, for the other principal pamphlet on Bodenham to represent her witchcraft as familial, even sexual; this assimilates her to Lambe's reputation as a whoremaster who supplied Buckingham with women.[12] This does not signify exciting unruly female sexuality recuperated as witchcraft, but the opposite: witchcraft (understood as a business) recuperated as whoredom. Anne Bodenham evaded the image of the formless body, only to have another figure of female chaos close on her from another direction.

Anne Bodenham claimed that 'she had learned much in Dr Lambe's service, and she reading in some of his books, with his help learned her art, by which she . . . had gotten many a penny'.[13] The London mob who killed Lambe may have made a link between magic and political culture rather different from the one being promoted by the absolutism of the Stuart monarchy. For them, Lambe's activities on behalf of the Duke of Buckingham were a sign of the illegitimacy of that grandee's influence.[14] In a lesser way, national and public issues were also entangled with the fate of Lambe's 'darling', Anne Bodenham, who was hanged in 1653, and whose trial is reported as 'a warning piece for England and Scotland'.[15] Certainly Bodenham's story contains some dramatisations of familiar tussles, some local and some national: between the godly and those keen to preserve traditional ways, between rural and urban, between masters and servants and especially in relation to the theme of the servant's treachery, always potent during the period of the English republic.[16] As the pamphlet narrative unfolds, it becomes clear that the story being told is tilted towards creating a portrait of Bodenham as the emblem of everything which Parliament and the English republic oppose: the abuse of power and privilege, social disorder, the sacrilegious 'traditional ways' of church-ales and alehouses, disorderly femininity, ungodliness amounting to diabolism.[17] All this inflection depends on the central trope of Anne Bodenham as Lambe's 'darling'; by reminding the public of Lambe, the pamphlet also recalls his master Buckingham and the worst excesses of Stuart rule.

The link between Bodenham and Lambe acted to authenticate Bodenham's power. She established herself not as a run-of-the-mill country cunning woman, but as a kind of female wizard. This was a much more theatrical role than that of village witch or cunning woman, involving authority and appearance of learning normally gendered male in the early modern period. The signs of this are her use of a scrying-glass, the incantatory circle and books rather than oral charms.[18] These gestures at Paracelsian magic involve Bodenham in the role of the mage who penetrates the secrets of nature, a role usually linked with a phallic gaze at a feminised object. The use of books and learned incantations, too, involves an appropriation of male rhetorics of authority. Anne Bodenham seems to have been able to borrow the role of male magus from Lambe, and with it the mage's authority. Her use of this role makes unequivocal her deliberate self-fashioning as a practitioner of magic. Unless the pamphlet is fabricated, Bodenham is an instance of a woman deliberately courting a witch's reputation.

Virtually the whole of the pamphlet about Bodenham is taken up with the deposition of Anne Styles. What survives is Styles's story, mediated by her godly interlocutor Edmond Bower, the author of the pamphlet, and by his separate account of meeting Bodenham herself. Anne Styles gives herself a leading, equivocal part in the story she tells. Acting first as Bodenham's client, and then as a kind of apprentice to her, Styles also portrays herself as Bodenham's principal victim, a prey to fits, possession and other signs of bewitchment. Like many women, Styles first consulted one of the cunning folk about a missing object, a silver spoon belonging to her master, Richard Goddard. The cunning woman in question was Anne Bodenham. Bodenham failed to recover the spoon, but soon Styles was back again, asking about some money on behalf of her master's son-in-law, a man named Thomas Mason. On this occasion, too, Bodenham managed to impress Styles without actually doing what had been asked of her.[19] What thrilled the maid was Bodenham's exotic rituals, and her books: 'She opened three books, in which there seemed to be several pictures, and amongst the rest the picture of the devil, to the Maid's appearance, with his cloven feet and claws'.[20] The appearance of the devil's picture seems to confirm for Styles that Bodenham can really conjure him. Bodenham also produces a crystal, or 'green glass' through which the maid sees all the affairs of her employers' household passing. Gradually, Anne Styles encounters more and more of Bodenham's theatrical repertoire: the magic circle, the cauldron, the demons Satan, Lucifer, Beelzebub, the summoning of a wind. After Styles's report, the family are impressed with Bodenham, resulting in increased contact between Styles and Bodenham as she is sent there more often. The master of the house sends 'to know whether a Master Rawley intended mischief against him, having lost money to him at cards'. Bodenham confirms this, and gives him a charm to keep him safe; 'and took a piece of paper and put therein yellow powder, and so made it up in a cross figure'.[21] She also provides him with charms against bailiffs, and performs a conjuration to see whether he will win his lawsuit against his father-in-law.

All these incidents reveal the tensions between the early modern household and the outside world. Faced with a potentially genuine wisewoman, the first instinct is to use magic as an art to find the mind's construction in the face, or more crudely, to spy on other people. Magic seems to the master of the house a way to get on in the world; it gives the man with access to it an edge. This was how it seemed to Lambe and Buckingham, too. More importantly, the consultations reveal stresses within the family, in the Rosewell–Goddard–Mason household which employed Anne Styles as a maid, tensions between generations around the question of money, illustrating the way the enterprise culture of early modern Britain could strain family relations. Reconstructing the family from the pamphlet, it seems that the older generation and their married children are at odds. For while Thomas Mason is engaged in a lawsuit with his father-in-law, Elizabeth Rosewell is afraid that her daughter-in-law Sarah is poisoning her, and sends Anne Styles to Anne Bodenham to find out whether her suspicions are justified. This is the undoing of both Styles and Bodenham. Initially, both are able to perceive and manipulate the fears and tensions of the family, but eventually they become scapegoats instead.

In her crystal glass, Bodenham shows Styles poison under the bed of one of the younger women, Sarah. Promising revenge, she makes up a potion for both daughters of vervain and dill, gathered by her demons from under the snow, and mixed with nail parings to 'rot their guts in their bellies'.[22] Bodenham stresses the need for maid and mistress to recite certain prayers and make the sign of the cross repeatedly when handling the draught, which added to their impression of its deadliness.[23] Eventually the daughters act against witch and maid. Bodenham has given Styles money to buy arsenic, to be put into the fire to prevent the poisoning. So when the daughters become suspicious, as well they might be when herbal tisanes are handed to them by family members frantically reciting the creed backwards, they point out that only Styles is known to have bought any poison. Unsurprisingly, Styles is sacked. Nonetheless, if she is to be believed, this may not have been altogether to the liking of Elizabeth Rosewell, who brought her her clothes and also some money for a final consultation with Anne Bodenham about the journey. The sign of the cross, the writing of the creeds and the powder in a cross shape may also suggest religious conflict between the family members, with the older generation less godly than the younger.

At this point, Bodenham apparently made an interesting offer. She 'earnestly desired the maid to live with her, and told her, that if she would do so, she would teach her to do as she did'. Bodenham was offering Styles the chance to follow in her footsteps as an apprentice to an older magic-user. At the time of her death, she was said to be eighty; she may have been searching for an heir. Understandably frightened by Bodenham's sudden transformation into a gigantic black cat, Anne Styles says no, and Bodenham then works a spell to ensure that Styles cannot give away her secrets: 'she must seal unto her body and blood not to discover her'.[24] Bodenham may have been thinking of her repertoire of unusually sophisticated magical tricks, whether or not learned from Lambe, but she may also have been thinking of the magistrates' probable reaction to her activities. Styles duly writes out a promise not to tell in her own blood, which is sealed with the gift of a piece of silver to Styles, and by two pins stuck through her headcloths. Like the rest of the repertoire of cunning spells in early modern England, this is a mixture of traditional magic (the pins) and more sophisticated demonological discourses (the blood pact), showing how Bodenham could synthesise diverse sources. Styles goes to London, but is followed by Mistress Goddard's sons-in-law, perhaps because they want to keep an eye on her. Importuned by them, she breaks her pledge of secrecy, with disastrous consequences. She falls into a trance, and on emerging is immediately seized by violent fits which continue even after she and Bodenham have both been imprisoned in Salisbury on poisoning charges. Her frenzies are so terrible that six men cannot hold her, and she believes them to be caused by the devil lodging inside her, tearing at her heart and bowels. Her possession signifies above all her involvement with Bodenham and her witchcraft. After a prayer session, Bower succeeds in transferring the malady from Anne Styles to Bodenham.

At one level, Styles's malady is the visible sign of Bodenham's witchcraft. Her dealings with the devil are marked first on Styles's body, and then on her own. At another level, both Styles and Bodenham were arrested on suspicion of poisoning, not for witchcraft. To the court at Salisbury, as opposed to Edmond Bower, Styles is not an injured innocent, drawn into Satanic circles against her will and thoroughly punished for it, but that bugbear of the middle and upper classes, the treacherous servant. It is not possible to reconstruct the quarrel in the Rosewell–Mason family in any detail, but it seems to have involved a wholesale rebellion of children and their spouses against aged parents, motivated by greed.

Elizabeth Rosewell's daughters-in-law were a latter-day Goneril and Regan, plotting to get rid of her in order to enjoy her estate. The fact that an intergenerational lawsuit was going on at the same time must have made Rosewell more nervous. This was exactly the kind of family strife which both sides pointed to as an outcome of misrule in the commonwealth; how, asked everyone, can family authority be maintained, when state authority is constantly called into question by the activities of the monarch/his rebellious subjects?[25] Like the image-magics and poison plots which courtiers feared in Elizabeth's reign, poison stands for danger from within the house or community. If Elizabeth Rosewell could not trust her servants to protect her, whom could she trust? In this context, Styles's convulsing body may have looked like a providential sign of God's judgement.

In prison, Styles sickens again, and before long both women are rolling and howling spectacularly. As always in possession cases, they are brought together, and the situation is resolved when the justice's clerk notices that Bodenham is wearing green silk string around her neck with a bag attached; it turns out to contain powder, white paper and seeds, and for Bodenham it plainly represents her power over the maid and perhaps over the devil, for when it is removed, she screams dramatically that 'her jewel was taken from her, her life was lost'.[26] Either Bower or Anne has recourse to the language of defloration to describe its loss; chastity is often a jewel, and to be undone is to be unchaste. In this case, the bag represents the opening of the witch's body which in Continental discourse was especially important for disclosing and hence ending her power over others.

But Bodenham is still not cowed. She attempts to escape custody by asking for liberty to fetch her book of charms, through which she might discover the whereabouts of a thousand pounds in the ground of Wilton, hidden by the old Earl of Pembroke. This is suspiciously like the kind of offer made by Lambe to his Worcester gaolers; either Bodenham or Bower is copying Lambe.[27] Bodenham is struggling for ale: she offers to make a toad jump out of her purse in exchange for six bottles and after being condemned to death, she blames Bower for her prosecution, and offers to give her books to a Salisbury grocer named Langley, and to teach him her art. Finally, she makes a wonderfully bad end. There is no sense in which she can be figured as repentant as an outcome of all this interrogation and intervention. She is resolved to be hanged, and asks to be buried below the gallows; she calls endlessly for drink, and Bower is shocked to report that 'but for restraint' she would have died drunk. She tries to obtain a knife and kill herself, not out of fear, but out of a wish to refuse the ceremonial of hanging. Her progress to the scaffold is equally unceremonious; she calls for drink at every house on the way, 'and was very passionate when denied', and on arrival at the scaffold, she tries to mount the ladder at once, and has to be held back by the clergyman. He presses her to confess and she utterly refuses. Finally mounting the ladder, she tries to turn herself off, but is prevented by the executioner. At the very last moment, she is defiant; he asks for her forgiveness, and she replies 'Forgive thee? A pox on thee, turn me off'.[28]

In Bower's story, this becomes the archetypal bad end, perhaps generic rather than true. Bodenham refuses to submit to Providence. Refusing the handling of church and state, she refuses divine authority.[29] To an audience of the godly, Bodenham is not agreeably feisty, but troublingly rebellious, though not all her neighbours might have agreed with this understanding of her defiance. It is significant in this context that the trial and execution took place in Salisbury, bastion of the godly, while Bodenham was from Fisherton Anger, part of what David Underdown has described as the more tradition-orientated, old-fashioned, anti-Puritan villages of the Wiltshire downs.[30] The other crucial point is the pamphlet account's emphasis on Anne's desire for drink, not a usual figure in accounts of witchcraft. To the godly Bower, the idea of dying drunk is frightful; the spectacle of Bodenham's desperation for drink is plainly intended as an awful warning of the dangers of drink directed at the defenders of church-ales and other dubious and vaguely Stuart pastimes.[31] Whether or not Bodenham really did see less harm in a few bottles of ale than did Edmond Bower, her representation here acts as a powerful way to link the drinking and 'church-ales' which the godly disliked with the despised figure of the witch.[32] Anne's drinking is a synecdoche of the old, careless ways which the godly tried to expunge from Wiltshire, often unsuccessfully. For the godly, such sins were always already linked with the devil and hence with witchcraft. Writing on Wiltshire in the late seventeenth century, Aubrey thought that the godly inhabitants of the 'cheese country' to the north were more likely to fear witches and night-hags.[33]

If Bower's account is true, however, it implies that Bodenham was not merely resisting her figuration as a witch, but also resisting a whole package of identities in favour of a defiant adherence to the old ways of the ungodly. Calling for ale on her way to the scaffold may have arisen less from a wish to die insensible as from the same refusal of godliness which led her to evade the clergyman stationed at the foot of the scaffold and the opportunity to fall in with his godly discourse in a public confession. As a woman of eighty, Bodenham might have been able to remember a time before the godly dominated affairs in Salisbury. To the diligent Puritan, her fierce display of bodily desire for drink, her reckless courage and her refusal to submit to state authority or the divine authority it represented would have seemed not only an awful warning, but also a sign of the difficulty of the task facing them in the region. Bodenham's 'witchcraft' may even have been part of that resistance. Though not portrayed as 'traditional' village witchcraft, or even as the traditional charming of the cunning woman, it nevertheless remains linked with the bad old world through the figure of Dr Lambe, emblem of royal corruption. Bodenham's loyalty to Lambe's methods may have been a signifier of her dislike of the godly, and in any case, what better way was there to annoy them than to set up in business as a practitioner of magic? There might have been much to be gained from being a witch, not only as a business, but also as a way of asserting a contested political and personal identity through troubled times. Bodenham's case shows just how weak and ineffectual the notion of pact witchcraft was as a means of controlling women and rendering them quiescent, for she first exploits elite discourses of conjuration and then summarily rejects godly interpretations of her actions. Bodenham got some pleasure and satisfaction from her self-fashioning as a witch, even if it also killed her.

This book has already looked at the emotional and narrative reasons why deponents might have wanted to figure one of their neighbours as a witch, but must also look at the way this process worked pragmatically. Even some court depositions, let alone narratives told directly to a wandering author or prison clergymen, were elicited by questioning, though less so than confession.[34] What might originally have been mild doubt, or even a different if related series of supernatural beliefs, becomes converted into the figure of a witch in questioning. While Anne Bodenham was unequivocally a cunning woman, other cases involved identifying as witch a neighbour who may never have purported to practise even the most benign magic. What is published as a piece of continuous prose may represent a negotiation between questioner and speaker. This itself grants unusual power to women of the labouring poor, whose opportunities to inflect what the clergy and the law said were ordinarily exceedingly limited.

Admittedly, some cases involve fairly straightforward acculturation (to use Muchembled's term): fairy-beliefs are converted into witch-beliefs, for instance, though even this represents a compromise between the deponent's sense of likelihood and that of the questioner. Often the deponent is saying things that the JPs find incredible.[35] Most JPs and clergymen are demonologists or sceptics, so any beliefs which do not fit either of these categories are more likely to be 'genuinely popular', and are also more likely to give rise to negotiation. 'Popular' beliefs are not single or stable. While some beliefs about witches are very old, others are more difficult to date, and still others are visibly changing in response to political, and social pressures. There were divisions within communities. As we have seen in Anne Bodenham's case, communities could be split between traditionalists and the godly, or between recusants and Protestants. Even old rhymes cited in good faith by one deponent are not necessarily widely trusted or known by others. Such divisions give opportunities for early modern deponents to insert their own beliefs and values into traditional stories and customs, or to assert their separation from them.

People in towns saw stage plays and read or heard ballads and pamphlets. Their neighbours were not their sole source of witch-beliefs and stories, though individuals might reinterpret the plots of plays and chapbooks to fit their own preconceptions. Nothing could have been more obviously 'foreign' or 'bookish' than the magic practised by Anne Bodenham, yet it impressed her fellow villagers as authoritative and was also part of her involvement in a local dispute. Some deponents seem actually to be influenced by stories of recent cases, and this is especially true of large and important local cases. Stories told by deponents or as confessions are often retold in that locale, sometimes becoming assimilated to more local beliefs as this happens. Deponents and accused alike did not passively spout an ideology of witchcraft common to all the Folk, but used a mass of 'elite' and 'popular' materials creatively to fashion their own stories about witches and reflect their own concerns, agendas and conflicts.

This can be shown by looking at the way witchcraft depositions and confessions reuse other material, material not naturally associated with witchcraft by the learned, but which came to be associated with it after being taken up in trials and also in polemics. I shall look at three instances: the reuse of Catholic beliefs in charms and spells, the reuse of fairy-beliefs in depositions and confessions concerning witchcraft, and the use of folktales. All three are 'old' beliefs; they predate the inception of the witchcraft statues. Their recurrence in witch-depositions shows that the figure of the witch does not spring straight from the head of Kramer or Sprenger, but is mediated by familiar materials. Though these materials were familiar, they were also fast becoming subjugated knowledges, however. Catholic rituals were proscribed; fairy-beliefs were located in the superstitious past by elite sceptics like Reginald Scot; folktales were part of a popular culture increasingly frowned on by the godly and smiled at indulgently by the educated elite. That such subjugated knowledges should be attached to the figure of the witch, nearly always a female figure, by women storytellers, is not altogether surprising. Women are characteristically the bearers of this kind of knowledge, the repositories of what has been lost, and the site of its shattering, uncanny return. As Cixous and Clément point out, 'each time there is a repetition of memories, a return of the repressed, it will be in a specific cultural and historical context'.[36]

When dealing with this collection of cultural hot potatoes, we must be cautious. For instance, Catholic materials as pretexts for witch-stories are common, but this is an area where reporters, from JPs to pamphleteers, had an interest in stressing these elements. This was definitely a matter in which the elite had a stake. Opponents of Catholicism tended to conflate it with witchcraft. Reginald Scot saw witch-beliefs as tinged with popery, while the exorcism crisis of the early seventeenth century confirmed Anglicans' worst fears about the fomentation of witch-fears by papists. It was common to decry popery and the mass as witchcraft, or simply to fail to make distinctions between them.[37] For the godly, papists were witches; indeed, anyone ungodly who practised traditional ritual might be viewed as trafficking with Satan. There seems no warrant for Edmond Bower's assertion that Anne Bodenham was 'much addicted to Popery'; her only popish gesture is a cross-shaped powder.[38] What he meant was that Bodenham was part of a traditional culture which still used rituals and practices which seemed tantamount to either devil-worship or Catholicism to their godly critics.

However, the accused often provided plenty of ammunition for such charges. The populace often saw Catholic prayers and rituals in terms of magic.[39] As recollection of an English Catholic church waned and the materials of popular worship were increasingly in the hands of ordinary people, without any institutional support, one of the aspects of the pre-Reformation Catholic church which survived best was its power to give supernatural agency to the believer.

Although the church had never been enthusiastic about believers using blessed bread or holy water for medicinal purposes, and although it always kept a wary eye on the self-fashioning of popular devotions, popular Catholicism was in good shape before the Reformation in part because it made itself available to relatively uneducated people, and this meant it could hardly avoid what the church hierarchy would have seen as misuse of Catholic rituals.[40] (In my own supposedly liberal, post-Vatican II Catholic childhood, I have seen young girls rushing in and out of church a hundred times on All Souls' Day to get the maximum number of souls out of purgatory. The girls were alight with a sense of their own power to command God.) What survived of Catholicism after the Reformation was its sense of drama, its use of props, its ritual learned prayers, all of which offered the laity a chance to act on their own behalf. These were the very things educated Protestant people found most repugnant. Yet this may not indicate an elite dictation of discourses to a cowed populace so much as a genuine anxiety on the part of the elite about what people made of the church's fragmentary survivals.

These survivals may have had particular appeal for women, denied supernatural agency even as a fantasy by mainstream Anglicanism. The prominence given in some surviving charms to the figure of the Virgin Mary bears this out, but what is more important is that such charms allow women the power to intervene in the supernatural. In a providential, predestinarian universe, the church was (at least in theory) dominated by men, and a male God controlled all events. By contrast, popular Catholic survivalism offered the individual believer a chance to alter or even compel the course of events, by healing, bewitching or unwitching. Midwives might have felt justified in a sense of bereavement at the Reformation, since Catholicism offered far more magical consolation to the woman in labour. One of the few midwives to be prosecuted for magic in England was Mistress Pepper, tried in Newcastle. She used a silver cross in healing, but though 'magical' by the mid-seventeenth century, this would once have been merely prayer.[41]

An instance of a dramatisation of the conflict between the Catholic church and the reformers through witchcraft comes from Essex in 1566. Agnes Waterhouse's familiar would only allow her to pray in Latin; at least, this was apparently the explanation she gave for refusing to pray. This is an unusual case for Essex, since in most cases the question of Catholicism did not arise so directly; it may be significant that it is so early. The 1566 pamphlet is replete with references to sending for the priest, suggesting a pre-Reformation world-view; Chelmsford, where the witches in this case were tried, was rather surprisingly still enjoying its Corpus Christi plays in the mid-1570s. Only five years before, a Catholic priest had been examined for hearing masses in Essex at New Hall.[42] Agnes Waterhouse cites her inability to pray in English as a transgression, but it is also obvious that it had only recently become one, and that Agnes was addressing a still-live local issue.

In other cases, the 'witch' is a cunning woman exploiting the forgottenness of

Catholicism and especially Latin to create an occult and magical impression. Mistress Pepper used a silver crucifix and holy water in her healing magic; some of the church relics buried by prudent presbyters at Elizabeth I's accession against the return of a Catholic monarch may have found their way into this kind of practice 'Boate [*beate*?] a god's name' was the distantly Latinate prayer of another northern suspect.[43] In still other cases, the witch is simply reusing terminology that once connected to an entire body of doctrine and practice in a decontextualised way. Even after the cult of the saints had been obliterated, the names of the saints might survive in invocations like the spell for recovering stolen goods by turning the sieve, or riddle: 'By St Peter and St Paul / If *X* has stolen *Y*'s *z* / Turn about riddle and shears and all'[44] This is very like the classic churning charm: 'Come butter come / Come butter come / Peter stands at the gate / Waiting for a butter cake / Come butter come'. The last of these seems to gesture at a greedy St Peter, one more like the clown of southern Italian folklore than the austere figure of elite medieval iconography. Being a churning charm, it is also a woman's charm. Yet all these charms are recorded in connection with witchcraft, which can only mean that over the course of an interrogation they had come to seem dubious even to their users.

Another instance of a popular confusion between Catholic survivalism and witchcraft comes from the huge Lancashire trial of 1613, unsurprisingly since Lancashire was thought to be a hotbed of recusancy. The pamphlet based on the trials contains two charms with obvious Catholic content. The first was used by Anne Whittle, alias Old Chattox, 'to help drink that was forspoken or bewitched':

> Three biters hast thou bitten
> The heart, ill eye, ill tongue,
> Three bitter shall be thy boot,
> Father, Son and Holy Ghost
> A god's name.
> Five paternosters, five aves
> and a creed,
> in worship of five wounds of our Lord.[45]

As Kittredge showed, this charm is a garbled version of one used for sick children earlier in the sixteenth century, and other versions of it have survived until relatively recent times in Scotland.[46] These charms, however, did not include the paternosters and aves which feature so prominently in Whittle's charm, and which make it read like an extract from a catechism or devotional manual which enjoins particular prayers for particular effects. Such prayers were a common part of medieval charms, but the idea was to say them in full.[47] If the prayers mentioned here are not just mysterious names, but are still being *said*, this reinforces Keith Thomas's argument that the medieval church provided comfort of a kind unobtainable after the Reformation. Whittle's charm is very close to one appearing as a spell against bewitchment in an early seventeenth century manuscript of magical spells, which concludes: 'say this 9 times over, and at every third time say a pater noster, an ave, and a creed.'[48] This charm either dates from pre-Reformation times or is deliberately harking back to them, as is Whittle. The five wounds are Whittle's addition; it may be significant that they were the insignia of the Pilgrimage of Grace, the series of northern risings of 1536–7 against Protestant reforms.[49] Although this was a long time ago by 1613, even by the standards of the venerable deponents Elizabeth Southern and Anne Whittle (both were over eighty), this may have given the five wounds special resonance in the north. This emphasises the role of the charm as a decaying record of half-forgotten history, being reduced to its power as sound by a process of forgetting its former context.

The second charm is recited not by an accused witch, but by the principal witness for the prosecution, the nine-year-old Jennet Device. Jennet said her mother taught her two prayers, the first (to get drink) was '*Crucifixus hoc signum vitam eternam*. Amen.' This garbled phrase might once have meant something like 'The cross of Christ gives eternal life', but it has become so detached from its original meaning as from its ritual context that assigning a meaning to it seems specious.[50] Even more intriguing is a prayer to cure one bewitched, which may be several prayers run together, by Jennet, by the JP or pamphleteer transcribing her words, or by Elizabeth Device herself or her daughter. I quote it in full, despite its length, because it constitutes an important instance of the conflation of religious ritual and magical ritual:

Upon Good Friday I will fast while I may,
Until I hear them knell
Our Lord's own bell;
Lord in his mass
With his twelve apostles good,
What hath he in his hand?
Ligh[t] in leath wand.[51]
What hath he in his other hand?
Heaven's door key.
Open, open heaven door-keys;
Stick, stick hell door.
Let chrism child
Go to it[s] mother mild.
What is yonder that casts a light so farrandly?[52]
Mine own dear son that's nailed to the tree.
He is nailed sore by the heart and hand
And holy brain pan.
Well is that man
That Friday spell can
His child to learn.
A cross of blue and another of red,

As good Lord was to the rood.
Gabriel laid him down to sleep
Upon the ground of holy weep;
Good Lord came walking by.
Sleepst thou, wakst thou, Gabriel?
No Lord I am stayed with stick and stake
That I can neither sleep nor wake.
Rise up Gabriel and go with me;
The stick nor stake shall never dere thee[53]
Sweet Jesus our Lord, Amen.[54]

Whether or not Jennet was telling the exact truth about her mother's use of this prayer, the text shows how culturally subjugated knowledges of the supernatural are open to one another, producing some very odd hybrids. Here, what were once prayers and devotions, sacred signs, are converted into magical rhymes, a process of conversion which at least partially depends on destroying their lucidity as the utterances of doctrine in order to make manifest their strength as words of power. This is in part a version of the notorious 'white paternoster', which was regarded as a papist charm by staunch Protestants. This 'prayer charm' is another instance, cited not in a witchcraft trial, but in a treatise on the survival of popery:

White paternoster, Saint Peter's brother,
What hast i'th' t'one hand? White book leaves
What hast i'th 'tother hand? Heaven gate keys.
Open heaven gate and stick hell gate;
And let every chrism child creep to its own mother.[55]

Early sixteenth-century conjurations by the Passion which enumerate 'the holy cross, nails three, crown of thorn' replicate the structure of the enumeration here. The prayer is also reminiscent of the devotions of popular (or once-popular) drama, including the miracle and mystery plays which were often remembered better by the laity than sermons. Some lines seem actually to be spoken by the Virgin Mary ('Mine own dear son that's nailed to the tree'); this part of the prayer is certainly dramatic, whether or not it derives from drama. In particular, the way stories in medieval dramas are interrupted by doctrinal assertions is replicated here.[56] These plays remained extremely popular even after the Reformation, and many locales signified as much by clinging to the plays or to the costumes or props which had been used in them. The words, too, might have been retained as objects of power by some who were not able to appreciate the cognitive attractions of Protestantism. The Catholic 'survivalists' in what the godly came to call 'the dark corners of the land' were especially keen to retain their playtexts; in Chester, Wakefield and York, plays were performed until the mid-1570s, so Elizabeth Southern, at least, might actually have seen one.[57]

At the same time, these prayers and sayings have been corrupted, and are now being enunciated by people who have little or no idea of the ecclesiastical or dramatic context into which they once fitted. As with the 'Latin' prayer, the corruption may take place at the level of the court records, the pamphleteer's transcription of them, or in the mind of the nine-year-old Jennet Device, or all three. In any case, the text before us is a series of fragmentary murmurs, containing names once rich in holy power but now containing only a remnant of that power. By weakening memories and releasing control of popular engagements with the supernatural, the reformers seem ironically to have brought about the very situation they feared: people mumbling spell-like prayers they did not understand, instead of reading their Bibles and accepting the instruction of the learned.

At any rate, that is how the pamphlet presents it. Thomas Potts, however, was writing for the London print market. His readers would have been expecting some signs of popery from the Lancashire witches. That this was so can be proved retrospectively. When various divines and privy councillors interviewed the suspects in the later Lancashire case of 1633, they were eagerly questioned about religion, praying and the Bible. It was the satisfactoriness of the women's answers which convinced the Bishop of Chester of their innocence.[58] The fact that the 1613 witches fulfilled Protestant expectations need not cast doubt on the veracity of Potts's report; he may merely be highlighting what his public expected to hear. If Potts's portrayal is accurate, then the 1613 witch-trial was in part a response to kinds of medieval magic that had come to seem indistinguishable from sorcery to Protestants. Like Anne Bodenham, the witches who used such traditional charms may have been consciously rejecting the new culture, rather than merely unable to say their prayers any other way. However garbled they became, the women would have known that such prayers were not regarded well by the Anglican church or the state; Jennet Device knew this too. Retaining a few magical charms might have been a way to resist the dominant culture.

Other strands of story and belief, also with their own rituals, were constantly woven into narratives of witchcraft, often in troubling ways, and these were beliefs in fairies, or spirits of the countryside. Some cunning folk claimed commerce with the fairies in an effort to distinguish themselves from witches. John Walsh was a cunning man, who under pressure stoutly denied that he had any familiars. But he claimed to have special access to the fairies, which enabled him to know whether people were bewitched:

> there be 3 kinds of fairies, white, green and black, which, when he is disposed to use, he speaketh with them upon hills whereas there is great heaps of earth, as namely in Dorsetshire. And between the hours of 12 and one at noon, or at midnight, he useth them, whereof, he saith, the black fairies be the worst.[59]

Later in his interrogation, it is apparent that his interrogators have interpreted this as a confession of pact witchcraft. Joan Tyrrye, a Somerset cunning woman, claimed to have met a fairy in Taunton market and 'come to him, thinking to make an acquaintance of him, and her sight was clean taken away for a time'. Joan's story is a reworking of the folktale of the woman who is blinded by the fairies after observing them.[60] The Civil War astrologer and cunning man William Lilly tells in his autobiography of conjuring the fairy queen for a terrified client, who ran away before she appeared.[61] Lilly was a celebrated figure, though a notorious one; Anne Bodenham excitably claimed that she could do as much as he with the right equipment. Here, however, he disavows witchcraft by replacing demons with figures that represent 'the old ways' and thus may signify his allegiance to Royalism. This too he shares with Bodenham. Finally, some Scottish witches, especially Isobel Gowdie and Bessie Dunlop, announced their belief in fairies, and told long tales of their interactions with them. Although this evidence was not taken seriously by the demonologically orientated elite, folktales also surface in trial depositions in the northern counties of England, as Miranda Chaytor has recently argued.[62]

All these people used the corpus of fairy stories in inventive ways to understand the practices of others or to legitimate their own. Such moves did not always work; the godly, at least, made no distinction between Robin Goodfellow and a demon, and a learned sceptic like Reginald Scot found both incredible. Fairy-beliefs were a sign of an outmoded structure of belief, always already on the point of disappearing, and hence associated, like folktales, with elderly, uneducated women. Consequently, courts and other interlocutors were more than likely to reinterpret a 'fairy story' as a story about some more up-to-date bugbear: a demon, a witch. The result was that some stories originally told as 'fairy stories' are re-presented as stories about witchcraft: this was true, for instance, of Joan Upney's confession about her familiar, discussed in the previous chapter. What Joan had was a mischievous sprite or brownie, not a demon who had appeared to get her soul. The villager might be just as incapable of understanding this as the educated person. Over time, some fairy-beliefs seem gradually to flow into witch-beliefs, making one discourse. Sometimes it is evident that what might once have been termed elfshot or the black fairy is now termed bewitchment, and fairies can sometimes be interchangeable with both witches and demons or familiars. For instance, a bewitched girl saw the witch who had afflicted her appear in one of her trances. The witch was wearing red and green, the fairy colours.[63] Thomas Darling initially saw vivid visions in his bewitched or possessed fits, crying out 'Look where the green angels stand in the window'. In folklore this was eventually rationalised as a way of identifying a witch: Addy reports that 'witches are dressed exactly like fairies'.[64] The bewitched child Margaret Muschamp sees angels in the form of doves and partridges, and sometimes like turkeys with faces like Christians. Bizarre though they sound, they gifted her both with the ability to survive without food for sixteen weeks, and with the power of prophecy and the ability to discern events taking place elsewhere.[65]

The accused witch Joan Willimot likewise muddled fairies and familiars, healing rites and bewitchment in a deposition in the case of Margaret and Phillippa Flower:

> This examinate saith, that she has a spirit which she calleth Pretty, which was given unto her by William Berry of Langham in Rutlandshire, whom she served three years, and that her master when he gave it unto her willed her to open her mouth and he would blow into it a fairy, which should do her good. And that she opened her mouth and he did blow into her mouth, and that presently after his blowing, there came out of her mouth a spirit which stood upon the ground in the shape and form of a woman, which spirit did ask of her her soul, which she then promised unto it, being willed thereunto by her master.[66]

Willimot adds that she never used the spirit to hurt anyone; like others who saw the fairies or similar, she seems to have seen herself as a healer and unwitcher.

Even more spectacular is the case of Anne Jefferies, a maid in a Cornish household.[67] She was nineteen in 1646 when one day, as she sat knitting in the garden when the family were out, 'suddenly there came over the Garden-hedge to her (as she affirmed) six persons, of a small stature, all clothed in green, which she called fairies'. Thereafter Jefferies experiences some of the classic symptoms of bewitchment: she falls into a convulsion, and 'in her sickness she cried out' that she saw 'them' going out of the window. Another woman in another place at another time might have meant a witch or familiar. Jefferies, however, begins to develop supernatural powers rather than to be subject to them. Her mistress is out and hurts her leg, and when she is carried home, Jefferies explains that 'she was heartily sorry for the mischance she had got in hurting of her leg, and that she did it at such a place (naming the place)'. Jefferies then cures the leg, 'by the blessing of God', and explains that the fairies came to her in the garden, asking if she has been 'put out' against her will'. When Jefferies answers yes, they remark ominously 'You [Jefferies's mistress; Jefferies is narrating the story to her] shall not fare the better for it'. They still sound like witches; Jefferies is well up in ominous prognosticatory discourse. But she portrays both herself and the fairies as healers too; the fairies provide a healing ointment with which Jefferies effects the cure. Jefferies also sings and dances with the fairies, and eats only their food. Soon she is making political and other prophecies: 'She prays very much and bids people keep the old forms of prayer, she says the king shall shortly enjoy his own and be avenged of his enemies'.[68]

Eventually, the elite get to hear of Jefferies. Some are intrigued: Hyde, later Earl of Clarendon, wrote eagerly 'I pray as soon as may be send me . . . some more of the prophetess of Bodmin'.[69] A long account of Jefferies's activities did reach him:

> she cures most diseases, especially the falling-sickness, and broken bones, only with the touch of her hand: she hath been before the committee and she

> bids them be good in their offices, for it will not last long, she hath been examined by three able divines, she gives a good account of her religion, and hath the Scriptures very perfectly, though altogether unlearned, they are fearful to meddle with her for she tells them to their faces, that none of them at all are able to hurt her . . . She was not seen to eat, but on Christmas day, and then she took bread and water.[70]

Others are troubled by the anomalousness of her sanitisation of witch-discourse, perhaps because they cannot accept her explanation of fairy agency. Clergymen appear and 'endeavoured to persuade her that they were evil spirits that resorted to her and that it was the delusion of the devil . . . and advised her not to go to them when they called her'. Jefferies tries to obey, but the fairies counter by quoting John's first Epistle 4.1: 'Beloved, believe not every spirit, but try the spirits whether they are of God, because many false prophets are gone out into the world'. However, this refutation does not satisfy everyone, and Jefferies is taken into custody by John Tregagle, a warm supporter of the Parliamentarian cause. Tregagle was suspicious of Jefferies. No doubt he was not overjoyed when the fairies told her that the restoration of the monarchy was imminent, since his estate had been confiscated by Royalists, who had also forced a loan from him.[71] But he also disdained her claims of supernatural power, and put her claim to eat only fairy food to the test by imprisoning her without food in his house. Like Anna Trapnel's amazing abstemiousness, Jefferies's fasts seem to have helped to authenticate her prophecies, which Tregagle was hoping to discredit. It remains unclear whether his attempt to prove her fraudulent was successful. Eventually, Tregagle had to let her go, and she was never formally charged with any crime; as such things go, she was lucky. But she was also cowed; therafter we hear nothing of her beyond her marriage. What is certain is that she refused to retell her story in 1697 when invited to do so by Moses Pitt, the son of her former employer. By that time, Jefferies knew that one might lose control of the self-fashioning process with disastrous results. Nonetheless, her story shows how a woman could use supernatural motifs to make herself an object of respect and even notoriety.

It is significant that both Anne Bodenham and Anne Jefferies began as servants, members of households from whose wealth and status they were excluded.[72] Perhaps the position of servant gave both women material for their fantasies, a goal to aspire to, while at the same time generating anger and resentment. Just as Bodenham's master followed Renaissance cynics like Ralegh's circle in seeing magic as a means to self-advancement, so these two servants may have found in the supernatural and its discourses their only hope of removing the class boundaries which would otherwise keep them lowly and unknown. This suggests that the figure of the witch could be an occasion for female self-fashioning in the full-blown Greenblattian sense; that is, it was an identity which allowed class boundaries to be crossed for those who otherwise found them impassable.

Finally, many stories show elements of folktales being reworked as part of court depositions. There was an overlap in any case between witch-beliefs and folktales; many folktales began as stories which warn children against unwary confrontations with witches, and they repeat the concerns expressed by women deponents.[73] As well, however, many depositions show traces of self-fashioning as heroes or heroines of popular stories. Upper-class women like Ann Fanshawe saw their lives in terms of the Platonic pastoral romances which constituted their leisure reading: ordinary men and women saw their lives in the narrative patters of popular stories. Two boys who were bewitched, both of whom later claimed to be faking, constructed their stories of witchcraft from recognisable folk antecedents.[74] The remarkable depositions of Anne Armstrong contain a number of folktale motifs. On a familiar path, Anne meets an old man who warns her about witches and instructs her in coping with their feast. Figures like this abound in folktale; for instance, the three golden heads at the well who feature in George Peele's *The Old Wives Tale*, which predates Anne Armstrong by over fifty years.[75] Thomas Darling went with his uncle to hunt hares in Winsell Wood. The boy was lost, and returned suffering from a bizarre illness whose principal symptoms were vomiting and visions, together with fits. When the possibility that he is bewitched is suggested to the boy, he explains that when lost in the wood, he met 'a little old woman who had a grey gown with a black fringe, a broad thrummed hat, and three warts on her face. While passing her, the boy 'chanced against his will to let a [fart] escape'. This angered the witch, and she replied 'Gyp with a mischief, and fart with a bell / I will go to heaven and thou shalt go to hell'.[76] This is a folktale adventure. Hunting hares is likely to bring about conflict with a witch, since witches of folktale often transform themselves into hares. The boy is alone and lost, in a wood, the sign of uncontrolled and therefore dangerous landscape. It is a also a place which *has* to be entered because it provides a living to the poor; the hares, similarly, are the kind of furred game with which a family might (illicitly) eke out an existence. There he meets with a being who could be one of many things: a fairy, an ogress, but in this case, a witch. Like many peasant tales before the Grimms and Perrault sanitised them, this one is scatological. The boy lets out a fart as the witch passes him, perhaps as a way of defying her. She replies with what sounds to us like a children's rhyme, but one full of menace. This kind of story could be understood by both adults and children, as the witch's reply to it shows. The accused witch in question, Alice Gooderidge, told the story otherwise, but also makes use of a more mildly scatological rhyme in replying to the boy; 'I met the boy in the woods, the first Saturday in Lent, and passing by me he called me the witch of Stapenhill, unto whom I said, 'Every boy doth call me witch, but did I ever make thy arse to itch?'.[77]

It is almost as if the young Edmund Robinson had read and benefited from the story told by Thomas Darling; his own tale is a tissue of folk material mixed with large lumps of local gossip. Yet these cultural materials are reshaped by Edmund's own complex and familial fears and desires:

> Upon All-Saints day last past, he being with one Henry Parker . . . desired the said Parker to give him leave to gather some Bulloes [wild plums], which he did; in gathering whereof he saw two greyhounds, viz. a black and a brown; one came running over the next field towards him . . . And the said greyhounds came and fawned on him, they having about their neck either of them a collar, to either of which collars was tied a string, which collars as this informer affirmeth, did shine like gold, and he thinking that some either of Mr Nutters or Mr Robinsons family should have followed them, but seeing nobody to follow them, he took the said greyhounds thinking to hunt with them, and presently a hare did rise, very near before him, at the sight whereof he cried 'Loo, loo, loo', but the dogs would not run, whereupon he being very angry took them, and with the strings that were at their collars tied either of them to a little bush at the next hedge, and with a rod that he had in his hand he beat them, and instead of the black greyhound one Dickinson's wife stood up, a Neighbour whom this informant knoweth. And instead of the brown one a little boy, whom this informant knoweth not.[78]

Understandably, Edmund tries to run away, but the woman holds him, and puts her hand in her pocket, pulling out 'a piece of silver much like to a fair shilling' and offers to give it to him to hold his tongue. He refuses, saying pluckily, 'Nay, thou art a witch'. She then produces 'a magic bridle that jingled'. She puts this on the boy-demon's head, and he becomes a white horse. Seizing Edmund, she mounts the horse and carries him to a new house 'called Houtons' [Hoarstones]. What Edmund remembers in detail about the witch-feast is the witches pulling on ropes to obtain food: 'flesh smoking, butter in lumps, and milk as it were sli[di]ng from the said ropes'. This Land of Cockaigne spectacle of piles of high protein and high fat food signify Edmund's preoccupation with his belly, understandable enough in a boy from a poor artisan family in a poor area. Yet this is also an old folk-fantasy: Edmund was also influenced by stories of fairy food in describing 'a young woman whom this informer knoweth not gave him flesh and bread upon a trencher, and drink in a glass, after the first taste, he refused, and would have no more, and said it was nought'. Edmund is showing the cunning of the folktale hero here, just as he earlier showed the cheek of a chapbook hero in refusing the witch's bribe. Eating the food of supernatural beings, especially fairies, put one in their power.[79] Similarly, the story of witches transforming themselves into hares and vice versa is one of the commonest pieces of folktale about witches in both England and Scotland.[80] Edmund's story of an incandescent woman who flew up the chimney, too, seems part of popular cultural apprehensions of ghosts. There may even be a hint of crypto-Catholic recollection in his narrative of Loynd's wife appearing like a radiant vision on the bridge, 'as though she had first been a lantern and after a woman'.[81] Edmund also uses another kind of women's tale, women's gossip. The women he names as witches are chosen because 'he heard the neighbours repute them for witches'.[82] For instance 'he heard William Nutter's wife say that Jennet Devys and William Devys had bewitched her; and it was generally spoken that Beawse's wife, who went a-begging, was a witch'. Edmund's narrative show him in a pleasingly plucky light. Not only does he defy a witch, refuse her attempt to bribe him into silence, and brave an entire sabbath of witches, he also shows knowledge and presence of mind, refusing to gorge himself on the witches' food, and escaping from their clutches. Heroically he fights a demon disguised as a small boy, who is therefore unnaturally strong.

Edmund later explained that 'he had heard the neighbours talk of a witch-feast that was kept at Mocking Tower in Pendle Forest about twenty years since [1613], to which feast divers witches came, and many were apprehended, and executed at Lancaster, and thereupon he framed those tales concerning the persons aforesaid, because he heard the neighbours repute them for witches'.[83] All these sources are female discourses. As Edmund later said, 'he heard tales and reports made by women, so he framed his tale out of his own invention'. As he later explained, the occasion for the story was also familial: 'he invented the said tale for that his mother having brought him up to spin wool, and also used to fetch home the kine but did not do it, but went to play with other children, and fearing his father or mother would beat him, he made this tale for an excuse'.[84]

Whether Edmund saw himself as cheeky Jack the Giant Killer, or as the discoverer of a fairy mound, he cast himself as the saviour of his family. (Ironically, he did help their fortunes, but not quite in the manner of the stories.) This reflects and assuages his guilt. The boy-saviours of folktales were dead losses economically before their supernatural encounters. Jack and the Beanstalk, for instance, is an idle layabout, and simple too. As Edmund told it, he resembled these Lazy Jacks in idling when he should have been working. He should have been spinning wool, a common form of piecework for women and children in poor rural families, or fetching the cattle home. Having neglected these duties to play, Edmund is guilty and apprehensive. Although parents in the past were just as loving as modern parents, early modern family relations are inseparable from the internal economy of the household. There was an unwritten contract of emotion as well as duty between parents and children. Edmund had broken this contract by preferring to play rather than work, and he was guilty as well as afraid of his parents' anger and their punishment. His story arises from that fear and guilt, as well as being an attempt to displace it. In it, he removes the cause of guilt by acting the part of the returning child-hero, initially lost but then recovered, while displacing his fear of his mother's anger into the figure of the violent and controlling Frances Dicconson, the witch who takes him in hand to the sabbath.

Yet Frances is also the good mother, the food-provider who offers Edmund lavish viands. She is his mother's rival as well as her image, cajoling as well as threatening. Edmund is not only Lazy Jack: he is also a lost babe in the woods, an infant who must be nourished. Frances Dicconson is his potential saviour. Oscillating between fantasies of wily power and fear of helplessness, Edmund's selves demand different mothers: a humble, grateful dupe for Lazy Jack and a nurturer for the lost boy. The witches' identities reflect the instability of Edmund's desires. Edmund's story and the witch-figures central to it embrace a cluster of familial conflicts ranging from the economic to the emotional. It offers a fantasy way out of those conflicts: Edmund rescues his family from economic privation by escaping the witches and bringing back tales of luxurious viands.

This is also the role the story played in 'real life'. Edmund's father, according to John Webster, soon began a career of exploiting his son's tale:

> the boy, his father, and some others besides did make a practice to go from church to church that the boy might reveal and discover witches, pretending that there was a great number at the pretended meeting, whose faces he could know, and by that means they got a good living, that in a short space the Father bought a cow or two, when he had none before.[85]

As Edmund himself said, finding that he was believed, he grew more and more confident about his story. How could he not, when it was not only raising his status in the family, but also proving the family's salvation? How could he not, when the story had not only staved off his parents' wrath and his own guilty feelings, but had also offered him a way to abject the fantasy image of his bad mother? Meanwhile, Edmund's mother drops out of our story when Edmund becomes a newsworthy commodity. She is silenced both in reality and in fantasy, speaking only through Edmund's desires. Often, the early modern mother can only be glimpsed through the distorting mirror of the son's fantasies. She is a figure in his story, but also its author, the tale-teller whose folk materials are reshaped in her son's tale into a story about her. The materials of folktale were kept in circulation by the shared concerns which they expressed and managed. The stories had meaning because they expressed common concerns: how to deal with those much more powerful than you, the cunning needed to live at the bottom of a hierarchical society, the constant desire for both food and money, and the inability to imagine them on the scale enjoyed by the rich, so that, for instance, abundance can only be signified by huge amounts of food.

In all these cases, the agency of deponents and witches is visible as a process of rewriting cultural materials. Confession, too, was a process of rewriting. The early modern legal system was particularly reliant on the witch's confession. We tend to think of witches' confessions as wrung from them or even dictated to them. Early modern people knew that confession was not a single act, but a series of negotations between the accuser and the accused, which would gradually result in increasing agreement on the parameters of 'the truth' and eventually would issue in a statement or series of statements as part of the trial evidence. The JPs and the accused went through a forensic rhetorical investigation to arrive at truth in a disputed matter. Their relationship would veer from the conspiratorial to the adversarial: JPs could use the full repertoire of devices available in rhetoric, which included sudden changes of tack, while the accused, as a witch and therefore an unrepentant sinner, was always liable to be seen as worryingly 'hard', needing to be broken down, to be opened up and thus normalised.[86] Often the confession retained material unassimilable by the categories of the learned, traces of the agency of witch rather than questioner.

In her first confession, or rather, as we should say, in her first interrogation, the St Osyth witch Ursula Kempe makes a minimalist confession which traces and normalises her involvement in magic without accepting accusations of *maleficium*. Ursula confesses that

> troubled with a lameness in her bones, and for ease thereof, [she] went to one Cock's wife of Weeley, now deceased, who told this examinate that she was bewitched, and at her entreaty taught her to unwitch herself, and bade her take hog's dung, and charnell, and put them together, and hold them in her left hand, and to take in the other hand a knife and to prick the medicine three times, and then to cast the same into the fire, and to take the said knife and to make three pricks under a table, and to let the knife stick there. And after that to take three leaves of sage, and as much of herb John (alias herb grace) and put them into ale and drink it last at night and first in the morning; and that she taking the same had ease of her lameness. The same examinate saith that one Page's wife and one Gray's wife, being either of the lame and bewitched, she being requested and sent for to come to them went unto them. And saith that she knew them to be bewitched and at their desires did minister unto them the foresaid medicine, whereupon they had speedy amendment.[87]

Ursula remembers this charm in great detail, which suggests that she did use it often. No other part of her confession is so detailed; she is not as interested in her alleged demons as she is in the niceties of which hand to hold the knife in and which herbs to use. Interestingly, either she or Darcy get one of these wrong; herb John is probably John's wort, with vervain and dill a basic remedy against bewitchment, but herb of grace, as all readers of *Hamlet* know, is rue, not the same plant. This points to the limitations of Ursula's skill as a cunning woman; she is not the herbalist witch of neo-Pagan fantasy, but someone who has learned one charm. Or it may point to the limitations of Darcy. The charm is recorded very fully, in something of the spirit which led Reginald Scot to report on popular superstition at voluminous length, but Darcy may not be familiar with what he is recording.

According to Ursula, this charm was the extent of her self-image as a witch, and it tallies with what she tells Grace Thurlow, that she can unwitch but cannot witch. At this point, the severe and demonological Darcy evidently takes over with leading questions about pact witchcraft, and Ursula agrees to the charge of keeping familiars. We could see this as a simple case of Brian Darcy gaining the initiative, and this is certainly how he presents it, since this redounded to his credit. However, we could also see Ursula's developing confession as analogous to the growth of belief in magic described by Tanya Luhrmann among modern witches. Luhrmann shows that well-educated, sophisticated people are slowly introduced to a discourse and a world-view in which magic does make sense, and they thereby come to interpret their own actions in the light of these discourses. So if they hold a ritual for more money, they search for evidence that it has succeeded. They 'find' such evidence, which reinforces their belief.[88] In a similar way, Ursula's movement towards accepting the idea that she could perform magic begins when she is taught a single charm by a cunning woman. Magic use nearly always begins outside the self, with someone teaching or introducing the witch to a magical practice. Like ancient constitutions, spells were always already located in a more authoritative past. The charm's iterability means that Ursula can try it herself on her neighbours, and this gives her an identity as a magic-user. In the course of the confession process, what appears to happen is that this identity, to which Ursula has consented and which she fashioned, is transformed by Brian Darcy into a different identity in a different interpretative system. Having accepted her own identity as a magic-user, Ursula is unable to impose this on Darcy, for whom all magic use is witchcraft. So she must either accept the identity he offers, as a black witch, or disavow any contact with magic. Having once acknowledged an identity as a magic-user to the court and also to her community, this is difficult for her. Moreover, she also believes in her own powers as an unwitcher and healer, and is unwilling to disavow that identity.

Many witches try to hold a line which acknowledges minimal magic use but refuses charges of malice; this rarely works once learned demonological discourses are involved. The cunning woman Joan Guppy tried to buttress her claim with a list of people she had helped by her cunning magic. Anne Bodenham claimed to have 'done hundreds of people good, and nobody ever gave her an ill word for all her pains'.[89] This kind of defence was enhanced by the kind of careful use of gender ideology which Ursula Kempe's testimony lacked. One especially articulate self-defence came from Joan Prentice, arraigned at Chelmsford in 1589. Prentice's confession refuses to acknowledge that she traded her soul for her familiar's services; instead she insists that she only offered it a drop of her blood. She confesses that she told it to spoil the drink of Mistress Adams, but on the more serious charge of bewitching a child to death, Prentice produces an interesting denial. When the ferret familiar appeared, and demanded to know her will, she replied

> 'Go unto Master Glascock's house, and nip one of his children a little, named Sara, but hurt it not'. And the next night he resorted unto her again and told her that he had done as she willed him, namely, that he had nipped Sara Glascock and that she should die thereof. To whom she answered and said 'Thou villain! What hast thou done? I bid thee to nip it but a little and not to hurt it, and hast thou killed the child?' Which speech being uttered, the ferret vanished suddenly, and never came to her since.[90]

This is a carefully shaped story, dramatic, conflictual, tragic. Prentice sets the scene by telling of her previous conflict with her familiar over her own soul, which lends credibility to her account of their final conflict. She is careful to say that she explicitly told the ferret not to hurt the child, and her account of her own words to it on its return stresses her surprise as well as her horror at what it has done. As well, these words signify a clear break between Prentice and her diabolic companion; it is unemotional, indifferent, undramatic in its reportage, while Prentice is impassioned and involved. This difference is re-marked twice; when Prentice calls the ferret 'villain' and when it disappears never to return. Prentice is also careful to locate her horror and anger in the ferret's act of murder rather than its disobedience. In representing herself in this story, she seeks to ally herself with respectable opinion against the callous malice of the ferret. This case shows how a woman in the disempowered position of witch-suspect was able to use verbal and storytelling skill to shape for herself an identity which showed her in the best possible light while acceding to the demand for confession, repentance and reparation. The fact that the act of killing a child was unacceptable to her represents her not as a counter-mother but as a woman with all her maternal feelings in place.[91] This is a clear case of a narrative that represents a compromise between the story of the accused and the questions put to her; Prentice admits to the crime, but subtly replaces the blame for it on the demons who acted on her behalf. Like Anne Bodenham and Ursula Kempe, she did not convince the court.

Other suspects also sought to represent themselves in ways which showed that they shared the notion of the good wife and mother which underpinned the fantasy of the witch. Elizabeth Lowys, for example, denied most of the specific charges of *maleficium* brought against her by neighbours, and also produced a more elaborate self-defence when asked particularly about the bewitching of a lamb:

> [when asked] whether she confessed that she killed a lamb by witchery, [she] yelled 'might it chene, must it be fed with the meat of children?' when it was a-feeding with milk and whitebread. She admitted that she said that she came unto the house where a woman was feeding a lamb with milk and white bread and spake 'what, must it be fed with whitebread and milk?' and what then when the woman put up the lamb, and the next day it died, by eating with white bread and milk overmuch.[92]

As Macfarlane points out, this suspect represents herself as correctly rebuking the extravagance of the woman feeding the lamb. The food is inappropriate because it is child-food. All is not well before the suspect comes on the scene; instead, she enters upon and names a scene of disorder. It is this transgression and not witchcraft which causes the lamb's death. Elizabeth Lowys represents herself as the maternal figure, concerned that child-food should be wasted on a lamb, in opposition to the lamb's owner, who is both excessively maternal in the wrong way and wastefully extravagant. This deponent, Lowys asserts, has failed to make correct distinctions between animals and children, has failed to order her environment as a woman should.[93] Amy Duny took a similar line when quizzed about her impact on the health of Samuel Pacy's child. When asked about its illness, she replied, 'Mr Pacy keeps a great stir about that child, but let him stay until he hath done as much by his children, as I have done by mine.' When pressed for details, she added 'She [Mistress Pacey] hath been fain to open her child's mouth with a tap to give it victuals'.[94]

All these women, deponents and witches, were not the passive repositories of either godly demonology and misogyny or the gender ideologies which often subtended them, though they sometimes chose to use those ideologies to help their case, much as a woman in a modern court case might take care to dress 'respectably'. Rather, from the self-fashioning of Anne Bodenham as a kind of occult businesswoman to the self-defence of Amy Duny as a good mother rather than a bad antimother, witches were women who scripted their own stories, at least in part. The way they did so, and their opportunities to do so successfully, were often constrained by a variety of factors, including (godly) assumptions about what women should be. Women like Anne Bodenham certainly got into trouble by defying such notions, not because of misogyny, but because ideas about 'proper' behaviour (for men as well as women) were caught up in a national struggle to control what we should now call lifestyles. Other women, like Ursula Kempe, though apparently less transgressive, got into the same trouble, and their attempts to get themselves out of it by a flexible response to their inflexible interrogators were not always successful. The accused did not always win the battle. But she usually fought for her life, both in the literal sense and in the sense that she struggled to incorporate some fragment of what she was to herself, what her own fantasy of herself as witch was, into her official confession. The fact that we can sometimes see a trace of this self-fashioning is a tribute to the courage and discursive skill of women accused of witchcraft.

NOTES

1 *The Apprehension and confession of three notorious witches, arraigned and by justice condemned at Chelmsford*, 1589, printed in *Witchcraft in England 1558–1618*, ed. Barbara Rosen, Amherst: University of Massachusetts Press, 1991, p. 186. Upney's case is discussed in more detail later in relation to her belief that her toads were like fairies. Her indictment concerns *maleficum* rather than a pact: 'Joan Upney, of Dagenham, spinster, indicted for murder by witchcraft. On 20 November 1588 at Dagenham she bewitched Alice Foster so that she languished until 14 April 1589 and then died. On 27 Mar. 1588 at Dagenham she bewitched Joan Harwood so that she languished until 24 August and then died' (J. S. Cockburn, *Essex Indictments: Elizabeth I*, London: HMSO, 1978, p. 339). The pamphlet does not deal with either event, suggesting that it is more interested in demons than in death.

2 See also the Flower case of 1618, Mother Sutton and her daughter Mary of Milton Mills, Bedfordshire, in 1616 (*Witches apprehended, examined and executed*, 1616), Agnes Browne of Guilsborough, Northants, and Joan Vaughan her daughter.

3 *Depositions from York Castle*, ed. James Raine, Surtees Society, vol. 40 (1860), p. 38, hereafter *YD*.

4 Could it be a congenital disease? wondered George Best, having seen a black child born in England, thus ruling out environmental factors. Richard Hackluyt, *The Principal Navigations, Voyages, Traffics and Discoveries of the English Nation*, ed. James McLehose, 12 vols, Glasgow, 1904, vol. 7, pp. 262–3.

5 See the excellent discussion on women, work and trades in Olwen Hufton, *The Prospect Before Her: A History of Women in Western Europe*, vol. I: 1500–1800, London: HarperCollins, 1995, pp. 91–3.
6 *The examination and confession of certaine wytches at Chensford*, 1566, in Rosen, *Witchcraft*, p. 73.
7 *The wonderfull discovery of witches in the County of Lancaster*, in Rosen, *Witchcraft*, pp. 364–8; *Witches apprehended, examined and executed, for notable villaines by them committed both by land and water*, 1613, sig. A4.
8 *The examination and confession of certain witches at Chelmsford*, in Rosen, *Witchcraft*, pp. 75–6. This seems to be a literal grandmother, though it may refer to Eve, the first woman.
9 *Dr Lambe revived, or witchcraft condemned in Anne Bodenham*, 1653.
10 Lambe was famous as the wizard of the Duke of Buckingham. For more about Bodenham's case and its inflection by Lambe's reputation, see below.
11 Anne Laurence, *Women in England 1500–1760*, London: Weidenfeld & Nicolson, 1994, pp. 125–37.
12 *Dr Lambe's darling: or, strange and terrible news from Salisbury*, 1653.
13 Edmond Bower, *Dr Lamb revived, or witchcraft condemned in Anne Bodenham, a servant of his, who was arraigned and executed at the Lent assizes last in Salisbury*, 1653, p. 7.
14 For Lambe's link with Buckingham, see *A briefe description of the notorious life of J. Lambe, otherwise called Dr Lambe*, 'Amsterdam' [probably London], 1628. This is a pamphlet about his life which gives details of his conjuring rituals; these sound remarkably like Bodenham's practices. Lambe eventually overreached himself by raping a woman of Southwark, and on 13 June 1628 was set upon and beaten to death by a London crowd on his way home from seeing a play at the Fortune. His death was very widely observed (see John Millington to Gilbert Millington, 21 June 1628, and the diary of public events both in *CSPD* 1628, vol. 102, nos. 57, 58, and a letter from Joseph Mead to Sir Martin Stuteville, 21 June 1626, cited in Gerard Bentley, *The Jacobean and Caroline Stage*, Oxford: Clarendon, 1956, vol. 1, p. 267). There was also a stage play, already old in 1633, when it was revised to cash in on the brief fashion for witch-plays set by the Lancashire witch-trial of 1633/4 (see Chapter 9), and a ballad entitled ironically 'The Tragedy of Dr Lambe' (*Pepysian Garland*, ed. Hyder Rollins, Cambridge: Cambridge University Press, 1922, p. 280). His death was widely seen as proleptic of Buckingham's end: see Francis Nethersole's letter to Elizabeth of Bohemia, 19 June 1628, which reports Lambe's death as a sign of Buckingham's unpopularity, and the jingle 'But Charles and George do what they can / The Duke shall die like Dr Lambe', was popular, probably after the fact (cited by Roger Lockyer, *Buckingham: The Life and Political Times of George Villiers, First Duke of Buckingham*, London: Longman, 1981, p. 451.)
15 There are two principal sources for Bodenham's case: Bower's pamphlet, the main source used here, and a shortened version of Bower's account, entitled *Dr Lambe's darling, or strange and terrible news from Salisbury, being a true relation of the contract made between the devil and A. Bodenham*, by James Bower, cleric, 1653. 'James Bower' may be a printer's error for Edmond Bower. As well as being shorter, this pamphlet is much more sensational, portraying Anne 'flying in the air' at '40 miles an hour' and also detailing her transformation into a wide range of animals. These details may be culled from the depositions which Bower does not bother to transcribe.
16 Annabel Gregory's study of a case of witchcraft in Rye also makes a witch-charge the outcome of quarrels between traditional and godly factions: 'Witchcraft, politics and "good neighbourhood" in seventeenth-century Rye', *Past and Present*, 133 (1991),

pp. 31–66. Here, however, it is a godly woman who is accused of witchcraft by her traditionalist neighbours.

17 On the conflict between traditional and godly in Wiltshire, see David Underdown, *Revel, Riot, and Rebellion: Popular Politics and Culture in England 1603–1660*, Oxford: Oxford University Press, 1985, and Ronald Hutton, *The Rise and Fall of Merry England: The Ritual Year 1400–1700*, Oxford: Oxford University Press, 1994.

18 Bower's account of Bodenham's activities is not a piece of fiction, but a (slanted) attempt to report what her customer Anne Styles and Bodenham herself told him. Since this pamphlet differs so substantially from the generic witch-narrative of the Civil War years, it seems unlikely that it is solely a printer's or author's fabrication.

19 As a godly minister, Bower would have been reluctant to acknowledge that witchcraft had any real effect for those who deliberately resorted to it.

20 Bower, *Dr Lamb*, p. 2. The 'book' may have been another witch-pamphlet, in a wonderful moment of self-reflexivity, and it may even be that Bodenham learned some of her magic from such books.

21 Bower, *Dr Lamb*, p. 34.

22 Aubrey cites a charm: 'Vervain and Dill / Hinder Witches from their will'; this suggests that Bodenham may have seen herself as an unwitcher. John Aubrey, *Remaines of Gentilisme and Judaisme*, ed. James Britten, Folklore Society (1881), p. 231.

23 This is the only sign of Bodenham's alleged Catholicism.

24 Bower, *Dr Lamb*, p. 10.

25 On this point, see Christopher Durston, *The Family in the English Revolution*, Oxford: Blackwell, 1989, and my D. Phil thesis, 'Gender, power and the body: some figurations of femininity in Milton and seventeenth-century women's writing', Oxford, 1991, section 3.

26 Bower, *Dr Lamb*, p. 31.

27 *The notorious life*, p. 8.

28 Bower, *Dr Lamb*, pp. 31, 34.

29 On the behaviour expected of the accused at executions, see J. A. Sharpe, 'Last dying speeches: religion, ideology and public execution in seventeenth-century England', *Past and Present* 107 (1985), pp. 144–67.

30 Underdown, *Revel, Riot, and Rebellion*, p. 94. Underdown lists an instance of traditional tolerance of activities which the godly might have found shocking, a tithingman who regularly plays bowls on Sunday.

31 Bower's pamphlet, and to a much greater extent its synopsis as *Dr Lambe's darling* are part of a genre of godly warning literature, of which the best-known example was Thomas Beard's treatise, which went through numerous seventeenth-century editions; *The theatre of Gods judgments*, 1597, rept. by Edmund Rudierd as *The thunderbolt of Gods wrath*, 1618.

32 On drink and church-ales, see Underdown, *Revel, Riot, and Rebellion*, pp. 92–4.

33 *The Natural History of Wiltshire*, ed. John Britton, 1892, p. 11.

34 'Hack' authors like Henry Goodcole and Edmond Bower claimed to get their stories from the accused and convicted witch; see Chapter 9 for Goodcole's claims, and for the genre of providential narrative. Miranda Chaytor makes a strong distinction between depositions elicited by questioning and those offered voluntarily in 'Husband(ry): narratives of rape in the seventeenth century', *Gender and History*, 7 (1995), pp. 379–81.

35 Robert Muchembled, *Popular Culture and Elite Culture in France, 1400–1750*, Baton Rouge: Louisiana State University Press, 1985, and *Sorcières, justices et société aux 16e et 17e siècles*, Paris, 1987.

36 Hélène Cixous and Catherine Clément, *La Jeune Née*, in English as *The Newly Born Woman*, trans. Betsy Wing, Manchester: Manchester University Press, 1986, p. 6.

37 Martin Ingram, *Church Courts, Sex and Marriage*, Cambridge: Cambridge University Press, 1992, p. 96.
38 Bower, *Dr Lamb*, p. 15.
39 J. C. Atkinson, *Forty Years in a Moorland Parish*, 1891, p. 59, cites this belief as late as nineteenth-century Yorkshire; priests of the old church are seen as powerful conjurors.
40 For the health and variety of traditional religion before the Reformation, see Eamon Duffy, *The Stripping of the Altars: Traditional Religion in England 1400–1580*, New Haven: Yale University Press, 1992.
41 *YD*, p. 127.
42 Alan Macfarlane, *Witchcraft in Tudor and Stuart England*, London: Routledge & Kegan Paul, 1970, p. 77. Other Essex cases of witchcraft with a recusant theme are mentioned by the Puritan sceptic Thomas Ady, *A candle in the dark*, 1656, pp. 58–9.
43 *YD*, p. 65. Boate is an archaic word meaning permission, entitlement, help, but this does not prevent it from being a corruption of *beate*.
44 *YD*, p. 82, unnumbered note.
45 Thomas Potts, *The wonderful discoverie of witches in the County of Lancashire*, 1613, in Rosen, *Witchcraft*, p. 363, recited by Anne Whittle, alias Chattox herself. See also the editions of G. B. Harrison, London: Bodley Head, 1929, and the annotated edition of James Crossley, *Chetham Society*, vol. 6 (1845).
46 George Kittredge, *Witchcraft in Old and New England*, New York: Russell & Russell, 1929, p. 39.
47 See for instance the charm recited by Isabel Muir of Bishop Wilton in 1528, which ends 'and after these words say xv Pater noster, xv Ave Maria, & three credes', *York Fabric Rolls*, Surtees Society, vol. 25, p. 273, cited in Ewen, *WD*, p. 446.
48 Bodleian Library, MSS Bod e. Mus 243 f.4. The manuscript is entitled *A book of experiments taken out of diverse authors*, and is dated 1622. The full charm is as follows: 'If any three biters have thee forbidden/With wicked tongue or with wicked thought/or with wicked eyes all ye most, I pray God be thy boot/In the name of the father, & of the son, and of the holy ghost. God that set virtue between water and land, be thy help and succour with this prayer that I can, for Jesus sake and charity, Amen'. Since this postdates the trial, one might argue that it is based on Whittle, so I quote the text here to show that this version is much fuller than hers.
49 D. M. Palliser, 'Popular reactions to the Reformation', in *The English Reformation Revised*, ed. Christopher Haigh, Cambridge: Cambridge University Press, 1987, p. 96.
50 What may have happened is this: the nine-year-old Jennet Device is repeating as a garbled phrase or Latin-sounding gibberish a Latin prayer she heard her mother or grandmother say. The pamphleteer Potts, with or without the extra help of a court reporter who made notes from the depositions, has made what he could of what he heard.
51 Literally, 'light in a slender wand', but it is difficult to be sure of the meaning where the whole text is so unstable.
52 Farrandly: a northern dialect word meaning comely or becoming; hence one might modernise as 'beautifully'. Such dialect words make the whole prayer more likely to be authentic.
53 Dere: frighten, daunt.
54 Potts, *Discoverie*, pp. 366–7.
55 John White, *The way to the true church*, 'Preface to the reader', in Eamon Duffy, *The Stripping of the Altars*, p. 583. White was not exactly unprejudiced; he was a notorious hater of papists. The white paternoster survived as a charm until the late nineteenth century or later: Sidney Oldall Addy, *Household Tales with Other Traditional Remains*, 1895, p. 21, reporting on the north of England.

56 On the popularity of these plays, see Robert Whiting, *The Blind Devotion of the People: Popular Religion and the English Reformation*, Cambridge: Cambridge University Press, 1989, pp. 199–201; Duffy, *Stripping of Altars*, 106–8, 579–82; and Christopher Haigh, *English Reformations*, Oxford: Oxford University Press, 1993, pp. 37–8.

57 On continued performance of the plays, see Palliser, 'Popular reactions', p. 103

58 For further discussion of the 1633 case, see Chapter 9.

59 *The examination of John Walsh before Master Thomas Williams, in Exeter*, 1566, in Rosen, *Witchcraft*, p. 68.

60 R. Holworthy, *Discoveries in the Diocesan Registry*, Wells, n. d. Tyrrye's deposition is dated 1555.

61 William Lilly, *A History of His Life and Times*, pp. 102–3.

62 Robert Pitcairn, *Criminal Trials in Scotland*, 1833. I am grateful to Miranda Chaytor for mentioning this in a personal letter to me on 15 August 1995.

63 *YD*, p. 93.

64 *The most wonderful and true story of a certain witch named Alse Gooderige of Stapenhill*, 1597, p. 1; Addy, *Household Tales*, 1895, p. 74. Ruth Tongue shows that in Somerset both red and green are regarded as unlucky: Ruth L. Tongue, *Somerset Folklore*, ed. K. M. Briggs, London: Folklore Society, 1965, p. 150.

65 *Wonderfull news from the north, or a true relation of the sad and grevious torments inflicted upon the bodies of three children of Mr George Muschamp by witchcraft*, 1650. The pamphlet is by Mary Moore. At times, the birds seem to speak to and for the mother, too, showing how the psychic and the social are unstably entangled in these texts.

66 *The wonderful discoverie of the witchcrafts of Margaret and Phillippa Flower*, in Rosen, *Witchcraft*, p. 377.

67 Anne's story is retold in a letter by Moses Pitt, the London printer who was a child in the yeoman household which employed Anne, in William Turner's *A Compleat History of the Most Remarkable Providences, Both of Judgement and Mercy*, 3 vols, 1697, vol. II, pp. 116–20. The letter is dated 3 December 1696. A bizarrely Victorianised account of Anne is offered by the normally more reliable Robert Hunt in *Popular Romances of the West of England*, London, 1865, and this in turn is cited by Katherine Briggs in *A Dictionary of Fairies*, Hanmondsworth: Penguin, 1976, pp. 239–41.

68 Letter in Bodleian Library, MSS Clarendon 29, fo. 102, dated 12 February 1647.

69 Letter in Bodleian Library, MSS Clarendon 2466, vol. II, p. 347, dated 16 March 1646/7.

70 Bodleian Library, MSS Clarendon 29, fo. 102.

71 On Tregagle, see Barbara C. Spooner, *John Tregagle of Trevorder: Man and Ghost*, Truro: A. W. Jordan, 1935. Ironically, Tregagle became the most famous of all Cornish bogymen after his death.

72 See Miranda Chaytor and Jane Lewis, 'Introduction' to *Working Life of Women in the Seventeenth Century*, by Alice Clark, London: Routledge & Kegan Paul, 1982, pp. xxxi–xxxii.

73 For further discussion, see Conclusion.

74 The sceptical polemicist Harsnett claimed that Thomas Darling confessed to him that he had faked the signs of possession, but Darrell claimed that this confession had been obtained with threats of torture (*A declaration of egregious popish impostures*, 1603). Edmund Robinson, of course, confessed that he was faking after interrogation in London; see Chapter 9 for the details.

75 Peele's play is usually dated to 1590. Miranda Chaytor's detailed study of Anne Armstrong is forthcoming.

76 *Alse Gooderidge*, p. 4. This was a Darrell case, so one must be especially cautious, but it is hard to see how the details and structure of this story confirm his claims as exorcist. Unlike some pamphlets, this does not attempt to record Darling's exact words, and no doubt the story has been shortened, but what remains does not seem to have been expanded in any way. The witch who answers in rhyme is also found in the Denham tracts; 'Your loaf in my lap/and your penny in my purse/You are never the better/And I am never the worse'. *Denham Tracts*, vol. I, p. 82.

77 *Alse Gooderidge*, p. 25.

78 The examination of Edmund Robinson son of Edmund Robinson of Pendle Forest eleven years of age, taken at Padham before Richard Shuttleworth and John Starkey Esqs, two of His Majesty's JPs within the county of Lancaster, the 10th day of February, 1633, printed as appendix to John Webster, *The displaying of supposed witchcraft*, 1677, p. 347; other copies include BL, MSS Harleian, 6854, fo. 26v; also Bodleian, MSS Dodsworth, 61, fos 45–47v (as a cross-check), Rawlinson D 399, fos 211–2v (rough), and BL MSS Add. 36, 674, fos 193, 196 (many omissions). See also Chapter 9 for more on this case.

79 Katherine Briggs, *A Dictionary of Fairies*, Hanmondsworth: Penguin, 1976, pp. 143–4.

80 The implication is that the greyhounds will not course the hare because she too is a witch and one of themselves. Katherine Briggs, *A Dictionary of British Folktales*, 4 vols, London: Routledge & Kegan Paul, 1970–1, cites numerous examples.

81 Lancashire was known in the south as a hotbed of recusancy, and quarrels about this may lie at the root of the entire case; they certainly influenced the 1613 prosecutions; see Christopher Haigh, *Reformation and Resistance in Tudor Lancashire*, Cambridge: Cambridge University Press, 1975, and 'The continuity of Catholicism in the English Reformation', *Past and Present*, 93 (1981), pp. 37–69.

82 For Edmund Robinson's subsequent recantations of his confessions, see *CSPD* 1634, pp. 141 and 152. His final recantation took place on 16 July.

83 Potts mentions this at sig. C3r; Edmund gave a fascinating portrait of gossip about witchcraft when he deposed that 'he heard Edmund Stevenson say that he was much troubled with the said Dicconson's wife in the time of his sickness, and that he suspected her, and he heard Robert Smith say that his wife, lying upon her deathbed, accused Jennet Hargraves to be the cause of her death; and he heard William Nutter's wife say that Jennet Devys and William Devys had bewitched her; and it was generally spoken that Beawse's wife, who went a-begging, was a witch, and he had heard Sharpee Smith say that the wife of John Loynd laid her hand upon a cow of his, after which she never rose', 16 July, Re-examination of Edmund Robinson Jr, taken before George Long, *CSPD* 1634, p. 152.

84 Examination of Edmund Robinson the younger, of Newchurch, co. Lancaster, aged 10 yeares or thereabouts, taken by George Long, Justice of the Peace for Middlesex, by command of Secretary Windebank, *CSPD* 1634, p. 141.

85 Webster, *Witchcraft*, p. 277. Edmund Robinson senior was, he explained, 'a waller' by trade and 'but a poor man', p. 277. When examined by a critical London judiciary, Edmund Robinson senior protested that he had never believed his son's story, far less exploited it: 'Examinant gave no credit to him, but sharply rebuked and corrected him. Nevertheless, the boy continued in a constant affirmation thereof even with tears, insomuch that examinant imagined he had seen some vision or something that had troubled his mind, but he never believed anything that the boy spoke concerning the same.' Examination of Edmund Robinson, of Newchurch, co. Lancaster, mason, taken before George Long, justice of the peace for Middlesex, by command of Secretary Windebank, *CSPD* 1634, p. 144.

86 For early modern ideas about confession and interrogation, see Chapter 9, and John H.

Langbein, *Torture and the Law of Proof: Europe and England in the Ancien Régime*, Chicago: University of Chicago Press, 1977; William Lambarde, *Eirenarchia*, 1588, p. 220; John Bossy, 'The social history of confession in the age of the Reformation', *Transactions of the Royal Historical Society*, 5th series, 25 (1975).

87 *A true and just record of the information, examination and confession of all the witches, taken at St Oses in the Countie of Essex*, 1582, in Rosen, *Witchcraft*, p. 114.

88 Tanya Luhrmann. *Persuasions of the Witch's Craft*, Oxford: Blackwell, 1989.

89 Bower, *Dr Lamb*, p. 27.

90 *The apprehension and confession of three notorious witches*, 1589, in Rosen, *Witchcraft*, p. 187.

91 Prentice was arraigned at the 1589 Trinity assize at Chelmsford. The indictment reads: 'Joan Prentice of Sible Hedingham, spinster, indicted for murder by witchcraft. On 10 Feb. 1589 at Sible Hedingham she bewitched Sarah Glascock so that she languished until 28 Mar. and then died' (Cockburn, *Essex Indictments: Elizabeth*, p. 335). Despite her careful statement, Prentice was found guilty, and sentenced to hang. Though the pamphlet does not reproduce the depositions of witnesses, claims of child-bewitchment were taken very seriously in this case, and in the two discussed in the following pages.

92 The depositions for this 1564 case are transcribed in full in Macfarlane, *Witchcraft in Tudor and Stuart England*, p. 309.

93 The indictment reads: 'Elizabeth Lowys, wife of John Lowys of Great Waltham, husbandman, indicted for murder by witchcraft. On 15 April 1564 she bewitched John Wodley, aged 3 monts, of Chelmsford, so that he died on 16 april. On 25 Apr. 1564 she bewitched Robert Wodley of Chelmsford, husbandman, so that he died on 1 May. On 20 Apr. 1564, at Great Waltham she bewitched John son of Gregory Canall yeoman, aged about 3 years, so that he died on 1 May' (Cockburn, *Essex Indictments*, p. 172). She was found guilty on all counts, but herself pleaded pregnancy at the assizes on 21 July. She was therefore imprisoned, and remanded in custody on 30 March 1565, pending inspection by a jury of matrons. They decided she was definitely not pregnant, and she was hanged (Cockburn, *Essex Indictments*, pp. 194, 211).

94 *A Tryal of witches at the assizes held at Bury St Edmunds*, 1682, pp. 9–11.

Part III

Witches on stage

7 Elizabethan stagings

The witch, the queen, class

'Mother, whose witches always, always
Got baked into gingerbread'

Sylvia Plath, 'The Disquieting Muses'

The premises of historical criticism of early modern drama have been revised by a decade of new historicism and cultural materialism. An earlier generation of critics were sure that being historical meant reading large numbers of literary texts, tacitly assuming that such texts 'reflected' the ideas and morality of their era. Cultural materialism and new historicism put the case rather differently, arguing for a vision of the theatre as marginal to and therefore subversive of the power regimes of the early modern polity, or, more pessimistically, seeing the Globe as a disseminator of state ideology. Even these opposing theories, however, share a faith that the theatre is somehow at the heart of the making of meaning in the early modern period. At a moment when the literary text is being marginalised – by the arrival of media studies on the one hand and by rejections of canonical texts on the other – historicism has sometimes seemed to offer a way of maintaining arguments for the importance of literary texts without having recourse to (discredited?) aesthetic judgements. To put it unkindly, cultural materialists accused of destroying the canon have actually been beavering away to find new methods of saving it. If we can no longer quite bring ourselves to see *The Tempest* as the serene triumph of Shakespeare's poetic art, at least we can read it as crucial in the development of the discourse of colonialism. Apparently modest claims for the role of literary texts in disseminating 'meaning' have a narcissistic end: save our jobs. The desire to keep the literary text in the foreground has led to some distortions of social history in an effort to bend discourses around so that they lead to Shakespeare. At worst, history becomes a pathway to the concerns of the text, while the text is reduced to an *exemplum* of social historical trends, trends described so vaguely that almost any early modern text might represent them. Seeing textual relations in terms of 'the circulation of social energy' rather than in the old strict hierarchies of text and source has enabled some critics arbitrarily to select texts, and relate them to any literary text. The results are then elevated into a truth about early modern culture, often on the basis of just one or two cultural survivals. In the case of witchcraft, recent criticism compares *Macbeth* to a range of primary and secondary 'historical' material covering a hundred years and at least five countries. This is not merely 'bad' historicisation; it simplifies the early modern period, patronising early modern people.

Throughout the preceding chapters, many literary critics will have been awaiting the transition to 'proper' literature with impatience, wondering how early modern positions can be understood in terms of the loved and familiar playtexts which have shaped their understandings of early modern witchcraft. For literary critics, both primary and secondary histories are quarries, places to seek reminders or clarifications of already known and always already central literary artefacts. When we say 'witch', we can hardly help thinking of *Macbeth*'s witches, however we judge them politically or aesthetically. It is hard for a literary critic to hear any new story without at once trying to fold it back into the old. However much we crave novelty and surprise, we want to be surprised not by the unfamiliar, but in relation to what we already know; new readings of old texts, not new texts for old. This process of surprise feeds our egos; how rich, how many-sided, are the texts we work on, in comparison with the dry, transparent materials over which historians must labour! However, the witch-stories told in earlier chapters will not render themselves sufficiently malleable to be fitted into the plot-paths left by the drama of witchcraft. The light they shed on drama is by negation. Contextualising a play concerning witches means recognising its place in a contest of meanings, seeing it as taking sides in a series of overt and covert disputes. But it also means recognising the points at which drama seeks to or inadvertently succeeds in uncoupling itself from or transforming the discourses upon which it draws, including both elite and popular discourses.

This is not to argue that such transformations, where they occur, are invariably aesthetic improvements. Rather, as I shall argue specifically in relation to *Macbeth*, the result may actually be less complex, less fascinatingly ambiguous, less surprising in plot, less conceptually lucid, than in the 'original' discourse. Moreover, the transformations in question are not in the case of witch-plays always driven by ideological or discursive power. As critics have always known, these appropriations are also driven by a sense of decorum, constraints of genre, questions of plot and plausibility, and commercial considerations. Stories about witches and tropes of witchcraft are often part of an attempt to bring to the stage some of the spectacle of popular print and perhaps oral culture, while *also* catering to the educated audience's fascinated dislike of these spectacles. In order to begin to see what the true place of the stage might have been in witchcraft discourses and debates, we must divest ourselves of the assumption that its place was central.

One way to do this is to look at the lack of correspondence between witch-trials, convictions and executions and the popularity of witchcraft as a topic in drama. Surviving records indicate that prosecutions and convictions for witchcraft peaked under Elizabeth, began to decline under James, and declined still more sharply under Charles.[1] This pattern does not correlate at all with the treatment of witchcraft as a stage topic, even when the lost plays we know about are taken into account. Plays concerning witches were not especially popular until the 1597 boom. Then there is another, larger boom in 1611, and an even more short-term series of revivals around the Lancashire witch-case of 1633, a case which is exceptional in a variety of ways, not least because it is the only large-scale prosecution of the Caroline era. Consequently, literary critics have been much more eager to report that James I tightened up the witchcraft statutes on arriving in England, because this allows us to make a correspondence between drama and 'reality', or at least between drama and a realm of power. Critics who want to argue that witch-hunters may have got their demonological information from the stage face a problem, since all evidence actually points in the opposite direction. The more witches were represented on stage, the more sceptical the London populace grew. The relation between the stage and the social order in the case of witchcraft is more complex than the simultaneous display of shared discursive practices, more teasingly evanescent than mere resistance to an identifiable dominant discourse, more pragmatic and commercial than the loyal replication of royal ideology, and also more idiosyncratic than a map of social or theatrical trends might indicate. I want to test the complexity of this relationship on the few Elizabethan plays to figure the witch as a character or topic of discourse.

As we have seen in the case of Anne Bodenham, witchcraft was itself potentially theatrical. It could involve reciting lines, opening books, acting out rituals, using props. To be sure, this case was not typical, but being a village witch involved behaving in well-known ways, opening the possibility of 'acting'. Opposing the witch is also theatrical; counter-magic involves recitation, ritual and the projection of emotion. The knowledge of witchcraft is itself comparable to generic knowledge; recognising a witch involves a process of identification by type not unlike the process of recognising the melancholic, the malcontent, or the clown on stage. It also caught up the householder in interpreting a familiar narrative, testing her knowledge of plots and plausibilities.

All this has long been recognised; by, for instance, theatrical controversialists of the late sixteenth and seventeenth centuries. Thomas Nashe ambiguously defends the stage by arguing that 'brave Talbot' is brought back to life by its necromancy, and Heywood celebrates the 'bewitching' power of plays to mould the hearts of the spectators. The theatre's opponents too called the plays diabolic: Philip Stubbes wrote that that 'plays were first invented by the Devil', claiming that those who went to theatres also repaired to brothels and to 'Satan's Synagogues, to worship devils and betray Jesus Christ'.[2] These figurations involved a selection from the various images of witches available. Nashe and Heywood's idea of bewitchment reflects the *dramatist's* idea of the witch: Nashe's necromancy derives from *Medea* and from Lucan's Erictho in the

Pharsalia, both sources for later plays, while Heywood's bewitching stage is proficient in love magic, as stage witches usually were, and as the witches of Ovid, Virgil and Theocritus were too. This classical figure of the witch also surfaces in some antitheatrical polemic, as when Philip Stubbes says that only men enchanted by Circe or Medea would dress as women, or Stephen Gosson called the audience Circe's beasts. Most often, however, the stage's opponents drew on learned discourses of demonology shunned by the stage's defenders, often interpereting them by godly lights. William Rankins understands acting itself as a form of possession.[3] The celebrated story about the performance of *Dr Faustus* in which the actors fled because they became convinced that there were one too many devils among them reflects a godly fear that all incantations involve interaction with the powers of darkness. The controversialists who used this figure were not sharing common beliefs, but disagreeing about what witches and drama did. What is striking is that these understandings of the stage as witchcraft, or witchcraft on stage, alike neglect the popular views of witchcraft still dominant in the English countryside. The dramatists were equally neglectful. Both the stage itself and debates about its magic reflect a social gulf between writers and populace, a gulf which the stage may have widened. More importantly, such figurations, however contested, show that a link developed in the minds of early modern writers between magic and theatricality. This created the possibility of a number of plots and self-representations. The kind of showy performativity extensively analysed in terms of cross-dressing also developed around the witch and the magician.

This indirect and subtle understanding of theatricality as a form of hocus-pocus or diabolism, does not inform us about theatrical representations of witches and magic except to show that such figurations were explicitly self-referential well before Prospero drowned his books. In using magic and witchcraft as tropes for itself, the theatre was invoking its own peculiarly idiosyncratic figurations of the witch, rather than referring to the authoritative discourses then in circulation about her. Apparently unmoved by legal, medical, ecclesiastical, theological, demonological and even royal discourses, the theatre's witches remained uninflected by the sometimes stupendous power struggles centring on the figure of the witch. Nor was the stage sticking resolutely to a popular cultural understanding of the witch; it would be generous to the point of being misleading to imply that the witch's chief dramatic architects had much idea of popular belief structures. Plays do not reflect any single discourse of witchcraft, but instead manufacture not one but many literary witches of their own that have only a tangential relation to the figures in other people's texts, much less the figures on the scaffold at Tyburn. This means that we cannot organise the stage into a taxonomy of institutions suddenly afflicted by an early modern 'gender crisis'. We cannot see plays and playhouses driven by a dominant gender ideology or by uncertainties about the fissures in dominant gender ideology. Dramatists *are* reacting to the gendered discourses of the stage and writing, especially the effeminisation of 'acting' and the feminisation of cultural authentication under the rule of a queen, because these inflect their own identities. Dramatists are less interested in witches – either as a social topic or as a terror of the night and a threat to the realm – than they are in their own identities when they produce their witch-figures.

Plays in which witches or witchcraft figure have a complex relationship with their already contested social and discursive pre-texts, and where that relationship demonstrates the agency of the theatre, there is commercial exploitation without great intellectual seriousness, and the transformation of belief into occasions for comic scepticism. If plays do not merely reflect but produce meaning, then the impact of witch-plays on early modern audiences was to widen the gap between popular and elite culture, and also between town and country, scepticism and belief, print culture and oral storytelling, educated and noneducated, civic and rustic, science and superstition, men and women. These distinctions were not (yet) social realities, but they were beginning to be manufactured discursively, and one of the functions of the witch in ideology is to help to fix the valuelessness of the negative term in each binarism. The actual growth of scepticism in the latter half of the seventeenth century may have had at least a little to do with the stage.

In order to understand how the stage witch was invented, I shall offer a narrative account of the way the figure develops. The witch of the Elizabethan stage gradually emerges from a mass of supernatural figures: sorcerers and sorceresses, classical witches, wise women, prophetesses and fairies. While 'real' witches were being hanged in unprecedented numbers, the stage was not especially interested in their fate, seeing the witch as one among many supernatural figures who could be offered as functions of comic and tragic plots of unexpected revelation which the dramatists enjoyed. Admittedly, the 'witch' was not always defined very clearly in popular culture either. While the term had serious legal meanings and implications, ordinary people were often unsure of where its boundaries lay, and were apt to find them less significant than the elite. Jennet Device and Edmund Robinson could draw on a mixture of popular Catholicism, folktales, fairies, popular witch-lore, drama and elite witch-lore to construct a story. Anna Trapnel could be hailed as prophet of the millennium in London and accused of witchcraft in Cornwall, while Anne Jefferies could be greeted as a true prophet by some and persecuted by others.[4] The roles of prophet, confidante of the fairies and witch might be distinct to some, indistinct to others. It was the elite who rushed about making new distinctions to try to bring this disorderly mass under some discursive control, as they were later to do with sexual behaviour. Dramatists furthered the muddle, but then partook of the categorisation process, so that as the sixteenth century wears on types become more distinct. The destination of this process is the emergence of the witch as a clear and recognisable stage 'type' from the muddle of magical figures in which she first appears and to whom she relates, and the way this connects to questions of gender in the political and social realms. The chief agent for this emergence is

Shakespeare, but it was made possible by the publication of Reginald Scot's *Discoverie of witches*, which became the dramatists' principal source.

The magical figure best known to literary critics is the sorcerer, who really deserves more serious treatment than he has received. The stage sorcerer engages with apprehensions about humanism and the power of print and rhetoric, most powerfully in *Dr Faustus,* and these engagements are heavily marked by assumptions about the connection between such topics and the masculine. Medieval enchanters of the Merlin type, who feature most prominently in romances and chronicle plays, are powerful and unequivocally prophetic. Merlin and his cognates are also the bearers of knowledge about the nation, and consequently their prophetic and storytelling abilities are reliable. (By contrast, 'cunning women' in plays of the same date are charlatans.) It was this role of 'national magician' for which Elizabeth selected that walking compendium of Renaissance magicians' roles, John Dee. She may not have shared Dee's imperialist mission to civilise the world through magic, but she did accept Dee's antiquarian researches, which located the Tudor monarchs as the heirs of Brutus and Arthur.[5] Like the tormented humanist-magician, the medieval sage reproduces critical assumptions about the gendering of knowledge; he can act as the repository of knowledge about the historical past and the national future precisely because he is male, just as the humanist-magician can also be the one who knows. *Sir Clymon and Sir Clamydes*, with its magician, Sir Brian Sans Foy, and Rowley's *Birth of Merlin* both celebrate the enchanter as the true author of British greatness and confounder of false magicians.[6] A third kind of magician also relates to epistemology, but in this case the growing empirical movement, which understands nature as a feminine space to be worked on by the male intellect. This image derives from magical discourse, on display in Robert Greene's *Friar Bacon and Friar Bungay.* Anthony Munday's *John a Kent and John a Cumber*, by contrast, shows sorcerers tricking people into and out of love affairs.[7] These magicians are hocus-pocuses, not real magic-users, using their skills to trick people.

Such figures overlap with the figure of the cunning woman, creating a range of problems which centre on the impossible task of defending the gender of the sorcerer-king against the creeping incursion of figures of effeminisation, luxury, duplicity and other tropes of femininity. The sorcerer must not only avoid becoming a witch; he must also avoid the least trace of femininity. This anxiety is a Jacobean development, arising at least in part from the pressure put on the discourse by James I's appropriation of the role of magus or royal sorcerer as a figure for the providential absolutism of his rule. In portraying himself and having others portray him as Solomon, James was deliberately conflating the roles of king and magus, for Solomon was both.[8] It is this ruler-sorcerer whose masculinity is asserted strenuously in Prospero and in Peter Fabel of *The Merry Devil of Edmonton*. In the same year, however, Barnabe Barnes's *The Devil's Charter* represents the figure of the magus as synonymous with feminine and even homoerotic tyranny and duplicity, using it as part of anti-Catholic polemic.

The play is violently pro-James and pro-Protestant, but it is also problematic for James's habitual self-representation as benificent magician-king.[9] More explicitly troubling is the Caroline posterity of the magician in Milton's Comus, a figure who turns Shakespeare's Prospero inside out in an astute countdown of all his darkest traits. Comus, lustful, luxurious, spendthrift, corrupting, is the magician-absolutist taken to extremes.

Elizabethan dramatists were also preoccupied with negotiating the relations between gender and rule, but these identities were differently constellated when Elizabeth occupied the throne. It was just as difficult to separate the figure of the witch from the queen as it was to separate James's benign royal magus from charlatans and devil-worshippers. However, while the Jacobean stage was preoccupied with witches just as the nation was losing interest in them, the Elizabethan stage was almost silent about them while the nation, and especially the court, were working themselves up to fever pitch. As C. L'Estrange Ewen points out, the surviving records suggest that witchcraft prosecutions and executions peaked in the 1580s and 1590s.[10] Some of the elite's anxieties related to their worries about the queen, the unclear succession and the threat from Spain. The witch-alarm began with the discovery of three female wax figures in August of 1578, found buried in a London dunghill, with bristles stuck through the heart. The Spanish ambassador reported the widespread dismay thus caused; it was assumed that the poppets were an attempt on the queen's life by witchcraft. The queen excluded witchcraft and sorcery from a general pardon given the same year.[11] The trial of the witches of Windsor, who had also used poppets, was examined by the Privy Council, who asked Sir Henry Neville and the Dean of Windsor to look into its wider implications, since 'there hath lately been discovered a practice of that device very likely to be intended to the destruction of her Majesty's person'.[12] The iterability of the royal image, so crucial to royal authority, became a problem, just as it did with counterfeiters, whose activities likewise troubled the queen's right to determine her own representation and to decide which images of her should count as authentic.[13] However, the sudden panic about witches and the queen also expressed more pressing political anxieties.

All these concerns imply an opposition between the queen and witches. Witches, acting on behalf of the devil (or Spain, or the pope) were assumed to be interested in removing her. Yet matters were not always so clear-cut. These concerns overlapped with the queen's last serious entry into marriage negotiations, with the Duc d'Alençon, which also involved tremendous stress for Leicester and his faction, fearful of a Catholic prince, Catholic toleration, and a Catholic heir. Their concerns were expressed, albeit crudely, by John Stubbs' notorious pamphlet *The discovery of a gaping gulf*; it is no coincidence that this pamphlet goes out of its way to portray a Catholic woman ruler, Catherine de Medici, as a witch, surrounded by 'familiar spirits'.[14] Elizabethan paranoia could accuse Catholics of political and other sorcery, but such figurations reflected on Elizabeth too. Catherine's witchcraft glanced not only at her religion, but at her anomalousness as a female ruler. The image of Catherine as sorceress in the power of the devil stood ready to *become* an image of Elizabeth if she accepted Alençon. Handily, it was a figure of female transgression and foreign control, since the elite did not believe that a witch was capable of any power without the devil.

While nobody in England seems seriously to have entertained the idea of Elizabeth as witch, Catholic propagandists were keen to present her as leagued with Satan. There was an opportunity in the fact that her mother, Anne Boleyn, had been accused of witchcraft; everyone knew that witchcraft descended in the female line.[15] This may be one reason that Scottish Catholics saw her as 'cozened by the devil' in signing Mary Queen of Scots's death warrant.[16] Fear of being leagued with Catholic propagandists might explain the stage's silence on a subject which was preoccupying the realm. Fear of the queen herself and of her disapproval must also have limited the possibilities, especially after the punishment of Stubbs and his printer. It would not have been politic, and it might have been frightening too, to create a powerful but evil female figure, one who could dominate the entire stage, and it might not have been possible to do so while keeping the figure entirely separate from the queen. Even Acrasia's defeat by a very thoroughly masculine humanist must have been covertly satisfying at fantasy level for the increasingly insecure men around Elizabeth. Effeminised courtiers lost in a daze of love foretell the disastrous rhetoric of the Essex faction, with their emphasis on the need for a real man as king.[17] The pressure exerted by Elizabeth on a masculine identity so fragile that it was unable to tolerate the equation of power with femininity in any sphere made the witch more of a problem, and perhaps more of a threat. Taken together with the politicisation of the figure in relation to the queen, it is not surprising that few were game enough to portray witches and sorceresses.

It was hard to maintain the distinction between the queen and the witch, partly because of Ralegh's link between Elizabeth and the moon, and dramatists' interest in classical witch-lore. Ralegh's representation of Elizabeth as the perpetually chaste moon was a response to the failure of the Alençon marriage negotiations. Usually read as an unequivocally positive image, Helen Hackett has recently pointed to the moon's dark side.[18] Significantly, the figure of the moon-goddess Diana was linked with the witch-goddess Hecate. In the English translation of Vincenzo Cartari's *Le imagini colla sposizione delgi dei degli antichi*, Robert Linche writes that Diana is triform; 'with some she was called Diana, with others Hecate' he adds.[19] Hecate is the goddess entreated by Medea and Theocritus's sorceress; she gives her name to the leader of the Weird Sisters in the revised *Macbeth*, and Middleton's witch is called after her.

This classical link makes it appropriate that the most classical of all Elizabethan witch-plays is also the one most directly concerned with the queen. John Lyly's *Endimion, or the Man in the Moon*, was written in 1584–5, in the aftermath of Alençon and after the sudden burst of anxiety about witchcraft. It was performed at court in 1585, and also at Paul's by a company of boy actors,

Paul's Children, in 1588. Lyly, a humanist turned courtier who was a client of both Burghley and the Earl of Oxford, has been represented by Richard Helgerson as a prodigal, a writer fearful that fiction-writing wastes time and talent that should productively be devoted to national interests and provident humanist patronage relations.[20] One might add that these images are gendered. Lyly is among those who are intent on figuring the romance discourse as directed at women while sharing a joke with his male peers about women's flightiness and incapacity, a joke which seems an attempt to explain away his own involvement with fiction.[21] Useful work involves converting men to virtue; prodigality equals entertaining ladies. This points to a certain nervousness about the boundaries of gender. Nonetheless, Lyly's fear of effeminisation did not prevent him from passionately hoping (in vain) for personal notice from the Queen, illustrating the way the humanist discourses of male patronage buckled under the strain of supporting a woman ruler at their apex. Lyly might have been invented to exemplify the pressure placed on (downwardly mobile) man when faced with a powerful woman.[22]

Lyly's play is beset by tension between flattery and its dark undertones, which keep bursting out with rage at failure to control the powerful and win their acknowledgement. In an important discussion of the play, Philippa Berry argues that Lyly's efforts to make a distinction between Cynthia, the powerful queen-object of Endimion's hopeless longing, and the witch Dipsas fail because it is Dipsas who incarnates the bodily reality of the (undesirable) ageing Queen Elizabeth.[23] Dipsas's body, ironically blazoned by her clown lover Sir Thopas, is the antithesis of of the Petrarchan ideal: 'In how sweet a proportion her cheeks hang down to her breasts like dugs, and her paps to her waste like bags!', he muses besottedly. However, the image is not only (a)sexual: Dipsas is also represented as past childbearing through her aged breasts, a fact which may have weighed more heavily with Elizabethans contemplating Elizabeth than her beauty or lack of it. The absence of any possible heir of the body had been the nightmare of the Burghley faction with whom Lyly was associated. In figuring an ageing female body, the play focuses regretfully on Elizabeth's obsolescence as a vehicle for maternity and royal continuity. The natural *continuity* of heirs has to be replaced with a notion of *timelessness*. Dipsas's age also signifies mortality, and Lyly's assertions of the timelessness of Cynthia's rule have a desperate ring. The Queen's death is marked on the ageing female body. Like her childlessness, it points to a blind future of frightening uncertainty.

At the same time, the obsolescence of the old woman's body is presented as a function of Dipsas's other limitations. In a paean to Elizabeth's characteristically Tudor fantasies of absolutism, Lyly follows the queen's own self-fashioning in distinguishing her spiritual motherhood of the nation from the physical barrenness which besets other women.[24] Dipsas and Cynthia are doubly differentiated. First, they have separate spheres of activity. Arrayed as Cynthia (Sky), Tellus (earth) and Dipsas (witch-world of night), the three at first suggest a triple goddess, Diana–Selene–Hecate, a triple lunar goddess representing the phases of the moon. Yet the three are not really understandable in this way. There is no question of Cynthia sharing the sphere of the moon with the others; she dominates it alone. Tellus, on the other hand, represents a feminised vision of the world as a site of seductive and prodigal temptation, problematic for the young men like Endimion who might become entangled in their desires. Dipsas, however, lacks a sphere of influence of either kind. Cynthia is goddess and queen; Tellus is seductress and figure of the world; Dipsas is just a village witch, with abilities magnified only to fairy-tale and not to allegorical level.

Throughout the play, the three are differentiated in terms of the conventions of comedy and not in terms of mythography, where differentiation is impossible to sustain. Dipsas is light relief, central to the comic love plot concerning Sir Thopas, the comic foil of Endimion, and the equally comic subplot involving her separation from Geras, her husband. Desire for Cynthia is the purest of neoplatonic passions for excellence; Tellus hopes to provoke the most prodigal Petrarchan excess (I. 2. 60ff); Dipsas is desirable only to comic effect. Dipsas is confined to the subplot, and thus distinguished from Cynthia. Dipsas is divided from Cynthia by social class. Cynthia is a queen, and Dipsas is a local cunning woman as seen by the learned. Dipsas's very first speech makes gargantuan Medean claims for her magic, but adds that 'there is nothing that I cannot do, but that only which you would have me do; and therein I differ from the gods' (I. 4. 22-5). Though this answer is perfectly true, it also comes from the discourse of tricksterdom and cozenage. *Endimion* was probably written and was certainly revised after Reginald Scot's *Discoverie of witchcraft* appeared, with its long list of juggling tricks to gull fools.[25] Lyly may have been first among the many dramatists to quarry it as a source, for at this point the text seems to be playing with the idea that witches are primarily cozeners.

This sceptical element became a leitmotif of witch-plays. It was an outcome of the relationship which grew up between dramatists interested in the supernatural and Scot's treatise. Even dramatists with quite different projects writing in different genres, even those writing on 'real-life' cases, consulted Reginald Scot. Even those writing explicitly to flatter James I, who was hardly Scot's greatest fan, continued to use his work. Like Holinshead's *Chronicles*, Scot's book became one of those compendia of plots and metaphors which virtually generated a discourse of its own. It is significant that the first play to feature a witch in a major part was not written until after the publication of Scot's treatise, some three years after the beginning of the witch-panic at court. Scot's thesis that witches are all mad or tricksters must especially have suited the stage, since the notion of witchcraft as a form of theatre created an appealing overlap between drama and the witch. In a piece of self-fashioning which may also have been intended to refute Puritans keen to equate theatres with demon-worship, the dramatists collectively sought to construct the witch, a figure whose witchcraft was at least partially understandable as theatrical spectacle. This vision was offered to dramatists by Scot, and they seized it gratefully. Along with Scot's multiplicity of stories of cozenage and his constant repetition of the minutiae of popular superstition, however, dramatists began to absorb his scepticism. Consequently, Lyly's play also offers the *real* power of witchcraft as something that can easily be defeated by the particular constellation of virtues represented by Cynthia. To put it crudely, it is as if Lyly, far from fearing the witch, is offering her defeat as a kind of reassurance, overtly for those worried about the Queen's life, and covertly for those half afraid of Elizabeth's own power. The play works to reduce the witch's power, exactly like the later *Masque of Queens*, which tackles the same problem of how to distinguish queenly power from that of night-hags, and is beset by some of the same anxieties about the effeminisation of the court.

By the time Lyly wrote his later play *Mother Bombie*, he had almost given up hope of preferment from the queen. Perhaps this is why *Mother Bombie* is almost a rude rewriting of *Endimion*, where Cynthia is deliberately and defiantly conflated with the cunning woman.[26] What is so strenuously kept apart in *Endimion* is allowed to melt together. While in *Endimion* it is Cynthia who takes control of the narrative, putting Dipsas in her proper place as a married woman, in the later play her role as unraveller of the plot is handed over to the witch. It is Mother Bombie who knows best, and who orders events justly. The play portrayal of a cunning woman is rare: Mother Bombie apparently has little posterity, though she is mentioned in later plays. This may be unduly subject to the injustices of time, for a number of witch-plays from the sixteenth century have been lost. One of these, *Mother Redcap*, may possibly have been about a cunning woman, but may also have been a representation of the case of Alice Gooderidge and Elizabeth Wright, both tried in 1597.[27] They were an appropriate subject for the theatre, for this was the first case in which the Puritan exorcist John Darrell was involved: the possessed boy in this case called the witch 'Mother Redcap'.[28] Lyly's difficulties with both Elizabeth and the witch suggest that others may have been reluctant to attempt representations too close to home; this may be why other sorceresses in Elizabethan drama are very strictly classical: Medea in Greene's *Alphonsus* (1591), and Melissa in his *Orlando Furioso* (1592?).[29]

Hence the surviving stage witch is almost purely Shakespearean. In virtually every one of his thirty-seven plays, witchcraft is a topic, a metaphor, a joke, a story, a half-formulated reference point, a piece of the plot. From the Lapland sorcerers imagined in *Comedy of Errors* to the 'witchcraft' which brings Hermione to 'life' in *The Winter's Tale*, the idea of magical intervention or bewitchment is crucial.[30] This interest may not have been widely shared among other dramatists, but it has become a crucial part of the image of the Bard in the modern world. The witch, the fairy and the other supernatural baggage carried around in Shakespeare's plays are vital parts of the image of a Merrie Rural Englande which his name still evokes in the breasts of the sentimental. A world where spry village spinsters believed in pert fairies and dapper elves is cuter than a world in which they incinerated themselves trying to cook their pancakes over a fire of bedstraw. Witches and fairies go with thatched cottages, knot gardens, maypoles on the village green and the other appurtenances of the organic society, village-style. The witch, as we have seen before, figures the distance we have come from the darkness of that past, but she also helps to idealise it by figuring its worst threat as an empty one. No nuclear weapons or gangs of muggers lurk round the Elizabethan corner; instead, there is the exciting and fundamentally powerless figure of the old hag.

It is odd that Shakespeare's witches should have been thus awkwardly fitted in to a fantasy of social history. His own understanding of the place of the witch in both history and nationhood was rather different. In the first two of his history plays, *Henry VI Parts I and II*, scenes of witchcraft and conjuration occur and are figured as blockages of good rule, of a kind which come from the nation's enemies.[31] Remembering, however, that Elizabethan rhetoric characteristically conflated the person of the monarch with the body of the state, it is not surprising to find that this figuration of the witch, like Lyly's, is not unrelated to the queen. While it is possible to read Joan la Pucelle's initial confrontations with Talbot as encounters between reality and paranoid fantasy, this possibility is very thoroughly removed by the sensational uncovering of her identity as witch in the final act.

It is crucial that this is 'history', presented as having in some way really happened, for this is one of the trajectories taken by the two surviving plays based on 'real' cases. In *The Witch of Edmonton* and *The Witches of Lancashire* sceptical positions are made available and then erased by the stage display of the witch's practices.[32] Joan enacts her conjuration, and this constitutes the principal revelation or discovery of the truth of witchcraft to the audience. A discovery, is of course a dis-covery, an unmasking or dis-closing, a bringing of the interior working into the light of the public gaze. Discovery was the term used by both sceptics like Reginald Scot and believers like Henry Goodcole to define the rhetorical protocols of their figuration of witches. Politically – as a threat to the queen – witches were a menace precisely because their art made it possible for them to work in secret. When Joan is revealed as a witch rather than a pragmatic French opponent of the field, a military threat becomes a threat from within.

The conversion of the other from a foreign army into a witch represents an inside-outing of the threat of the other, from the masculine realm of war (in which Joan is a virago) to the feminine realm of sorcery. This play comes after Armada year and during the siege of Rouen, but also after a number of plots against the queen's life using sorcery or the equally private poison; many of these involved an alliance between foreign foes and traitors at home. The Florentine banker Roberto Ridolfi was the go-between in an elaborate scheme involving a Spanish invasion from the Netherlands, an English rebellion, and the deposition and murder of Elizabeth. Francis Throckmorton's plot of 1583 involved a French invasion and the murder of the queen. Elizabeth was also the target of an early gunpowder plot in 1587, which aimed to blow her up in bed, while Roderigo Lopez was to try to poison her in 1594, and Squire to kill her by smearing the pommel of the saddle she used with deadly substances.[33] It was the job of the Elizabethan secret service to discover such links between inside and outside and to expose them; it is the role of this secret service that the theatre takes up. The alliance between the powers of hell and the military might of France is uncovered in the person of Joan as witch.

It is as an amazon that Joan manages to conceal her witchcraft; far from being allied, the images of virago and witch are opposed, because the play is not driven by gender anxiety but by political fears with a less direct relation to gender.[34] In terms of nationhood, witchcraft and Amazonian invasion are opposite threats; one is invisible, the other visible. Since one is public, the other private, one could interpret these as gendered; certainly it was the *sphere* of witchcraft (among other things) that marked the witch as feminine. Here, however, this is overdetermined not by the problem of the queen's sex, but by the assumption that without witchcraft Joan could never have gotten ahead. Exactly the same thing happens in *Henry VI Part II*. The Duchess of Gloucester is a kind of virago by her language, but what that language attests is her marginality, her distance from the military and macho ways of political action: 'Were I a man, a duke, and next of blood / I would remove these tedious stumbling-blocks / And smooth my way upon their headless necks' (I. 2. 63-5). The lines prefigure Lady Macbeth, another virago symbolically allied with witchcraft. Witchcraft is the resort of women because it symbolises the only way they can work politically; by stealth, in secret, rather than on the public field of battle or debate. The only way that a woman like Joan can enter these public spaces is by witchcraft, an irony which explains her sudden reduction to feminine helplessness when she loses her powers. If this reduction glances at Elizabeth as a woman rather than as embodiment of the English nation, it is only to fantasise a realm where the rules of gender hold good with no troubling exceptions.

Just as Joan's conjuring signifies 'real' threats to Elizabeth posed by the alliance of secret and foreign powers, so the Duchess of Gloucester's eventual conjurations with Margery Jourdain look back to the threat to Elizabeth believed to be posed by those who threatened to do her horoscope to determine her date of death. A 1581 statute made it an especial offence to try to predict the queen's future. This was the result of claims that Norfolk had been influenced to join the Ridolfi plot by a prophecy. Francis Babington, too was convinced he could succeed because of his reading of one of the Merlin Prophecies.[35] It was against the politicised prophecy that the Earl of Northampton wrote in his *Defensative against the poison of supposed prophecies*, first printed in 1583. There were also a mass of prophecies and bad auguries in Armada year, many of which directly concerned the queen.[36] While Jackson and Marcus see the witches of the *Henry* plays in terms of the Jacobean witch-discourses incarnated in the North Berwick trial of 1591, one might more plausibly argue the opposite; that *Macbeth*'s obsession with the overlap between witchcraft and prophecy harks *back* to the last two decades of Elizabeth's reign and its heavily politicised ancient prophecies. Certainly it is the act of 1581, which specifically forbade prophesying the queen's future 'by witchcraft, conjurations, or other like unlawful means whatsoever', which is evoked in *Henry VI Part II*, along with the kinds of prophecies it was intended to suppress. In the play, these are amphibologies, or ambiguities, like the prophecies in *Macbeth*, stories which could be read as prophecies of success or failure, precisely the kind of prophecy believed to be politcally dangerous because likely to incite rebellion.[37] However, just as the disclosure of Joan's witchcraft nullifies her threat to the state, so the witch Margery Jourdain proves the undoing of the Duchess of Gloucester's plotting; it is surveillance of her that leads to the Duchess's arrest. The witch again works to signify a narrative occasion for a threat to the state whose revelation equates with neutralisation. What might have seemed an alarming alliance between members of different classes is swiftly the means by which such problematic links are broken.

Shakespeare's witches were part of a growing divison between urban and rural, peasantry and bourgeois middle class, which allowed the latter to begin to idealise and sweeten their image of the former. This happened most obviously through pastoral, but also through the appropriation of chivalric romance for a figuration of civilité, the politicisation of the figure of the shepherd in Spenser and Milton, and conversely the conservative defences of old holiday pastimes and traditional hospitality under James and their codification into a *Book of Sports* that disseminated royal ideology.[38] Just as few of these projects undertook to represent the 'true' or authentic views of those who actually plied the homely slighted shepherd's trade, so Shakespeare's plays are not especially interested in faithful representations of popular beliefs. The exception may be *The Merry Wives of Windsor*, which does attempt to represent the lives and customs of a group of the middling sort – innkeepers, doctors, magistrates, citizens and citizens' wives, parsons – in a highly specific locale. No other Shakespeare play is set in an English town known to members of the audience; here airy nothing has been given some very local habitations indeed. There is a long standing, and probably incorrect tradition that *Merry Wives* was written at Elizabeth's request. She had asked for a play about Falstaff in love.[39] More convincingly, Leslie Hotson has argued that the play was written especially to be performed at the Garter Feast of 23 April 1597, one month before the knights themselves were to be installed at Windsor. Both these views share an important perspective: the play anatomises the middling sort, from which Shakespeare himself came, for the eyes of their betters.[40] They present the middling and their lives as a space of allegorical and symbolic representation of the deeds of their betters – Anne Barton rightly sees the play as a kind of antimasque of the Garter – but the play also holds those lives and beliefs up as objects of curiosity and vehicles for the symbolism of unruliness and chastisement. The bourgeois thus symbolically participate in the Garter ceremony, but in a manner that is already contained by the fact that they are anatomised with such precision. The play is aristocratic not only because Fenton's eventual success in marrying Ann Page signifies a kind of appropriation of middling (cash) value by the aristocracy, but also and more importantly because of Elizabeth's figurative role as both Diana to Falstaff's Actaeon and as spectator who embodies the social hierarchy.[41]

The witch of Brainford, like the fairies of Windsor and Herne the Hunter, never appears in the play. Instead, the play sets out systematically to show that these creatures are the inventions of (feminine) cunning allied with (masculine) superstition. The truths which lie behind them are female resourcefulness, male sexual desire, and sheer theatre – costumes, special effects and the like. The fairies are both masks and a masque: they conceal the identities of the wives, and they act as a stage spectacle. As tricksters who lure a greedy man to come to the wood and be deceived in his hopes, they recall the notorious cozener Judith Philips, who swindled a member of the middling sort of Hampshire by promising to introduce him to the Queen of the Fairies. Having persuaded him to prepare a chamber for the queen hung with linen and decorated with gold candlesticks, and having extracted the sum of fourteen pounds in gold from him, Philips plays her trump-card:

> This Judith caused him and his wife to go into the yard, where she set the saddle on his back, and thereon girteth it fast with two new girths, and also put a bridle upon his head, all which being done, she got upon his back in the saddle, and so rid him three times betwixt the chamber and the holly tree.[42]

Ann Page's suitors are left to cool their heels in the wood while Anne gets away; Judith's 'rich churl' here is left 'quaking in the cold' while Judith 'vanishes away', 'as the old wives say night-spirits do'. The figure of the woman riding the man is the staple popular image of the world turned upside down; it comes from exactly the compendium of plots that Shakspeare uses in *Merry Wives* to humiliate Falstaff and Master Ford, as well as Ann Page's suitors. The pamphlet's robust tone, reminiscent of *fabliaux*, can help us to understand the diversity of plots which the supernatural could generate. Not all witches or fairies must be serious-faced representations of supernatural or political matters. Like the play, the story of Judith Philips sees the supernatrual as a series of masquerades which can be assumed by women to trick men.

The fairies of *Merry Wives* recall the all-singing, all-dancing fairies who danced on to interrupt the action in plays like Lyly's *Gallathea* and *Endimion*, and they look forward to the dancing witches of the Jacobean stage.[43] Like the fairies of *Endimion*, and like the Weird Sisters, they speak in octosyllabic couplets. What is distinctive in *Merry Wives* is the fakery of the fairies and the presence of the fairy queen. She is 'played' by Mistress Quickly, who even in this incarnation is not a figure readily associated with semipaternal wisdom, perpetual virginity, or just rule. The figure of the fairy queen, associated with Elizabeth very firmly by 1597, makes this a dangerous dream. However, just as in Lyly's play the queen was divided from Dipsas by the insuperable bounds of class, which prevent a confluence along lines of gender, so here the antics of the duplicitous though fiercely chaste fairy queens, and the 'fairy quean' Mistress Quickly, are separated from Elizabeth by their location among the middling sort. Although the last passage in the Folio text explicitly alludes to the queen in connection with these false fairies, Mistress Quickly borrows the appropriate rhetoric of the literary and dramatic fairies which were Shakespeare's invention two years earlier in *A Midsummer Night's Dream*:

> Search Windsor Castle, elves, within and out.
> Strew good luck, oafs, on every sacred room,
> That it may stand till the perpetual doom
> In state as wholesome as in state 'tis fit,
> Worthy the owner and the owner it.
>
> (V. 5. 55-9)

The passage is so close to the fairy finale of the *Dream* that one might suspect Shakespeare of adroitly cannibalising his own work; the 'fairies' enter a palace by night and admire it, so that fairy order and aristocratic order confirm each other. Despite the change of register, Mistress Quickly is not really going to dance through the castle at Windsor; nor is she going to dance in it, under any circumstances. It is the precise location of the play in the social hierarchy that allows Shakespeare to debunk some of the most cherished and dangerous images of the reign. This includes the image of the witch of Brainford, here reduced in the first instance to nothing but impersonation, an incident of cross-dressing which may recall *Macbeth*'s bearded women by figuring the ambivalence of the witch's gender, but also reminds us of the witch's theatricality. The 'witch of Brainford' is nothing more than a costume, a hat and cloak.

The play goes on to figure the witch as the fantasy of one especially paranoid man. Master Ford is not of course an upstanding Elizabethan patriarch, but that figure of fun, the jealous husband, whose jealousy is based on his sexual incompetence. By associating witch-beliefs with such a figure, the butt of popular jokes and an embodiment of all that the carnivalesque antimasque wishes to expel, Shakespeare disassociates himself and the court from them. Witch-beliefs, he seems to say, are the figments of an idle brain; the very name of the witch's habitation, Brain-Ford, seems to signal her origins in Master Ford's head.[44] So sceptical is the play that even Master Ford dislikes the 'witch' primarily because he (with ironic perspicuity) sees the identity of 'witch' as a cover for sexual licence. 'We are simple men,' he laments, 'we do not know what's brought to pass under the profession of fortune-telling. She works by charms, by spells, by the figure, and such daubery as this is, beyond our element; we know nothing' (IV. 2. 172-9). Though Ford conflates the witch with sexual licence, feminist critics have been wrong to assume that the play endorses his vision, and that this somehow glances back at Elizabeth in the way that *Endimion* or the *Faerie Queene* cannot help doing. Mistress Ford's militant chastity and the 'true' identity of the witch mean that 'she' cannot be understood in such terms. Ford's words focus not on the unruly female body, but on the cover story: they render witchcraft part of a world of female stories and practices designed to deceive the eyes of men, seen as women's gulls whether clients, lovers or husbands. The witch is not alarming because she has supernatural powers, but because 'she' is representative of the power of female storytelling. It is this female power to invent and stage supernatural stories which constitutes their principal weapon against their importunate suitors and suspicious husbands. Against this prodigality of invention, the crude desires of Falstaff and the equally crude violence of Master Ford are not only ineffectual, but made to appear part of a drama over which they have completely lost control.

If the court had really been palpitating with fear of witches in 1597, this would have been a very impolitic piece of writing, even given the safe distance established by class between the witch and the queen. It would have been daring to the point of suicide, in fact, since the witches who were regarded as the most dangerous to the queen, the witches who used poppets, had themselves come from Windsor. What seems more likely is that the 'witch-vogue' of 1597 was made possible by the *resolution* of the tensions around the figure of Elizabeth which had fractured Lyly's play and troubled Shakespeare's histories through the distance of class. Taken together with the growth of scepticism, however, this had the effect of turning the witch-beliefs of the populace into a compendium of fantastic or untrue plots to be quarried and mined by dramatists. The principal *copia* of such plots was Reginald Scot's *Discoverie of witchcraft*, a sceptical work, but one which recounted beliefs, and it duly produced sceptical dramas which told breathlessly sensational witch-stories. This ensured that the stage would play a part in separating popular and high culture at the very moments when it might otherwise appear to bring them together. Although Shakespeare is not the first to divide the witch from other women along lines of class and the rhetorics and protocols which go with it, he is the most important, for it is in his plays that we find the precursors of our own ideas of witches as signs of a vanished and feminised primitivism.

NOTES

1 This was first established by C. L'Estrange Ewen's study of witch-trials (*Witch Hunting and Witch Trials*, 1929 hereafter *WH*); more recently, see Ann Laurence, *Women in England 1500–1760*, London: Weidenfeld & Nicolson, 1994, p. 218.

2 Thomas Nashe, *Pierce Penilesse His Supplication to the Devil*, in *The Works of Thomas Nashe*, ed. R. B. McKerrow, 5 vols, Oxford: Blackwell, 1966–74, vol. I, p. 212; Philip Stubbes, *The anatomy of abuses*, 1583, ed. F. J. Furnivall, p. 143; Stubbes is making the classic equation between Jews and witches common to demonologists and Puritans. See Laura Levine, 'Men in women's clothing: antitheatricality and effeminisation from 1579 to 1642', *Criticism*, 28 (1986) pp. 123–8; Stephen Greenblatt, 'Shakespeare and the exorcists', in *Shakespearean Negotiations: The Circulation of Social Energy in Renaissance England*, Oxford: Clarendon, 1988.

3 Thomas Heywood, *An Apology for Actors*, 1612, sig. B4r; Stephen Gosson, *School of abuse*, p. 10; William Rankins, *A mirror of monsters*, 1587.

4 On Trapnel, see *Anna Trapnel's report and plea*, 1654, 'To The Reader'; on Jennet

Device, see Chapter 6, on Edmund Robinson see Chapters 6 and 10, and on Jefferies see Chapter 6.

5 John S. Mebane, *Renaissance Magic and the Return of the Golden Age*, Lincoln and London: University of Nebraska Press, 1994, p. 86. See also *The Private Diary of John Dee*, ed. J. Orchard Halliwell, Camden Society, 1842, pp. 18–21.

6 *Sir Clymon and Sir Clamydes*, 1570/80, authorship uncertain; William Rowley's Jacobean chronicle play, *The Birth of Merlin*, in *Shakespeare Apocrypha*, ed. C. F. Tucker Brooke, London: 1908.

7 *Friar Bacon and Friar Bungay*, 1589?, in *The Plays and Poems of Robert Greene*, ed. John Churton Collins, Oxford: Oxford University Press, 1905; Anthony Munday, *John A Kent and John A Cumber*, ed. Arthur E. Pennell, New York and London: 1980.

8 James as Solomon: see Graham Parry, *The Golden Age Restored*, Manchester: Manchester University Press, 1985, pp. 31–2.

9 *The Merry Devil of Edmonton,* 1607. Barnabe Barnes, *The Devil's Charter*, 1607.

10 See Ewen, *WH*, pp. 180–5.

11 *Statutes of the Realm*, vol. 4, part I, p. 659.

12 *A rehearsall both straung and true*, in *Witchcraft in England 1558–1618*, ed. Barbara Rosen, p. 83ff, and see Rosen's headnote. See also Reginald Scot, *Discoverie of witchcraft*, 1584, 16. 3.

13 The witch using a poppet does not appear in drama until Dekker's *Whore of Babylon* in 1604, where the plot is to kill the queen. It is followed by the use of poison, also a deadly method which works from a distance, and the one used by the Ridolfi plotters.

14 *The discovery of a gaping gulf*, sig. D4. We might also note the presence of the Continental demonologist and political theorist Jean Bodin in Alençon's train until 1 February 1581/2. He visited Parliament, and attended the trial of the Jesuit Edmund Campion.

15 *CSPD*, Henry VIII 10, p. 70. All her life Elizabeth resisted being identified with her mother in favour of being seen as her father's daughter, an understandable response, since her mother was represented as an anthology of the featrures of a 'bad woman'. See Leah Marcus, *Puzzling Shakespeare: Local Reading and its Discontents*, Berkeley: University of California Press, 1988, pp. 54–6.

16 Leah Marcus wrongly states that Elizabeth herself was seen as a witch. This statement is now being cited by others, despite the fact that Marcus's evidence is very weak: *Puzzling Shakespeare*, pp. 81 and p. 235, n. 56.

17 On the effeminate courtiers of Acrasia's bower, see Patricia Parker, *Literary Fat Ladies: Rhetoric, Gender, Property*, London: Methuen, 1987, ch. 4.

18 Helen Hackett, *Virgin Mother, Maiden Queen: Elizabeth I and the Cult of the Virgin Mary*, London: Macmillan, 1995, pp. 182–6.

19 Vincenzo Cartari, *Le imagini colla sposizione delgi dei degli antichi*, Venice, 1556, Robert Linche, *The Fountain of Ancient Fiction*, sig. H3v. This conflation is also asserted by Thomas Heywood, *Gunaikaeon, or nine books of various history concerning women*, 1624, pp. 15–6.

20 John Lyly, *Endiminion, or the Man in the Moon*, in *The Complete Works of John Lyly*, ed. R. Warwick Bond, 3 vols, Oxford: Clarendon, 1902; Richard Helgerson, *The Elizabethan Prodigals*, Berkeley: University of California Press, 1976.

21 See Helen Hackett, '"Yet tell me some such fiction": Lady Mary Wroth's *Urania* and the femininity of romance', in *Women, Texts and Histories 1575–1760*, ed. Clare Brant and Diane Purkiss, London: Routledge, 1992, pp. 39–46. On Lyly as a ladies' man, see Juliet Fleming, 'The ladies' man and the age of Elizabeth', in *Sexuality and Gender in Early Modern Europe*, ed. James Grantham Turner, Cambridge: Cambridge University Press, 1993, p. 159.

22 On Lyly see G. K. Hunter, *John Lyly: Humanist as Courtier*, Cambridge, MA:

Harvard University Press, 1962. On Elizabeth and her courtiers see Louis Montrose, '"Eliza Queene of Shepherds" and the pastoral of power', in *Renaissance Historicisms*, ed. Arthur F. Kinney and Dan S. Collins, Amherst: University of Massachusetts Press, 1987, pp. 34–64.

23 Philippa Berry, *Of Chastity and Power: Elizabethan Literature and the Unmarried Queen*, London: Routledge, 1988, ch. 5.

24 On motherhood see Hackett, 'Yet tell me', pp. 118–9, and 164–5.

25 Scot's treatise was first printed in 1584, and was not entered in the stationer's register. Lyly's play is usually dated 1584–5.

26 John Lyly, *Mother Bombie*, in *Complete Works*. Mother Bombie may originally have been based on Scot's Mother Bungy of Rochester, *Discoverie*, 16.3.

27 Alice Gooderidge is also discussed in Chapter 6.

28 *The most wonderfull and true storie of a certain witch named Alse Gooderige*, 1597, p. 31. Though both appear in 1597, the play probably postdates the trial, since Henslowe does not mention it till December. The play is mentioned in Henslowe's *Diary* (ed. W. W. Greg, pp. 82, 83, entries for 22 and 28 December 1597 and 5 January 1598); and in Thomas Heywood, *The Wise Woman of Hogsdon* I. 2. There is a pub called 'Mother Redcap' on the A40 between Beaconsfield and High Wycombe. Another lost Elizabethan witch-play, *The Witch of Islington,* may have been about a real case (Henslowe's *Diary*, 14 July 1597, p. 54). Finally, a lost play called *Black Joan* may have influenced Shakespeare's puzzling Pucelle in *1 Henry VI* (Henslowe, inventory, in *Henslowe's Papers*, ed. W. W. Greg, p. 121.) All these references seem to point to a mini-vogue for witches in 1597.

29 *Fidele and Fortunio, or The Two Italian Gentlemen*, 1584, an adaptation of the *Il fidele* of Luigi Pasqualigo,1575, also contains a classical witch in the person of Medusa.

30 *The Comedy of Errors* I. 2. 97–102; II. 2. 190–202; III. 2. 149–61; IV. 3. 45–82.

31 Phyllis Rackin has recently offered a useful analysis of these plays in terms of history and gender in *Stages of History*, London: Routledge, 1990, ch. 4.

32 In those later plays too, the familiars desert the witches in moments of crisis, as if to demonstrate the contingency of the witch's power. This deflates the witch, in this case Joan, to her 'proper' place as a woman, and the play does jump up and down on her by figuring her as a desperate coward as well. On this see Gabriele Bernhard Jackson, 'Topical ideology: witches, Amazons and Shakespeare's Joan of Arc', in *Women in the Renaissance: Selections from English Literary Renaissance*, ed. Kirby Farrell, Elizabeth Hageman and Arthur F. Kinney, Amherst: University of Massachusetts Press, 1988, pp. 88–117. However, Jackson overstates the play's interest in the question of gender, which is subordinate to the question of power and nationhood.

33 On plots against Elizabeth, see Christopher Haigh's useful summary: *Elizabeth I*, London: Longman, 1989, pp. 144–5.

34 For two different readings that see the play and Joan's witchcraft in terms of fear of gender, see Jackson, 'Topical ideology', and Leah Marcus, *Puzzling Shakespeare*, ch. 2. Both see Joan as a figure of the queen.

35 See Keith Thomas, *Religion and the Decline of Magic*, Harmondsworth: Penguin, 1971, p. 480, and *CSPD*, 1547–80, p. 430.

36 See Thomas, *Religion*, p. 481, and Gareth Mattingly, *The Defeat of the Spanish Armada*, London: Cape, 1959, ch. 15. Of course not everyone accepted them as valid.

37 For the amphibology or ambiguity of ancient prophecy, see George Puttenham, *The Arte of English Poesie*, ed. Gladys Doidge Willcock and Alice Walker, Cambridge: Cambridge University Press, 1936, p. 261. Edward Coke, *Institutes*, iii, ch. 5, cited by Thomas, *Religion*, p. 470; Francis Bacon, 'Of Prophecies', in *The Essayes or Counsels, Civill and Morall*, ed. Michael Kiernan, Oxford: Clarendon Press, 1985, p. 114.

38 Raymond Williams, *The Country and the City*, London: Collins, 1964; David Norbrook, *Poetry and Politics in the English Renaissance*, London: Routledge, 1984; Don Wayne, *Penshurst*, Ithaca and London: Cornell University Press, 1983; Leah Marcus, *The Politics of Mirth*, Chicago: Chicago University Press, 1986.

39 This is first suggested by John Dennis in 1702. He also says the play was written in fourteen days.

40 Richard Helgerson argues in a recent paper for a political interpretation of the play that implicates Elizabeth as monarch in the process of determining the action: his reading sees the queen as paralleling the role assigned her in Lyly's *Endimion*. 'The laundry basket, the witch, and the queen of the fairies in Shakespare's Windsor', paper given at the 'Texts and Cultural Change' conference, Reading, 18 July 1995.

41 For Elizabeth's role in the drama in detail, see Peter Erickson, 'The Order of the Garter, the cult of Elizabeth, and class–gender tension in *The Merry Wives of Windsor*', in *Shakespeare Reproduced*, ed. Jean Howard and Marion F. O'Connor, London: Methuen, 1988, pp. 116–40. On Falstaff as Actaeon and Elizabeth, see Leonard Barkan, 'Diana and Actaeon: The myth as synthesis', *English Literary Renaissance*, 10 (1980), pp. 317–59.

42 *The bridleing, sadling and ryding of a rich churle in Hampshire*, 1594. Reprinted in Rosen, *Witchcraft*, pp. 217–18. This case and others like it went on to influence the role played by Doll Common, alias the Fairy Queen, in Jonson's *Alchemist*.

43 *Gallathea* II. 3. 1–8. *Endimion* IV. 2. 26ff; the most preposterous intrusion is in *Lust's Dominion*, where Oberon turns up in the midst of Senecan carnage with a troupe of dancing fairies to give an unheeded warning (III. 2).

44 Brainford is the spelling in the Folio text; the 1602 quarto, which seems to have removed parts of the play's local and occasional specificity, gives the real name, Brentford (IV. 2. 66–7). The name may also have been suggested by a comic poem, *Gill of Brentford's Testament*, which includes a grotesque woman's bequest of farts to her curate, with other curses (see Arden edition, p. lxii). As Patricia Parker has shown, there is always more than a trace of the fat lady about Falstaff; *Literary Fat Ladies*, ch. 1.

8 The all-singing, all-dancing plays of the Jacobean witch-vogue

The Masque of Queens, *Macbeth*, *The Witch*

> Dostoyevsky's devils tell us: I'm nothing but an obsession. And then: I am the nothing that manifests itself as obsession. I am your obsession. I am your nothing.
>
> Octavio Paz, *On Poets and Others*

A protocol has been established: one must always begin on witchcraft and drama with James I, the king who argued for the reality of witches' compacts with the devil, and believed that he had himself been the target of witches' machinations. James was personally involved in prosecuting the witches who had tried to sink his ship, showing miraculous knowledge of what he and his bride said on their wedding night. Taking place in Scotland in 1591, this trial showed the influence of Continental theories of diabolic pacts and sexual transgression, unlike most English trials. Torture was used to extract confessions, including the Scottish practice of thrawing (or wrenching) the neck with a rope. Taken together with the prosecution's reliance on evidence from the accused, torture rendered the giving of evidence a matter of bodily and vocal articulation: that is, bodies were turned into texts, were made to speak, were read, and the results displayed.[1]

However, James was inspired to go beyond the normative theatricality of a witch-trial. Despite his anxiety about the power of witches, James showed signs of seeing the accused witches as a show staged for his benefit. The king's interest was caught by the evidence given by Agnes Tompson. Tompson deposed that

> upon the night of All Hallows Eve last, she was accompanied as well with the persons aforesaid as also with a great many other witches to the number of two hundred, and that all they together went by sea, each one in a riddle or sieve, and went in the same way substantially with flagons of wine, making merry and drinking by the way in the same riddles or sieves, to the kirk of North Berwick in Lothian, and that after they had landed, took hands on land and danced this reel or short dance, singing all with one voice: Commer ye go before, commer go ye / If ye will not go before, commer let me. At which time she confessed that this Gillis Duncan did go before them playing this reel and dance upon a small trump, called a Jew's trump, until they entered the kirk.[2]

After hearing this, James was 'in a wonderful admiration',

> and sent for the said Gillis Duncan, who upon the like trump did play the said dance before the king's majesty, who in respect of the strangeness of these matters took great delight to be present at their examination.

Tompson's evidence, with its mass of detail, allows the listeners to visualise – almost to witness – the witches' journey. However, James wants more. He summons Gillis Duncan to perform the dance for him, summons her not as a witness but as an entertainer. She is asked to *act out* her own behaviour, to turn the case against her into a theatrical event, to transform a tune which might have been freighted with occult significance into a pastime for a ruler.[3] We should pause to note that this was a woman who had perhaps been tortured, had certainly been terrified, asked to perform the 'crime' which would cost her this pain as a species of entertainment. We do not know what Gillis thought, but we do know what James said. What delights the king about Gillis's performance is 'the strangeness of these matters'. Like other societies, early modern society is compelled to define itself in terms of a constantly adjusted figure of otherness, an otherness which could represent that which society hoped to avoid or repress. Yet although stagings like this one presume strangeness as their *raison d'être*, they also work to *produce* the performer as other. By becoming a performer, Gillis Duncan established a series of relationships between herself and the king. He watches; she is what he watches. James estranges her from the court, who become the spectators who attend her performance. He also becomes her symbolic master; she now exists only to please him, to offer him wonder and strangeness. James is master of the witches who had threatened to master him. He restores the hierarchy and order threatened by the witches. The witchcraft that seemed dangerous when secret becomes visible as a performance. James's command turns the forensic and rhetorical proceedings of the court into an explicitly ideological drama, a drama in which symbolism replaces truth, and meaning is re-created – one might almost say recreated. This affirms royal power as the privileged spectator and interpreter of a spectacle offering otherness only to be dispelled by legitimate authority. In the moment of commanding Gillis Duncan's song, James becomes the author of his own masque and antimasque. Her dance is the origin of the many all-singing, all-dancing witches subsequently offered to king and commonwealth in Jacobean drama.

At the same time, James's staging is *reductive*. Complex narratives which have shape and meaning in popular culture and female household spaces are reduced to a single story of witchcraft as an all-but-incomprehensible song. This reductiveness comes about when women's stories of witchcraft are appropriated to serve male political, social and intellectual agendas, or (to put it differently) when witchcraft is staged as a theatrical spectacle of otherness which exists to subtend the maintenance of hierarchy and order. It is *not* a natural or an inevitable outcome of 'early modern witch-discourses', but a highly specific *intervention* in those discourses, one which serves particular interests. James's investment in staging witchcraft as a royal command performance functions to confirm his own role as discerning interpreter. In fact the king 'interprets' nothing; one might even reverse the usual readings and opine that he is reduced to helpless silence by the song he orders. The song-and-dance show does not move forward the narrative of the trial. Seemingly a mere delay, a frivolity, it is as if James were deliberately trying to play the role of the effete absolutist interfering in the affairs of the law. No wonder, then, that after becoming king of England, James discovered another and more effective way to use witchcraft cases to establish his position as discerning interpreter of visual, aural and other signs. Always eager to appear abreast of intellectual fashion, James did not regard *Daemonologie* as his final or only word on the subject of witchcraft. Tacking to catch a fresh intellectual breeze, he was soon just as ready to deploy scepticism as belief in examining cases of witchcraft and possession, asserting belief in the case of the Essex divorce and scepticism in numerous cases of possession, carefully unmasked as fraudulent by the detective powers of the king.[4] Using the forensic discourses of interrogation and observation, and the nascent discourses of the medicalisation of hysteria, James tried to ground the monarch's authority in new science as well as old superstition. For instance, James intervened to get Elizabeth Jackson released after reading Edward Jorden's medicalising account of Mary Glover's 'possession' as a form of hysteria.[5] In his pamphlet on Mary Glover's 'possession', Jorden presents Glover's hysterical body and speech as an object of the knowing eye and ear of empiricism. Such stagings appealed to James; they offered an even more powerful means of defining the observer as the possessor of knowledge and interpretative skill than the discourses of Continental demonology. When in 1605 James encountered another case of possession involving a young woman named Anne Gunter, he at once enlisted the help of Edward Jorden to determine the genuineness of the case, showing his respect for Jorden's theories of hysteria.[6]

Such stagings of empiricism's triumphs over the supernatural are still figured by historians as a civilising break with the rhetorics of demonology which are valued in the case of Gillis Duncan. Placing the discovery of hysteria side by side with the revision of Gillis Duncan's dance-tune, however, suggests continuity rather than change. The fraudulent or hysteric woman offers herself as a more secure object of enquiry than the witch, since she is stripped of all power before examination. At the same time, the gaze of the empirical observer is invested with greater power than the gaze of the spectator, for the empiricist can tell the difference between acting and being, determining the truth that the body and gestures may seek to conceal. Gillis Duncan and Mary Glover are both presented as spectacles, objects of the knowing look. Both look forward to Charcot and the figuration of the female body and rambling speech of the hysteric as disorderly or carnivalesque spaces which ceaselessly transgress the bounds of decorum.[7] This presentation offers them as figures of disorder, figures against whom order can be defined. Such presentation allows the king to become the site of interpretative truth set over against a disorder which is not mysterious, but completely comprehensible in the authoritative discourses of science and medicine. At the same time, this new interpretative power allowed James to re-present himself – in Habermas's useful term – as Christlike and even Godlike in his power to tell truth from fiction. Like a precious gem sensitive to poison, James could act as a touchstone of genuine virtue. No role could have been more suitable for an absolutist king.

However, when witchcraft was less ambiguously staged as a masquing spectacle for the king's enjoyment, the author of the antimasque was apparently not James but Anne of Denmark.[8] In inspiring Jonson to create an antimasque for *The Masque of Queens*, Anne might initially strike us as nothing but a woman voicing a discourse of male power, for arguably there is a huge gap between witchcraft as woman's fantasy and the Jonsonian masque as Anne's fantasy. Rather, Anne seems merely to be voicing James's fantasy, if indeed she really suggested the trope of witchcraft and not merely the need for some disorder. However, when the masque is examined closely, it can be seen that there is a certain tension between the female fantasies of witchcraft discussed in previous chapters and the male fantasies of witches exemplified in James's stagings and writings.

When Jonson stated his own intentions for the masque, he explained his understanding of the antimasque:

> since the last years I had an antimasque of boys, and therefore, now, devised that twelve women, in the habit of hags or witches, sustaining the persons of Ignorance, Credulity, &c, the opposites to good *Fame*, should fill that part; not as a *Masque*, but a spectacle of strangeness, producing multiplicity of gesture, and not unaptly sorting with the current and whole fall of the device.[9]

For Jonson, the witches represent opposition, especially to good (feminine) fame. Jonson thus casts the figure of the witch into the space of otherness in which alternative cultures are rehearsed; the re-iteration of witchcraft in the masque is to serve explicitly simply to define its opposite in positive terms. That opposite is not the virtuous wife and mother as such, but knowledge. Jonson sees the witches not as allegories of women's power, but as figures for ignorance, groundless suspicion and credulity; opposites of learning, rationality and civility. The three abstract nouns Jonson chooses connote popular culture as seen from above, and partake of the sceptical humanist discourses on witchcraft produced by Scot and Gifford. This discourse sees witch-*beliefs*, not witchcraft, as a threat to learning because witch-beliefs exceed the terms of rationality. Learned Jacobean discourse is one of the first to figure women as the bearers of a subversive popular culture which challenges the high. Thus, as represented in the masque, Jonson's witches present the court with a spectacle of a popular culture the court has outgrown, an opportunity to look *down* on a set of beliefs no longer current. This discourse is not in tension with the king's own intervention in witchcraft, since by the time *The Masque of Queens* was being produced James had changed from endorsing Continental fantasy to exposing cases of witchcraft and demonical possession as fraudulent.[10] Jonson's masque makes a direct appeal to James's newly trained empirical eye.

Anne of Denmark's role may be crucial here. For according to Jonson, her motive for suggesting he use the device of the antimasque was her knowledge that 'a principal part of life in these spectacles lay in their variety'. It is unclear whether Jonson refers to variety between or within masques, but in either case Anne's reasoning figures the antimasque as a novelty. The court was being entertained with a new spectacle drawn from but also distanced from popular culture, the spectacle of the witch. The importance of spectacle rather than story, with its recollections of the king's appropriation and staging of Gillis Duncan's dance, is emphasised by Jonson's stress on the word 'gesture', a stress repeated in his description of the hags' dance:

> at which with a strange and sudden music they fell into a magical dance full of preposterous change and gesticulation, but most applying to their property, who at their meetings do all things contrary to the custom of men, dancing back to back and hip to hip, their hands joined, and making their circles backward, to the left hand, with strange fantastic motions of their heads and bodies.[11]

Preposterous literally means having in front what should come behind, and as Patricia Parker shows, it is a standard rhetorical figure for disorder of thought or feeling.[12] Here preposterousness is part of a general display of reversal and inversion. But as Peter Stallybrass has pointed out, there is nothing natural or inevitable about the use of such logic; in each case, the structure of same and other has to be created and mapped onto more labile or shifting circumstances.[13]

In keeping with the logic of otherness, it looks at first sight as if the masque's authors did everything they could to mark a difference between the carefully calculated display of witchcraft and the virtuous ladies of fame who dispelled the witches. As if to emphasise the distinction between Bel-Anna and her ladies and the hags, the latter were actually played by men. We might read this as an ironic emblem of the appropriation of the witch for male display and fantasy. Certainly the witches of the antimasque are readable as a reconstruction of cultural materials wrenched from a variety of contexts and reassembled into a general figuration of female power gone wrong. This stew of ingredients draws impartially on English popular culture, learned treatises on Continental pact witchcraft, ancient literary texts and other dramas from a perspective which flattens out the differences between these discursive spheres and understands *all* witches simply as emblems of that feminine disorder which signifies popular unreason. The crude opposition between order and disorder was a vital piece of early modern mental equipment, a grid which could be imposed over any story or event. One ideological function of the court masque genre was to make this tool for easy thinking available to the court. The witches of *The Masque of*

Queens are a muddle of otherness, as declared by the Dame who announces the group's intentions in the following pantomimic terms:

> I hate to see these fruits of a soft peace
> And curse the piety gives it such increase.
> Let us disturb it then, and blast the light;
> Mix hell with heaven, and make Nature fight
> Within herself; loose the whole hinge of things,
> And cause the ends run back into their springs.[14]

Apart from the specific allusion to James's foreign policy, this is a very general evocation of disorder indeed. The means by which the hags will bring disorder about are marginally more concrete, though again they muddle together several different fantasies of witchcraft simply to maximise the grisly effect. The hags produce the emblems of their power, a repertoire of herbs and medicines that could be seen to mirror – albeit very distantly – the anxieties registered in women's stories of witchcraft, anxieties about control and acculturation of dangerous substances. However, it seems more likely to derive from straightforward borrowing from the classics, and hence from a misogynist reinterpretation of women's anxiety, one which fears women because of their power over food and the household, and thereby associates them with poisoning.

Similarly, the two references to child murder in the witches' song could be read as a faint trace of the deep maternal anxieties encoded in women's fantasy of the witch. These two references are elliptical, and flat, however:

> 5th hag: Under a cradle I did creep
> By day, and when the child was asleep
> At night I sucked the breath, and rose
> And plucked the nodding nurse by the nose.
> 6th hag: I had a dagger; what did I with that?
> Killed an infant to have his fat.
> A piper it got at a church-ale
> I bade him again blow wind in the tail.[15]

The Fifth Hag's method of killing the infant (sucking its breath) sounds like a distorted form of the cures performed by cunning women. But the story of the Sixth Hag diverts attention from the theme of maternity to issues of paternity and illegitimacy in a way which indicates the substitution of a male agenda for a female fantasy. The child killed is a bastard gotten at a church-ale; a child of lawlessness and festival, and thus already 'given over' to the disorder represented by the witches. By contrast, in English popular culture the children killed by witches are legitimate and wanted, and the persecution of the witch is intended to mark the difference between her and them.

But this faint trace of the women's stories is subsumed beneath a mass of more sensational material, which seems to justify its inclusion by representing the grotesque rather than by reference to any actual popular discourse of witchcraft.

Dead children become simply one exhibit among many. A charnel-house skull, pieces of the bodies and clothing of a hanged murderer, and various inedible bits of animal creep by us. The specificity of a dead child is lost, becoming one more shlock-horror signifier of a world turned upside down. The hags' stories, like their dances, exist as preposterousness, backward in both senses. One can imagine the Jacobean court enjoying this spectacle rather as the upper classes used to enjoy the *News of the World* murder trials, or as the *Sunday Sport* is popular in some Senior Common Rooms.

What kind of figures succeed in dispelling this half-comic, half-nauseating world of feminised disorder as imagined by men? Female figures of course: the figures of female fame who dispel the hags are themselves possessed of many of the hags' most daunting qualities.[16] The queens are themselves figures of violence, often violence against men; indeed, often violence against *husbands*. As well as man-slaying Amazons, the queens include the unusual figure of Valasca, Queen of Bohemia, who, as Jonson puts it; 'to redeem her sex from the tyranny of men . . . led on the women to the slaughter of their barbarous husbands and lords' (643–54). Bel-Anna, or Queen Anne, is said to sum up the qualities of all these warlike queens. Jonson and Jones pointed up these Amazonian references with their costume design, a bodice adapted from armour, a helmet in quasi-Roman style, and boots.[17]

But although perfectly capable of representing disorder and domestic rebellion, the Amazons of the masque are not so figured.[18] Their martial strength is devoted to dispelling the feminised disorder of the witches. Whatever the history of the figures, they are shown as antagonists of feminised barbarism; their power is the power of civility and true fame, a power which is capable of overcoming the primitiveness and corporeality, the ignorance and superstition of untutored femininity. This is a remarkable tribute to Anne of Denmark, but it offers her a role only as the civiliser of *women*. The women in question, the hags, are not finally dispersed by the arrival of the masque of queens. Instead, they are yoked to the queens' carriage, drawing the queens toward triumphant finales. The popular culture represented in the figures of the hags is *literally* subordinated to the rule of the queens' classicised high culture. The spectacle of the hags drawing the queens' carriages is a self-referential trope for what Jonson does with the figure of the witch; the power of popular superstition is subordinated in art, lending it vitality.

The subordination of women's fantasies is precisely what allows women to gain and retain power on other, more prestigious terrains. The queens' appropriation of the power of the hags recalls Athena's adoption of the head of the unchaste and monstrously feminine Medusa as her aegis, her emblem and fetish, a story gestured at by Jonson through the figure of Perseus the gorgon-slayer. As Stephen Orgel points out, Jonson's interest in the figure of Medusa is ostensibly nothing more than an investment in the heroic and emphatically male virtue of Perseus, her slayer.[19] At first glance it seems as if this figure of masculine virtue is about to appropriate the women's power:

> I did not borrow Hermes' wings, nor ask
> His crooked sword, nor put on Pluto's casque
> Nor on my arm advance wise Pallas's shield
> (by which, my face aversed, in open field
> I slew the Gorgon) for an empty name.
> When Virtue cut off Terror, he got fame.
> And if when Fame was gotten, Terror died
> What black Erinyes or more hellish pride
> Durst arm these hags now she is grown and great
> To think they could her glories once defeat? (346–55)

Perseus's speech recalls concerns about patrilinearity and male identity allowed to surface in Jonson's retelling of child-murder by witchcraft. Patrilineal family values are also asserted in lines about the subordination of Bel-Anna's power to the king's: 'Far from self-love, as humbling all her worth / To him that gave it' (402–3). Nonetheless, it is the queens and not Perseus who eventually obtain and control the witches' power, just as Athene obtained Medusa's power. The spectacle of the hags drawing the queens' chariots, occurring after Perseus's explication, is crucial for returning the masque to the central figure of Anne, whose power is alone praised in the final speech.

Despite the distortion of the tropes of popular witchcraft to fit them into a spectacle of otherness, Jonson's masque becomes Anne's when it voices the representation of a powerful femininity set over against not masculinity, but an alternative femininity which would usurp its power. In this way, Anne's fantasy surprises by its closeness to those of ordinary women. Of course, there are critical differences: female concerns about household and children are transmogrified into male concerns about legitimacy, legitimation and the female body, and the hags represent an unruly popular culture dispelled by the interpretative powers of learned princes and poets. Nonetheless, a masque which sets out to laugh at the popular ends by ironically voicing the same concerns.

It might seem odd to treat Macbeth after *The Masque of Queens*; traditional literary histories see Shakespeare as Jonson's inspiration and not vice versa, since *Macbeth* was certainly on stage at the Globe in 1606. However, the version of *Macbeth* which survives is the product of later revision; attempts to bring the text back to the putative purity of its first staging can only be conjectural. What survives is a play reworked for the witch-fashion set by Jonson's masque; in this Borgesian sense, Jonson is Shakespeare's precursor and not vice versa. The wish to return the play to pre-Jonsonian origins is reflected in the contextualisations offered for its dramatistion of witchcraft. Since James is actually alluded to in *Macbeth* in the scene where the witches display Banquo's heirs, conventional wisdom sees the witches as a compliment to him; or, as we might put it today, as a staging of violent misogyny for the benefit of a patriarchal absolutist paranoid about women's powers. It is traditional to see the witches of *Macbeth* as addressed to the crusading paranoiac of *Newes from Scotland* rather than the sceptical debunker of the claims of the possessed.[20] Certainly, the witches in *Macbeth* are not offered as a display of ignorance and superstition as Jonson's hags are, and their appeal to the king's interpretative power is different. Jonson's hags invite the king to see *through* them as a theatrical display which minimises the figure of the witch; the witches of *Macbeth* are equivocal or unreadable texts, which the *characters* must but cannot interpret successfully.[21] Because the play lacks any interpretative figure who can make sense of events, correct interpretation of the witches in *Macbeth* lies outside the play itself, privileging the spectators in general and one (royal) spectator in particular.

However, Shakespeare's representation of witchcraft steers clear of any endorsement of the notions of Continental pact witchcraft central to *Daemonologie*. The knowledge embodied in James's writings and speeches at the Scottish trial is *not* the knowledge which the play privileges as the correct way of interpreting the witches. Jonson's hags make constant appeals to James's learning; Shakespeare addresses himself to the king's newer preoccupation with the words used, the gestures made by the lying witnesses in possession cases. As *prophets*, rather than as witches, the Weird Sisters raise the questions of meaning and truth which James had begun to understand as central to witchcraft.

Rather than presenting a single discourse as the 'answer' to witchcraft, Shakespeare refuses any such direct solution, insisting that the menace and the pleasure of witchcraft as a spectacle lies ultimately in its destabilising inscrutability. At the same time, the witches are an awkwardly compressed mass of diverse stories, inscrutable in another sense. Or existing simply to be scrutinised: the witches of *Macbeth* are a low-budget, frankly exploitative collage of randomly chosen bits of witch-lore, selected not for thematic significance but for its sensation value. Pandering shamelessly to the novelty-hungry news culture of Jacobean London, and to a court and intellectual elite increasingly eager for narratives of folklore which would demonstrate their separation from a credulous peasantry, the witch-scenes brazenly refuse any serious engagement with witchcraft in favour of a forthright rendering of witches as a stage spectacular. These all-singing, all-dancing witches bear about as much relation to the concerns of village women as *The Sound of Music* does to women's worries about childcare in the 1990s. Shakespeare buries popular culture under a thick topdressing of exploitative sensationalisation, unblushingly strip-mining both popular culture and every learned text he can lay his hands on for the sake of creating an arresting stage event. Learned interpretations of the play which eagerly make sense of the witches and relate their activities cogently to the main action are untrue to the play's unbridled sensationalism, which looks less appealing once the listener is conscious of the female voices suppressed.

The muddled signifier that is the witches does have effects. If we read the witches' confusion as an unavoidable part of a play where confusion is a preoccupation, we can see how the witches sometimes seem to figure that confusion 'intentionally'.[22] The play encourages slippage between definitions of the witch which made sense in village society and definitions of the witch which made sense to a learned sceptic like Scot and definitions of the witch which made sense to European demonologists and their followers and definitions of the witch which made sense to humanist scholars. This slippage has been replicated by many of the critics who, taking up the challenge of outdoing Macbeth which the play appears to set, have tried to interpret the witches. For example, Peter Stallybrass argues that the Weird Sisters 'have features typical of the English village witch'; what he means by this becomes clouded when he elucidates it in terms of their physical appearance, sourcing this to Reginald Scot, as if Scot were a disinterested observer of village life rather than a writer with the particular interests and agendas of Protestant scepticism. For Scot the recognisability of witches was a sign that their accusers were prejudiced, but his is not the interpretation offered by the play. Stallybrass's strategy is further exposed when he speaks of Shakespeare's reluctance to '*reduce* the play's witches to village widows.[23] This assumes that such a portrayal would automatically *be* reductive; actually, the imaginings of village women are far more complex than the Weird Sisters. Stallybrass's view uncritically reflects the Jacobean dramatists' scepticism about 'popular' superstition as nothing but a set of stories with commercial value. *Shakespeare* could only find significance in the stories of village witchcraft if they became signs of events in the public sphere; failure to churn butter or the death of a child hardly matters unless it signifies something about where Scotland stands. The *stories* of village witchcraft become metaphors for events elsewhere, and the significance they had for their original tellers becomes a layer of meaning beneath the text, a memory-trace which the play does not encourage us to uncover. The effect of the witchcraft scenes in which tropes of village witchcraft are used depends on the stories and events half narrated in them *remaining* utterly unreadable and inscrutable, so that the stories themselves function not as metaphors for *real* concerns and anxieties, but as signifiers of impenetrability and strangeness, signs of fog, filthy air, and foul is fair.

In becoming a kind of enactment of unreadability, the play draws attention to a current problem in feminist readings of early modern drama, which currently always sees scopophilia as bad, and theatrically problematised identities as good. The fact that witchcraft was a role did not always make it an interesting subversion of gender boundaries. Once convicted and hanged, the witch's opportunities for exciting unfixings of the assumptions of others were rather limited. Besides, the transformation of a witch into nothing but a theatrical event suggests that patriarchy may actually have an interest in theatricality. Such roles can become a way of mocking identities and beliefs that may feel authentic to other people. If you were (someone who believed they were) a witch, or a person who believed a witch had killed your child or taken away your livelihood, the term 'witch' might not be a spectacular curiosity, but a real part of your identity. Could it be that this authentic or 'real' witch was more awkward and unmanageable as a signifier than the theatrical display of sorcery? Shakespeare may have been shadowing James's move away from detecting 'real' witches to detecting witches as the forgeries of fraudulent actors.

At the same time, the signifcance of the play's reductiveness can only be understood if we are willing, speciously enough, to recover the traces of the stories of village widows in a text which seeks to deny them. I will start with the witch's colloquy in Act I, scene 3:

> 1st Witch: Where has thou been, sister?
> 2nd Witch: Killing swine.

The reference is so brief that any reading feels like overexpansion. Witches attacked pigs in village stories, but here those stories are condensed into a single gesture. Read in the context of the witches' first appearance as enigmatic weatherworkers and prognosticators, the single word 'swine' gestures less at an English village context than at the elaborate pig-fictions of Continental demonology, which systematically conflated notions of the pig's uncleanness with groups deemed beyond the pale, including Jews and witches.[24] The last thing that is conjured up here is a domestic animal, a plump porker on which a family might depend for winter protein; rather, the pig is already reduced to a metaphor of disorderliness and uncleanness. This tiny fragment of introit prepares us for the longer story of 'village' witchcraft on which one of the Sisters then embarks:

> A sailor's wife had chestnuts in her lap
> And munched and munched and munched; 'Give me,' quoth I
> Aroint thee, witch, the rump-fed roynon cries.
> Her husband's to Aleppo gone, master of the *Tiger*;
> But in a sieve I'll thither sail
> And like a rat without a tail
> I'll do, and I'll do, and I'll do.

We could react to this by seeing it as an allusive version of women's trial stories, and thus we could respond by reconstructing a 'popular' story of witchcraft from the text, filling in its lacunae so that it reads as follows. The witch asks for food, and is rudely refused. The food she asks for is a staple of the diet of the poor; bread was sometimes made with chestnut flour when wheat was scarce. Having refused the witch, the sailor's wife replies with something like an averting charm; 'Aroynt thee, witch' is not common parlance, and seems like words of power designed to dismiss the witch.[25] But the witch is not to be got rid of so lightly. Like all witches, she has supernaturally close knowledge of the family's affairs; she knows where the husband's ship sails. And she plans a revenge, a revenge which will destroy the family's livelihood; not the standard one, but there are cases which predate the play in the West Country trial records of witches wrecking ships by creating storms.[26]

The Third Witch's speech is thus inscribed in terms of popular witch-stories, and it may be that some at least of the audience would have heard it in these terms. Nonetheless, it also transforms such conceptions. There are already signs that female anxieties are being replaced by male anxieties. The witch does not strike directly at the female domains of body, household and children, but indirectly through the husband. Her power over him is sexualised, as numerous feminist critics have pointed out; it is the power to drain the moisture from his body, exhausting his vital essence.[27] This notion of witchcraft does not figure in women's stories, but is crucial to the fantasies of demonologists. In *Macbeth*, women's stories are put to work as part of the more grandiose male narrative of the play; the Third Witch's tale foregrounds metaphors of rebellion, threats to patriarchy, disorder in nature. Because the story presents itself as a series of metaphors, what was rich, complex and coherent in the stories of village women is reduced to signs of vague disorder here. The passage also gestures, apparently randomly, at a recent news story which had nothing to do with witchcraft, the ill-fated voyage of the *Tiger*. This investment in the topical and novel, irrespective of context, points to the sensationalism which flattens out any deeper coherences in the hag's story in the interests of novelty.

This flattening effect is partly brought about by the singsong, incantatory quality of the last three lines. The witch ceases to tell a story, and begins to speak in irregularly rhyming octosyllabic lines, the metre of witch's songs, like the song of Gillis Duncan that so intrigued James. When the Third Witch resumes her narrative of revenge she speaks entirely in this idiom of incantatory verse. As the play continues, the verse comes to signify the witches' collective difference from other characters in the play, and by extension their difference from ordinary men and women. Interestingly, rhyming couplets with very short lines were one of the hallmarks of the representation of witches on the Jacobean stage; they are also used in *The Masque of Queens* and in Middleton's *The Witch*, while in *The Witches of Lancashire* the culprits speak in couplets to each other and in blank verse or prose when passing incognito as ordinary women. Like the villain's black hat in a western, the octosyllabic couplet became a simplistic convention which divides evil from good. In the world of uncertainty that is *Macbeth*, the one thing we and the other characters can be sure of is that the witches are *witches*, and not simply rather odd old women. Their speech is marked off from that of the other characters in a manner which insists on their iconic status and also on their difference from the human.[28] They are not ordinary women who have sinned, but a special class of being, like monsters or mermaids. Banquo's words on their appearance confirm the witches' ontological oddity using the language of unreadability:

> What are these
> So withered and so wild in their attire
> That look not like the inhabitants of the earth
> And yet are on't? Live you, or are you aught
> That man may question? You seem to understand me,
> By each at once her choppy finger laying

Upon her skinny lips. You should be women
And yet your beards forbid me to interpret
That you are so.

Banquo is labouring to interpret the witches, and his comments on them stress their indeterminacy. The witches inhabit a borderland between clearly marked states. They are on the earth, but they do not look like its inhabitants, they should be women but they have beards. Similarly, their words are ambiguous, inviting a variety of interpretations. The witch-figure can stand for nothing concrete, but must evoke the disorder of the play's notion of order by indeterminacy. Ironically, this failure of interpretation becomes an interpretation: indeterminacy, and hence chaos, *is* the witches' meaning. This simple interpretation is supported by the impossibility of finding a coherent pretextual context for the witches; the fact that their accoutrements, language and behaviour are borrowed from hither and yon without regard for truth or theory reinforces their metaphoric status as figures of and for confusion. They shimmer uncertainly because they are both authentic prophetesses and village witches seen from above, both Weird Sisters or Fates and beard sisters, or stereotypes from Scot.

Although Banquo says the witches understand speech, they do not respond to his questions or Macbeth's. They do not engage in conversation. They make statements, a function of their status as prophets, since they have anticipated all encounters. Their refusal – or inability – to interact with people further marks their words as different from those used by others; they make hieratic or prophetic statements, not communicative utterances. Even when the witches have disappeared, Macbeth and Banquo remain uncertain about them rather than newly certain about the future; they debate their vanishing, and argue about whether they dissolve into air or earth. Are they fairies? Fates? This is precisely the kind of sceptical, probing debate that the learned members of the audience might have been expected to engage in. Although the two thanes do not reach any conclusion (naturally, since the whole point was to urge the audience to enter the interpretative fray), Banquo's position does evolve into providentialist scepticism not unlike Reginald Scot's as the play proceeds. Since Banquo is the representative of James, this suggests that the king was being asked to authenticate his rule as lawful rather than tyrannical precisely by taking up a sceptical position, or rather that Shakespeare understood how discourses of scepticism could naturalise the king's absolutism as privileged spectator more naturally than discourses of paranoid belief.

This becomes more evident in the witches' later appearances, appearances which also reveal that James does not quite have it all his own way with his text, and also that another set of interpretations was possible for those with different knowledges and agendas. The cauldron scene is probably the scene people remember most clearly from the play. It is usually seen in relation to Continental sabbaths, in which unbaptised babies were said to be boiled to make flying-ointment. *One* of the unsavoury ingredients piled into the 'charmed pot' by the

Weird Sisters confirms this: 'Finger of birth-strangled babe / Ditch-delivered by a drab' (IV. 1. 30–1). The babe in question has been strangled at birth by its prostitute mother, who as an unmarried woman has given birth to it in a ditch, perhaps because fleeing the boundaries of her own parish; it is therefore unbaptised, and unbaptised or chrism children were sought by witches for their potions, because of their extreme vulnerability to evil. The results of the spell also echo and adapt flying-ointment; here too the result of the mixture is supernatural power, prophetic rather than ambulatory. Time rather than distance is annihilated. So far, so coherent: however, the scene also borrows from all over the place: from Lucan's Thessalian witch in the *Pharsalia*, who prophesies for a would-be usurper by reanimating a corpse; from the lore of teeny-weeny fairies which Shakespeare helped to create; from Shakespeare's own *Henry VI Part II*, where Margery Jourdain and others conjure up spirits to give them clairvoyant knowledge of the future. The play's Continental borrowings are not especially privileged; they do not offer a way to understand the text. Continental narratives are merely one possible source of raw materials among others.

The cauldron scene also contains a deformed trace of English women's anxieties, centring on its preoccupation with food and babies. Mocked as popular superstitions, those anxieties are also reshaped as male fears. The list of noxious substances read out by the witches, which constitutes the incantation, is a *recipe*, albeit a parodic one; this becomes more tenable when we recall that books of housewifery were often composed in rhyme in the early modern period, as an *aide-mémoire*, and when we remember that some counter-magical charms were preserved in recipe books.[29] The injunction 'Cool it with a baboon's blood / Then the charm is firm and good' alludes especially clearly to discourses of cookery; the imperative verb echoes injunctions like 'bake in slow oven'. Cauldrons, now linked with witches thanks to the memorability of this very scene, were once simply the ordinary cooking ustensil of those too poor to own an oven.[30] The witches' cauldron is a reminder of women's control over food production. Like village witches, the witches of *Macbeth* use this power to reverse it; instead of transforming the natural into the cultural, they produce the unnatural. The list of cauldron ingredients is selected to give a *frisson* of shock rather than to follow English or Continental practice; the sole point is to transgress the boundaries of the acceptable and clean. All that the ingredients have in common is their repulsiveness. This is the sensationalism of the Jacobean stage at its worst.

The trace of the family cooking-pot visible in the witches' cauldron draws attention to a sphere of feminine power separate from sexuality but equally threatening to men. Cooking at this point in the play represents other forms of misfeeding, since the purpose of the potion is to produce the prophecies which will deceptively lure Macbeth to his death. The witches' potion is 'cooked' in the sense of 'cooking the books'; constructed to deceive innocent men. The underlying metaphor here may be poison, death served up in the guise of friendship, as it is to Duncan. Poison also represents women's power to intervene decisively in public affairs by using their power over food preparation.[31] The effect of the witches' cookery is to give them power over Macbeth, to reverse gender norms, to pluck a kingdom down, but also to remove a tyrant, right a wrong, restore lawful rule.

In all these ways, then, the cauldron as cooking-pot registers some distinctively *male* anxieties arising from the buried trace of tropes of female anxiety embedded in witch-stories. The cauldron is not just a cooking-pot. It is also a womb, a space from which metaphorical and actual children are born. The 'children' in question are the speakers and the embodiments of the tellingly ambiguous prophecies which the entire rite is designed to produce.[32] The cauldron's firstborn replicates its contents; an armed head is a severed souvenir reminiscent of the bits of murderers and heretics which have gone into the stew. But it also recalls the world of military hack-and-slay and tyranny created and inhabited by Macbeth. Hence this 'child' is most truly Macbeth's son, the more so since it is himself, foretelling his last appearance as a severed head. The second apparition is a child, and a newly born child at that, covered in the blood which signifies his unnatural separation from the mother. This violent separation from the maternal marks the unnaturalness of the witch's cauldron as a mechanism of birth, but also offers the child-prophecy as an unreadable fantasy of autotelic male identity, forever separated from the mother. In other words, the second child gestures at a fantasy of male power which the witches are specifically seen to trouble; a fantasy of man finally divided from the troubling and troubled mother/wife. This fantasy is strengthened with the appearance of the third child, who represents not just the power of the king over nature, but a genealogy produced apparently exclusively from the male figure of Banquo.

Of course, this is what the figures signify when 'read' correctly by Macbeth. But when first introduced, they *seem* to signify the opposite of what they really portend: the possibility of dismemberment or death, eternal attachment to woman, the limits of royal/male power over nature. Ironically, these fears become Macbeth's shaky safeguards in the witches' hands, but as it turns out, such fears are fantasies. In actuality, as the play understands, men *can* be born without woman, and man's power over nature extends to uprooting whole forests.[33] In the world of the play, the latter is natural, and women's role in the generation and birth of children is associated retroactively with the unnatural rule of the Macbeths. In general, then, the children of the cauldron represent male fears which paradoxically and harmfully become male fantasies, dreams-come-true which annihilate Macbeth. What has vanished from the scene is any sense of *female* fears or fantasies about the person of the witch. The witches remain 'bad' mothers, but bad mothers dealing in dead and symbolic children rather than real ones. Anxieties about a maternal power which would replace the mother's own role are displaced into anxieties about relations between a deformed maternity and a paternity that would be autotelic. What had once been women's stories and agendas are repackaged as affairs of the male heart, and as affairs of state.

Even this makes too much of a scene primarily mocking and comic in content. The cauldron contents also signify the ridiculousness of popular superstition; the witches' ingredients are grisly, but they are also infantile in their dirtiness, silliness, elaborateness, a list to recall Scot's bugs to frighten children. They are not a sincere list of what someone really thought witches might use, but a piece of infantile Gothic. Their messiness, disorder and rather simplistic otherness, involving a body-part from every racial or religious Other available, do indeed invert order, but they also act as a comic inversion not of the values of the absolutist court, but of the good sober carefulness and containment of the *bourgeois* household and its economics of prudence and containment. These strands of mockery give the court the opportunity to elevate itself above both peasants and godly city matrons. But for those in the know about the court, there is a pointer to its own less lovely excesses; the witches represent the unnaturalness of the Macbeths' tyranny, a tyranny which blocks the circulation of power, creating some nasty spillages. Cunningly offering its ambiguity as a way to sell itself to opposing schools of thought on witchcraft, *Macbeth*'s nasty witch-brew palters with the audience in a double sense as well; it offers both king and commons a chance to feel superior to each other.

Even *this* reading may be excessively earnest for a scene staged to end with the words 'And now about the cauldron sing / Like elves and fairies in a ring'. Here as elsewhere, fairies signify that part of popular superstition readable as emphatically over. In concluding the manufacture of a spell with a trope which compares the witches to fairies, the Weird Sisters are bracketed as figments of the dramatic imagination. In doing this, Shakespeare credits himself with inventing figures which are recensions of other people's half-remembered stories, from Lucan to ordinary women. The *frisson* of fear that the witches still have for some Bardophiles is an echo of the fears of others, the others who originally wrote and believed the stories. However, *we* can credit Shakespeare with granting witches and fairies the diachronic signficance they still have for us. The sheer banality of Hecate's lines, especially 'like elves and fairies in a ring' points to the joint infantilisation of octosyllabic couplets and the supernatural. Both are now associated not with childhood, but with a naive and pre-electronic childhood of times past. Ironically, the witch-stories written for today's more knowing and sceptical children contain the most sophisticated readings of the tone of *Macbeth:* the comic witch Meg appropriates the language of the Weird Sisters, chanting 'Bubble bubble, rock and rubble, oil boil and cauldron bubble'.[34] This points to the cultural power of Shakespeare's witches, but also to their aesthetic impoverishment. The Weird Sisters are nothing more and nothing less than *Macbeth*'s missing comic sub-plot.

The complex intertextual relations of the third of the witch-vogue plays, Middleton's *The Witch*, complicate any discussion of its representation of witchcraft. The play has historically been seen in relation to *Macbeth* because two of its songs, and a dance known as 'The Witches Dance' occur in it and also in the Folio text of *Macbeth*.[35] It has also been suggested that *The Witch* was a hastily written attempt to cash in on the vogue for witchcraft created by *The Masque of Queens*, and that properties, costumes and even stage effects were imported from that masque.[36] More recent criticism has suggested that *The Witch* is a response to and covert staging of the Essex divorce case and the Overbury poisoning trial; it has even been argued that the play's notorious failure was a consequence of censorship.[37] All these readings of *The Witch* subordinate it to another text deemed more original and authoritative: whether seen as fashionable, exploitative, or scandalous, *The Witch* is always seen as a recapitulation of a story from elsewhere.

The tangle continues; it has been suggested recently that the revised edition of *Macbeth*, which may have been the work of Middleton, was a response to the dramatic success of *The Masque of Queens*, while it has also been argued that the hags in *The Masque* may have been played by members of the King's Men, the parts taken by male actors and not women or boys. Without attempting to resolve the purely scholarly problems of dating and revision raised by this criticism, I want to begin to explore the intertextuality of *The Witch* from a different, less determinist point of view. Rather than seeking to establish the strict *order* in which the various intertexts of witchcraft caught up in *The Witch* were composed, I want to explore their discursive relations and the different ways in which the figure of the witch is caught up in them. All three texts are indeed entangled, perhaps past disentangling. The Folio version of *Macbeth* is marked by the songs and dance from Middleton's play, though other markings are less easy to source. There are resemblances between the witch-scenes in Middleton's play and the antimasque of *The Masque of Queens*, even if these are not strong enough to allow for an argument of direct borrowing. What seems to unite these texts is a similar *approach* to the staging of witchcraft, an approach which also has much in common with *Macbeth*, as opposed to later 'realist' dramas like *The Witch of Edmonton*. For example, all three dramas present cauldron scenes in which a list of noisome ingredients is read out.

Part of this approach was a response to James and Anne's rule. Yet the *Masque*'s painstakingly marked separation between legitimately powerful ladies and hags was deconstructed by the revelations which accompanied the Essex divorce case and the Overbury poisoning case. Frances Howard, accused of consulting cunning men and women to ensure her husband's copulatory impotence and to procure poison for Overbury, was one of the women actors in *The Masque of Queens*, one of the women whose virtue and fame was to dispel ignorance and vulgarity represented by the hags. The scandal of Frances's behaviour lay in her failure to continue in the role in which the masque had cast her. She was aligned with the hags as a figure of feminised disorder. The incessant dramatisations of Frances Howard's story by her contemporaries and its appropriation and reappropriation for duty on various ideological agendas were made possible by the success of texts like *The Masque of Queens* in establishing such distinctions. The anxiety Howard provoked, too, is an anxiety always already present in the masque itself, which as we have seen cannot guarantee to maintain equivocal and fragile bounds.

Critics have also found traces of Frances Howard's story in *The Witch.* However, attention has been focused on the scholarly problem of dating to the exclusion of the historical problem of discourse. Critics have tended to argue that the play must be based on (or alluding to) the Essex divorce hearing or the Overbury poisoning trial, turning the play into a kind of *roman à clef.* Attention has therefore centred on the place of impotence-causing witchcraft in the play, while the representation of witches themselves has been ignored. This tendency to treat Frances Howard's trials as a way to ground the play's otherwise puzzling meanings is neatly reversed in David Lindley's recent work. Lindley argues rightly that it would be equally accurate to see drama as one of the factors which shaped attitudes to Frances Howard as it would to see Howard as the source for dramatic attitudes.[38] Rather than insisting that Howard is the origin of all plots, it might be reasonable to see the figure of 'Frances Howard' as shaped by the plots of others.

For Lindley, then, both the trials (and ancillary texts) and the plays of the early seventeenth century are part of the *same* set of assumptions about gender, and both trials and plays work to reproduce these assumptions. The fact that an impotence-inducing drug is present in *The Witch* should not lead us to read the Essex divorce hearings as the play's source; rather, we should 'read' the play as a reproduction of the *same* male anxieties that surface in the trial. Lindley's strategy *seems* an exemplary way of restoring historicity to both play and trial. But although his analysis of Frances Howard's construction restores her to her place as a product of Jacobean ideology, there are a number of less spectacular problems with the relation between *The Witch* and the trials, problems which are easy to overlook because they are not ostensibly central to the trials or the play in the way that the figure of Howard is. It is probably inevitable that a well-meaning male historian searching for a female role model of truculence should have hit on Frances Howard, but it is nonetheless depressing that Lindley fails to notice the other women caught up in her plots, women less able than she to escape their socially determined closure. Frances Howard got off lightly in comparison with what Middleton's text does with another figure from the divorce and poisoning case.

This is the so-called 'cunning woman', Anne Turner, the woman whom Howard allegedly consulted about keeping her husband impotent, attracting the desire of Carr, and poisoning Overbury. One of the results of historians' lack of interest in Turner is that we thereby neglect one of the few instances of a relationship between the one of the 'better sort' and the cunning folk in the early modern period.[39] The relation between Turner and Howard is especially interesting because it involves an entire network of cunning people. There was also a second 'cunning woman' involved in the Essex divorce case: Mary Woods, said to have cozened Frances Howard of a jewel of great value in exchange for poison. According to Woods, the poison was aimed at Essex.

Another woman witness, Isabel Peel, gave evidence that Woods was a cunning woman who had cozened a number of women with promises of husbands or pregnancies.[40] These discourses of conspiracy figure all the women involved as part of a terrifying network of secret power, power capable of destroying the order of society. The fact that nobles and common people were involved and in alliance made the prospect more terrifying, for Anne Turner could be figured as always already transgressing class boundaries in her ambitious upward mobility.[41]

If the fashioning of Frances Howard has been suppressed, the equally flagrant fashioning of Anne Turner in interrogation, trial, execution *and drama* has been even more neglected. This is partly owing to the aristocentrism of literary critics' historicisation. The real cause, however, is that popular views of witchcraft are a subjugated knowledge in seventeenth-century dramatic texts. Middleton does not offer to reproduce the concerns of Anne Turner or her clientele. Instead, he transforms Turner into an almost unrecognisable and practically inhuman monstrosity, the witch Hecate. Hecate is not 'based' on Turner (though this is as plausible as it is to argue for a direct correlation between Frances Howard and any of the play's characters or events). Nonetheless, Hecate in the play can be found *doing* all the things of which *Turner* (rather than Frances Howard) was accused. What Middleton does is to reshape the agent who performs transgressive acts into a symbol of transgression. Hecate is less a witch than the *embodiment* of witchcraft, witchcraft made into action or made capable of action. In order for the witch to move from female plot-conspiracy to dramatic plot or narrative, she must be utterly transformed. As such, 'she' represents a way of involving the witch in a different kind of plot, a dramatic plot. As I shall show shortly, the whole point about Turner's narrative of witchcraft in her confession was its *secrecy*. Hecate, one might say, is like Anne Turner turned inside out. What is hidden in Turner is fully displayed in Hecate. As well, the edifying aspect of Turner's story is its ending. Not only is she punished with death, but she dies the 'good death' desired by crowds attendant on the spectacle. She is repentant and reintegrated into the community. Hecate, however, survives the play and undergoes neither retribution nor repentance. Paradoxically, this treatment of the witch-figure eliminates any sign of women's agency and control over their own story.

In order to understand how and why the gap between Anne Turner and Hecate looms so large, it is necessary to understand the way in which *The Witch* rewrites and reshapes popular stories of witchcraft in general. Middleton's notorious dependence on Reginald Scot's *Discoverie of witchcraft* meant that he was influenced by Scot's contempt for popular beliefs, and his wish to display them as grotesque and farcical. In particular, Scot's misogynist distaste for women – as marked as anything that can be unearthed in the most hostile and excitable Continental sources – has the effect of linking witch-beliefs with a feminised popular culture which can then be stigmatised by virtue of its very femininity.[42] Scot's treatment of the St Osyth case reveals with especial clarity the tendentiousness of his approach to the 'problem' of witchcraft and its capacity to silence the voices of women. As we have seen, the stories of women witnesses at this trial reveal a coherent set of assumptions about what a witch was, or a set of workable fantasies about what a witch could be. In Scot's hands, however, the trial becomes a discourse voiced exclusively by the JP Brian Darcy, exemplifying Darcy's absurd faith in the sayings of a bunch of credulous peasant women. Take, for example, Scot's account of the role familiars played in the case; in fact, the demons reported by accused and witnesses alike must have disappointed Darcy, hoping for luscious Continental pact witchcraft. The familiars represented were not sexual demons, but the standard creatures described in English witch-cases: animals with pet and child-names. Scot, however, does not comment on this discrepancy; all that interests him is that *Darcy* has flouted providentialism by accepting their existence:

> Now, how Brian Darcies he spirits and she spirits, Tittie and Tiffin, Suckin and Pidgin, Liard and Robin, etc., can stand consonant with the word of GOD, or true philosophie, let heaven and earth judge.[43]

Middleton borrows on more than one occasion from Scot's synopsis of the St Osyth trials.[44] For example, Hecate's invocation of spirits appears to be drawn directly from the passage from Scot cited above: 'Titty and Tiffin / Suckin and Pidgen, Liard and Robin / White spirits, black spirits' (I. ii. 1–4). This is Hecate's very first appearance, so that the image of her – and consequently, the play's notion of what a witch is – is dominated by Scot's reading of the St Osyth trial. Scot's providential scepticism is transformed by Middleton into stage comedy and burlesque. Hecate is presented as comically rather than sinisterly grotesque; she does not have any power over the public sphere, and her power in the private sphere, though real, is devalued as trivial by virtue of the very fact that the play's lengthy displays of witchcraft 'lore' are not fully integrated into the main plot.

Like Jonson in *The Masque of Queens*, though in the different context of the public stage, Middleton offers the audience a display of signifiers of witchcraft detached from meaningful context and thus available as curiosities and wonders.[45] Like the witches in *Macbeth*, Hecate's appearances are staged as a queasy mixture of decontextualised village witch-stories muddled with the more striking and spectacular features of Continental lore – and here, too, Scot is often Middleton's source.[46] What Middleton mostly draws from Scot are *lists* – ingredients, familiars – and the list becomes, as it does in *Macbeth*'s cauldron scene, a principal way of signifying witches by metonymic logic. For example, the list of magical herbs, which derives from Scot, is a kind of love potion designed to allow Hecate to 'have' the Mayor's son at the next mounting: 'They're down his throat / His mouth crammed full, his ears and nostrils stuffed / I thrust in *eleoselinum* lately, / *Aconitum*, *frondes populeus* and soot' (I. 2. 40–3). The herbs have little to do with traditional love medicine; instead, most are poisons, including *aconitum* (wolfsbane) and *Solanum Somniferum* (deadly nightshade).[47] Scot cited the recipe as one for miraculous or aerial transportation rather than as a love charm. This does not matter to Middleton's intended effect as long as the ingredients sound both nasty and magical, but it illustrates the fundamentally unserious and purely spectacular character of Middleton's representation. The numerous sexual transgressions which more than anything unite witch-plot and main plot are similarly decorative. Hecate's power to dry up generation ought to be a serious threat, as should her incestuous relationship with her son, but no *frisson* of real fear or disorder attends these revelations as Middleton presents them.

Similarly, Hecate's invocation of familiars is strikingly detached from any magical purpose: 'urchins, elves, hags, satyrs, pans, fauns, Silens, Kit-with-the-candlestick, tritons, centaurs, dwarves . . . the hellwain, the fire-drake, the puckle. Ar ab hur hus!' (I. 2. 101–5). The list is derived directly from Scot's list of 'bugs' 'with which our mothers' maids have so fraid us'.[48] Critics usually comment derisively on Middleton's reiteration of Scot's list of bugs, without noticing the fact that learned sceptic and playwright share a contemptuous attitude towards the beliefs they recount. Scot associates 'bugs' with 'our mother's' maids', with femininity and the lower orders. Listening attentively to such stories, and feeling afraid, is linked with childhood. Middleton's presentation of Hecate is in keeping with Scot's text, in that his very carelessness about magic and belief denotes an unwillingness to take it seriously. No wonder then that Middleton's Hecate rarely succeeds in producing the kind of *frisson* of fear with which one associates the witches in *Macbeth*, or even the Erictho of *Sophonisba*.

Perhaps this is not surprising, since Hecate is not a 'real' person, but a *witch*. Critics have often been puzzled about the fact that Middleton named his witch for a classical goddess; this reflects the reduction of the witch to a symbolic figure.[49] That is, Middleton, like Shakespeare and Jonson, eschews any notion of the witch as an old woman tempted into malice by demons, much less any idea of the witch as problematic member of the village community. Hecate is schematically divided from society; she exists only in the midnight world of her own abode and the witches' meeting places. She has no place in the larger society or familial structures which she serves and disrupts; even though she has a son/lover, this does not amount to social integration, but is yet another signifier of her apartness, her disorder. She has no place in the play's codes of moral retribution, discovery and restitution: she is entirely excluded from the denouement, and gets off scot-free, in itself a sign that she metaphorises a threat which is located elsewhere. The idea of Hecate arrested and charged with witchcraft by a properly constituted court is somehow farcical.[50] By detaching her from society, Middleton can turn her into a reflection of it, since her excessive displays of desire and rage externalise the preoccupations of the main characters, while comically deflating them.

The play's connections with the Essex divorce case and Overbury poisoning case make its detachment seem odd, however. If we are to understand the play as a rewriting of or a series of references to these topical events, then we must understand Hecate as Middleton's representation of the kind of witch to whom the great might have recourse: as his version of Anne Turner. Middleton did not set out to offer a recognisable portrait of Turner, or even of the Essex divorce case or Overbury trials. The question of the play's date is difficult to resolve with any certainty, and it may be that the play was written in ignorance of the role Anne Turner played.[51] Hecate is emphatically not represented as a person, a social being with her own desires and interests. However, Hecate plays the role in *The Witch* that Anne Turner played in the accounts of the Overbury trials; she represents the intervention of supernatural knowledge or belief into domestic and social affairs. More simply, she is a witch consulted by her social betters for advice about love and sex. Middleton's portrayal of Hecate does owe something to the stage figure of the cunning man or woman, of the kind featured in *The Alchemist* and in Heywood's *Wise Woman of Hogsdon*. These incarnations of learned scepticism are recognisable by the subtle forensic skill which they deploy to extract information from their clients which can then be re-presented as prophetic knowledge. Hecate's skill in extracting information from Sebastian about his quest while dressing this up as her own foreknowledge is part of this tradition.

But if Hecate bears some relation to the stage figuration of the cunning man or woman, and also some relation to the figure of Anne Turner, there are also a range of contrasts between Hecate and Turner, contrasts which exemplify the gap between the stage figure of the witch as cobbled up by Jacobean dramatists and the complex lability of the experience of a witchcraft accusation in Jacobean culture. Hecate's multiplicity and internal contradictoriness may seem striking, but she pales in comparison with the contradictoriness of Turner. It is more accurate to speak of the *figures* of Anne Turner, to read 'Anne Turner' as a set of competing and conflicting constructions of wayward femininity fashioned by herself and by her interlocutors, storytellers, gossipers and other interested reporters. Turner's own voice can also be heard intermittently, diligently ventriloquising the discourses of submission and repentance which offered her a way to evade the shaping discourses of the court while conforming to the demand for a retributive ending.

Looking more closely at Turner's representation during her trial, there are two striking features: one is Turner's relentless efforts to present or stage herself as modest and virtuous, offering a demeanour that is a fascinating interpretation of seventeenth-century notions of what female virtue was; the other is the equally stubborn wish on everybody's part to figure her actions as symbolic transgressions of gender and societal norms, rather than acts of diabolically inspired witchcraft. Misogynist though the latter discourse is, it does not depend on the work of Continental demonologists for its misogyny. Rather, it deploys the basic discourse of inversion used by seventeenth-century culture – including Continental demonology – to represent the normative and the deviant.

The Jacobean misogynists' 'reading' of Turner is heavily dependent on a scene which bears an uncannily close resemblance to Middleton's play. As we have seen, Middleton's primary means of representing witchcraft is via lists of objects and ingredients selected less as genuine illustrations of particular spells than as figures of witchcraft itself. Similarly, Anne Turner's prosecution opens with a rather muddled list of magical objects found in her possession:

> There was also showed in court certain pictures of a man and woman in copulation, made in lead, as also the mould of brass, wherein they were cast, a black scarf also full of white crosses, which Mrs Turner had in her custody . . . there were also enchantments shown in court, written in parchment, where in were contained all the names of the blessed Trinity, mentioned in scriptures, and in another parchment, +B+C+D+E, and in a third likewise in parchment were written all the names of the Holy Trinity, as also a figure, in which was written the word Corpus, and upon the parchment was fastened a little piece of the skin of a man. In some of these parchments, were the devils particular names, who were conjured to torment the Lord Somerset and Sir Arthur Mainwaring, if their loves should not continue, the one to the countess [i.e. Frances Howard], the other to Mrs Turner.[52]

We have some opportunity to see how Jacobean men read these revelations in the letter of Thomas Bone to Sir John Egerton, giving an account of the trial. Bone writes:

> the imagery and spells were all produced and expounded, and the very same spell (and in the very same paper) that were used to unite and continew the love of the too much honored couple, the very same (*mutatis mutandis* only) were put in practice by Forman at the instance of Mris Turner to catch the knight Sir Art[hur Mainwaring] for herself.[53]

For Bone, the crucial point is that Turner and Frances Howard use the *same* spell to control men's desires and to bind their lovers to them. He is less interested in the list of items than in reducing it to one key item. But the list itself also has significance. The first thing to strike the reader is the mixture of religious and sexual imagery; the names of the Trinity jostle with figures of copulating couples, and word magic brushes up against sympathetic magic. Although this *seems* chaotic, however, it actually makes a strong appeal to the right-thinking Jacobean reader. The religious images figured are readable as Catholic, especially the scandalous figure of the word *Corpus* coupled with a small piece of a man's skin. Ordinary Jacobean witch-pamphlets produced in the wake of the Counter-Reformation exorcism controversy were at pains to try to ally Catholicism with diabolism, usually by figuring Catholic worship and iconography as too close to magical practice for comfort. There was emphasis on the witch's use of Latin, for example, or emphasis on the place of the old religion in her alleged spells.[54] The fact that Turner was herself a Catholic was duly given prominence.[55] The other striking thing about the list of objects is its apparent randomness; it is offered less as material evidence at Turner's trial for the poisoning of Overbury than as a series of signifiers of Turner's witchcraft and its power over men.

Another kind of list also characterises the courts' attempts to arrive at a single and stable representation of Anne Turner's actions in terms of Jacobean notions of order and disorder. As part of his peroration, the Lord Chief Justice

> told Mrs Turner that she had the seven deadly sins: viz, a whore, a bawd, a sorcerer, a witch, a papist, a felon, and a murderer, the daughter of the devil Forman; wishing her to repent, and to become a servant of Jesus Christ, and to pray for him to cast out of her those seven devils.[56]

Turner is figured as a synecdoche of all vices; sexual and religious sins are conflated just as sexual and religious images are mingled in the list of charms. This discourse represents Turner as the embodiment of vice in general and female vice in particular. This careless blending of vices also arises from the tendency of the story to cast Turner as a go-between, an agent, a signifier of nothing in herself but a facilitator of the crimes of others; she has no meaning in herself, but always points beyond herself at the crimes of those with whom she was associated. It is true that Turner obtained the services of cunning men for Frances Howard; at her trial she claimed that after the death of Simon Forman she and Howard had recourse to another conjurer, Dr Savery, in an effort to ensure Essex's continued impotence.[57] The (unreliable) word of James Franklin declares that Turner also orchestrated the traffic through Frances Howard's bedroom door.[58] It is this figuration of Turner as bawd which is developed in Francis Osborne's play *The True Tragedy Lately Acted at Court*. Osborne's treatment of the theme makes it apparent that the figure of the bawd represents Turner's problematic class mobility, her inappropriate and unacceptable self-fashioning.

Ironically, the metaphor of the seven deadly sins becomes the occasion for an appeal to sanctioned supernatural practice; Coke prays that devils be cast out of Turner, an office usually performed by a minister, over which the Counter-Reformation Jesuits claimed special authority, but an office also sometimes claimed by the cunning men and women called in to cure illness, a category into which Turner has, for Coke, literally *fallen*. Ironically, however, Coke's reference to exorcism has the effect of comprehensively disempowering Turner; she has not herself acted, but has been acted through by devils; she has not herself exercised power, but had it exercised upon her by the legions of Satan. This standard Continental method of refiguring witches as the powerless dupes of wily demons glances less at Middleton's witch, who like village witches is the *embodiment* of evil, than at 'realist' dramas like *The Witch of Edmonton*, which seek to rationalise away the witch's powers. Curiously, Coke's words also glance back at Reginald Scot's scepticism, for Scot is precisely sceptical *about* the power of strange old women in villages to do real harm.

The two lists taken together figure Turner as nothing more than a kind of moral *exemplum*, a visible and readable narrative of the vice of witchcraft brought to light by diligent examination. It is crucial that the contents of the lists be dramatically *disclosed*; the trial is a revelation of what had been unrecognisable. The pamphlet literature on the case reflects this discourse of revelation: for example, the anonymous Civil War pamphlet *Truth brought to light and discovered by time* (1651).[59] By contrast, Hecate's status and powers are never in doubt, always displayed for the audience.

But if the trial of Anne Turner, like the other Overbury trials, was in more than one sense a show trial, Turner herself resisted becoming the object of this kind of scrutiny. An incident at the opening of the trial reveals Turner's attempt at self-fashioning as the virtuous but wronged woman:

> Sir Ed. Coke . . . told her, that women must be covered in the church, but not when they are arraigned, and so caused her to put off her hat, which being done she covered her hair with her handkerchief, being before dressed in her hair, and her hat over it.[60]

Evidently Turner had appeared in a hat; this is presented as a breach of protocol (Turner mistakes the court for a church) but Turner's 'mistake' is actually indicative of her tendency to see her role in moral terms, a tendency shared by her accusers. Her response is to insist that her head be covered, a figuration of herself as modestly closed to scrutiny. However inappropriate such a piece of self-fashioning, it contributes to the repentant and virtuously feminine persona that Turner strove to establish throughout the trial and right up to the scaffold steps. Even before the trial began, Turner was exercising this persona when she petitioned the Lord Chief Justice on 12 October 1615, begging for a speedy trial or release on bail for the sake of her fatherless children.[61] Similarly, she represented herself in her confession as actuated by appropriate feelings of loyalty towards her mistress, Frances Howard.[62] Far from figuring herself as the willing disrupter of the social order, Turner was able to present herself as reinforcing it. Figuring herself as a caring mother, a loyal servant and a modest woman was her way of seeking to rebut the allegations of sexual and social misconduct levelled at her by the prosecution. It also represents Turner's attempt not to be consigned to the symbolic space marked out for her by Edward Coke's lists; it represents her attempt to retain control of the presentation of her identity in the face of attempts by others to redraw it along new and sinister lines. Part of this process was, paradoxically, Turner's confession of complicity in the crime of poisoning Overbury, and her implication of others.[63] Turner's willingness to produce a confessional discourse rerpresented her only chance to figure herself as other than the collage of satanic signifiers assembled by the prosecution. Pressure to talk and confess might be seen as stemming from plays like Middleton's, in which the witch is not a speaking subject but a loosely held collection of signifiers, a museum display of grotesquerie.

Turner finally took the public stage at her own execution, where her behaviour aptly exemplified the seventeenth-century ideal of repentance and contrition.[64] John Castle, writing to James Miller, stressed Turner's repentance:

> If detestation of painted pride, lust, malice, powdered hair, yellow bands, and all the rest of the wardrobe of Court vanities, if deepe sighs, teares, confessions, ejaculations of the soul, admonitions of all sorts of people to make God and an unspotted conscience alwayes our friends; if the protestations of faith and hope, to be washed by the same Saviour, and by the like mercies that Mary Magdalene was, be signes and demonstrations of a blest Penitent, then I will tell you that this poor broken woman went *a cruce ad gloriam*, and now enjoys the presence of hirs and our Redeemer.

The fact that Turner had herself been responsible for introducing the fashion for yellow ruffs to the Jacobean court gives extra point to the reference.[65] Turner's transformation from fashionable lady to penitent is exemplified in the contrast between the meanings assigned to her 'extravagant' dress and the language of her repentant body and tongue. The rhetoric of the description reduces Turner to an *exemplum*, but Turner initiated such rhetoric herself when in her confession she attacked the court, wished the king better servants 'there being nothing amongst them but malice, pride, whoredom, swearing, and rejoicing in the fall of others', and wondered that the earth did not open to swallow so wicked a place. Thomas Tuke also saw Turner's end in exemplary terms; for him, her example could instruct others in true repentance, while even Edward Coke gloated that 'she that was before an example of wickedness was now become a zealous persuader to Christian piety and goodness'.[66]

The execution was written up in broadsides which render Turner's story a piece of morally exemplary tale-telling. *Mistress Turner's Farewell to All Women*, for example, offers paired images of 'Mistris Turner' and 'Lady Pride'; Lady Pride is dressed in the height of court fashion, while Mistress Turner wears sober and godly gear.[67] The very titles suggest that Turner has been transformed into an allegory of repentance, a figure whose virtuous contrition cancels out and contrasts with the allegory of female pride, excess and sexuality. At the same time, the paired portraits offer Lady Pride as a figure of sexual exposure; her breasts are bare to the nipples. Mistress Turner, on the other hand, is well covered; this is a trope for modesty, which also returns us to Turner's wish to evade becoming an object of display and forensic discovery. When she came to speak at her execution, Turner figured her death in terms of self-discovery and self-realisation: 'for by that meanes she came to know her self, and was made truly penitent'.[68]

This self-staging differentiates Turner from Hecate, who glories in her own sinful visibility. Neither female figure is likely to appeal much to the modern feminist reader, and they cannot be arrayed in terms of the right-on and the right-off. Turner sacrifices her power as cunning woman for subjectivity, the power to speak and be heard and understood, while Hecate represents the unpleasant truth that in the Jacobean public sphere, the only way for a woman's power to be visible was through her reduction to a signifier of disorder. For Anne Turner, and to some extent for Frances Howard, the alternatives were as stark as that, and it is fair to say that the figure of Hecate and her stage companions in *Macbeth* and *The Masque of Queens* helped to increase the pressure, even if only slightly. Moreover, their grotesque presence shows how horribly insensitive Jacobean drama could be to the social events being acted out all around it.

NOTES

1 On James's role in determining practices at this trial, see Christina Larner, 'James VI and I and witchcraft', in *Witchcraft and Religion: The Politics of Popular Belief*, Oxford: Blackwell, 1983, pp. 7–15.

2 *Newes From Scotland, declaring the damnable life and death of Dr Fian*, 1591, reprinted in *Witchcraft in England 1558–1618*, ed. Barbara Rosen, Amherst: University of Massachusetts Press, 1991, p. 195. See also Robert Pitcairn, *Criminal Trials*, Edinburgh, 1833.

3 For a similar transposition into theatre, see Stephen Greenblatt's account of Samuel Harsnett in 'Shakespeare and the exorcists', in *Shakespearean Negotiations*, Oxford: Clarendon, 1988, pp. 94–128, esp. pp. 108–9.

4 For readings of the politics of James's rhetoric of witch-beliefs, see Stuart Clark, 'King James's *Demonologie*: witchcraft and kingship', in *The Damned Art: Essays in the Literature of Witchcraft*, ed. Sydney Anglo, London: Routledge & Kegan Paul, 1977, pp. 167–73; Lucia Folena, 'Figures of violence: philologists, witches, and Stalinistas', in *The Violence of Representation: Literature and the History of Violence*, ed. Nancy Armstrong and Leonard Tennenhouse, London and New York: Routledge, 1990, pp. 219–38; unfortunately, neither Clark nor Folena considers the politics of James's conversion(s) to scepticism.

5 On James's involvement in the case of Mary Glover, see Henry Paul, *The Royal Play of Macbeth*, New York: Macmillan, 1950, pp. 98–103, 111, and Michael Macdonald, *Witchcraft and Hysteria in Elizabethan London: Edward Jorden and the Mary Glover case*, London: Tavistock/Routledge, 1991, pp. xlviii ff.

6 Macdonald, *Witchcraft*, p. xlviii; Paul, *Royal Play*, pp. 118–27; C. L'Estrange Ewen, *Witchcraft in the Star Chamber*, 1938.

7 See Mary Russo, 'Female grotesques: carnival and theory', in *Feminist Studies/Critical Studies*, ed. Teresa de Lauretis, London: Macmillan, 1986, pp. 213–29; Claire Wills, 'Upsetting the public: carnival, hysteria and women's texts', in *Bakhtin and Cultural Theory*, ed. Ken Hirschkop and David Shepherd, Manchester: Manchester University Press, 1989, pp. 130–51. See also Chapter 3.

8 John Donne says in a letter that the king 'left with the queen a commandment to meditate upon a masque for Christmas (*Letters to Several Persons of Honour*, 1651, p. 143); Jonson himself credits Anne with the inspiration for the antimasque. See Barbara Lewalski, *Writing Women in Jacobean England*, Cambridge, MA: Harvard University Press, 1993, pp. 35–7, and Marion Wynne-Davies, 'The queen's masque: Renaissance women and the seventeenth-century court masque', in *Gloriana's Face: Women, Public and Private, in the English Renaissance*, ed. S. P. Cerasino and Marion Wynne-Davies, Hemel Hempstead: Harvester, 1992, pp. 79–104. See also Suzanne Gossett, '"Man-maid, begone!" Women in masques', in *Women in the Renaissance: Selections from English Literary Renaissance*, ed. Kirby Farrell, Elizabeth Hageman and Arthur F. Kinney, Amherst: University of Massachusetts Press, 1988, pp. 118–35.

9 Ben Jonson, *The Complete Masques*, ed. Stephen Orgel, New Haven and London: Yale University Press, 1969, pp. 122–3.

10 See Paul, *Royal Play*, pp. 141–8

11 Jonson, *Masques*, p. 134.

12 Patricia Parker, *Literary Fat Ladies: Rhetoric, Gender, Property*, London: Methuen, 1987, pp. 67–9.
13 Peter Stallybrass, 'The world turned upside down: inversion, gender and the state', in *The Matter of Difference: Materialist Feminist Criticism of Shakespeare*, ed. Valerie Wayne, Brighton: Harvester, 1991, pp. 201–20. This essay revises his earlier essay on *Macbeth*, which did assume a logic of inversion to be inevitable.
14 *The Masque of Queens*, in *The Complete Masques*, ed. Orgel.
15 *The Masque of Queens*, pp. 158–65. For church-ales in a real case, see Chapter 6.
16 This point was recently made by Lewalski in *Writing Women*, p. 37.
17 The surviving costume designs of Anne and her ladies are reproduced in Stephen Orgel, *The Illusion of Power: Political Theatre in the English Renaissance*, Berkeley: University of California Press, 1975, figs 8, 9 and 10.
18 For a study of the possible figurations of the Amazon in Elizabethan and Jacobean drama, see Simon Shepherd, *Amazons and Warrior Women*, Brighton: Harvester, 1981.
19 Orgel, 'Jonson and the Amazons', in *Soliciting Interpretation: Literary Theory and Seventeenth-century Poetry*, ed. Elizabeth D. Harvey and Katherine Eisaman Maus, Chicago: Chicago University Press, 1990, pp. 126–31. Gossett also reads the masque as a misogynous fantasy of taking power away from women, p. 123, as does Jonathan Goldberg in *James I and the Politics of Literature: Jonson, Shakespeare, Donne and their Contemporaries*, Baltimore and London: Johns Hopkins University Press, 1983, p. 88.
20 For an account of James's engagement with multiple cases of possession exposed by him as fraudulent, see Paul, *Royal Play*, pp. 75–127. Dymphna Callaghan has recently argued that the play stages a conflict between scepticism and belief, 'Wicked women in *Macbeth*: a study of power, ideology and the production of motherhood', *Reconsidering the Renaissance*, ed. Mario A. Di Cesare, Binghamton, NY: Medieval and Renaissance Texts and Studies, 1992, pp. 355–69.
21 On the importance of equivocation and ambiguity in *Macbeth*, see, among others, Steven Mullaney, 'Lying like truth; riddle, representation and treason', in *The Place of the Stage: License, Play and Power in Renaissance England*, Chicago: Chicago University Press, 1988, pp. 116–34. On the significance of interpretation in witchcraft and magic generally, see Greenblatt, 'Shakespeare and the exorcists', pp. 108–9, and Karen Newman, 'Discovering witches: sorciographics', in *Fashioning Femininity and English Renaissance Drama*, Chicago: Chicago University Press, 1991, pp. 65–6.
22 Shakespeare's conflation of classical goddesses and early modern witches has often been noted, but most commentators have tried to sort it out rather than simply point it out; see, for instance, W. C. Curry, *Shakespeare's Philosphical Patterns*, Baton Rouge: Louisiana State University Press, 1937, and Anthony Harris, *Night's Black Agents: Witchcraft and Magic in Seventeenth-Century English Drama*, Manchester: Manchester University Press, 1980. Harris provides a depressing instance of criticism which assumes village witch-beliefs involve the 'trivial', pp. 38–9. Mischieveously and disingenuously, Terry Eagleton argues that the witches are really the heroines of the play, *William Shakespeare*, Oxford: Blackwell, 1986, ch. 1. This reading has been surprisingly influential among the historically naive.
23 '*Macbeth* and witchcraft', in *Macbeth*, ed. Alan Sinfield, London: Macmillan, 1992 (first published 1983), pp. 29–30, emphasis mine. For a similar confusion, see Sarah Beckwith, 'The power of devils and the hearts of men: notes towards a drama of witchcraft', in *Shakespeare in the Changing Curriculum*, ed. Lesley Aers and Nigel Wheale, London: Routledge, 1991, pp. 143–61. Literary critics have often relied on Stuart Clark's piece 'Inversion, misrule and the meaning of witchcraft' (*Past and Present*, 87 [1980], pp. 98–127) for their interpretive framework, largely because its rhetoric of inversion fits with the ideas of the early modern stage as carnival so popular with the post-new historicist Renaissance scholar.

24 Peter Stallybrass and Allon White, *The Politics and Poetics of Transgression*, London and New York: Methuen, 1986, ch. 1.

25 Cf. *King Lear* III. iv. 129: 'And aroint thee witch, aroint thee!', used by Edgar in a similar context of exorcism. Scholars are still unsure of the origins of the phrase, but its obscurity (in this play above all) may be part of its power.

26 Usually identified as deriving from *Newes from Scotland*; James believed his life had been threatened by the witches' attempts to raise a storm at sea (Rosen, *Witchcraft*, p. 197). However, there are similar cases in the English records: in 1601, a Devon woman named Anne Trevisard was accused of causing a ship to founder after a sailor's wife had insulted her (C. L'Estrange Ewen, *Witchcraft and Demonianism*, 1933, pp. 194–5). Weatherworking is more usual on the Continent; see Luisa Accati, 'The spirit of fornication: virtue of the soul and virtue of the body in Fruili, 1600–1800', trans. Margaret A. Galucci, in *Sex and Gender in Historical Perspective*, ed. Edward Muir and Guido Ruggiero, Baltimore and London: Johns Hopkins University Press, 1990, pp. 110–40. Nashe illustrates the influence of these continental ideas on English intellectuals in *The Terrors of The Night*, 1594, *The Works of Thomas Nashe*, ed. R. B. McKerrow, 5 vols, Oxford: Blackwell, 1966–74, vol. I, p. 359.

27 'I'll drain him dry as hay/Sleep shall neither night nor day . . . Weary seven nights nine times nine/Shall he dwindle, peak and pine'. See Janet Adelman, '"Born of woman": Fantasies of maternal power in *Macbeth*', in *Cannibals, Witches and Divorce*, ed. Marjorie Garber, *Selected Papers from the English Institute*, Baltimore: Johns Hopkins University Press, 1987, and Marjorie Garber, *Shakespeare's Ghost Writers: Literature as Uncanny Causality*, London and New York: Methuen, 1987.

28 By contrast, the plays which do not seek to dismiss all witch-beliefs do not use verse in this way. Plays like Dekker, Ford and Rowley's *Witch of Edmonton*, which is an account of a contemporary witch-trial, do not use singsong verse to separate witches from the rest of the village community, but tend to emphasise their ordinariness, their indistinguishability from other villagers. Elizabeth Sawyer speaks in blank verse like everyone else, sometimes in prose. Similarly, plays like Heywood's *The Wise Woman of Hogsdon* and Lyly's *Mother Bombie*, which portray witches as tricksters keen to extract money painlessly from the gullible, do not present witches as inhabiting a different verse form from everyone else.

29 See for example, Thomas Tusser, *Five Hundred Points of Good Husbandry*; and see Stephen Mennell, *All Manners of Food: Eating and Taste in England and France from the Middle Ages to the Present*, Oxford: Blackwell, 1985; on magic in recipe books, see Richard Kieckhefer, *Magic in the Middle Ages*, Cambridge: Cambridge University Press, 1990, p. 9.

30 See Caroline Davidson, *A Woman's Work is Never Done: A History of Housework in the British Isles 1650–1950*, London; Chatto & Windus, 1982, ch. 1.

31 On the Overbury case, see David Lindley, *The Trials of Frances Howard*, London: Routledge, 1993.

32 For a case involving prophetic witches, see Paul, *Royal Play*, pp. 115–17. The fatal ambiguity of the prophecies in *Macbeth* is the one clear sign of a direct appeal to James's turn towards scepticism; there is a humanist discourse of long standing which sees prophecies as a menace to order because of their verbal disorder and ambiguity; of especial interest in this respect is *A Defensative against the poyson of supposed prophecies* by Henry Howard, Earl of Northampton, 1583; the Earl of Northhampton was one of James's principal supporters and later courtiers. See Diane Purkiss, 'Producing the voice, consuming the body: seventeenth-century women prophets', in *Women/Writing/History*, ed. Susan Wiseman and Isobel Grundy, London: Batsford, 1992, pp. 139–58, esp. 154–6, for a more sustained account.

33 Rebecca Bushnell points out that Macbeth's femininity is linked with the traditional

image of the tyrant in 'Tyranny and effeminacy in early modern England', in *Reconsidering the Renaissance*, ed. Di Cesare, pp. 339–54.

34 Helen Nicoll, *Meg and Mog*, London: Picture Puffins, 1972, p. 10.

35 J. M. Nosworthy, *Shakespeare's Occasional Plays: Their Origin and Transmission*, London: Edward Arnold, 1965, pp. 24–45. Nicholas Brooke argues, following Gary Taylor, that Middleton was responsible for revising *Macbeth* (*The Oxford Shakespeare: Macbeth*, Oxford: Oxford University Press, 1990, pp. 57–9).

36 W. J. Lawrence, 'Notes on a collection of masque music', *Music and Letters* (1922), and 'The mystery of *Macbeth*', in *Shakspeare's Workshop*, 1928, p. 28–33.

37 A. A. Bromham, 'The date of *The Witch* and the Essex divorce case', *Notes and Queries*, 225 (1980), 149–52, and also Gareth Roberts, 'A re-examination of the magical material in Middleton's *The Witch*', *Notes and Queries*, 221, new series 23, (1976), pp. 218–19. Ann Lancashire, '*The Witch*: stage flop or political mistake?', in *Accompanyinge the Players: Essays Celebrating Thomas Middleton*, ed. Kenneth Friedenreich, New York: AMS, 1983, pp. 161–81 argues that the play may have been censored. Relations between the Overbury case and Middleton's *The Changeling* have also been suggested, by J. L. Simmons, 'Diabolical realism in Middleton and Rowley's *The Changeling*', *Renaissance Drama*, new series, 11 (1980), pp. 135–70, and Christina Malcomsen, '"As tame as the ladies": politics and gender in *The Changeling*', *English Literary Renaissance*, 20 (1990), pp. 320–39.

38 Lindley, *Frances Howard*.

39 Significantly, those relations more fully investigated feature male protagonists: Ralegh and Harriot, Dee and his clients. There are precedents for English noblewomen consulting cunning women for love charms; there is, for instance, the sixteenth-century case of Frances Throgmorton, who in 1559 is said to have consulted a cunning woman for a love potion: Keith Thomas, *Religion and the Decline of Magic*, London: Harmondsworth: Penguin, 1971, p. 278.

40 For the predominance of love magic on the Continent, see Mary O'Neil, 'Magical healing, love magic and the Inquisition in late sixteenth-century Modena', in *Inquisition and Society in Early Modern Europe*, ed. and trans. S. Haliczer, London: Croom Helm, 1987, pp. 88–114, and Lyndal Roper, *Oedipus and the Devil: Witchcraft, Sexuality and Religion in Early Modern Europe*, London: Routledge, 1994, ch. 6. Mary Woods: *The Letters of John Chamberlain*, ed. N. E. McLure, Philadelphia, 1939, vol. I, p. 449; *SP* 14/72/53; *SP* 14/51/133.

41 Much was made of Turner's affair with Sir Arthur Mainwaring. Other fantasies sprang up thickly around the question of class boundaries and their maintenance; see, for example, Davenport's story of a plot to poison the Royal Family at a christening at which a baby of Anne Turner's sister would have been passed off as Frances Howard's: Chester City Record Office, MSS CR 63.2.19. fo. 5, cited by Lindley, *Frances Howard*, p. 165. See also *CSPD*, 1615, for the idea that the poisoners had also done away with Prince Henry; Mainwaring is referred to as the Prince's 'carer'.

42 On Scot's limitations, see also Chapter 3, above.

43 Scot, 'A discourse upon divels and spirits', appended to *The discoverie of witchcraft*, 1584.

44 See, among others, *The Witch*, ed. W. W. Greg and F. P. Wilson, Malone Society, Oxford University Press, 1950 for 1948; David George, 'The problem of Middleton's *The Witch* and its sources', *Notes and Queries*, 212, new series 14 (1967), p. 209; Roberts, 'A re-examination', pp. 218–19; Roberts argues that Middleton also borrowed directly from the St Osyth pamphlet; even if this is accepted, it is plain that his reading was filtered through Scot's.

45 Hecate also resembles Erihtho in Marston's *Sophonisba*, especially since both are

consulted for love charms and are themselves sexually transgressive. See Chapter 10 for a discussion of classical witches in relation to early modern dramas.

46 See for example the way Middleton's recital of ingredients from Scot's flying potion suddenly turns to a story of village witchcraft and a witch's revenge on those who refused her: 'They denied me often flour, barm and milk/Goose-grease and tar, when I ne'er hurt their churmings [churnings]' (I. 2. 53ff).

47 Scot, *Discoverie*, X. 8, and Middleton, *Witch*, I. 2. 40–5ff.

48 Scot, *Discoverie*, VII. 15. The final evocation 'a ab hur hus' comes from Scot's charm against toothache (XII. 14).

49 A trace of Hecate the goddess seems to survive in an oblique reference to moon-worship (V. ii. 96–7), which also looks back to Elizabethan witch-dramas like *Endimion*. Middleton may have been directly or indirectly influenced by those classical texts like Theocritus' second idyll which depict love magic in association with Hecate; for an analysis of these, see John J. Winkler, 'The constraints of desire: erotic magic spells', in *The Constraints of Desire: The Anthropology of Sex and Gender in Ancient Greece*, London and New York: Routledge, 1990. Generally, however, he is just as cavalier with classical sources as with contemporary popular culture.

50 Charles Lamb once remarked that it would take a brave constable to arrest the Weird Sisters.

51 It is very difficult to detach Reginald Scot's discourse on love charms and copulatory impotence from the assumptions on display in the cases of Frances Howard. Scot records in detail, and therefore promulgates, the Continental understanding of witches as those who impede 'the vertue of generation', and he specifically mentions 'images, herbs etc' as the extrinsic agents by means of which this is done (Scot, *Discoverie*, V. x).

52 T. B. Howell, *A Complete Collection of State Trials*, vol. II, *1603–1627*, pp. 932–3. Turner's trial began on 7 November 1615, and she was hanged on 14 November. In the intervening time, she made an elaborate confession to Dr Whiting, and was reconciled with the Church of England.

53 Thomas Bone's letter to Sir John Egerton, *The Egerton Papers*, ed. J. P. Collier, Camden Society, vol. 12 (1840), pp. 470–3, esp. p. 473. The letter is dated 'Thursday evening', i.e. 9 November.

54 For instances, see Chapter 6.

55 Coke accused both Anne Turner and Sir Thomas Monson of Catholicism as part of their prosecutions; Frances Howard, too, was suspected of Catholic leanings.

56 *State Trials*, p. 985.

57 Savery claimed that Turner offered him a reward for trying to induce Sir Arthur to marry her; when the reward was not forthcoming, he vowed to betray her dealings to Sir Arthur and accuse her before the Arches court of loose conduct (*CSPD*, 1615, p. 321.)

58 Franklin was the apothecary who supplied the poisons (*State Trials*, p. 933). For Franklin's testimony see *Historical Manuscripts Commission Salisbury MSS*, 22, p. 29; Turner loathed Franklin and begged not to be executed with him 'for he is so foule' (*SP* 14/83/20). Francis Osborne, *The True Tragicomedy Formerly Acted at Court*, trans. John Pitcher and Lois Potter, ed. Lois Potter, *The Renaissance Imagination*, vol. 3, New York and London: Garland, 1983.

59 See also Richard Niccols, *Sir Thomas Overburies vision*, 1616; *The bloody downfall of adultery, murder, ambition*, by contrast, uses apocalyptic rhetoric to attack the disparity between appearance and corrupt reality. There is an excellent discussion of the politics of the Overbury stories and publications in Linda Levy Peck, *Court Patronage and Corruption in Early Stuart England*, London: Unwin Hyman, 1990, pp. 175–81.

60 *State Trials*, p. 931.
61 *CSPD*, 1615, 1 October 1615, p. 315.
62 See for instance Turner's claim in her confession to Dr Whiting that she concealed the poisoning of Overbury for the sake of the Countess, 'whom she loved as her own soul' (*CSPD*, 1615, p. 327). By contrast, there is Turner's more critical comment that 'my love to them and to their greatness hath brought me to a dogged death' (*SP* 14/83/20). Some of Turner's statements on this subject represent an attempt to enlighten the court about the inequality of the patronage relationship and her own relative lack of freedom of choice: at her trial, for instance, she complained that she 'had no other means to maintain herself and her children, but what came from the countess' (*State Trials* p. 936).
63 Lyndal Roper, 'Witchcraft and fantasy in early modern Germany', *History Workshop Journal*, 32 (1991), pp. 19–33. See also Elizabeth Hanson, 'Torture and truth in Renaissance England', *Representations*, 34 (1991), pp. 53–84.
64 For seventeenth-century ideas about how the condemned should behave, see J. A. Sharpe, 'Last dying speeches: religion, ideology and public execution in seventeenth-century England', *Past and Present*, 107 (1985), pp. 144–67.
65 Middleton also alludes to Turner and the yellow bands in *The Widow*, V. i: 'That suit would hang him, yet I would not have him hanged in that suit though, it will disgrace my masters fashion for ever, and make it as hateful as yellow bands'.
66 Birch, *The Court and Times of James I*, vol. I, p. 333; Thomas Tuke, *A treatise against painting*, 1616, p. 52, Bodleian Library, MSS Willis 58, fo. 226.
67 *Mistress Turner's Farewell to All Women*, printed for John Trundle. Reproduced as Plate 9 in Lindley, *Frances Howard*. See also *Mistress Turner's Repentance*.
68 *SP* 14/83/33.

9 Testimony and truth

The Witch of Edmonton and *The Witches of Lancashire*

> Then there were books, oh such books, with such titles: Broomsticks, or the Midnight Practice. Spells and How To Bind Them. Merlin's 100 Best Bewitchals. Were-Wolves, by One of Them. Shape-Changing for All, by M. Le Fay. At the end of the shelf was a small red book: Why I Am A Witch, by Sylvia Daisy Pouncer. 'I say', he thought 'this is confession; she glories in it. I'll write to the Bishop. I don't care if it is sneaking. She has no business to be doing this kind of thing'.
>
> John Masefield, *The Midnight Folk*

James I moved from paranoid investigation of the truth of witchcraft to sceptical debunker of the claims of the possessed, while the staging of witchcraft grew more and more sensational around him. This sensationalisation sought to ride the eddies of changing ideas of witchcraft rather than to fix them. It reflected the growing and amused scepticism of the learned, while incorporating half-understood fragments of once-cogent popular beliefs into its glittering and getpenny rhetoric. Although the elite everywhere were becoming more sceptical of the claims of accusers all over the country, with a resultant fall in the number of prosecutions, the growing scepticism did not produce new unanimity. Rather it arose from gaps and fissures in the seventeenth-century understanding of what truth was and how it could be procured. James, admittedly, was motivated chiefly by a cynical wish to display himself to best advantage as a truth-finder, but others, including his son Charles, were more interested in the genuine discovery of truth. In Charles's case this interest seems to have extended well beyond what was politically useful and even into realms of political danger. But where and how was truth to be found? There was a clash between providential ideas of the discovery of truth by the agency of providential revelation, humanist notions of truth as the product of forensic rhetoric, and new empirical notions of the uncovering of truth by diligent scientific enquiry. Stage-plays, however, could respond only by presenting truth as the outcome of layers of plot. Nevertheless, plays as well as other discourses were eager to turn the uncovering of the truth about the witch into a saleable commodity. The witch's guilt or innocence was the truth which the procedures of the witch-trials and the witch-texts sought to uncover, but this discovery could also become the basis for dramatic plotting. The witch-dramas of the later seventeenth century, which often preferred to exploit the sensationalism of actual trials in a new attempt to present themselves as true, explored the conflicting orders of truth through plot. All these discourses, including the most arrantly sensational plays, tried to oppose their truth to the commercial exploitativeness and crudity of other and especially popular accounts of witchcraft; that is, truth came to seem the opposite of sensationalism governed by consumer demand. In the process, it also came to seem the opposite of the popular superstition thought to be catered for by such populist publications, the popular superstition held up to ridicule in plays of the early Jacobean witch-vogue. Then as now, popular superstition was always apt to be feminised, and the eventual result was to construct an idea of the superstitious as crude, unlearned, ugly, illiterate, irrational and deeply unfashionable, an idea then promptly equated with both the witch's female accusers and with the supposed witch herself. This process can be seen in *The Witch of Edmonton*, which draws on the godly reluctance of Henry Goodcole to construct Elizabeth Sawyer herself as the self-deceiving blockage to understanding the truth about witchcraft, even though she is also a truth-teller, or scold. The dramatists construct a narrative of the revelation of truth which relies on establishing the spectacle of revelation via a witch's recognisable staged behaviours and speeches in opposition to the questionable truth of testimonies, thus drawing on an epistemological procedure becoming established in the courts. Nonetheless, the theatricality of being a witch, usually an index of falsity, cannot altogether be banished from the play, any more than can the discourses of commerce and commodification. *The Witches of Lancashire* understands that truth is difficult to obtain, but nevertheless offers to substitute the stage spectacle of witchcraft – somewhat outrageously – for the truth of the body valorised by the courts, while following scepticism in calling into question the truth of testimony or confession.

We in the late twentieth century often valorise realism as a mode of truth-telling, which makes it difficult for us to see these plays independently of our criteria for judging docudramas. Consequently, there is a tendency on the part of critics to assume that *The Witch of Edmonton* is truthful by modern standards. That is, it is seen as representative of popular witchcraft, so that social histories like Macfarlane's or intellectual histories like Stuart Clark's can be mapped straight onto it. It is also seen as sceptical about witchcraft and sympathetic to the witch involved, a position that we in the late twentieth century think of as the epitome of good faith. By contrast, *The Witches of Lancashire* is usually stigmatised as prejudiced. All this suggests is that we have learned to cope with ease with the presentation of truth in *The Witch of Edmonton*, which has become naturalised as 'the truth' and as authoritative, whereas the sensational comic carnival of *The Witches of Lancashire* strikes us as fictional, and also as vulgar, low, superstitious. In this we are reflecting (rather than reflecting on) prejudices and ideas which the plays themselves helped to solidify, rather than investigating how that solidification process occurred around the figure of the witch. Actually, of course, neither play really offers the truth about witches, both drawing freely on a range of more-or-less old-hat stage figurations of witches set by the plays of the witch-vogue which I have just been discussing, so that even Elizabeth Sawyer ends up in the usual business of providing love-potions for yobs who fancy their betters. Manipulating the plays to fit them into a Whiggish narrative of dawning Enlightenment evades the historical specificity of their engagement with truth. At the same time, our own insanely sensationalist era leaves us poorly placed to see how early modern people grappled with the problematic relations between displaying and discovering truth raised by both plays, but also by the events they draw on.

Elizabeth Sawyer is a name that will be familiar to most people from Dekker, Ford and Rowley's play, *The Witch of Edmonton*, first performed in 1621 at the Cockpit. Apart from the play, the story of Elizabeth Sawyer is known to us in just one pamphlet, Henry Goodcole's *The Wonderful Discovery of Elizabeth Sawyer A Witch.*[1] To seventeenth-century Londoners, however, the name of Elizabeth Sawyer might have been familiar from a much greater diversity of texts. Goodcole contrasts his own pamphlet with the 'most base and false ballads, which were sung at the time of our returning from the witch's execution.' The improvisations of this literature attract his disapproval because they abandon plausiblity for sensation: 'I was ashamed to hear such ridiculous fictions of her bewitching corn on the ground, of a ferret and an owl daily sporting before her, of the bewitched woman braining herself, of the spirits attending in prison'.[2] At the same time, Goodcole's own pamphlet was dependent on Sawyer's manufactured notoriety for its success, as were Dekker, Ford and Rowley. Goodcole's anxiety springs from the increasing divergence of opinion about the kind of truth to be determined in cases of witchcraft which characterized the seventeenth century. The Lancashire witches were indeed famous by the time Heywood and Brome staged their play on the topic. Commercialisation of this particular sensation was by no means confined to the lower orders of London. Even before the Privy Council got involved in a kind of appeals procedure, even before the original assize trial in Lancashire, the principal witness for the prosecution was turned into a kind of travelling show. Edmund Robinson, whose story of his encounter with a witches' sabbath in Pendle Forest sparked the scare, was trundled around the local churches by his father so that he could attempt to point out the faces of anyone he had seen at the gathering. Once the story had become a topic for the Privy Council and the king, once the witch-suspects arrived in London, themselves becoming objects of display for official and unofficial examiners alike, their story was circulated in many forms, elite and popular: letters, circulated manuscripts of the depositions and confessions at the original trial, ballads, many old plays dressed up with new and topical allusions to the current case.[3] In Oxford, Thomas Crosfield saw a puppet show of 'the witches of Lancashire over against ye Kinges Head, their tricks, meetings', along with other enetertainments such as a lion, a tableau of the destruction and rebuilding of Jerusalem, and a hocuspocus.[4]

Dramatists were therefore only one group involved in the displaying of witchcraft: also involved were witches' accusers and their families, judges and justices, the witches themselves, their relatives, printers, pamphleteers like Goodcole, puppeteers, ballad-writers, the king, the court, the clergy, and the medical profession. All wanted to display different aspects, but all were keen to hold witchcraft stories or persons up to popular view. How did attempts to explore ideas of truth and testimony sit with the topic of the witch as a novelty, newsworthy? The displaying of witchcraft might involve laying bare the truth of it, but might equally mean merely showing it to a public excited by novelty and news. The plays therefore recycle general questions about truth and belief which are tackled in different ways and with different results by every text which offers to disclose a truth about the witches in question. The case of the Lancashire witches gives us the opportunity to see how the chance to be listened to and celebrated also motivated child-witnesses. Edmund Robinson's remarkable fantasy repays closer study than I can give it here; I have suggested elsewhere that Edmund turns his fear of parental cruelty into a fantasy of a cruel witch, thus achieving the resolution of displacing his hatred and fear of his parents onto the witch, and similarly displacing their anger against him onto the witches.[5] Later he was spurred on by the same factors that influenced Margaret Johnson: 'at first he framed these tales to avoid his mother's correction for not bringing home her kine, but perceiving that many folks gave ear to him, he grew confident in it more and more'. Edmund's story is not made up out of nowhere; he draws on a range of popular cultural materials, including folktales, gossip, slander, and the witchtales of 1613, slowly melting into the general corpus of local legend.[6] An object lesson in how to construct a plausible narrative using cultural materials, Edmund Robinson could have given pointers to Brome and Heywood, if plausibility had interested them. If Edmund's story was refined with adult assistance by the time he told it at the Assizes, it obeyed local laws of plausibility and believability which may have been different in Lancashire and London. What worked on the London stage might not have done for Edmund's self-staging, and vice versa. As we know, the Edmund Robinson Show was a hit with the jury, but the judges gave it a bad review; perhaps its recusant undertones were less appealing to them than to the jury, but also because Edmund's self-staging appeared to them as just that: a performance in a play possibly written by somebody else.

The critics of torture, so speciously dominant in our image of witch-trials, sometimes described it in theatrical terms. Richard Verstegan's *Theatrum Crudelitatum haereticorum nostri temporis* (1587) offers the scene of torment not as a scene of truth, but as a display of cruelty. Such texts are usually accompanied by illustrations which make literal a disclosure of pain and torment, but also turn the scene into a spectacle. Yet this spectacle was absent from the scene of English witchcraft. On the Continent, and in Scotland, torture was used very frequently in cases of witchcraft, but in England there seems not to have been one single occasion where the torture of a woman for suspected witchcraft was licensed. Torture is the deliberate use of pain designed to produce a confession as a legal and accepted part of the process of interrogation. When critics like Gail Paster claim that witches in England were 'tortured' by being watched for the arrival of familiars, which inadvertently involved sleep deprivation, they miss the historical point. In any case, such practices were rare outside Matthew Hopkins's reign of terror.[7] Other repellent practices which may have occurred, such as swimming witches, were not usually sanctioned by law, and were in any case a trial by ordeal, not a milder form of torture but a completely different forensic process. In our anxiety to be sympathetic to those accused of witchcraft, we must be careful not to muddle cruelties together, for only by retaining some sense of their specificity can we hope to understand them and their meaning for women. The point of torture is not only that it hurts, but that the pain is supposed to elicit true speech.

Asking questions about the absence of torture from the English scene has led to further questions about the truth of witchcraft and how it was constructed in a range of literary and nonliterary texts in the mid-seventeenth century, centring on the case of Elizabeth Sawyer and the play which emerged from it, *The Witch of Edmonton*, and the case of the Lancashire witches of 1633 and its dramatic representation, *The Witches of Lancashire*. The absence of torture from English witchcraft is the key to understanding the epistemological problems posed by the witch and the conflict between the various kinds of representation which tried to solve that problem. The problem arose from a collision of ideas; the increasingly complex standards of legal, scientific and rhetorical proof clashed with popular superstitions which understood the community as the guarantor of truth. The elite began to distance themselves from popular superstitions, as a mark of social elevation, but needed a secure way to tell truth from falsehood on the terrain of belief. These epistemological problems could be addressed in three ways. The confession of the accused could be valorised as an absolute truth guaranteed by its status as providential revelation, an outcome which at least gave women a chance to talk and be heard; the truth of the body could be substituted for the dubiety of the truth of a woman's tongue, which allowed scientific discourse to interrogate popular superstition; or forensic humanist and Puritan rhetorics of disclosure offered the truth of witchcraft as that which could be separated interpretatively from the mass of popular superstition. However, all these texts had to work to distinguish their 'truth' from the commodified sensationalism of the popular marketplace, where ballads jostled with puppetshows in offering thrills to a public in love with the pleasures of news. Publishing a confession, or for that matter a display of scientific or rhetorical acumen, did not mean informing the ignorant; it meant entering into undignified competition for truth with the sensation-monger. The stage, most sensational of all, was also a competitor, and the shadow of theatricality, fakery and acting haunts all the other possible proofs mentioned. The plays based on real cases are the dark doubles or shadows of the more authentic discourses on which they draw. Yet they offer their own form of truth, since domestic dramas work by a process of discovery or revelation of the nature and identity of witches, so that at the level of plot they seek to establish the truth about witchcraft. Both tried to use the truth of the body and also the truth of the tongue, witchmarks and confessions, but both raise more problems than they solve in the context of the theatre. As if in depair, both plays are in the end content to fall back on sensationalism, the revelation of theatricality of witch-identity and the spectacle of magic as an outcome of stage skills.

Henry Goodcole, like most men who interrogate witches, has had a bad press from feminism. With a few exceptions, feminism has tended to equate him with much more irrational and severe figures like Matthew Hopkins, and even to call him a torturer. Usually regarded as the prejudiced, overly religious interrogator, Goodcole seems to be set up for Dekker, Ford and Rowley to rise above. He is also regarded as the purveyor of disinformation, the man who covered up Elizabeth Sawyer's defiance and replaced it with an eroticised fantasy of compliance.[8] This does little justice to Goodcole or to his early modern audience, who were not especially credulous about confession or interrogation, and who were quite aware that people could be frightened into telling lies. Goodcole is drawing on very powerful ideas about the saving power of truth, ideas widely shared by the crowds attending executions.[9] His interest in this truth is not altogether disinterested; as we shall see, truths like this had a market value. Nonetheless, the fantasy in which Goodcole invests is less of eroticised or sadomasochistic reverie than of discursive saviour and restorer of spiritual health. 'For my part,' he writes in his *Apology to the Christian Readers*, 'I meddle here with nothing but matters of fact, and to that end produce the testimony of living and dead'. Goodcole offers Sawyer's confession as the truth which refutes not only the popular rumours which surround her, but also her denials at her trial. The latter is mainly important for Sawyer, since Goodcole sees her cursing and denials as providentially designed to produce the truth of her guilt:

> thus God did wonderfully overtake her in her own wickedness to make her tongue to be the means of her own destruction . . . out of her false swearing the truth whereof she little thought would be found, but by her swearing and cursing blended, it thus far made against her that both Judge and Jury, all of them grew more and more suspicious of her (p. lxxxvii).[10]

Later, Sawyer's confessing tongue will providentially produce another kind of truth, the kind which restores her to God. For Goodcole, the confession purports to have absolute spiritual value rather than legal validity; he understands the legal system of conviction and execution only as an instrument of the providential unfolding of divine truth. Elizabeth Sawyer's interrogation by her confessor is not an act of unfeeling cruelty, but a way of encouraging her to utter the stories that can return her to the Christian community from which her diabolic pact had exiled her. Goodcole presents himself as motivated, like the Continental inquisitors, not by a disinterested desire for abstract truth, but for truth as a means of salvation and reintegration. For him, Sawyer's confession is not a weak-kneed renunciation of her identity under pressure, but a recovery of the true self she had lost by diabolic pact.

For those of us who would like to see the confessions of witches as male fantasies forced into women's mouths by violence, like scolds' bridles, Goodcole and Sawyer are an awkward team. The truth of her confession had value as a commodity. This was not Goodcole's only attempt at presenting a true confession. Unable to attend university or to gain preferment in the church until late in life, Goodcole eked out a living as a chaplain attending condemned prisoners in Newgate, publishing their confessions to augment his income. His distinction between his own serious work and the ballads which produce stories 'fitter for an ale-bench than for a relation of proceeding in a court of justice' and his criticism of 'lewd balladmongers' who are wrongly allowed 'to creep into the printer's presses and people's ears' might read as a denunciation of his more lurid competition rather than a sincere distinction between himself and the vulgar. Thus his strictures about the lies told by such people problematise the truth of his own text. Witchcraft itself could be dismissed as an implausible fiction by some of Goodcole's readers, and Goodcole's assertions about it rest heavily on the confession of Elizabeth Sawyer, unsupplemented by any depositions from her neighbours. Sawyer's last appearance on the scaffold could be read as a carefully staged promotion of Goodcole's fiction rather than as the urgent truth of the dying speech. Outside providential discourse, confession was neither as reliable nor as providential as Goodcole tried to make it seem. Theatricality keeps erupting into areas from which it has been carefully banished.

This becomes even more obvious when we turn to the Lancashire witch case of 1633/4, the case that inspired Heywood and Brome's play. One at least of the accused witches who was eventually brought to London was not named by the original child-witness, Edmund Robinson; she came forward voluntarily to confess to witchcraft after no interrogation or questioning by anyone. Margaret Johnson's confession illustrates the extent to which playing the role of witch could be pleasurable for early modern women, as well as having some commodity value for them; a reputation for witchcraft could extract courtesy as well as food from neighbours. This is not to suggest that Johnson was not speaking the truth as she saw it. Seeing the advantages of being a witch were not incompatible with thinking that you were one. Johnson and the Elizabeth Sawyer of the play may have been alike in wishing to turn their passive misery as poor and abused women into a mode of aggressive power. Johnson told that she 'was brought thereto upon some vexations of her bad neighbours';[11] in particular, she claimed to have entertained special animosity against Henry Heap, her neighbour, who 'called her a witch before she was one, whereupon her spirit willed her to hurt him, but she assented not'. It is almost as if she has been influenced by *The Witch of Edmonton*. Johnson plays the already-scripted part of a witch, perhaps after being cast in it by some of her neighbours, and she plays it with gusto. Johnson lays great stress on the sexual seductiveness of the devil, going beyond most pamphleteers in sensationalism. The devil appears 'in the similitude of a man apparelled in a suit of black tied with silk points', and 'with her consent' he 'defiled her by committing wicked uncleanness'. She reiterated this at her second confession, claiming that 'he called himself Mamilion, and most commonly at his coming had the use of her body'. This is only one aspect of her bodily relations with Mamilion – she also suckles him, and this might seem a shocking act of incest. Though would be nice to think that the link between the two bodily unions is that Mamilion is a fantasy of satisfaction of desire, the metaphor seems rather more depressing than this since Johnson protests that she does not enjoy it much. As a poor woman, Margaret Johnson has nothing but her body to offer in exchange for commodities or services. She can lend her feminine body to be used for the pleasure of another. Her fantasy of a demon-familiar does not change this. The part she scripts for herself is always based, as it must be, on her own life and her own experiences. The connection between sex and suckling is that Margaret Johnson pays for the devil's services with her *body*, even though she knows that the compact is over her *soul*. Or does she? As we shall see, this was precisely the debatable point for early modern discourses about witchcraft in the mid-seventeenth century.

Confessing to witchcraft offered Margaret Johnson the opportunity, not usually offered to women, to be centre-stage for a while, to speak about desire, to speak about maternity, to speak about her dreams, and to be listened to attentively by her neighbours, and by the better sort. Yet as Goodcole's pamphlet shows, confession and testimony are subject to this difficulty; once a gap opens up between the person speaking the words and the 'I' of the narrative, the authenticity of confession is lost; performance and authentic confession are opposites.[12]

Torture arose on the Continent in response to new and rational notions of truth and proof. These ideas replaced older beliefs about a providential truth allowed to emerge through the trial of the body in ordeal or combat. Although these trials came to seem irrational, they usually produced a clear outcome. By contrast, a rationalist rather than a providential understanding of truth as the outcome of a process of reading and reflecting on a morass of testimony was much less certain, and often produced an outcome which depended on interpretation.[13] Ordeals and combat relied on the truth of the body and the power of providence to make a moral truth manifest through the body as sign, but the new rational trials required that the truth be made manifest in language, and language not providentially guaranteed. This was especially true of witchcraft cases, where conviction often rested on the confession of the accused. While witnesses' depositions might be guaranteed by oath, confessions were not taken on oath since no one could be asked to swear their own death. Torture, however, offered to guarantee the confession of the accused, in part because it resembled the abandoned ordeals and combats, but mostly because (in accordance with ancient lawcodes) it was seen as a way of helping the accused to speak the truth.[14] It filled the ontological space in forensic rhetoric with a postulation of certainty, not because early modern judges did not know that pain could make people confess to anything (they did) but because they saw such confession as the product of *incompetent* use of torture.

In England, however, torture was not used in witch-cases, though it was used for a wide range of felonies considered milder than witchcraft, including burglary and assault.[15] Despite this, there is often a self-congratulatory note in discussions of English witchcraft; unlike the Europeans, we of course were too just and humane to use torture on the hapless accused. In fact, there were other, less flattering reasons for the absence of torture in English witch-cases. Torture was not used much in England because the laws of evidence here were so crude that the problems and ambiguities that torture was used to overcome on the Continent simply never arose. Juries (as opposed to judges) retained some of the 'inscrutability' of the ordeal; defendants could be convicted on less evidence than was required as a mere precondition for interrogation under torture on the Continent.[16] Nonetheless, just as England's elite eventually imbibed a watered-down version of the Continental idea of witchcraft, so by slow degrees they came to embrace a few parts of the Continental, neo-Roman idea of evidence. Manuals of instruction for justices of the peace, a literature which begins to multiply in the late sixteenth century, point to the shift from an investigative jury to an investigative justice of the peace, who takes down depositions and presents evidence for the prosecution. Worries about the truth of testimonies are heavily underlined in this literature, stressing the importance of taking evidence under oath, but this safeguard is not available for the accused, since no one can be bound to accuse him- or herself. Hence the confession of the accused should ideally be verified by witnesses under oath, and vice versa.[17] As a result of these anxieties, the Continental idea of torture began to be entertained, reaching a peak during the second decade of James's reign, but also used extensively in the 1590s, especially in cases of treason, where it was used to uncover the principal actors in complex plots.[18] The very terminology – actors, plots – should alert us to a possible corollary in the uncovering of the truth of plot on stage. However, torture was also understood more simply as an expedient to recover an otherwise elusive truth in quite ordinary cases of felony. A burglar named Rice was ordered to be tortured in 1567, 'whereby he may be the better brought to confess the truth'.[19] Torture was often ordered in cases where prosecutors felt they *knew* the truth; the early modern phrase for this was 'vehement suspicion'.

Torture is repeatedly equated in recent theoretical literature with the epistemological rhetoric of scopophiliac discovery, that is, with anatomy classes, with the *Novum Organum*, and so on. Francis Bacon is cited as an empiricist who advocated torture in a letter to James concerning an apprehended sorceror.[20] Feminist readings have demonstrated that the logic of empirical enquiry invented by Baconian science is relentlessly gendered; the object of study and examination is almost invariably a feminised site, whether it is nature or that configuration of internal anatomy which can be feminised, while the enquirer is always male.[21] If we map this discourse onto torture in the way suggested by Elizabeth Hanson, one would expect to find a particular willingness to torture women, and especially witches, whose bodies are in any case possessed of mysterious and threatening powers requiring investigation. Moreover, witch-cases presented a particular epistemological problem, since signs and wonders which could confirm the confession were more difficult to recover. Finally, the confession came from the unreliable tongue of a woman. All this would fit with Elaine Scarry's theory that the incontestable truth of bodily pain is a supplement to the perceived lack or unreliability of language; in Scarry's thesis, torturers torture in order to reinforce a belief of which they are themselves unsure, to fill an epistemological gap.[22] An expectation that witches would be tortured would also chime with far cruder feminist understandings of witchcraft as woman-hating. We might also want to see torture as related to the rhetorical practices surrounding the publication of the events of witch-trials. Witchcraft cases were always accompanied by a forensic rhetoric of discovery which contrasted the secret or hidden practices of witches with the exposure of discourse or print, exposure that could lead to knowledge and understanding. Standard discourses of humanist profitability could expand to include the witch as the object of knowledge, rhetoric and proof, and these discourses too were gendered, since the knowledgeable reader was assumed to be male. The pamphlet on the 1613 Lancashire witch-trials was accompanied by a preface which asserted that 'it is necessary for men to know and understande the meanes whereby they [witches] worke their mischief, their hidden mysteries of their devilish and wicked Enchantments, charms and sorceries, the better to prevent and avoid the danger that may ensue'.[23] It might look as if the torture of witches is so overdetermined as to be inevitable.

And yet we find just the opposite, an extreme reluctance to torture female suspects in general, and witches in particular, at a time when witchcraft prosecutions, patriarchal paranoia and torture warrants all reached a peak in the last years of the sixteenth century and the first decade of the seventeenth. Even the notorious, half-mad Matthew Hopkins did not attempt to torture suspects, relying on other methods to provide evidence to support confession. There were very few cases of torture involving women, and even these show some sense that women's bodies could not be made to speak in this way. Whipping was the standard recourse if the prospect of the torture of a woman or a child was raised, which suggests that women's legal status as minors protected them.[24] However, no records survive of accused witches being whipped in order to extract a statement from them. There were a few cases where practitioners of magic were put to torture. All of them were male: one was Samuel Peacock, a former schoolmaster alleged to have attempted 'to infatuate the King's judegement by sorcery' (1620), while the last Jacobean warrant for torture was issued against James Crasfield, who had predicted a rebellion in 1622.[25] Although sorcerors, especially those somehow tainted with treasonous activities, could be tortured, a suspected witch was not a natural candidate.

It was when confession was not forthcoming that real difficulties arose. Some of those accused in Lancashire in 1633 stoutly denied all charges. All those interested in the case were faced with a choice between the word of the defendants and the testimony of Edmund Robinson, the chief witness for the prosecution. What happened is instructive: the Privy Council had the witches carefully interrogated, and then ordered a search for witchmarks to be carried out by a team of midwives and doctors. Similarly, Elizabeth Sawyer was searched by a specially appointed jury of matrons, and the searchers apparently found 'a thing like a teat, the bigness of the little finger, and the length of half a finger, which was branched at the top like a teat, and seemed as though one had sucked it'.[26] Village midwives often examined the accused for a mark. England alone had searches for witchmarks, and England practically alone in Western Europe did not have torture. A coincidence? Perhaps not. Charles I was doing something crucial in ordering a serious medical investigation of the Lancashire suspects. He was agreeing that the truth of the body could supplement the truth of the tongue where providence seemed slow in revealing the difference between truth and lies; he was installing science as a supplement to a defectively operating providential unfolding of truth. The epistemological discourse of discovery which could have spawned a practice of torture instead spawned a medicalisation of witchcraft which itself contributed to the scepticism which accompanied the arrival of empirical considerations at the English court. The witchmark became conceivable as a site of scientific truth at the moment when empirical science was trying to invent an authoritative rhetoric for itself out of a mixture of juridical rhetoric and ancient medicine. The witchmark, which could claim to be the bastard child of juridical and medical truth, was its ideal *exemplum*, because on it, as on the bodies of the possessed, a struggle for scientific as opposed to traditional or superstitious truth could be staged. By admitting the possibility of a witchmark, empiricism enabled itself to prove its impossibility, a tack it also took with other supernatural phenomena. But in admitting such a possibility, science was opening the floodgates of fantasy, and a dark tide of anxiety rolled in. For the witchmark was not the creation of empirical science, but of popular anxiety.

As we have seen, early modern medical writers believed that breastmilk was the blood which had been nourishing the foetus in the womb. Clean, nourishing blood was separated or skimmed off from the impure blood which continued to be shed from the womb as lochia, drawn up to the breasts in a large vein, and purified by the heat of the heart, literally by maternal love. The breast was therefore a redeemed and redeeming part of the leaky and polluting body of the childbearing woman. However, the blood or milk was still linked with the lower body, so anxieties about its state proliferated. Anxieties about the borderline between humans and animals, between clean and unclean, translate into the elaborate fantasy of the witch and her suckling familiar.

In *The Witch of Edmonton*, Dekker, Ford and Rowley focus on Sawyer's ability to shift the boundaries between animal and human for the entire village.[27]

Her idea of a witch is someone close to animals: 'I have heard old beldames / Talk of familiars in the shape of mice, /Rats, ferrets, weasels and I wot not what, / That have appeared and sucked, some say, their blood' (II. 1. 102–5). For Sawyer this is the essence of witchcraft. The witch's punishment of her enemies involves forcing them to cross the lines between animal and human: Old Banks, for instance 'cannot chuse, though it be ten times an hour, but run to the cow, and taking up her tail, kiss (saving your worship's reverence) my Cow behind; that the whole town of Edmonton has been ready to bepiss themselves with laughing me to scorn' (IV. 1. 53–8).[28] Sawyer also casts her enemies as sucking animals, however: calling one 'a black cur / That barks and bites, and sucks the very blood / Of me, and of my credit' (II. 1. 111–13).[29] Even at the end she calls them 'dogs' (V. 3. 41). They in turn represent her as a 'beast'. Yet this seems less a definition of witchcraft than an understanding of the low social status that led everyone to plague Sawyer in the first place.

By contrast, Henry Goodcole uses the witchmark as sign of transgression to the full; it is a teat on the lower body, near the polluting anus, suckled by a devil in the shape of a dog. Goodcole's exhibition of the mark is not a sign of prurience; the mark is a synecdoche of the bodily truth which supports and grounds the truth of Sawyer's words to him. Its presence is thus paradoxically her damnation and her salvation. Some characters in the play emulate this discourse: Sir Arthur Clarington avers to the Justice that 'far and near she's bruited for a woman that maintains a spirit that sucks her' (IV. 1. 90).[30] However, in the play Sawyer's body is presented as more prone to 'leak' words than blood: she offers the 'teat' to her familiar, but also apologises for being dry through cursing (IV. 1. 154–7). At the level of character, this means that Sawyer is choleric, overflowing with the hot blood of the dog days, blood that is dried up by her furies. She is the stage-type of the elderly shrew, whose humours make her cursed. Dramatically, the play substitutes the sound of cursing for the sight or site of the witchmark, a bodily truth which is difficult to show on stage. Instead, the play valorises the truth of the body *as* speech; cursing is an expression of the hot blood which would otherwise leak out or be fed to the dog. The fact that the dog-demon arrives as Sawyer is cursing is usually read socially: cursing is a transgression of gender roles. But it can also be read medically: cursing is a sign of hot red blood overflowing, a sign to which a familiar is naturally attracted.

This continues the medicalisation of the witch begun by Reginald Scot and continued by Edward Jorden.[31] However, the play also valorises the truth of another kind of speech, the speech of confession, especially when figured via the stage confession or soliloquy. The authenticity of this form of speech is what 'proves' Sawyer to be a witch, especially given the frequent displays of her inner thoughts and feelings in it. However, it is these early speeches which attract the modern audience, used to seeing soliloquy as the revelation of the inner self. The play is not interested in witchcraft as self-actualisation, but in an idea of witchcraft drawn from George Gifford, for whom pact witchcraft involved the damnation of a witch destined to be damned in any case, and unable to draw on any diabolical powers.[32] In order to follow his providential narrative, the dramatists abandon the idea of confession as spoken revelation of truth which Goodcole so valued, and also reject the detailed specularisation of the body. Instead, the guarantor of truth turns out to be action, in thoroughly predestinarian form. In the event (or plot), Sawyer is damned. This is apparent in the one (edited) spectacle retained in the play, the spectacle of the condemned witch before her execution. Whereas for Goodcole this is a moment of real repentance and social reintegration, for Dekker, Ford and Rowley it is a moment when predestined damnation can be proved by display, since their Elizabeth Sawyer is not fully repentant, still choleric with her neighbours (V. 3. 41).[33]

The king and Privy Council, trying to resolve the problem of whom to believe in the case of the 1633 Lancashire witches, relied heavily on empirical proof in the form of the witchmark. However, the connection between that proof and the emergent rhetoric of empirical science becomes apparent in the appointment of the King's physician Sir William Harvey to lead the team of doctors and midwives who would examine the suspects for witchmarks.[34] In another sense, too, Harvey was ideally placed not to find witchmarks, because it was he who had begun the process of demolishing the understanding of the female body on which the idea of suckling familiars depended. Harvey discovered the circulation of the blood in 1628, which understood the heart as simple pump, not a purification chamber.[35]

The eventual party consisted of five physicians and ten female obstetricians acting under Harvey's direction. They found 'nothing unnatural' on Jennet Hargraves, Frances Dicconson or Mary Spencer, but on Margaret Johnson they discovered 'two things which might be called teats, the first in shape like the teat of a bitch, but in their judgement being nothing but the skin drawn out as it would be after the piles on application of leeches; the second being like the nipple or teat of a woman's breast, but without any hollowness or issue for any blood or juice to come from thence'.[36] The teats are described in language which recalls anxieties about breasts and breastfeeding. Margaret Johnson's first mark appears like the teat of a bitch, but it is really a pile to which leeches have been applied. The force of the comparison to the teat of a bitch seems to be to debunk too-hasty classification of teats on the basis of their resemblance to animal teats; Harvey's rhetoric is doing battle with popular readings of the mark. The dismissal of the second teat on grounds of its unconnectedness to any vein or vessel is also significant; the examiners had ceased merely to look, and were applying stringent standards of function to the witchmark. Their rhetoric indicates that they are not only seeking to judge the truth of the witchcraft accusation they are investigating, but also of the empirical method; the witch-mark is supposed to demonstrate the truth of science, even as science demonstrates the truth or fictionality of the witchmark. It contrasts with the much more laconic notes of the Lancashire midwives who had examined the same women: 'Jennet . . . 1 mark in her secret place . . . Francisca, Dicconson, 3 marks in her secrets . . . Margaret Johnson, 1 mark or pap betwixt her seat and secrets'.[37] The midwives emphasise the location of each mark, on the lower body near genitals or fundament. This is the rhetoric of anxieties about breastfeeding and the maternal body. But could it be dispelled by the truth-telling of the scientists? Admittedly, Charles I did issue a pardon for all the witches, but three years later they were still incarcerated in Lancaster Castle.[38] Why?

While the careful medical epistemology of Harvey's team's report on the witchmarks might have appealed to Charles, it did not strike a chord with everyone. Other kinds of display may have carried more weight and offered more authenticity, thus creating a different truth. For although some, like Goodcole, continued to worry about the corruption of truth at the hands of rumour, sensation and press display, others saw those instruments of display as a way to make truth visible when it had been obscured. Paradoxically, the theatre might have had a role to play here. Characteristically the locus of socially destabilising lies for those enthusiastic about a providentialist unfolding of truth via authentic signs and wonders, it could also be seen as a way of conveying otherwise obscure truths to a deluded populace by members of the elite imbued with a humanist notion of its educative properties. When it suited them, some of the elite seemed more than willing to cast aside the protocols of epistemology by substituting for them a theatrical display. This is even truer if we accept Herbert Berry's idea that some members of the Privy Council might have set the King's Men on to write *The Witches of Lancashire* in an effort to register the guilt of the witches with the public and protest the sceptical climate of the court.

However, this thesis seems unlikely in the context of Nathaniel Tomkyns's letter describing the performance of the play he witnessed at the Globe in the summer of 1634.[39] Of the play he writes that

> though there be not in it (to my understanding) any poeticall genius of art, or language, or judgement to state or tenet of witches (wch I expected) or application to virtue but full of ribaldry and of things improbable and impossible; yet in regard it consisteth from the beginning to the end of odd passages and fopperies to provoke laughter, and is mixed with diverse songs and dances, it passeth for a merry and excellent new play.

This suggests that the early modern gentleman or lady was a sophisticated reader of different discourses about witchcraft. Tomkyns is in no danger of taking the play to be sober 'truth'; he reads it as merriment whose pleasure largely comes from its variety. The remainder of his description of the play is taken up with a list of its spectacles, its staging of magic tricks, a series of visual fantasies notable for their strangeness or newsworthiness, but not notable for their plausibility. This is not contrasted with the ongoing newsworthiness of the accused women themselves, who remain in gaol ('the witches still being visible'), but aligned with it; the women themselves are nothing but a site of interest or merriment. He is consigning witches to a realm of popular superstition, and in this he is recognising the similarity between *The Witches of Lancashire* and the plays of the sceptical Jacobean witch-vogue.[40]

Nonetheless, the play does engage with the question of truth. The first scene is a debate between rationalist scepticism and popular superstition. It begins with a debate about whether a hare is a disguised witch, and continues with Squire Generous's denunciation of mannerly hypocrisy in favour of old-fashioned plainness. At first, truth is associated with the sceptics, but the plot is organised around a series of spectacular revelations of supernatural activity. These revelations are offered as the hidden truths towards which the plot has been building, the authentic showing of real witchcraft, but because the revelations are based on spectacle, they are also disclosed as the full exploitation of the resources of the theatre. We see some *Macbeth*-style witches sitting around talking in those octosyllabic couplets; we see them eating a Land of Cockaigne-like bounty of meat and fat, and we see them obtain this bounty from the wedding feast. It was these stage spectacles that stuck in Tomkyns's mind, but they stuck in his mind as spectacles, not as serious truths about witchcraft. Heywood and Brome take the trope of truth by seeing and use it to justify display. Squire Generous's scepticism is based on the absence of sight: 'you will believe nothing but what you see', says his servant Robin contemptuously, arranging to show him (though not the audience) the transformation of his wife from horse to woman. It is all so familiarly stagey that what is on display is not truth, but spectacle: for once it really is not *a priori* certain that drama is about anything but itself.

Yet the play also wants to punish the scepticism that its own theatricality encourages, while separating itself from the popular. Although popular superstition is constantly stigmatised as low or base, it is also shown to be the only correct way to interpret evénts. Squire Generous, the best-educated character and the only unequivocal member of the better sort, finds his scepticism is thoroughly punished by the revelation that his wife is a witch. The play does not seem the amused display of popular error that one finds in the plays of the earlier seventeenth century. It is as if the stage has become uncertain about separating itself from supernatural belief, as if this would make it too less believable. In a different way, the dramatists of *The Witch of Edmonton* also assault truth by equating witchcraft with acting. They stress the witch as a *role* in the morris dancing in *The Witch of Edmonton*: 'Have we e'er a witch in the morris?', asks young Banks eagerly, but the First Dancer assures him that only Maid Marian and the hobby horse will be represented. 'Faith, witches themselves are so common now-a-days that the counterfeit will not be regarded. They say we have three or four in Edmonton besides Mother Sawyer.' The Second Dancer puts in 'I would she would dance her part with us' (III. 1. 7–14). The morris dancers propose that a woman who is really a witch should act as one, exactly what happens in the play. Like Margaret Johnson, Elizabeth Sawyer becomes increasingly absorbed in *acting* as a witch: in her scenes with young Banks, for instance, she throws herself into the *part* of the sinister old crone who can give a love potion. The scene is full of asides which point up the distinction between self and role: 'I must dissemble the better to accomplish my revenge', Sawyer tell the audience, and 'we shall have sport', she says, observing her power to trick Banks (II. 1. 208, 224). When she finally promises, 'what art can do, be sure of', we are not sure which art she means (II. 1. 233). What eventually happens to Banks, too, is not so very different from what happens to the luckless suitors in *The Merry Wives of Windsor.* He is fobbed off with a theatrical replica of his love. And just as Margaret Johnson appears to have been influenced by stage-plays of Sawyer, so Sawyer's mutterings over the love-potion cannot help but remind us of Middleton's *The Witch.* Despite its ostensible realism and seriousness, then, *The Witch of Edmonton* too eventually shows the figure of the witch to be a role; at one point, Old Banks (mis)identifies Sawyer with Mother Bombie, the benign wisewoman of Lyly's Elizabethan comedy of 1590 (IV. 1. 200), while later he miscalls her Gammer Gurton, promising to 'have at your needle of witchcraft', referring to the 1557 comedy's heroine (who was not a witch).[41]

Many modern critics have taken *The Witch of Edmonton* for realism and hence for social truth, and yet it cannot help pointing flagrantly at its own theatrical history and at the theatricality of witchcraft itself. The shifting colour of the Dog, signifying its unreliability and deceptiveness, points to the instability of identity, and this is further emphasised by his curiously lengthy explanation of how he comes by bodies to use. The Dog's final and apocalyptic speech of intent seems in godly mode to equate theatricality with the devil: 'I'll . . . get a noble countenance/Serve some Briarean footcloth-strider/That has a hundred hands to catch at bribes/But not a finger's nail of charity.'[42] The point of this scene is to deny the truth of the body, to present the body as prone to mistake, fluid, rotten with tricks, impossible to know, ripe for deceit. Yet what provokes this outburst is Young Banks' horror at the Dog's willingness to suck the polluted blood of witches: 'to creep under an old witch's coats and suck like a great puppy! Fie upon it!' (V. 1. 173–4). In the context of anxieties about breastfeeding it is no surprise to hear Young Banks's epithet for this practice: 'beastly'. Despite Dekker, Ford and Rowley's avoidance of any spectacle of the perversely lactating body of the witch, it is that body, in the end, to which they uneasily revert. Neither play can decide what should count as truth, or how truth, theatre and the supernatural can coexist best, whether truth lies in the slipperiness of language or the fakery of stage spectacle, whether the female tongue or the female body is the most obviously forked and frightening. Usually, the stage is read as complicit in witch-hunting, but these plays are uneasy about exactly what they wish to endorse or how to read or write the increasingly cloudy figure of the witch. We are used now to hearing that the theatre was an ideological arm of everything we dislike in seventeenth-century power relations, but one could conclude with a question which might point to the benefits of showing witchcraft up as epistemologically uncertain. Can it be a coincidence that the most horrible, bloody and rabidly misogynistic witch-trials ever appearing in England, the

Matthew Hopkins trials, trials which turned on the discovery of witchmarks, took place at the time when the London theatres were closed by the Parliamentarian regime?

NOTES

1 No records of Sawyer's trial or indictment in Middlesex survive. Barbara Hamilton's forthcoming Master's dissertation surveys all the surviving witchcraft records for Middlesex.

2 Henry Goodcole, *The wonderful Discovery of Elizabeth Sawyer a witch*, 1621. The pamphlet is reprinted in *The Works of John Ford,* ed. William Gifford with additions by Alexander Dyce, 3 vols, London, 1895, vol. I, pp. lxxxi–cvii.

3 Letters: in Lancashire, see Sir William Pelham to Lord Conway, 16 May 1633 (*CSPD*). Anecdotes: Sir William Brereton gave an account of the affair to the Queen of Bohemia in the Hague on 3 June (*Travels in Holland the United Provinces England Scotland and Ireland*, ed. Edward Hakins, Chetham Society, vol. 1 (1844), pp. 43–4. Manuscripts of depositions: these survive in at least four manuscripts and one printed transcription; though these can be divided into two clear and related groups, this does suggest that manuscripts circulated fairly freely, and Brome and Heywood certainly had access to some of them. Ballads: at least two were registered, both now lost: *Prophane Pastimes of the Witches Mad Humours*, and *The Witches Dance*, both registered 22 August, 1634. Both seem to reflect the jokey tone of the play. Plays: as well as Heywood and Brome's play, there was the revival against which the King's Men petitioned on behalf of Heywood and Brome, probably *Dr Lambe and the Witches*: 'A Peticon of the Kings Players complayning of intermingling some passages of witches in old playes to ye pr[e]judice of their designed comedy of the Lancashire witches, & desiring a prohibition of any other till theirs be allowed & Acted. Answered p[er] Reference to Blagrave in absence of Sr H. Herbert/July 20 1634' (Malone Society Collections, vol. ii, p. 410, from the Lord Chamberlain's Petition Book, LC 5/183, and see postscript) *The Witch of Edmonton* might itself have been revived for this occasion, as Onat suggests (*The Witch of Edmonton*, ed. Etta Soif Onat, New York: Garland, 1980). Allusions: see, for instance, Thomas Nabbes, *Tottenham Court* (Prince's Men, 1634) I. 2. B[v], and John Kirke, *The Seven Champions of Christendom* (Prince's Men, 1635), 235–8.

4 Thomas Crosfield, *The Diary of Thomas Crosfield*, ed. Frederick S. Boas, London, 1935, p. 79, 10 July 1633, fo. 72[r].

5 Edmund Robinson's confession: the fullest text is in John Webster, *The displaying of supposed witchcraft*, 1677, p. 347ff, used here, but it is also transcribed in BL, MSS Harleian 6854, fo. 26[v], and also in Bodleian, MSS Dodsworth 61, fos 45–47[v]; a less polished version is in Rawlinson, D 399, fos 211–12[v], and BL, MSS Add. 36–674, fos 193, 196; the last has many omissions. Katherine Briggs, *A Dictionary of British Folktales*, 4 vols, London: Routledge & Kegan Paul, 1970–1, cites several instances of witches transforming themselves into hares. See Chapter 6 for more on Edmund Robinson.

6 Webster, *Displaying*, p. 277.

7 Gail Kern Paster, *The Body Embarrassed: Drama and the Discourses of Shame in Early Modern England*, Ithaca: Cornell University Press, 1993, p. 254.

8 E.g. Paster, *The Body*, pp. 253–4, and Viviana Comensoli, 'Witchcraft and domestic tragedy in *The Witch of Edmonton*', in *The Politics of Gender in Early Modern Europe*, ed. Jean R. Brink, Allison P. Coudert and Maryanne C. Horowitz, Kirksville: *Sixteenth Century Journal Publications*, 1989, especially pp. 43–5. Both muddy the waters by comparing the play with Continental materials and materials from much earlier and later trials. Kate McLuskie's reading is much more nuanced, in *Renaissance Dramatists*, London: Macmillan, 1989, pp. 63–6.

9 J. A. Sharpe, 'Last dying speeches: religion, ideology and public execution in seventeenth-century England', *Past and Present*, 107 (1985), pp. 144–67.
10 *Wonderful Discovery*, p. Lxxxvii. This is not to suggest that Goodcole's report of Sawyer's words is *really* truthful in the sense of being accurate, or purporting to be, by the standards of modern ethnography. Goodcole does not purport to transcribe Sawyer's exact words, but does go bail for the validity of her meaning.
11 *CSPD* 1634, p. 141.
12 Greenblatt claims that 'performance kills belief; or rather acknowledging theatricality kills the credibility of the supernatural'; 'Shakespeare and the exorcists', in *Shakespearean Negotiations*, Oxford: Clarendon Press, 1988, pp. 96–114.
13 See Edward Peters, *Torture*, Oxford: Oxford University Press, 1985. Elizabeth Hanson's 'Torture and truth in Renaissance England', *Representations*, 34 (spring 1991), pp. 53–84, is fascinating, but flawed by a lack of knowledge about the use of torture in cases of ordinary felony.
14 See Page duBois, *Torture and Truth*, London: Routledge, 1991.
15 Of seventy-four cases where a warrant was issued in the sixteenth and seventeenth centuries, twenty-two – more than a quarter – deal with ordinary felony, mostly murder and theft (John H. Langbein, *Torture and the Law of Proof: Europe and England in the Ancien Régime*, Chicago: University of Chicago Press, 1977, p. 88); the other cases concern state crime.
16 Maitland, vol. II, 660–1, cited in Langbein, *Torture,* pp. 77–8.
17 Or, William Lambarde suggested, it could be verified by 'signes, which discover him; such as by having blood, or the goods about him, the measure of his foot, the bleeding of the dead body', William Lambarde, *Eirenarchia*, 1588, p. 220; on confession, see John Bossy, 'The social history of confession in the age of the Reformation', *Transactions of the Royal Historical Society*, 5th series, 25 (1975).
18 Langbein, *Torture,* p. 90.
19 Langbein, *Torture,* p. 88.
20 See for instance Hanson, 'Torture and truth', drawing on duBois on ancient Athens, pp. 54–5.
21 See e.g. Evelyn Fox Keller, 'Baconian science: a hermaphroditic birth', *Philosophical Forum*, 11 (1980) pp. 299–308; Ludmilla Jordanova, *Sexual Visions: Images of Gender in Science and Medicine Between the Eighteenth and Twentieth Centuries*, London: Harvester, 1989; and, more recently, Jonathan Sawday, *The Body Emblazoned: Dissection and the Human Body in Renaissance Culture*, London: Routledge, 1995.
22 Elaine Scarry, *The Body in Pain*, Oxford: Oxford University Press, 1985.
23 Thomas Potts, *The wonderful discoverie of witches in the County of Lancashire*, 1613, ed. James Crossley, Chetham Society Publications, vol. 6 (1845), sig. B1^{v}.
24 In the Chester records is a case of a young woman ordered to be whipped for some form of religious crime on 2 June 1581 with a torture warrant, but a man in such a position would have been given much more severe torture with the rack or the boots. Langbein, *Torture*, p. 106.
25 Langbein, *Torture*, p. 139; on Peacock see Bacon's letter to James I, in *Life and Letters of Bacon*, ed. J. Spedding *et al.,* vol. 14: pp. 77–9.
26 Goodcole, *Elizabeth Sawyer*, citing the report of the jury; this is one of the points where Goodcole's text is closest to straightforward reportage, though it is still synopsis rather than transcription, p. xci.
27 Goodcole, *Elizabeth Sawyer*, p. xcvii.
28 This seems to be an allusion to or use of George Gifford, *A Dialogue concerning witches and Witchcraft,* 1593, p. 113. See Onat's comments, in *The Witch of Edmonton*, ed. Etta Soiref Onat, p. 340.

29 She also calls her persecutors 'a bed of serpents' (IV. 1. 29) and 'base curs' (IV. 1. 76).

30 'There's a pretty tale of a witch, that had the Divels mark about her, God bless us, that had a gyant to her son, that was called Lob-lie-by-the fire, didst never hear it George?' (III. i. 439).

31 Ann Ellis Hanson, 'The medical writers' woman', and Anne Carson, 'Putting woman in her place: women, dirt and desire', both in *Before Sexuality: The Construction of Erotic Experience in the Ancient Greek World*, ed. David M. Halperin, John J. Winkler and Froma I. Zeitlin, Princeton: Princeton University Press, 1990, pp. 309–38, and 135–8. On hot blood and crime, see Natalie Zemon Davis, *Fiction in the Archives: Pardon Tales and Their Tellers in Sixteenth-Century France*, Cambridge: Polity, 1987.

32 *Witches and witchcraft*, and *A discourse of the subtle practices of devils by witches and sorcerers*, 1587. On the tendency to overstate Gifford's scepticism, see Chapter 3.

33 Webster alludes to the witch who suckles her familiar; Marcello is questioning Flamineo about the role he played in procuring his sister, Vittoria, for the pleasure of Brachiano: 'You, 'tis said / Were made his engine, and his stalking-horse / To undo my sister': Flamineo replies: 'I made a kind of path / To her and mine own preferment./ Marcello: 'Hum! Thou art a soldier / Followest the great Duke, feedest his victories / As witches do their serviceable spirits / Even with thy prodigal blood' (*The White Devil,* III. 1. 33–40). This compares the witch's suckling to fornication and political corruption, as well as to war and bloody service. It casts a new light on the link between Macbeth's bewitchment and his military violence. And it also reveals the meaning assigned to familiars suckling there; it is an admixture of bodily fluids, a taking-in of one person's body by another, and hence a blurring of social and other hierarchies.

34 Harvey was just the man for the job. A later story shows how for him empirical enquiry via dissection connected with disproving the powers of witches. He 'proved' that an old woman's toad was not a demon by luring her out of the room and then dissecting it. She returned and he triumphantly showed her that it was a normal toad – only dead. He was very surprised when she seemed unenthusiastic about this proceeding, flying at his face like a tigress. Alarmed, he was only able to extricate himself by an expedient lie, saying that he had come to test her for witchcraft, but had found her innocent. See Wallace Notestein, *A History of Witchcraft,* 1911, pp. 161–2, and *Gentleman's Magazine*, 1832, part I, pp. 405–10, 489–92.

35 On Harvey see Luke Wilson, 'William Harvey's *Praelectiones*: The performance of the body in the renaissance theatre of anatomy', *Representations*, 17 (1987), pp. 69–95.

36 *CSPD*, 1634 p. 129.

37 C. L'Estrange Ewen, *Witchcraft and Demonianism*, 1933, pp. 241–7.

38 Pardon: said to be issued on 30 June 1634, by Thomas Whitaker, *An History of the Original Parish of Whalley*, Blackburn, 1801, vol. I, p. 187; Witches' imprisonment: HMC Tenth Report, vol. IV, p. 433; Henry Burton, *A Narration of the Life of Mr Henry Burton*, 1643, pp. 16–7.

39 Somerset Record Office, DD/PH 212/#12, transcribed in full in Herbert Berry, 'The Globe bewitched and *El Hombre Fiel', Medieval and Renaissance Drama in England,* 1 (1984), pp. 212–3.

40 Kate McLuskie points to the way witch-plays reflect a split between popular and high views of witchcraft in *Renaissance Dramatists*, pp. 66ff. The plays do not altogether resolve the issue.

41 The use of these particular names, neither very appropriate, suggest the dramatists' carelessness with matters of witchcraft; one popular superstition was much like another, one old woman also like another.

42 V. 1. 183–6. Briarean footcloth-strider: Briareus was a hundred-headed giant in classical mythology; the allusion means a rider of a caparisoned horse.

10 The witch on the margins of 'race'

Sycorax and Others

What is foreign is that which escapes from a place.

Michel de Certeau, 'Montaigne's "Of Cannibals: The Savage 'I'"'

The witch is always located on the edges, at the margins. The village witch works through thresholds, doorways, liminal states. She attacks in such spaces, or in debatable open country or forests. Though she may be part of social networks and interactions, she is problematic in relation to them. The stage-witch, too, is conceptually and topographically removed from the centre of the dramatic action; either she is isolated from community affairs or she is geographically located elsewhere. The Sicilians are willing to speak of witches only as 'the ladies from outside'.[1] These different kinds of ex-centricity are all used to define the witch in the different layers of discourse she occupies. I now want to add two further layers of discourse, layers which show the figure of the witch being appropriated for explanatory and ideological purposes in new topographies. These new topographies, and the discourses used to interpret them, in turn inflected the representation of the figure of the witch in a pair of crucial though neglected witch-dramas. The first of these new layers is the Renaissance reception of classical witch-texts, and the second is the tentative discourses of exploration, discovery and colonialism in the New World. The two plays are Marston's *Sophonisba* and Shakespeare's *The Tempest*, both of which contain the story of a witch who is marginal to but also important for all the other stories the text wants to tell and the stories it does not want to tell, and whose narrative marginality is reciprocally reflected in her geographical and ethnic alterity. This alterity is also interpreted by and through the figure of the nearly absent witch.

As well, however, I want to point out how classical witch-texts are currently neglected as pre-texts of the witch-dramas of the early modern period, partly because of a preference for immediate and more directly 'social' contexts. Classical texts were a crucial part of early modern thinking equipment, at least for the opinion-forming classes, though ancient texts were also interpreted in ways shaped by social and ideological contexts. In the case of the New World, the classics offered an interpretative schema which did not always elucidate, and sometimes complicated, relations between the invaders and the peoples they encountered.[2] In the case of *The Tempest*, classical pre-texts offered a series of alternative narratives to the one that unfolds in front of us, alternatives that allow us to understand better what is at stake in that narrative. *The Tempest* is haunted by a series of ghostly stories of encounters with foreign witches on foreign soil, including the soil of the New World. Yet these encounters can never take place. Sycorax is not there, but always already banished from the scene of action. Prospero's masque for Ferdinand and Miranda lacks an antimasque not because it is unfinished, but because the confrontation between rule and misrule has already been staged and misrule already banished, not by Prospero, but by the same providential agency which ensures his arrival. Yet the shadowy form of the witch haunts the scene from which she was removed.

We might read Sycorax's evanescence as Shakespeare's attempt to write his way out of the witch-trend he had created, where virtuous patrilineal rule is opposed by embodied hags who sing and dance and invite a sceptical reading. In this sense, the neglect Sycorax has suffered from modern critics is a correct response to her marginality, and modern productions which eagerly make her visible by borrowing from *Macbeth* overlook Shakespeare's willingness to revise his own work. In Peter Brook's deliberately provocative production of 1968: 'the monster-mother is portrayed by an enormous woman able to expand her face and body to still larger proportions . . . Suddenly, she gives a horrendous yell, and Caliban, with black sweater over his head, emerges from between her legs: Evil is born'. Similarly, Derek Jarman's *Tempest* features a Sycorax who nurses Caliban at her pendulous breast; she is 'an obese naked sorceress, heavily made up and smoking a hookah'.[3] Both these sensational depictions show themselves insensitive to Sycorax's invisibility, her instability and ultimate unknowability. All interpretation of her risks the same obfuscation, which means making dark. Brook and Jarman cannot resist conflating Sycorax willy-nilly with as many images of feminine and ethnic darkness as they can lay their hands on. Admittedly, Prospero sometimes does the same, but reducing Sycorax to a mere figure of otherness who simply defines Prospero by negation does no justice to the complexity and precision of the text's intertextuality. Critics, even the best, have not always been immune to this tendency. In particular, a simplistic understanding of the witch as a Bad Woman has shaped understandings of Sycorax as much more unproblematic in relation to both Prospero and Caliban than she really is.[4] This oversimplification no doubt explains why Sycorax is always excluded from discussions of the representation of witchcraft on the Jacobean stage. If she is mostly excluded from discussions of *The Tempest* as part of discourses of colonialism too, this is explicable in the light of our tendency to follow early modern explorers in seeing Indians of importance as male. However, we are not following their witch-discourses in seeing all witches as 'white'.

To begin the journey which will lead to Sycorax, we must look first at the entanglement of Old and New World discourses. One of the most alarming aspects of the New World for both explorers and invading colonists was Indian religion. The encounter with a different supernatural world was crucial to European understandings of what they were doing in the Americas and who they were meeting there. Faced with the need to think their way into what Michel de Certeau terms 'an insurmountable alterity', Europeans struggled to comprehend and sometimes chose to evade the sheer strangeness of the Indians' diverse world-views in a variety of ways which contain their own contradictions. Within single narratives, Europeans move from denying that Indians had any religion, interpreting their religion as ancient paganism, interpreting it as demon-worship *because* it was like ancient paganism, interpreting it as proto-Christianity, and interpreting it as witchcraft. Diverse understandings of witchcraft – as the demon-worship of all non- or pre-Christian societies, as the superstitions of the unlearned, as a series of tricks to keep power and keep one's place in society or to make money, as a sign of the devil's power over the world, as the hallmark of Roman Catholicism/Protestantism – surface in the New World texts which interpret the Indians as witches or demons. There was no single dominant figure of the witch who could explain the Indian.

The explanation of witchcraft was one among many means by which Europeans sought to familiarise an otherwise unbearable challenge to their world-view, for how could Providence be unfolding as it should be when here was a whole continent of people who had never heard of Jesus Christ and whose religious beliefs necessarily upset the European Christian observer with different understanding of the sacred? While Thomas Harriot may have borrowed from the urbane and curious ethnocentricity of Herodotus, others took their cue from more anxious Greek and Roman texts such as Athenian and Roman epic and tragedy.[5] These ancient world nationalisms sited the viewer at an extreme distance from barbarians constructed as his opposite. Witches were plentifully distributed around these classical epic and dramatic margins, and this is not insignificant for early modern understandings of Indian religion and being. The understanding of Indians as witches fitted in with these attempts to understand the New World via the classics.

However, interpreting native religion as witchcraft, while reassuring in explaining alterity away by reinscribing it in a different system of value, also provoked fresh fears and gave them expression. A whole continent of demon-worshippers! This fulfilled the worst fears and deepest longings of Calvinist pessimism, and it provided new ways to interpret Old World witches too. The mutually interpretative relation of witchcraft discourses and those of New World ethnography can be seen in two texts. In Jean de Léry's Huguenot history of the Tupinamba of Brazil, there is a long quotation from Jean Bodin's work of demonology, a quotation which both describes and interprets the festivals of the cannibalistic Tupinamba women. Léry concludes:

> I have concluded that they have the same master; that is, the Brazilian women and the witches over here are guided by the same spirit of Satan; neither the

> distance between the places nor the long passage over the sea keeps the father of lies from working both here and there on those who are handed over to him by the just judgement of God.[6]

One effect of this is to feminise the material native world. Yet a note of relief is audible: the signs of witchcraft, so familiar to the believers among the Continental elite, act not as genuine alterity, but as a reminder that European man is used to this sort of thing, has met and dealt with this perfectly recognisable Other before. How cosy the Other looks in the face of alterity! Metaphorically, this feminine witch-world remains under the controlling surveillance of the father of lies, whose presence oddly reassures because he is familiar and recognisable and male. They say that when abroad, even an enemy will be greeted as an old friend, sheerly because he is familiar. Satan here sounds just like the colonists, gallantly undeterred by the distance across the sea. Like a missionary, he labours to guide the otherwise incomprehensible natives; like reason, he struggles to subdue the bodily femininty of the natives.

This discovery that the enemy at home is somehow more comfortable than the enemy abroad is a classic response to alterity. Conversely, James I in *Daemonologie* cites the prevalence of the devil in the New World as proof that those devoid of Christianity are in the grip of demons; 'The wild parts of the world' afford great opportunities for mischief because 'where the Devil finds greatest ignorance and barbarity, there assails he grossliest'.[7] This uses the 'discovery' of the devil in the New World to locate him in the Old World. The wilderness, where the ignorant and the barbarous live, is the devil's abode; as far away as possible conceptually and geographically from James, his books, his court, his city. James uses the information that witches abound in the New World to locate witchcraft among the uncivilised in Europe, and to make an opposition between civilisation and diabolism. Ironically, this was the discourse which was eventually to demolish witchcraft beliefs among the elite. Notions of witchcraft came to seem primitive and rustic, and it is no coincidence that this followed the dissemination of the knowledge that New World natives believed in witchcraft and magic.

In writing thus, James was not drawing solely on Protestant sources. Though keen to label the Spanish cruel, and eager to believe every blood-drenched word of de las Casas's account of their doings, the English at Roanoke and later at Jamestown and in New England lived in fear of finding the local Indians like the Aztecs, and the colonists at least knew of the discourses produced about them by the Spanish. Precisely because early travellers and colonists were always a little vague about where they were, native peoples were muddled with each other. Stories like those of the Inca 'witches' discovered by Polo de Ondegardo, witches who fly through the air, speak to the devil, and know what cannot be known by natural means, may have circulated among the English as well as among the Spanish.[8] De Ondegardo writes that 'about these witches . . . there are a great many of them, and differences between them. Some are adept at making potions of herbs and roots in order to kill those they give their concoctions to. Those who perform this kind of witchcraft are almost always women.' De Ondegardo's suspicions were confirmed when some Andean women did confess to witchcraft after interrogation, confessions that represent a negotiation between the way the Andeans perceived their relations with the supernatural and European expectations of witches.[9]

Those expectations were on view again in Europeans' interest in New World cannibalism. This may have been fuelled by expectations about witches and demon-worshippers. Old World witchcraft was linked with cannibalism in that witches were supposed to devour babies, and in classical texts to use dead bodies in magic. This made it seem natural to assume that 'where the anthropophagi do inhabit, are many spirits, which do the people there very much harm'. José d'Acosta wrote of the Aztecs that

> all their ceremonies were cruel and hurtful, as to kill men and spill blood, are filthy and beastly, as to eat and drink to the name of their idols, and also to piss in the honour of them, carrying them upon their shoulders, to anoint and besmear themselves filthily, and to do a thousand sorts of villainies, which were at the least, vain, ridiculous, and idle, and more like the actions of children than of men. The cause thereof is the very condition of this wicked spirit, whose intention is always to do ill, provoking men still to murders and filthiness, or at the least to vanities and fruitless actions, the which every man may well know, if he duly consider the behaviours and actions of the devil, towards those he sets to deceive.[10]

The Incas' willingness to sacrifice their own children especially upset Europeans: Samuel Purchas called it 'most unkind and unnatural'.[11] Perhaps because they had read some of these texts, or others like them, some of the English in Virginia were willing to believe the worst of their natives. John Smith printed the first account of Powhatan's murder of the 'black boys', whom he believed were eaten by the tribe. William Strachey, trying to rationalise what he interpreted as the natives' penchant for human sacrifice and cannibalism, wrote that 'it may well be by the subtle spirit the malicious enemy to mankind whom therefore to pacify and work to do them good (at least no harm) the priests tell them do these and these sacrifices unto, of these and these things, and thus and thus often, by which means not only their own children but strangers are sometimes sacrificed unto him'.[12] Jamestowners saw Powhatan worship as merely 'many devillish gestures with a Hellish noise'.[13] In these texts, European witchcraft interprets Indian religion.

It did not always require a Spanish precursor to arouse this kind of anxiety. Martin Frobisher's party on its second voyage met an Eskimo woman whom they suspected of being either a devil or a witch; they took off her buskins to see if she had cloven feet:

> Two women not being so apt to escape as the men were, the one for her age, and the other being encumbered with a young child, we took. The old wretch,

> whom diverse of our sailors supposed to be either a devil, or a witch, had her buskins plucked off, to see if she were cloven footed, and for her ugly hue, and deformity, we let her go; the young woman and the child we brought away.[14]

The hint of scepticism in this account is amplified in Jamestowners' view that native religion was 'only superstition, which we hope by the grace of God to change into true religion'. This aligns the natives with ignorant peasants at home, as does Le Mercier's account of a fortune-teller among the Huron:

> an old woman, a sorceress or female soothsayer of that village, said she had seen those who had gone to the war, and that they were bringing back a prisoner. We shall see if she has spoken the truth. Her method is by pyromancy. She draws for you in her hut the lake of the Iroquois; then on one side she makes as many fires as there are persons who have gone on the expedition, and on the other as many fires as they have enemies to fight . . . It is thus that the Devil amuses this poor people, substituting his impieties and superstitions in place of the compliance they ought to have with the providence of God, and the worship they ought to render him.[15]

The English colonists were not always comfortable with their interepretation of native religion, and some struggled to make sense of nations of devil-worshippers, just as they had tried to understand the difference of witches at home. Trying to interpret native religion with a set of tools derived from the Church Fathers, John Smith noted that 'all things that were able to do them hurt beyond their prevention they adore with their kind of divine worship . . . But their chief God they worship is the devil. Him they call Oke and serve him more of fear than love. They say they have conference with him, and fashion themselves as near to his shape as they can imagine.'[16] Smith sees the Indians' devil-worship as devil-fear, a traditional Christian humanist interpretation of all religions other than Christianity, yet here Smith is projecting some of his own fears onto the Indians, not least the fear of 'going native'. There is another aspect of Smith's account that comforts scared white settlers, but scandalises them too: since whites came to glory in being among those who could do the natives hurt, Smith's account implies that in that role they became their own supreme Other, the devils falsely worshipped by the natives. As is well known, the tribes of the Eastern woodlands took whites for shamans. When Father Le Jeune exposed a shaman among the Montagnais in 1637, the shaman's followers could only marvel that the French were 'greater sorcerers than they were'.[17] The French were cast as devils when they had sought to cast themselves as Satan's opponents; exactly the dilemma confronting Prospero. Impersonating or being taken for the feared other gave some relief to the terrified, while offering the sceptical an opportunity for internal mirth at the Indians' expense, another way to deal with difference.

These responses to native religion using the witch-discourses of Western

Europe helped Europeans to cope with the imaginative challenge offered by the spectacle of religious difference on a wide scale. They evolved over time: the responses of first explorers and settlers like Frobisher and Smith were less complex and contradictory than those of later settlers. As the contradictions worsened, especially around the question of the colonists as indistinguishable from what the Indians feared, and the Indians (therefore) as indistinguishable from what the colonists feared, the collapse of systematic differentiation produced some unpleasant side-effects for Indians and colonists alike. This was especially true where the natives were seen to embody the worst imaginable transgressions of the European mind. Colonists were terrified of the spectacle of Indian violence and atrocities: one described seeing an Indian bearing as a trophy an embryo 'torn from its mother's pregnant womb, and elevated upon a stick or pole, as a trophy of victory'.[18] This recalled the powers of witches and devils, since both elite and populace at the time saw witches as women unnaturally interested in unbaptised babies.

In this context of fear and projection it is scarcely surprising that Salem's witch-crisis was blamed on the Indians, 'whose chief Sagamores are well-known unto some of our captives, to have been horrid sorcerers, and hellish conjurors, and such as conversed with Demons', wrote Cotton Mather.[19] When a woman named Mercy Short was possessed by the devil, she described him as follows: 'he was not of a Negro, but of a tawney, or an Indian colour: he wore a high-crowned hat . . . and had one cloven foot'. Mary Toothaker also claimed that the devil appeared to her 'in the shape of a tawny man', while another told of attending sabbaths with both the French Catholics and Sagamore Indians. Another suspect described the devil bluntly as 'a thing all black like an Indian'.[20] (By contrast, and showing that not all the culture shock was on one side, the devil often appeared to Andean women as a Spaniard.) By the late seventeenth century, discourses of ethnicity and the supernatural were so entangled that Mercy Short and Mary Toothaker's notions of witchcraft arose from and were shaped by their terror of Native Americans, not as a concept, but as an actuality. Although that moment was still far off when the first English settlers began to arrive in Virginia, it was foreshadowed in their discourse and in their willingness to borrow even the hated Spaniard's rhetoric to reduce the otherness of the natives to manageable proportions.

Europeans who understood Indian religion as devil-worship or witchcraft were able not only to project their fantasies of otherness and misrule onto the native figures. They were also able to partake of a cultural distance and its codes which was already emerging in Europe around the question of witchcraft. The literate were already inclined to see themselves as distinct from a populace construed as gullibly victimised by shrewd demons or robbed by charlatans performing tricks. This made it possible to begin to compile anthropological taxonomies of the superstitions thought to characterise benighted underlings, superstitions which in the very act of compilation were distanced from the compiler.[21] As we have seen, the stage – private and public – could play the role of cultural anthropologist. The taxonomical tools and sense of distance established in these discourses stood Europeans in good stead when interpreting Indian activities. Descriptions of Powhatan ceremonies and of the activities of Huron shamans and their divinatory practices recall Reginald Scot and Montaigne, with their efforts to chart popular superstitions and the practices associated with them. As Frank Lestringant has pointed out, it was these Enlightenment discourses which ultimately went furthest in denying respect to Indian notions of the supernatural. The Enlightenment rationalised the uncanniness of Léry's cannibals and transformed them into nature's noblemen. In place of Léry's stunned vision of unimaginable human otherness, the philosophers projected onto the natives the phantasms of the European imagination, thus reducing their religion to mere trickery and imposture.[22] At least Cotton Mather had the grace to be afraid.

Looking at this proto-anthropological discourse suggests a simple grounding of Sycorax in the European capacity to equate native American woman with Old World witch. Yet we should be cautious about proceeding to such a judgement, and not only because many of the texts I have cited were unknown to Shakespeare. To us, calling the Indians witches can only be a mark of prejudice, jumbling innocence and evil. We make clear, sharp distinctions between witches and natives, based not on fantasy and reality, but on evil and neutrality. But for early modern Europeans, the analogy came naturally to mind because both the category of witch and the category of native were elastic enough to contain one another. Like early modern genre categories, the categories of otherness available were not as distinct to Shakespeare as they might have seemed to us. Just as Caliban can be Wild Man and Caribee, monster and servant, peasant and slave, so Sycorax can be both witch and Indian woman, both monstrous hag and former resident of Algiers, both native and immigrant to the island. It has often been said that the discourses of 'race' and imperialism were evolving together, that *The Tempest* stands at the earliest point of contact between literature and those discourses. I argue the opposite: *The Tempest* represents the last moment of innocence in which the New World had yet to be interpreted and could be caught up in Mediterranean and demonological topographies without outraging the sense of cultural and geographical difference. Sycorax represents not the first but the *last* moment at which a New World native woman, an Old World witch, and a classical world witch might be the same thing, the last moment in which vagueness about the New World could generate meaning.

The dizzying newness of the New World was constantly managed by attempts to conflate it with understood categories. This was achieved principally through the classics, because the classics, together with the Bible, constituted the master discourses of the period. Yet the classics had to be interpreted. Relations in discourse between classical and New World geographies, spectacles, narratives and practices were not inevitable; they had to be made. The result was to add to the muddle mentioned above; the New World could be seen in terms of the classics, and actually conflated with them, understood as the pastoral land of simple and homely shepherds of the idyll, the home of the Amazons described in classical texts, or the resting place of the classical deities chased out of Europe by the coming of Christianity. (As Bartolomé de las Casas reasonably observed, they had to go somewhere.)[23] What to Peter Hulme is *The Tempest*'s dual topography of Mediterranean and Caribbean could also be understood as two interchangeable frames of reference. We assume that if the play is about the New World then it cannot be about the Mediterranean; that if it is about the Mediterranean, then it cannot have anything to do with the crisis of discourse around the New World. The distinction between one island and another is simpler for us than for Shakespeare, because Shakespeare's world had not yet understood the utter difference of place, though it had been shocked by it. As Derek Walcott's *Omeros* shows, the entanglement of Ithaca and St Lucia can seem resonant today. Yet Walcott's poetry is marked by its extraordinary geographical precision, its loving use of both classical and Caribbean topography. The Renaissance was the opposite. Even quite late in the sixteenth century, texts could be remarkably vague about the difference between Old and New Worlds.[24] The 1556 edition of Cartari's compendium of classical mythology for the use of writers and artists refers in passing to the idols of people inhabiting the islands recently found by the Spanish, assuming they belong with the other pagan idols. By the 1615 edition, Cartari had added a full appendix on the gods of Mexico and Japan.[25] Marston's *Sophonisba* and Shakespeare's *Tempest* were written in this hiatus between this moment of astounding vagueness and the moment of clarification, in the pause when information and narratives thickened, sorting out some problems and clouding others. Some writers exploited the confusion for reasons of their own, siting flattering Amazons on the new continents and imagining the terrain as a classical pastoral as well as an English heaven.[26] Others sought to clear up the muddle, but could only have further recourse to different classical authorities to do so. Classical texts offered to decipher the New World, for had not the ancients too travelled and met barbarians? The New World threw retrospective light on the ancients, confirming some authorities and qualifying others. In any case, there was not *one* single classical text to be used to interpret the whole experience of conquest and colonisation. Instead, conflicts sprang up between different interpretative schema used by different texts, while other writers ignored the nice differences between Strabo and Diodorus to borrow more lavishly from a general set of tropes, figures and metaphors no longer fully attached to any particular name or text.

Both Marston and Shakespeare create witch-figures who gesture at geographical and ethnic marginality by pointing back to a range of other classical texts. Both Marston's Erictho and Shakespeare's Sycorax draw on other witches understood as 'foreign': Circe, Medea and Dido. Circe and Medea have a lot in common with each other. Both are from Colchis, lunar, manslaying, seductresses, and both embody a fear of miscegenation, emasculation, and the disruption of primogeniture which reflect both Marston's and Shakespeare's concerns with good rule. Circe and Medea are products of ancient Athenian ethnocentrism, readable as emblematic of the liminal geographic and ethnic space of the witch. Medea in particular must have sprung to mind as the possible *telos* of a voyage in search of gold in strange and unexplored territory. Reporting on the island of Goa, *The Moderate Intelligencer* writes that 'if any island deserves the name of Colchos, from whence the Argonauts are said to have fetched the Golden Fleece, 'tis surely that of Goa'.[27] There are places where the Pocahontas story as understood by Europeans gestures at Medea's romantic treachery to her people. Medea is racially, geographically and religiously other than the Greeks. As Edith Hall has shown, Medea is moved further and further out towards the periphery of Greek ethnicity by the Athenians; she began as the Greek Agamede of the *Iliad*, but her barbarisation is the result of the tragedians' efforts.[28] Especially interesting for *The Tempest*, Pindar's fourth Pythian ode locates her origins as North Africa. Shakespeare probably did not know Pindar: his prime sources would have been Ovid and Seneca. They, however, have merely amplified what the Greeks set in motion: Medea is linked with the periphery wherever the centre locates itself. Medea's barbarisation does not confine itself to geographical relocation, however. Both her actions and her magic are understood in terms of ethnic alterity. She is most barbarian when she subordinates her feminine instincts as a mother to her desire to dominate, reversing the protocols of gender in Athens and London. Normative gender behaviour becomes the guarantee of ethnic sameness or canniness. This Medea violates not only by her rejection of maternity for power, stressed by Seneca, but also by her magic, stressed by Ovid.

We know that Seneca influenced the shaping of Shakespeare's late romances; his Medea may have been in Shakespeare's mind in a series of plays that deal with parents and children.[29] We know that Ovid's Medea was in Shakespeare's mind too.[30] Medea's invocation to Hecate and night in the *Metamorphoses* includes claims to complete mastery of nature; 'my magic song / rouses the quiet, calms the angry sea / . . . I move the forests, bid the mountains quake / The deep earth groan, and ghosts rise from their tombs / Thee too, bright moon, I banish, though thy throes / The clanging bronze assuage'.[31] She also 'summoned the deities of earth'. These incantatations, echoed by *The Tempest* in a surprising manner in Prospero's famous speech, figure Medea as part of a fantasy of omnipotence. In Prospero, such words and claims are not simply an undoing of laboriously established differences between himself and Sycorax. They arouse the spectre of going native, a spectre inextricably linked with questions of desire and hence of gender, a spectre dramatised in the figure of Medea, who is the desiring woman with whom Jason becomes entangled. Living on the outside, it is said, means living outside the law, occupying a position from which it is possible to escape its workings – or control them. This is the terror of the ladies from outside, whether outside was the Americas or Colchis.

Unlike the mobile Medea, Circe is always already other, the inhabitant of an island she rules. It may be that the hazy reference to New World islands in

Cartari reflects not only Bermoothes and Caribees, but also the voyages of Odysseus. Like the New World, Circe appears like home: a virtuous woman, weaving diligently, she lures Odysseus's men into an illusion of homeliness or canniness. This illusion of sameness turns out to be like the early descriptions of America as paradisal England. What seems canny turns uncanny in an instant. Circe's transformation of men into beasts is proof of femininity's power to render categories and identities unstable; Circe, like the Witch of Edmonton, crosses clearly marked lines between the human and the animal. Her drugging draught is a precise figure for going native; it makes Odysseus's companions forget their native lands, and thereafter they are stranded on her island, unable to imagine a destination and an end to their stories. When Odysseus's men recover their memories, they also recover remembrance of Ithaca; they flock about him like calves about their mother, as if he in his body were the land they have just been able to remember.[32] The story of Circe could be understood as an encounter with a strangeness so powerful that it overmasters the beholder.[33]

The release of desire could also be moralised in terms of gender. Circe was primarily an image of illicit female desirability which released men's longing to forget themselves. From Petronius's rewriting of the Circe story in *Satyricon*, where Encolpius is obsessed with his beautiful but fickle girlfriend Circe, to Verdant languishing in Acrasia's Bower of Bliss, forgetting his arms and his knighthood, Circe represents the otherness of femininity, and her trace of ethnic otherness is subsumed as a metaphor for her lovers' loss of place and identity in her. These losses can be further understood in terms of patrilinearity, recently argued to be the Renaissance idea of 'race' by Lynda Boose.[34] The irruption of the mother into the scene of paternal self-replication is figured by Circe's power to transform men into monstrosities. This recalls Medea's ability to transcend motherhood by literally exterminating the patriarchal line. A late version of Circe's story makes explicit these themes of loss of the shaping power and fixed identity of masculinity and fatherhood. In it, Circe becomes the mother of an unknown son of Odysseus, a son so unknown that he repeats the crime of Oedipus by accidentally killing his father on Ithaca and marrying his father's wife, Penelope.[35] This late story makes visible the underlying themes of the *Odyssey* and Ovid, and these are also themes explored in the story of Sycorax. In the *Odyssey* Circe too is a witch in a story told by someone else, by her conqueror. All we know of her comes from Odysseus, just as all we know of Sycorax comes from Prospero.

The Thessalian witches of Lucan and Apuleius reflect and rewrite the Athenian tendency to locate the witch's origins in the far north. Drawing on both the *Odyssey* and the various Medeas of antiquity, Roman writers fashioned a locale for witches peripheral to what they saw as the centre. Thessaly, marginal to the Roman world, became associated with witchcraft and wildness, a Roman heath. In the *Pharsalia*, Marston's chief source for his Erictho in *Sophonisba*, Lucan creates witches who resemble Ovid's Medea in their exclusion from the normal rules of supernatural decorum and behaviour. Lucan's Thessalian witches can stop time, suspend natural law, and foil the gods; 'postponed by lengthened night/ the day comes to a halt; the ether does not obey the law / the racing universe is paralysed once the spell is heard; / and as Jupiter drives on the sky on its speedy axles/he is amazed that it does not move'.[36] They incarnate the scandalous sense of female power strenuously denied by humanist sceptics, the power to interfere with the providential working of narrative.

Jonson's *Masque of Queens* used Lucan's text while denying the hags' power. Marston alters the scope of their power to fit humanist preconceptions of gender.[37] In Lucan, Sextus is driven to consult the witch of Thessaly by ambition, but in Marston's play the desire to possess a state has been transformed into the desire to possess a woman, a convention followed by Middleton's *Witch*.[38] Whereas *Macbeth* retains the public and political function of the witch from its pre-text in Lucan's ghoulish and corpse-loving hag, Marston substitutes a signifier of tyranny and usurpation for the thing itself.[39] Tyranny was associated with lust, and especially with illicit lust.[40] Despite its consciousness of her peripheral location, Marston's play takes the figure of Erictho as emblem of tyranny without reference to any New World encounters. The Thessalian setting figures battle, and is distant from the seat of empire, that's all (like the heath in *Macbeth*, out the same year). In *Sophonisba*, tyrant summons a witch to help him govern an unruly female who refuses to submit to his desire. His eventual copulation with Erictho in a bedtrick symbolises the impropriety of their association: the uncanny is mistaken for the canny, and allowed into the domestic realm. Sophonisba's chaste body emblematises the impenetrably virtuous state; the witch's theatricality confirms her power as the opposite of such clear bounds. The witch, taken straight from Lucan, inhabits a periphery because this is part of understanding her as a witch; topography interprets witchcraft.

An early sixteenth-century Italian tragedy of *Sofonisba* by Trissino contains a prologue which includes Sophonisba's recital of the story of Dido, whose misplaced love and suicide prefigure the action. This brings us to the last of the classical witches of ethnic alterity who lie behind the shadowy figure of Sycorax. As Margo Hendricks and Patricia Parker have both noted, Dido's North African origins were not acknowledged by the Renaissance as a 'problem' of ethnicity.[41] Nonetheless, Carthage is relentlessly figured in Roman literature, and especially in Virgil, as the ethnic and geographical opposite of the Roman centre. Its queen, Dido, is a figure of virtuous female rule, a Sophonisba-like figure whose bodily bounds are coextensive with the bounds of Carthage. She is also a seduced and betrayed woman, an *un*chaste suicide, whose dead body becomes a sign of the future wars between Rome and Carthage and the obliteration of her city.[42] Dubious in respect of virtue and rule, Dido is also ethnically debatable, neither securely one of us nor overtly different, combining in her diverse legends roles as chaste guarantee of the state and disorderly witch who threatens it. Matters are further complicated by the haunting of Dido's story by Circe and Medea, as well as by the stories of the chaster women who successfully ground empires by their suicides.[43] Like Circe, like Medea, Dido greets a band of travellers in trouble; like them, she engages in an affair with the leader marked as illicit to the point of miscegenation. Like their affairs, this one ends badly, in further transgression, in the reinforcement of difference rather than its acceptance. Dido's presence in *The Tempest* as a none-too-comprehensible joke should not blind us to her overarching influence on the plot and its unfolding.[44] Above all, Dido is from North Africa. She is close to being a witch of Argier.

To cover her suicide, Dido pretends to consult an Ethiopian priestess whose charms can release some from love while bringing it on others.[45] Dido's willingness to invent such a lady and to follow 'her' advice by demanding that her pyre be arranged as a love spell can be read as signs of witchcraft. To play the part of the witch, as Dido is doing, is to undo at a stroke her ethnic sameness, revealing herself to be African too. It is worth noting, however, how Dido's witch-story confirms the essential plot of the classical witch: she is ethnically other, located on the margins of the known world, expert especially in love magic, but also capable of political intervention through the personal, for the love affair between Dido and Aeneas is always a public matter. Like Circe, the witch is a character in a story told by somebody else, a character who is not real. For all these reasons, she may remind us of Sycorax. But she may also remind us of another, earlier Shakespearean story of an African witch, or rather series of witches, a story told by a man as a cover for personal feelings not to be revealed. Othello's improvised fiction about the handkerchief he gave Desdemona does not merely recall the Dido legend. It also rewrites Circe, Medea and the link between witchcraft and ethnic alterity and geographical marginality. In taking up the story, Othello is apparently bowing to a discourse used most extensively by Brabantio, but inaugurated by Iago, a discourse which would associate his skin colour with the blackness of devils and his seduction of Desdemona with the witchcraft of love charms.[46] Iago speaks of Othello as 'the devil' first in terms of procreation, linking Othello with the incubuses who in Continental demonology seek mortal women to beget their children. Brabantio takes up the theme by expanding on the unnaturalness of Desdemona's passion as a sign of witchcraft, a move which conflates Othello's appearance with his supposed magical powers (I.1. 92, I. 2. 170–3).[47] Othello, however, defending himself against the charge of witchcraft, substitutes the art of storytelling for magic: 'This only is the witchcraft I have used' (I. 3. 168). This reply brilliantly turns Brabantio's linkage of ethnic alterity and witchcraft against him by linking them in a different and far more innocent way. Othello's otherness and his knowledge of the other is not occult knowledge, but publicly available to Desdemona or anyone as a story. Othello himself only becomes seductive along with the story by virtue of his role as teller and protagonist, roles which explicitly distance him from the others he combats and narrates. The magical transformation of the court room depends in part on making Brabantio's belief in literal witchcraft look naive. Explicitly, Shakespeare through Othello substitutes belief in pleasurable stories about witchcraft for belief in the real thing. Far more than Prospero, Othello *is* Shakespeare at this moment, patiently teaching the Venetian court that hearing a story is not the same as believing in witches. This scepticism allows the new witchcraft of story to be acknowledged by everyone: 'I think this tale would win my daughter too'. What Othello tells Desdemona is stories of other figures stranger than himself, 'men whose heads do grow beneath their shoulders' and the cannibals whose activities recalled European witches. He reminds the Senate that he is not the ultimate in insurmountable alterity, that the margins extend far beyond him.

In parentheses, one might note that the only time we see something like a trial for witchcraft dramatised on the Renaissance stage, the defendant is a man. Undoubtedly this reflects the origin of the charge in Othello's racial otherness: Indians, too, male and female, were called witches or devils impartially by Europeans for whom witchcraft was ordinarily gendered. However, in the story of the handkerchief, Othello restores this normative association, just as he appears to restore the association between ethnic otherness, North African location, and real magical powers which he was previously concerned to undo. Yet by telling the story, Othello also reasserts the role as tale-teller through which he previously undid these associations. It is the way in which the event rewrites earlier events which makes it so horrible. The handkerchief story is cruel to everyone; it torments Desdemona with the same seductive device that was once used to win her, a tale of otherness. Still sadder, it shows us Othello making a last desperate bid to push otherness away from himself in her eyes, to seduce her with a story of the marvellous as he did before. And for a brief instant, she responds with the kind of (feminised) noise of encouragement that had once drawn further tales from him; 'Is't possible?' she breathes, as if so lost in the tale that she has forgotten its application to herself. This is the authentic gasp of wonder (III. 4. 64). Othello's response, too, suggests that he is lost in his own tale; it is the reassurance of the storyteller: 'Most veritable'. He then adds 'therefore look to it well', and suddenly this has become a story that will cost lives. Othello's fiction of alterity is now attached to an object in Cyprus; it has been dragged into the play not as a wonder-tale, but as truth.

In that fiction, the handkerchief is triply mothered by Othello's mother, the 'Egyptian' who gave it to her and told her of its powers as a love charm, and the 'sibyl' who made it 'in her prophetic fury'. Medea-like, the sibyl presents as ethnically other when her occult powers are made to depend on frenzy or uncontrolled passion, the reverse of the wisdom or *sophrosune* which would connect her with Western knowledges. Frenzy connects the sibyl with Othello; her age reminds us of the Cumaean Sibyl of the *Aeneid*, but the way it is expressed, numbering 'two hundred compasses' of the sun's course partakes of discourses of travel literature and of Othello's definition by the choler-producing sun. The other two women are also distinguished from Desdemona by their ethnicity: the woman who gave it to Othello's mother is an Egyptian or gypsy, a woman in whom ethnicity implies innate magical powers, while Othello's mother is a practitioner of magic by virtue of the handkerchief.[48] All the figures are female, and it is thus that Othello struggles to maintain his own distance from the identity as racist other fashioned for him by Iago, Brabantio and others. However, as both Lisa Jardine and Karen Newman have noted, this self-definition in relation to an abjected or excluded femininity is precisely what eventually triggers the murderous rage which casts Othello most ineluctably as the stage Moor, carried away from true identity by the same animality discovered by Circe in her followers.[49]

The story is polysemic; it can also be read as Othello's yearning rediscovery of his (violent) roots in African culture, so that the purport of the entire speech is to cut Desdemona off from these dark and magical women, to isolate her by her colour as the Petrarchan object of desire, for whom the handkerchief can *only* be a misunderstood love token. In Othello's fantasy, Desdemona's desirability becomes the condition of her whorishness; better, then, the dark ladies who control desire by witchcraft than the elusive because exchangeable white commodity. Yet this division, too, is fictive. The magic of the handkerchief is built up from signifiers of European witchcraft: despite its laboriously detailed signs of otherness, the magic of the handkerchief is not far removed from the Weird Sisters' cauldron. Its dye – or colour – comes from mummy, one of the ingredients of the witches' spell, and its love magic is also practised by stage hags like Middleton's Hecate. Nonetheless, it offers an early instance of witchcraft and ethnicity joined together in a narrative which seeks to legitimate male power.

Othello is linked to *The Tempest* by the shadowy presence in both of a North African witch-mother.[50] Whereas Othello's mother has been noticed only recently, Sycorax comes trailing a cloud of critical investments which date back to the nineteenth century. When she is noticed it is in relation to other absent women, or to the 'problem' of Caliban's unstable ethnicity. She represents either race or gender, but not both. Her absence, not only from the play, but also from critical discourse, has been noted and regretted by a number of critics; Orgel, Thompson and Loomba most recently. All point out that Sycorax is only one of the play's absent women. The question I want to address is not why she is absent, but on what terms has she been present to critics and editors of the play. To explore this, I will focus on interpretations and explications of particular lines in the text of Prospero's story, lines which address the question of Sycorax's 'true' identity.

The only thing we learn about Sycorax's body, it appears, is that she is pregnant. Yet there is one line which appears to describe her: 'this blue-eyed hag was hither brought with child'. Because of a line in Webster's *Duchess of Malfi*, modern editors universally interpret the blue eyes as merely blue eyelids, signs of pregnancy.[51] Even Stephen Orgel concurs, though with a sense of discomfort. The discomfort seems amply justified. Prospero has just made a joke about Sycorax's pregnancy: 'for one thing she did / They would not take her life'. Why should he follow this with two references to her condition in one line, saying in effect, 'This pregnant hag was brought here, pregnant'? In the teeth of common sense, modern editors insist on reading this line as a datum about Sycorax's sexuality, or about her gender, rather than about her ethnicity. Nineteenth-century editors, not as committed to making Sycorax into the play's race lady, were more comfortable with the idea of Sycorax's blue eyes as signs of moral status. They suggested that blue irises are a sign of hag-like malignancy. Of the play's principal editors, only W. J. Craig has seen Sycorax's eyes in relation to ethnicity. He noted in Hakluyt a reference to native women 'marked in the face with blue streaks . . . round about the eyes'.[52] Is it we, and not Shakespeare, who are troubled by the idea of a hag from Algiers with blue eyes, anxious as we are (whatever our politics) to classify ourselves and everyone else absolutely into racial groups by physiognomy?

Yet the idea of blue-eyed peoples inhabiting Africa is a very old fantasy, often mapped onto the Berbers, for example. Relating to the fantasy of Prester John, the blue-eyed African promises a providential outcome to the conflict between West and Orient. Read in this way, Sycorax's blue eyes become guarantees that under the otherness of ethnicity and even race is a reassuring sameness. On the other hand, Sycorax's blue eyes, or blue eye, could also be an assimilationist trope of a more sinister kind. As numerous editors of *The Witch of Edmonton* point out, being one-eyed was a sure sign of witchcraft, and one could add that Scot (Shakespeare's principal *copia* of witch-stories) reports a popular belief that women with one blue eye and one dark are witches.[53] If so, Sycorax is marked by her blue eye as a witch, and Shakespeare, with characteristic insularity, assumes that a witch is a witch from Stratford to Algiers.

The same uncertainty prevails among editors about Sycorax's name. 'Sycorax' has been found more or less unreadable by many generations of editors. Copious annotations appear at the foot of the pages on which she is mentioned, but these remain uncertainly poised between political, supernatural and colonial discourses, each of which implies a different locale. Yet in a sense Sycorax exists nowhere, or nowhere but in Ariel and Prospero's story. This at any rate is literally true of her name. Nobody is sure what it means. The unreadability or meaninglessness of Sycorax's name suggests the inscrutability of New World peoples, while the way it looks readable and even familiar – the very thing that so teases editors – reminds us of Columbus thinking he understands the Indians he has just told us that he doesn't understand.[54] The usual denotation points towards classical origin, but also opens out in the direction of other classical witches. Yet none of these provide a programmatically exact model for interpreting her. Modern editors have all but given up the search for an explanation. Most give the usual etymology without much conviction, from *sus* (sow) and *korax* (crow); Frank Kermode rightly thinks this 'rather improbable' and suggests an allusion to Circe, born in Colchis of the Coraxi tribe. More recently, Orgel says bluntly that 'the name has never been satisfactorily explained', but suggests an epithet for Medea, 'the Scythian raven'.[55] He also suggests Scythia, often spelled Sythia.

All of these sound plausible without *explaining* the name Sycorax precisely. Nineteenth-century editors were equally baffled, even when they sounded sure of themselves. Francis Douce sees Sycorax as indebted to a passage in *Batman upon Bartheme* which gives the raven's name as Corax, while Lloyd comes up with an etymology which connects Sycorax with the word *psychorragia* or death struggle; *psychorrhax*, he suggests, means heartbreaker. Tackling problems of ethnicity head-on, Phillpotts suggests that 'as an Algerine witch', Sycorax would have an Arabic name, possibly Shokereth, the deceiver. Most wackily of all, Clement identifies Sycorax with Elizabeth I by deriving from it the etymology *sic o rex*.[56] Everyone looks for 'her' in the same places: on the borders of the Mediterranean, from North Africa to Greece, and in the languages and texts produced there. In other words, what we can know from the name Sycorax is that she has a classical name. As we have seen, this does nothing to define her ethnicity, precisely because early modern writers were accustomed to using classical texts as ways of understanding the New World.

None of these 'explanations' explain Sycorax. Yet everyone wants to explain her, either as a mother (pregnant and physically defined by her motherhood) or as a figure in an earlier story which fills in the gaps in this one. The first preoccupation explains the second; we want to know Sycorax because we are interested in her son, his ethnicity, his story. Sycorax is understood as nothing but the mother of Caliban, whose name, location and ethnicity have been so variously and intensely interpreted.[57] Recently, Valerie Traub argued that Gloria Naylor's *Mama Day* is a rewriting of *The Tempest,* refiguring Sycorax as a freed slave matriarch.[58] Like other narratives which are more obviously silent about Sycorax, this understands her as (Caliban's) pre-colonial self, the motherland from which the slave is taken and to which he is constantly trying to return: Sycorax's meaning is confined to her womb. When we fix the meaning of blue eyes in relation to Sycorax's status as mother, when we discuss her in relation to the play's other absent female family members, when we read her witchcraft as a metaphor for her motherhood, when we see her name as the indication of her son's ethnicity, we are untrue to the play. Sycorax is not introduced as Caliban's mother, but as Ariel's tormentor and defeater. She is unhelpful as the ground of Caliban's identity, since Prospero's interrogation of Ariel seems to point to its own unreliability. The faultiness of Ariel's memory is the occasion for the story's telling, but also problematises it since Ariel is Prospero's source for the story. Unlike other witches, however, Sycorax is not a spectacle: she 'appears' only as a story. In so far as Sycorax is ethnically other, she is so not by virtue of the spectacle of otherness, skin colour, but by virtue of the kind of narrative in which she is inscribed: one of barbarity, sexual unruliness and devil-worship in another place.

How does the play read if we see Sycorax as unknowable, or unreadable? What if her story exists to put out vagrant tendrils in many directions rather than to be tied to a particular point of origin? What if we allow identities to become unsteady in the light of the metaphoric interchangeability between the world of the witch, the ancient world and the New World? If we allow ourselves to see Sycorax as polyvalent, then we can bring together the associations of her name: *corax*: crow, raven; Colchis; Syrinx; Scythia; Circe; Scylla. All ill-omened beasts or witches or figures of monstrously transformed femininity; all located on the periphery of the known. So far, so explicable in terms of the now-familiar Renaissance tendency to lump together different patterns of otherness to make a syncretist symbol. Yet none of this appears to apply to Syrinx. She interprets another feature of these places and these women: all are objects of desire. Roland Greene suggests that Columbus interprets his encounters with natives in terms of a Petrarchan discourse of desire; 'on seeing and being seen, the natives recognise themselves as objects and flee like figures in an Ovidian turned Petrarchan myth, which casts the explorers in culturally appreciable roles – as Apollos and Actaons – that they are entirely willing to play'.[59] Yet how can Sycorax be an object of such desire when she no longer inhabits the island? when she no longer exists? when Prospero has never met her? Nonetheless, the idea that meeting a strange lady on an unknown seashore is an occasion for desire is well known to Prospero: Aeneas and Dido, Jason and Medea, Odysseus and Circe, Odysseus and Calypso, Odysseus and Nausicaa, are in his mind when he anxiously superintends Miranda and Ferdinand. So what has happened is that the troubling desirability of Sycorax, with her ethnic otherness and witch-powers, is displaced onto the sweeter and more manageable figure of Miranda, the only female object of desire that the play will allow. The dark lady is folded back into the whiteness of the Petrachan object of desire. Circe transformed men into beasts; in *The Tempest*, this narrative is inverted as a (black) witch is displaced by the unambiguously virginal white girl as object of desire.[60] Desirability is no longer a conduit for power, as it was for Medea, Circe, Dido. As it might have been for Sycorax, as it will not be for Miranda.

Generic reading means an audience interpreting events in the light of their expectations, or of the rules of narrative. The audience hold in their minds a range of alternative outcomes or plots, so that their choice can be compared with the dramatist's. What if the island were ruled by a witch (rather than a wizard)? What if the island's resident power were a witch like Circe or Medea, acting on her own desires? These are the kind of speculations indulged by the shipwrecked nobles, just as they were entertained by the New World voyagers both before and after meeting the inhabitants of the Americas. The surprise – for the nobles, for Ferdinand, for the audience – is the presence on the island of the canny or homelike rather than the uncanny. Only Caliban is left as a reminder of what might have been. However, Sycorax's son does not have her power; he curses Prospero in his mother's name, but with no result (I. 2. 339–40). Prospero's opponents for rule are not symbolic witches, but Machiavellian rulers from the real world. However, before we reify the play's separation of the realms of magic and politics, let us look at what would happen if Sycorax were a Thessalian witch. If Sycorax were still alive, the usurpers might seek her out for help. Caliban's lust for chaste Miranda, who also embodies rule of the island, recalls the tyrant's lust for Sophonisba, which makes him resort to Erictho. Eliminating Sycorax means eliminating both tyranny and the lust and improper desire of the tyrant As always, however, the fear of both mimicry (in Homi Bhabha's sense) and of 'going native' haunt the colonial text, just as they haunt Lucan's source-text and Ovid's. Prospero's rule on the island is possible because all these narratives are cancelled by Sycorax's death.

This is ideologically true too: the immediate usefulness of the story of Sycorax is to define Prospero's magic and to justify his control of Ariel. Most critics have agreed that Prospero's Paracelsian magic is not to be confused with witchcraft, but to be defined in relation to it.[61] Paracelsian magicians were certainly keen to distinguish themselves from witches.[62] Prospero's release of Ariel from the tree enacts a strain of highly gendered imagery implicit in Paracelsian magic and borrowed from its Neoplatonic pre-texts, imagery of the natural world as a womb or pregnant female body which could be opened and brought to birth by the male investigator. Francis Bacon promised that the new magic or science would lead to the power to control the seasons, creating fertility; Ralegh in *The History of the World* wrote of magic as 'the bringing forth of such effects as are wonderful to those that know not their causes'. Ralegh's metaphor casts the magician as a midwife, bringing things out; even in the Renaissance, many juggling tricks involved the opening of boxes, the revelation of what was hidden, the pulling of rabbits out of hats, all easily understood as births.[63] Ariel's space of enclosed imprisonment is highly feminised: he is enwombed, enclosed, and must be reborn in order to live. Ariel in the cloven pine recalls Caliban, locked in the body of his mother. Sycorax has made Ariel hers in the only way she can, by symbolically becoming pregnant with him as well as Caliban, but her mothering of him is bad because static; it brings his story to an end rather than inaugurating it. At least, this is how Prospero tells the story: Ariel has forgotten his release by father-Prospero, just as a baby forgets birth.

Magic could also be understood through colonialist and exploratory metaphors: Bacon, for instance, wrote of magic as storming the castle of nature and extending the boundaries of the human empire.[64] And the converse is also true: just as the play sometimes wants to offer magic as a symbol for politics and sometimes wants to oppose rule and conjuring, so it sometimes sees magic as a form of exploration or colonialism, and sometimes as making this unnecessary or taking off its edge. When Prospero explains that they would have starved if not for his art, or shows how he uses his skill to manipulate the unruly, magic becomes a solution to the problem of living in a new and wild place. It is magic which turns the colony into the potential utopia of Gonzalo's fancy. At the same time, Prospero's magic, and its extraordinary dubiety, cannot but remind us of the colonists who found themselves playing the role of Satan in their own fantasies by appearing as shamans, natural forces or 'missionaries' to the natives. Such identifications with Satan fit the ambivalence of Prospero's magic. Everyone has noticed his reference to necromancy in his renunciation speech. It seems to prompt his sudden *volte face* from enumerating his magical powers to announcing his intention of renouncing them (V. 1. 48–50). It recalls not just Medea, but Erictho, whose necromancy depends on her reuse of dead bodies. Prospero is not as strictly divided from the witch as her elimination from the narrative might suggest, and his relations with her look dubious if we can also see him as her 'master'. We might reasonably see him as her magical master, but the opposition that Prospero tries to make of this between himself and Sycorax is often too problematic to be sustained. It collapses so regularly that one must see these disintegrations as part of the play's strategy. Like everything else about Sycorax, including her presence or absence, her relation with Prospero and with her son Caliban is unsure.

As both Prospero and Caliban sometimes seem to know, the radical undecidability of Sycorax problematises Caliban's racial origins, class origins, and claim to the island, not least because he lacks a (known) father and therefore a secure name.[65] At the most basic level of dramatic typology, Sycorax does give Caliban a ready-made identity which is not often mentioned by critics, the identity of a witch's son. Her story as told by Prospero aligns him with other clowns born of witches, from Spenser's *Faerie Queene* through the Firestone of Middleton's *The Witch* to Maudlin's son in Jonson's *The Sad Shepherd*. In all these plays the witch constantly tries to obtain a beautiful, well-born and chaste woman for her son's lusts, without success. It is as if Caliban is acting as his mother's son, enacting this plot himself, when he tries to rape Miranda. Yet Shakespeare also rewrites the tradition of the witch's son as clown by endowing Caliban with poetry and feeling. As David Norbrook points out, one would ordinarily expect Caliban to speak in prose, like Stephano and Trinculo.[66] His blank verse is unique for a witch's clownish son: Firestone, for instance, speaks in prose and not in the mother-tongue of octosyllabic couplets. Even this endowment could be read as a way of domesticating the other, forcing 'our' language on him. This seems wrong; it might be better to see Caliban as a literary experiment. What kind of poetry would a witch's clownish son speak if poetry were invented for him? For, as noted by all, Caliban's language is not like other people's. Caliban's simple and touching poetic owes a little to the natural men of pastoral, especially to Theocritus's pathetic, dangerous Cyclops, in love with a woman for whom he can only be a monster, who influenced Virgil's *Eclogues*. Both these texts locate their simple shepherds in Mediterranean wildernesses where sorceries also abound. The whole point of Caliban, in speech and action, is his relative untameability, and his refusal to abandon the gods, speech and customs of his mother means that he remains his mother's son and refuses to become Prospero's. Yet Prospero is the one who taught him language.

This raises what Lynda Boose has recently identified as the very hallmark of early modern fear of the racial other. In patriarchy the son must resemble the father. For the early modern period, the son's identity was the principal guarantee of the father's in a manner most easily glimpsed in Shakespeare's *Sonnets* 1–16, in which looks and spirit are legacies to be handed on intact, with no feminine darkening, through the begetting of sons. The birth of monsters was one sign that the process had gone wrong.[67] Another, as Boose points out, was miscegenation. She argues that the horror of miscegenation resided precisely in its signification of a feminine disruption of patrilinearity. In George Peele's *The Battle of Alcazar*, a white man has a black son after marrying a black woman; the son is a demonic traitor. He is repeatedly identified with the devil: 'accompanied, as you now may behold / With devils coated in the shapes of men' (22–5), and at one point he recites an invocation which has some affinities with those of Medea:

> You dastards of the night and Erybus,
> Fiends, fairies, hags that fight in beds of steel
> Range through this army with your iron whips,
> Drive forward to this deed this Christian crew,
> And let me triumph in the tragedy,
> Though it be sealed and honoured with my blood,
> Both of the Portugal and barbarous moor (1230–8).[68]

Muly Mohammed, like Caliban, is exclusively his mother's son, which is why he can act out the role of the witch from elsewhere, Medea, in his invocation. Similarly, Wolfram's *Parzival* has a character called *Feirefiz* (*vairefils*) which means variegated son, or freckled whelp, as Shakespeare might have translated it. This variegated son, however, is less fully the son of his mother than is Muly Mohammed. As his name – and Caliban's – imply, he is a mixture, freckled rather than black. This mixed son is the father of Prester John, the mythical Christian king in Africa. As the father of Prester John, Vairefils is responsible for creating a (fantasy) bridge between alterity and home; is this Prospero's dream for Caliban, a dream too for the New World?[69] A true treaty-child? When Prospero says 'this thing of darkness I acknowledge mine' he is speaking the language of paternity, which is close to the language of ownership of slaves and the discourse of mastery of servants. The other romances involve recognition of a lost or forgotten child – *Cymbeline*, *The Winter's Tale*, *Pericles* – by an exhausted father, though in each case the child is a daughter. Here in the family plot Prospero is forced to recognise the difference of the child, forced to acknowledge a male child who does not resemble him. I am not suggesting that he is literally Caliban's father, but symbolically Caliban remains, as Adelman says, his mother's son, signifying precisely the threat symbolised by the black woman, of a failure in patriarchal self-replication. Prospero has tried to be a father to Caliban in the sense that he has attempted to remake Caliban in his image, but Caliban has refused to resemble his father, remaining tied to the earth of the island. Miranda's difference disqualifies her from representing this self-replication, though Prospero's anxiety about her chastity could be an outcome of the same logic.

So when Prospero is willing to see that a 'thing of darkness' may be his, we can read this as touching, an acknowledgement of an alterity which need not prevent contact, the beginning of a place where the language of paternity need not require self-replication. However, the father's identity still demands *either* self-replication or an interaction based on an almost apartheid-like acknowledgement of insurmountable otherness. Once the other is acknowledged to be unchangeable, racism and fear of miscegenation can begin in earnest, unbridled, unchallenged by any missions to alter, amend or convert. And what if the condition for this acknowledgement of alterity is the absence of the powerful mother? If Caliban can only be acknowledged as in some sense belonging to Prospero in the absence of Sycorax, to whose awesome competences Prospero has been unable to resist alluding just a few lines earlier, then things of darkness can only be acknowledged when they are fully disarmed of the appallingly dense alterity symbolised by the image of them as witches. Scepticism, then, brought about in part by such encounters between white and dark, made possible both contact and genocide, and both are foreshadowed in the play.

Shakespeare deliberately reduces the lady from outside to a story from the past. In working her up to full size, we are being false to the play, which insists that narratives which are dominated by Sycorax must be absent from the drama in order for its own narrative to unfold without impediment. In reconstructing Shakespeare's witches – Joan la Pucelle, the Witch of Brainford, the Weird Sisters, Sycorax – we are untrue to the plays. We must face it: we are much more interested in witches than early modern dramatists were.

NOTES

1 Gustav Henningsen, "The ladies from outside": an archaic pattern of the witches' sabbath', in *Early Modern European Witchcraft: Centres and Peripheries*, ed. Bengt Ankaroo and Gustav Henningsen, Oxford: Oxford University Press, 1993.

2 Anthony Pagden, *The Fall of Natural Man: The American Indian and the Origins of Comparative Ethnology*, Cambridge: Cambridge University Press, 1982. David Norbrook also points out that humanism was not always a colonialist's charter in relation to *The Tempest* in '"What cares these Roarers for the name of king?": language and utopia in *The Tempest*', in *The Politics of Tragicomedy*, ed. Gordon McMullen and Jonathan Hope, London: Routledge, 1992, pp. 38–9.

3 Alden T. and Virginia Mason Vaughan, *Shakespeare's Caliban: A Cultural History*, Cambridge: Cambridge University Press, 1991, pp. 191, 210.

4 Ann Thompson, 'Miranda, where's your sister? Reading Shakespeare's *The Tempest*', in *Feminist Criticism: Theory and Practice*, ed. Susan Sellers, Hemel Hempstead: Harvester, 1991, and Ania Loomba, *Gender, Race, Renaissance Drama*, Manchester: Manchester University Press, 1989, in otherwise excellent articles which at least point to Sycorax and to the play's other missing women.

5 On Herodotus and the New World, see among others Stephen Greenblatt, *Marvellous Possessions: The Wonder of the New World*, Oxford: Oxford University Press, 1991, ch. 5.

6 Jean de Léry, *De la demonomanie des sorcières*, 1578; *History of A Voyage to the Land of Brazil*, trans. Janet Whatley, Berkeley: University of California Press, 1990, p. 248. See Janet Whatley, 'Savage hierarchies: French Catholic observers of the New World', *Sixteenth Century Journal*, 17 (1986), pp. 319–30, and Michel de Certeau,

'Ethno-graphy, speech, or the space of the other: Jean de Léry', in *The Writing of History*, trans. Tom Conley, New York: Columbia University Press, 1988, pp. 232–4.

7 James I, *Daemonologie*, in *Minor Prose Works of King James VI and I*, ed. James Craigie, Edinburgh: Scottish Text Society, 1982.

8 On Inca witches see Irene Silverblatt, 'Andean witches and virgins: seventeenth-century nativism and subversive gender ideologies', in *Women, 'Race', and Writing in the Early Modern Period*, ed. Margo Hendricks and Patricia Parker, London and New York: Routledge, 1994, and *Moon, Sun and Witches: Gender Ideologies and Class in Inca and Colonial Peru*, Princeton: Princeton University Press, 1987. See also Sabine MacCormack, 'Demons, imagination and the Incas', in *New World Encounters*, ed. Stephen Greenblatt, Berkeley: University of California Press, 1993, p. 116

9 Juan Polo de Ondegardo, 'Errores y supersticiones', 1554, cited in Silverblatt, *Moon, Sun and Witches*, p. 172.

10 *The Natural and Moral History of the Indies*, ed. Clements R. Markham, London, 1880, first printed 1604, pp. 298–325, and cf. pp. 330–2, 337, 368–9, 370–1.

11 *Hackluytus Posthumus, or Purchas His Pilgrimage*, 20 vols, Glasgow: James McLehose and Sons, 1905, vol. I, p. 961.

12 John Smith, 'Map of Virginia', in *Jamestown Voyages 1606–1609*, ed. Philip L. Barbour, Hakluyt Society Publications, 2nd series, vols 136–7, Cambridge: Cambridge University Press, 1969, vol. 137, pp. 367–8, cited in Bernard Sheehan, *Savagism and Civility: Indians and Englishmen in Colonial Virginia*, Cambridge: Cambridge University Press, 1980, p. 46.

13 *Jamestown Voyages*, vol. 136, p. 143; vol. 137, p. 364.

14 'The Second Voyage', in Richard Hackluyt, *The Principal Navigations, Voyages, Traffics and Discoveries of the English Nation*, ed. James McLehose, 12 vols, Glasgow: 1904, vol. VII, p. 220.

15 François-Joseph Le Mercier, 21 June 1637, a report on a Huron ceremony to cure smallpox, in James Axtell, *The Invasion Within: The Contest of Cultures in Colonial North America*, Oxford: Oxford University Press, 1985, p. 190. Cf. also Jean de Brébeuf's letter of 27 May 1635, equating native witchcraft with devil-worship, in a move which replicates the acculturation discovered by Muchembled in Europe.

16 Axtell, *Invasion Within*, p. 13; see William Strachey in his *History of Travel into Virginia Brittania*, 1612, ed. Louis B. Wright, Hakluyt Society, 2nd series, vol. 103, London, 1953, pp. 88–9; Alexander Whitaker, *Good News From Virginia*, 1613, pp. 23–4.

17 Axtell, *Invasion Within*, pp. 98–9.

18 Axtell, *Invasion Within*, p. 311.

19 Cotton Mather, cited in David Stannard, *American Holocaust: The Conquest of the Americas,* Oxford: Oxford University Press, 1992, p. 230

20 Richard Godbeer, *The Devil's Dominion: Magic and Religion in early New England*, Cambridge: Cambridge University Press, 1992, pp. 200–1.

21 Reginald Scot's *Discoverie of witchcraft* was the first such work, but there were many more, including Thomas Browne's *Pseudodoxia Epidemica*, Montaigne's *Essays*, and in the late seventeenth century, Aubrey's *Miscellanies* and Robert Kirk's *Secret Commonwealth of Elves, Fauns and Fairies*, 1691.

22 Stephen Greenblatt, *New World Encounters*, ed. Stephen Greenblatt, Berkeley: University of California Press, 1993, p. xii.

23 For Las Casas, however, this commonality of experience enabled him to show that the Indians merely shared the common and miserable lot of humanity, prone to be tricked by illusions or idols; *Apologetica historia*, ed. Edmond O'Gorman, Mexico City, 1987, ch. 245.

24 Geographical vagueness about the New World: see Sabine MacCormack, 'Limits of

Understanding: Perceptions of Greco-Roman and Amerindian paganism in early modern Europe', in *America in European Consciousness 1493–1750*, ed. Karen Ordahl Kupperman, Chapel Hill: University of North Carolina Press, 1995, p. 80.

25 MacCormack, 'Limits' p. 87. See also Anthony Grafton and Nancy Siriasi, *New Worlds, Ancient Texts: The Power of Tradition and the Shock of Discovery*, Cambridge, MA: Harvard University Press, 1992.

26 *The discovery of the large, rich, and beautiful empire of Guiana*, 1596, reprinted in Hakluyt's voyages of 1598–1600; *Principle Navigations*, vol. X, pp. 366–7.

27 *The Moderate Intelligencer*, 29 December–4 January 1649, in *Making the News: An Anthology of the Newsbooks of Revolutionary England 1641–1660*, ed. Joad Raymond, Gloucestershire: Windrush Press, 1993.

28 Edith Hall, *Inventing the Barbarian: Greek Self-Definition through Tragedy*, Oxford: Clarendon Press, 1989, p. 35, 203, n. 9; see also *Argonautica*, IV, by which time she is right on the rim of the known world.

29 For Shakespeare's use of Seneca in the romances, see Erica Sheen, '"The agent for his master": political service and professional liberty in *Cymbeline*', in *The Politics of Tragicomedy*, ed. McMullen and Hope, pp. 59–65.

30 By the Roman era, witches had been firmly located in an imagined Thessaly, and Ovid explains that Medea's herbs and knife are Thessalian. *Metamorphoses*, 7. 264, 314; the word is *haemonia*.

31 Ovid, *Metamorphoses*, trans. A.D. Melville, Oxford: Oxford University Press, 7. 200ff.

32 *Odyssey*, 10. 410–17.

33 Ovid was interested in the moment of change (*Metamorphoses,* 14. 276–415); Horace, on the other hand, moralised the transformation as prodigality; we, he writes, without Odysseus's willpower, give in to our desires as consumers and fashionplates, transforming ourselves (*Epistles* 1.2, 17–31).

34 Lynda E. Boose, '"The getting of a lawful race"; racial discourse in early modern England and the unrepresentable black woman' in *Women, 'Race', and Writing*, ed. Hendricks and Parker.

35 See Richard Brilliant, 'Kirke's men: swine and sweethearts', in *The Distaff Side: Representing the Female in Homer's Odyssey*, ed. Beth Cohen, New York: Oxford University Press, 1995, p. 172.

36 Lucan, *Pharsalia,* VI, 461–5, trans. Susan M. Brand, Oxford: Oxford University Press, 1992; Thessalian witches also occur in Apuleius, *Metamorphoses* 2. 21–30, where too the witch is a necromancer.

37 Sources for the Sophonisba story include Livy, bk 30; Boccacio, *De claris mulieribus;* Petrach, *Trionfo d'amore* and *Africa*. There is also an early Italian tragedy of Sophonisba by Galcotto del Corretto, dedicated to Isabella D'Este Gonzaga in 1502, in which ancient history is clearly understood in relation to contemporary political events; Isabella D'Este's husband had been taken prisoner by the Venetians in 1510, and her son was taken hostage by the pope.

38 For a classical source for love spells, see Theocritus, *Idylls*, II, and see Virgil's adaptation of it in *Eclogue* VIII.

39 *Sophonisba* was entered in the Stationers' Register on 17 March 1606, having been performed at Blackfriars; it was apparently written in deliberate competition with Jonson's *Sejanus* (performed 1603, printed 1605). It must therefore be very close in date to *Macbeth*, and may precede it, influencing Shakeapere's reinscription of fates as witches and the linkage of witchcraft and questions of legitimate rule.

40 Rebecca W. Bushnell, *Tragedies of Tyrants: Political Thought and Theatre in the English Renaissance*, Ithaca: Cornell University Press, 1990.

41 Patricia Parker, 'Fantasies of "race" and "gender"; Africa, *Othello*, and bringing to light', in *Women, 'Race', and Writing*, ed. Hendricks and Parker, pp. 96–9.

42 On Dido's two identities, see my 'The queen on stage: Marlowe's *Dido Queen of Carthage* and the representation of Elizabeth', in *The Figure of Dido*, ed. Michael Burden, London: Faber, forthcoming.
43 See Stephanie Jed, *Chaste Thinking: The Rape of Lucrece and the Birth of Humanism*, Bloomington: Indiana University Press, 1989.
44 As Stephen Orgel shows, the joke is 'about' the two traditions of Dido's rule, but it is also 'about' the shipwrecked parties' expectations of colonial encounters and the role of the classics in shaping those expectations.
45 *Aeneid* 4. 481ff.
46 On Othello's submission to being fashioned by others, see Stephen Greenblatt, *Renaissance Self-Fashioning*, Berkeley: University of California Press, 1980.
47 All quotations from *Othello* are from the New Cambridge Shakespeare edition, edited by Norman Sanders, Cambridge: Cambridge University Press, 1984.
48 On the scene see Janet Adelman, *Suffocating Mothers: Fantasies of Maternal Origin in Shakespeare's Plays, Hamlet to The Tempest*, New York and London: Routledge, 1992, pp. 65–71, 275–6, 277; Peter Stallybrass, 'Patriarchal territories: The body enclosed' in *Rewriting the Renaissance: The Discourses of Sexual Difference in Early Modern Europe*, ed. Margaret W. Ferguson, Maureen Quilligan, and Nancy J. Vickers, Chicago: University of Chicago Press, 1986, pp. 137–40; Ania Loomba, *Gender, Race, Renaissance Drama*, Manchester: Manchester University Press, 1989, pp. 41–2; Anthony Barthelemy, *Black Face, Maligned Race: The Representation of Blacks in English Drama from Shakespeare to Southerne*, Baton Rouge: Louisiana State University Press, 1987.
49 Lisa Jardine, 'Why should he call her whore? Defamation and Desdemona's case', in *Essays in Interpretation*, 1990, pp. 124–53; Karen Newman, '"And wash the Ethiop white"', in *Fashioning Femininity and English Renaissance Drama*, Chicago: Chicago University Press, 1991.
50 Both plays are performed at court on All Saints' Day, in 1604 and 1611 respectively; despite my efforts, I cannot make much of the festive significance of these dates. Both were revived for the wedding of Elizabeth of Bohemia and the Elector Palatine. See John B. Bender 'The day of *The Tempest*', *English Literary History*, 47 (1980), pp. 235–58 on the significance of All Saints' Day.
51 I. 2. 269: *The Tempest*, ed. Anne Barton, London: Penguin, 1968; see also *The Tempest*, ed. Frank Kermode, Arden Shakespeare, London: Methuen, 1954, both citing Webster, *The Duchess of Malfi*, (II. 1. 67). Orgel concurs, but with a greater sense of discomfort; as well he might (*The Tempest*, ed. Stephen Orgel, Oxford: Oxford University Press, 1987).
52 Hakluyt, *Principal Navigations*, vol. VII, p. 209; W.J. Graig, ed., *The Complete Works of William Shakespeare*, Oxford: Clarendon Press, 1892, note on 1. 2. 269; Kermode, *The Tempest,* p. 167.
53 *The Witch of Edmonton* II. 1. 89; G. B. Harrison mentions this in his edition of Potts's *The wonderful discovery* (London: Davies, 1929) p. 55. I am not suggesting that this actually was a popular belief, but that it was a belief in circulation among dramatists.
54 Greenblatt, *Marvellous*, p. 54.
55 Natalis Comes says that Circe came from Colchis like Medea (*Mythologiae*, Frankfurt, 1584, pp. 570, 578). Orgel points out that elsewhere Shakespeare associates Scythia with cannibalism (at *King Lear* I. 1. 116–17).
56 Horace Howard Furness, ed., *The Tempest,* new variorum edition, Philadelphia, 1892.
57 Trevor Griffiths, '"This island's mine": Caliban and colonialism', *Yearbook of English Studies*, 13 (1988), pp. 159–80; Vaughan, *Shakespeare's Caliban*.
58 Valerie Traub, 'Rainbows of darkness: deconstructing Shakespeare in the work of Gloria Naylor and Zora Neale Hurston', in *Cross-Cultural Performances: Differences*

in Women's Re-Visions of Shakespeare, ed. Marianne Novy, Urbana: University of Illinois Press, 1995.

59 Roland Greene, 'Petrarchism among the discourses of imperialism', in *America in European Consciousness 1493–1750*, ed. Karen Ordahl Kupperman, Chapel Hill: University of North Carolina Press, 1995, p. 137.

60 This reading of *The Tempest* is informed throughout by Gayatri Spivak's 'Three women's texts and a critique of imperialism', in *'Race', Writing and Difference*, ed. Henry Louis Gates, Chicago: Chicago University Press, 1987. For an analysis of the metaphoric subtext of 'hue' as racially inflected, see Jonathan Crewe, 'Out of the matrix: Shakespeare and race writing', unpublished paper given at 'Texts and Cultural Change' conference, University of Reading, 19 July 1995. This substitution occurs to Caliban too: 'I never saw a woman / But only Sycorax, my dam, and she; / But she as far surpasseth Sycorax / As great'st does least' (III. 2. 98–100).

61 Ania Loomba discusses Sycorax as Prospero's other in *Gender, Race, Renaissance Drama*, pp. 151–3.

62 See for instance Agrippa's story of a witch's love magic gone wrong, *De occulta philosophia*, 1533, 1. 41, p. 47.

63 See Barbara Mowat, 'Prospero, Agrippa and hocus-pocus', *English Literary Renaissance*, 11 (1981), pp. 281–303.

64 Francis Bacon, *De augmentis scientiarum*, 4. 1. Sir Walter Raleigh, *The History of the World,* ch.11, sect. 2.

65 In writing this I am reminded of Hortense Spillers's justly celebrated argument that African-American slaves have had the mark of the father abducted from them in the voyage through the Middle Passage: 'Mama's baby, Papa's maybe', *Diacritics*, 12 (1988), pp. 1–12.

66 Norbrook, 'Language and utopia'.

67 See my doctoral thesis, 'Gender, power and the body: Some figurations on femininity in Milton and seventeenth-century women's writing', Oxford, D. Phil thesis, 1991, ch. 4.

68 George Peele, *The Battle Of Alcazar*, ed. W. W. Greg, London: Malone Society Reprints, 1907.

69 Wolfram von Eschenbach, *Parzival*, trans. A.T. Hatto, Harmondsworth: Penguin, 1980; Boose, 'Racial discourse', also discusses this story, but misreads it as a sign of the spotting or staining of the child by the mother.

Conclusion

Bread into gingerbread and the price of the transformation

Even the half-disregarded witches of early modern drama have enormous significance for us at the end of the twentieth century, but not the same significance that they had for their inventors. In laying hold of the witch, in making her our own, we have also lost her, or perhaps lost what she once was for her original owners. Now she stands like a country house, with so many additions from diverse historical periods that the original structures are no longer visible from any angle. For despite the subtleties of radical feminists, historians and modern witches, the dominant image of the witch is still of a shrieking hag on a broomstick, the Wicked Witch of the West.

The witch's consignment to the world of childhood infects historical accounts of her. She is the bogey of Western society's infancy, a feature of our early years as a culture. She exemplifies the dark ages, the primitive, the superstitious, the unenlightened. It is right for her to wear black, because her black clothes show she is from the deep, unknown past. She also represents the dark forces of unreason which may return at any moment to menace civilisation. But it is not so much she herself who represents these things. It is belief in her, belief in her power, and also a willingness to act on that belief by killing her. Because it is impossible for most of us to be who we are and also to accept the knowledges of early modern believers about the witch, those knowledges have to be understood in other terms, our terms.

The transformation of folktales which once embodied early modern knowledge of the witch into more anodyne tales for modern children offers a potted version of the narrative of this book; in them, we can see both how and why early modern knowledge of witches becomes subjugated. In what is most familiar, canny, even cosy, lies buried a trace of that which we now find absolutely alien. Yet we cannot see this trace. Admittedly, there is no single 'uncontaminated' wellspring of folktales which reflect a purely early modern perspective; all are reshaped by the interests and preoccupations of the folklorists who inscribed them.[1] Yet if the historicity and mutability of the folktale before inscription is neglected, there will be a concomitant neglect of the ways in which elements of folktales relate to a social context other than – and sometimes absolutely alien to – the one that inscribes them. The result will also be some interpretive mistakes, even by astute critics. In reading the role of witches in Grimms' tales, for instance, Ruth Bottigheimer lays great stress on the fact that witches do not perform acts of conjuration; overt magic is reserved for their 'good' opponents.[2] But early modern witches as represented in trial literature only rarely perform overt acts of conjuration; mostly their acts of magic are silent and unseeable, detectable only by half-hidden signs. Their village opponents, on the other hand, do often use conjurations, prophetic insights, written spells or magical talismans.

As Marina Warner has recently shown, neglecting the popular aspects of folk retellings and recitals means neglecting the stories of women.[3] Whether those women are early modern peasant women telling each other tales, middle-class women writers creating entertainments for their friends, nurses and governesses bringing the concerns of a different social class into the castle, or mothers assiduously reading fairy stories to their own children, folktales still speak to us in a female voice, the female voice whose fantasies about witches are visible in trial depositions. As early as the ancient world, certain kinds of stories were associated with an old woman narrator, stories Plato calls *mythos graos* or tales from the old woman, stories that Reginald Scot associated with a woman's culture which was now thankfully vanishing. One of the earliest European collections of such stories and legends, Basile's *Pentamerone*, describes its contents as 'those tales that old women tell to amuse children'. As late as the 1820s, John Clare described the scene inside a cottage in winter where an old woman tells tales while she knits or sews. Other tale-tellers were domestic servants: both Dickens and Stevenson had nannies who regaled them with frightening bedtime stories of murderers and witches.[4]

The neglect of the association between folktales and women tellers parallels the situation in early modern witchcraft studies. Just as women's role in shaping the witch of the trial literature has been erased, so women's place as narrators and shapers of folktale witches has been concealed. But when the two kinds of female-authored, though much-mediated, narrative are put together, it is not surprising to find considerable areas of overlap. Many folktales, even in late and uncomprehending versions, contain clear traces of women's fears of and fantasies about the witch and her powers. At the very least, both kinds of story come from a society of food scarcity, and a society where women are responsible for feeding the household.[5] Many folk stories warn of the dangers of accepting a gift of food, especially a luxury food such as fruit or cake, from a woman outside the immediate family. In 'Snow Drop', the earliest version of the tale which became better-known as 'Snow White', the wicked queen, who plainly has magical powers, prepares one last trap for her victim: a poisoned apple. 'The outside looked very rosy and tempting, but whoever tasted it was sure to die'.[6] 'Hansel and Gretel' is the best known of a group of stories in which two children are victims of their own and their parents' terrible hunger.[7] These two children, abandoned by their (step)mother, find an alternative and apparently miraculous source of food, a house made of luxury items: 'the cottage was made of bread and cakes, and the windowpanes were of clear sugar'.[8] The magic house is inhabited by a witch; it embodies and represents her magical power that she can create such an impossible dwelling and symbol of plenitude. The witch at first seems kind and considerate, but later reveals herself to be the opposite of the nurturer she seems; she is a devourer, not a substitute mother but an antimother:

> the old woman, nodding her head, said 'Ah, you dear children, what has brought you here? Come in and stop with me, and no harm shall befall you'; and so saying she took them both by the hand and led them into her cottage. A good meal of milk and pancakes, with sugar, apples and nuts, was spread on the table, and in the back room were two little beds, covered with white, where Hansel and Gretel laid themselves down, and thought themselves in heaven.[9]

Even this apparently simple fare offered by the witch represented a feast to the peasantry, especially in time of famine.[10] Such special foods were often associated with the alluring power of witches in the trial literature.[11] What is striking in the context of a story about children on their own is that the witch plainly adopts a charitable and even a maternal tone in relation to her offer of food and rest. The children's relief at having found a substitute mother is mirrored in the phrase 'thought themselves in heaven'; the luxuriouness of the food casts them in a familial relation whereby the witch offers to supplement the inadequate food-provision of the children's (step)mother and thus replace her. However, just as the (step)mother turns out to be insufficiently generous, so the witch turns out to be a counter-mother, not nurturative but consuming, not selfless, but devouring:

> The old woman had behaved very kindly to them, but in reality she was a wicked witch who waylaid children and built the bread-house in order to entice them in; but as soon as they were in her power she cooked them, ate them, and made a great festival of the day.[12]

The witch decides to eat Hansel and to keep Gretel to work, and as a result it is Gretel's feminine linkage with the kitchen and cooking that allows her to turn the witch from consumer to meal, baking her in the oven she prepares for Hansel.[13] Counter-magics involving burning bewitched objects or objects associated with the suspected witch are often mentioned in women's trial literature stories, and in that context Gretel's incineration of the witch seems a radical, fantasy version of such remedies, as well as replicating their magical reclamation of the role of mother and cook–food–provider.[14] Such a reading emphasises her peasant ingenuity as well as stressing her role as a warning to other girls and women. In 'Hansel and Gretel', as well as in trial stories, the role of housewife that Gretel reclaims is not entirely of women's own making, but socially enjoined upon them; nevertheless their investment in it means that women understand the witch as a threat to their mastery of the domestic sphere. Gretel, who has been cast out of her home by another woman (a particularly tough and common fate for a daughter) can symbolically, and ultimately actually, reclaim it by destroying her devouring antimother in a manner which asserts her own domestic and perhaps magical know-how.[15] Gretel's ability to cook the witch signifies her assumption of control over the food supply, her assumption of the role of mother, and thus she is able to guarantee the survival of her 'child' Hansel and herself, a survival that was twice threatened by another woman's assumption of that controlling position. Gretel's reward seems piffling only in a modern context; she is installed as sole controller of the domestic household, since her (step)mother has conveniently died, and can thus guarantee what had previously seemed precarious; her own survival and that of her brother. In context, 'Hansel and Gretel' offers a set of rules which are as rational in a society which believed itself plagued with witches as modern books on 'stranger danger' seem today. Its warnings made sense in a context where the magical capacity of food to cross the boundaries of the household or the body and invade the person was understood.

The witch who offered food also symbolically assumed the role of the child-victim's mother, since it was normally a maternal duty to offer food and to guard its integrity. This relation between the mother who will not or cannot provide food and her surrogate and dark double, the devouring witch, is manifest in one of the English 'Hansel and Gretel'-type stories, a story called 'Black Annis'. The relation is not simple; the witch is not merely a psychically disguised version of the 'bad' mother, but also her opponent and opposite. The 'bad' mother's ally in seeking to dispose of the children, she is also their abductor who goes beyond the 'bad' mother in taking control of them and using them to satisfy her own appetite. One might say that the witch represents a mother's fear that she is behaving like a cannibal in denying her children the right to feed from her, literally or figuratively; in a famine, in extreme poverty, it was (and is) the mother who is expected to go without food.[16] From the point of view of a mother, the witch is the social sanction which prevents her from abandoning her children. In 'Black Annis', the 'wicked stepmother' sends her three children out 'near Christmastide to gather wood'. The use of the stock phrase 'wicked stepmother' probably points to literary 'contamination' – the story was recorded in 1941, after Disney's *Snow White* – but Black Annis is a traditional figure, and behaves like the traditional ogre-witch, eating children who stray from the domain of civilisation because their parents are neglectful or have in some way abdicated responsibility. And as with the witch of 'Hansel and Gretel', when Black Annis is killed, the stepmother mysteriously disappears too, and the children return to find a feast of kippers and butter, signifiers of plenitude in a context of wartime rationing.[17] This late retelling of the Black Annis story – the figure was first recorded much earlier – demonstrates the resilience of the motifs of hunger and maternity in a context of privation, and also demonstrates the ongoing meaning of the witch-cannibal for women as a carrier of their fears about themselves and about their children.

By contrast, very modern retellings of the better-known Grimms' tales, however desperately authentic or deliberately colloquial, lose sight of this complex of symbolic significances, even when the retellings are by women. Knowledge is lost, even as its symbols are parroted: Snow White's fatal apple and the witch's food house are now flat features of the plot, or have had other meanings assigned to them at variance with – and sometimes the opposite of – the meanings which operated in the older social contexts of the stories. Serious warnings to be vigilant at the boundaries of the body, anxieties about food and survival in rural subsistence cultures, have become part of narratives which reflect *adult* anxieties about controlling and managing the 'greed' of children. Indicative of these misreadings and rewritings is the alteration of the witch's original bread house to a *ginger*bread house. A simple subsistence food is replaced by a teatime luxury. As a result, the lost children are no longer eating from need, but gorge themselves on food which would normally be rationed by caring parents. Unlike bread, gingerbread is not rationed because of scarcity, but because of notions of discipline and self-control – because it is desirable, in fact. The substitution of gingerbread for bread makes Bettelheim's reading of 'Hansel and Gretel' as the tale of *children's* oral cravings look credible, but this meaning has been added to the story recently, by *adults*, and forms part of the wish to control and manage children's bodily drives and desires which characterises the nineteenth-century's notion of civility.[18] In this context, the witch becomes the agent of the adults' wish that greedy children should be punished. The witch also represents, however, a terrorising symbol of what might happen if children's desires are left unrestrained by discipline; her uncontrolled orality is the presumed end-product of the indulgence which her cottage signifies.

Despite the unfashionableness of the idea that children's oral cravings need curbing, some very recent retellings are still plainly influenced by Bettelheim's theory that Hansel and Gretel simply project their own violent orality onto the cannibalistic witch; Helen Cresswell, for example, describes the childrens' encounter with the witch's house as follows:

> It was a little house with walls of gingerbread and a roof of cake and windows of frosted sugar. Hansel ran forward and broke off a piece of the roof in a shower of crumbs, 'Food!' he cried, his cheeks bulging, and Gretel too began to stuff her mouth with the rich, curranty cake.[19]

The page on which this passage is printed has margins filled with pictures of luxury foods, of the kind we would now regard as treats rather than necessities: sweets, cakes, tarts. It seems to be about greed. But it is also deeply nostalgic; even gingerbread seems more a relic of past times than an emblem of modern anxieties about children and eating, which centre far more on 'Americanised' convenience and fast food, or the 'empty calories' of crisps and fizzy drinks.[20] Though this modern Hansel and Gretel are behaving greedily, their greed is *not* modern, but part of a past presented as cosy with cake and other teatime treats, rather than as half-starved. Another way to put this is that in the retelling the children are transformed from subsistence-class peasants to middle-class children with plenty to eat. The witch, who is not illustrated in this retelling, appears in this context of plenty as a retributive force of oral greed. Similarly, versions based more closely on Grimms' later editions still use a rhetoric of uncontrolled orality: one version explicitly says that the children 'fell upon the house greedily' and refers to them 'gobbling the wall, breaking off huge chunks of cake'.[21] Unsurprisingly, the witch is a reflection of this greed; 'children were her favourite delicacy', says the text, emphasising that children are the witch's gingerbread. In such modern retellings, the foods the witch offers are given much less emphasis than the foods of which her house is made; they are not presented as luxuries, not revised from the original foods likely to impress an audience of peasant children. It is not the role of the witch as surrogate mother and food provider that interests modern retellers, but her role as greedy consumer, emblem of what the children may become or may already be.

Moreover, the witch actually restores a kind of normality by inviting the children to eat; the whole point of emphasising their attack on the house seems to be their determination of their own food consumption, their refusal of commensality. This is still a crime in modern households which resonate to cries of 'You'll spoil your dinner'. When Hansel and Gretel get home with their purloined treasure in these modern retellings, they do not have any kind of family meal; instead, they share their new-found *wealth* with Papa, pouring out jewels and gold onto the table. This re-emphasis ensures a restitution of the principle of sharing as a moral without reference to food, and also emphasises the reconstitution of the family as an economic unit with consumer power, rather than as sharing food consumption. This reflects adult fears that children will somehow escape the family and its controls, and escape it precisely as consumers with spending power.

It also turns the story of a witch into something like a story of 'stranger danger', since the witch is no longer a substitute demon-mother but a source of tempting wealth and the power it brings.[22] The motifs of maternity and hunger which had once shaped the tale are disfigured and flattened into psychoanalytic truisms. The witch becomes the *modern* idea of a 'bad mother', a greedy consumer who sacrifices children to her own needs and fails to discipline their oral cravings so that they become as monstrously greedy as she is. This modern monster-mother is a child abuser whose abuse is concealed from scrutiny by a veneer of kindness; she is also the alluring stranger who threatens the unity of the family by offering forbidden treats as snares for and metaphors of forbidden sexuality: 'Would you like a sweetie, little girl?' Because the historicity of the folktale is erased by its elevation to classic timelessness, no one notices the process of transformation and its frightening implications for our own witch-hunts and prejudices.

Thus even the witch of 'Hansel and Gretel' has been tugged in new directions by our demands, our desires, just as she was once shaped by the fantasies of early modern women. Those earlier fantasies are still present in vestigial form, but without further knowledge of the early modern context, they are no longer readable, and are liable to be recuperated as psychic symptoms or as inscrutable historical darkness. This process of transformation, which is not without its contestations, involves a series of noticeable losses. For the essence of the early modern witch is fear, and we no longer find the witch frightening. Charles Lamb might have said that it would have taken a brave constable to arrest the Weird Sisters, but most of us would see even those flying night-hags as sad, deluded old ladies, with such conviction that they might see themselves that way too, and go quietly. Even in the nursery the witch is no longer a terror. Yet unless we can for a moment understand what it is to fear the witch, we cannot understand her early modern incarnations. Anyone who wishes to feel such real fear might try reading 'Chips', a story told to the young Charles Dickens by his nanny Mary Weller.[23] The story is about a man whose family all sell their souls to the devil. He does everything he can to avoid doing so, but at last he is forced into the pact, and the devil kills him in the most awful way imaginable, with plenty of warning to draw out his fear and ours. It terrified the young Dickens, and it should strike fear into any sane reader, because it is about the inescapability of the discovery that you may yourself be the worst thing in the world. The real terror of the witch lies in this mixture of familiarity and unbearable strangeness. She represents what we cannot bear to acknowledge as ours, the feelings, violence, dirt and filth that we cannot own without destroying our pleased sense that we are good and kind and clean.

It is easy for us to feel superior to the early modern men and women who thus expunged their worst feelings and attached them to another person. Superiority should, however, be tempered with caution. Although we no longer fear the witch, we still have not owned those dark feelings. Rather, we have sanitised the witch, so that she can become acceptable, transforming her into another one of our better selves. Now she is clean, pretty, a herbalist with a promising career in midwifery, a feminist, as good a mother as anybody if not rather better than most, sexually liberated (without anything too kinky). If a constable did pluck up enough courage to arrest the Weird Sisters, we would probably feel indignant on their behalf rather than impressed with his nerve ('Free the three!'). It is Macbeth, with his broadsword militarism, who endangers us. We are all Romantics now, all more taken with sexy and cynical Vivian than with boring old Arthur and moralistic old Merlin. Vivian's transgressions are mild; to us, her sexuality is not a transgression at all, but a point in her favour. She is the mother of those near-pornographic fantasy creatures who roam freely in the films of Ken Russell, for whom the label 'witch' is simply an excuse for a lot of uninhibited nudity and nook. Any crimes grimier than this, like eating babies, can be dismissed as libels.

So much for our witches. They have made it impossible for us to avoid the little sin of dissolving literature into history. We cannot help but see the witches of *Macbeth* in terms of the social history of witchcraft, because we cannot help but see the social history of witchcraft in terms of the witches of *Macbeth*. Yet the longer one looks at the relations between playtext and trial text, the more complex these relations appear. It is mostly early modern literary writers who clump together figures of otherness to make one big Other of disorder. In doing so they weaken rather than strengthening the specificity of the images and stories they deal with, which might have very highly developed meanings in other contexts; you could even say that the stage contributes to acculturation, and it certainly contributes to the growth of the kind of scepticism that eventually ensures the end of the successful prosecution of the witch, though not the end of stories or beliefs. It does this despite or rather because of its real lack of interest in witches. You might see Shakespeare's writings on witchcraft as rather like Sylvia Plath or Martin Amis or D. M. Thomas using the Holocaust as a fictional metaphor for modern alienation; it is almost that exploitative, only rather less serious. You might see it that way, and thus repeat the mistake of seeing the horrors of earlier centuries in terms of our own.

The dark sister of the charming herbalist with the well-scrubbed pine table and the bunches of herbs drying in the rafters is for us nothing but a mass of bygone prejudices, a marker which divides us from the benighted and bigoted past into which we have abjected so much of our worst selves. The bright, steady lights of empirical history and symptomatic ego-psychoanalysis can illuminate that darkness (in which case it ceases to be dark). For if we can no longer feel fear when contemplating the witch, we can at least feel its supposedly more rational double, curiosity. All our witches are the daughters of the Weird Sisters, because all our witches, from the Witch of Atlas to Starhawk, are displays. All our witches exist to satisfy curiosity about witches, and I too am of that happy breed, having written this book to satisfy my own curiosity and in the hope that it will allow others to do the same. Our witches, like the Weird Sisters, are displays of lost lore, displays of a past always already going out of fashion, dissolving, requiring exorcism or preservation, but always requiring action on our part. This book, inevitably, is part of the process of keeping the witch in play, playing with her, creating new meanings for her so that she remains one of the dominant figures of our mental landscape.

NOTES

1 Robert Darnton, for instance, shows that those who analyse such stories without considering their transmission and historicity risk relying for their interpretation on details unknown in early versions of the tales: 'Peasants tell tales', in *The Great Cat Massacre*, Harmondsworth: Penguin, 1987. Jack Zipes, *Fairy Tales: The Art of Subversion*, London: Routledge, 1983; *The Brothers Grimm: From Enchanted Forests to the Modern World*, London: Routledge, 1988. Maria Tatar, *The Hard Facts of the Grimms' Fairy Tales*, Princeton: Princeton University Press, 1987, p. 49.

2 *Grimms' Bad Girls and Bold Boys: The Moral and Social Vision of the Tales*, New Haven and London: Yale University Press, 1987, pp. 40–50.

3 Marina Warner, *From the Beast to the Blonde: On Fairytales and their Tellers*, London: Chatto and Windus, 1994, pp. 12–20. This entire argument is indebted to

Warner's meticulous and exciting scholarship. See also Ruth Bottigheimer, 'Tale spinners: submerged voices in Grimms' fairy tales', *New German Critique*, 27 (1982), pp. 141–50, Karen E. Rowe, 'To Spin a Yarn: The Female Voice in Folklore and Fairy Tale', in *Fairy Tales and Society: Illusion, Allusion and Paradigm*, Philadelphia: University of Pennsylvania Press, 1986; Tatar, *Hard Facts,* Ch. 5.

4 Warner, *From the Beast*, Ch. 2, esp. pp. 13–18. Plato, *Gorgias*, 527a4; Marlowe, *Dr Faustus*, V 133; George Peele, *The Old Wives Tale*, 1590; Giambattista Basile, *Pentamerone*, trans and intro. Benedetto Croce, ed. N. M. Penzer, 2 vols, New York: John Lane, 1932, 1. 9; John Clare, *The Shepherd's Calendar*, ('January: A Cottage Evening', first published 1827); Jonathan Gathorne Hardy, 'The nanny as bard', in *The Rise and Fall of the British Nanny*, London: Weidenfeld & Nicolson, 1972, pp. 282–7. The idea of the nurse as the repository of popular legend is interestingly fictionalised by C. S. Lewis in Prince Caspian's nurse. See also Rowe, 'To spin a yarn', and for an interpretation of gender in the tales as told, see Peter Taylor and Hermann Rebel, 'Hessian peasant women, their families and the draft: a social historical interpretation of four tales from the Grimm collection', *Journal of Family History* (1981), pp. 347–78.

5 Eugen Weber also notes the predominance of food motifs in the Grimms' stories, in 'Fairies and Hard Facts: The Reality of Folktales', *Journal of the History of Ideas*, 43 (1981), pp. 93–113. For an excellent analysis of the motifs of orality, canibalism and maternity, but without reference to the context of witch-beliefs, see Maria Tatar, *Off With their Heads! Fairy Tales and the Culture of Childhood*, Princeton: Princeton University Press, 1992, Ch. 9.

6 'Snow Drop', from *German Popular Stories . . . collected by M. M. Grimm*, 1823, reprinted in Peter and Iona Opie, *The Classic Fairy Tales*, Oxford: Oxford University Press, 1974, p. 180. For analyses of the way different versions of the Grimms' story vary, see Zipes, *The Brothers Grimm* and Kay Stone, 'Three transformations of Snow White', in *The Brothers Grimm and Folktale*, ed. James M. McGlathery, Urbana: University of Illinois Press, 1991. There is no record of an originary English 'Snow White', but there is a late version which brilliantly reworks the Grimms' story in *The Penguin Book of English Folktales*, ed. Neil Philip, Harmondsworth: Penguin, 1992, pp. 102–10. The apple again plays a key role.

7 The principal English version of the theme of abandonment is 'Babes in the Wood', in which the hapless children simply die of exposure, and the French version is the more complex 'Hop O' My Thumb', in which a pair of ogres replace the witch of Grimm in threatening to devour the children. For an analysis of the French 'Le Petit Poucet' as retold by Perrault, see Darnton, *Great Cat Massacre*.

8 'Hansel and Gretel', from *Household Stories*, 1853, in Opie, *Classic Fairy Tales*, p. 242. The passage is substantially the same in the other principal English translation, that of Ralph Mannheim in *The Penguin Complete Grimms' Tales*, Harmondsworth: Penguin, 1984, first published 1977, p. 59. Though reflecting early modern concerns, this version of the story is late. I bracket (step)mother because in the original 1810 manuscript of the tale the woman is the children's real mother. Interestingly, this is a story known to have been originally told to the brothers by a woman, Dortchen Wild, the future wife of Wilhelm Grimm.

9 Opie, *Classic Fairy Tales*, p. 242.

10 See Weber, 'Hard Facts', pp. 98ff. The fantasy of a house made of food is typical of carnivalesque texts about the Land of Cockayne (see e.g. BL, MSS Harley 913) but the foods are staples such as bread, meat and fish.

11 C.'L'Estrange Ewen, *Witchcraft and Demonianism*, 1933 pp. 332–4.

12 Opie, *Classic Fairy Tales,* p. 242.

13 Maria Tatar also discusses the relation of the tale to 'reality' in *Hard Facts*, pp. 49–50.

14 The story may also refer to the folk-belief that burning a witch's body ended her power, a belief which subtended (but did not cause) the practice of burning witches in Germany. The wicked queen/witch in 'Snow White' also meets a fiery end in some versions of the tale, being forced to don red-hot slippers and to dance in them until she dies.

15 On patterns of abandonment and poverty as its cause, see John Boswell, *The Kindness of Strangers: The Abandonment of Children in Western Europe from Late Antiquity to the Renaissance*, Harmondsworth: Penguin, 1988.

16 On this idea in the early modern period, see Diane Purkiss, 'Producing the voice, consuming the body' in *Women/Writing/History*, ed. Isobel Grundy and Susan S. Wiseman, London: Batsford, 1992, and on the continuance of the notion, see Nickie Charles and Marion Kerr, *Women, Food and Families*, Manchester: Manchester Univeristy Press, 1988.

17 Katherine M. Briggs, *A Dictionary of British Folk-tales*, 4 vols, London: Routledge & Kegan Paul, 1970–1, vol. I, pp. 620–2. See also two further English stories in which a young girl is turned out to service by her uncaring parents and finds a job with a witch or bogle: 'The Green Lady' and 'The Old Witch', in Philip, *English Folktales*, pp. 58–68. Both stories turn on knowledge about food, meals and other household matters; both feature resourceful heroines who use this knowledge to triumph over the cruel witches and families. For a discussion of the way folk knowledge of witches crops up in less well-known stories, see Chapter 6.

18 Bruno Bettelheim, *The Uses of Enchantment: The Meaning and Importance of Fairy Tales*, Harmondsworth: Penguin, 1978, pp. 161–5, first published 1975. On nineteenth-century agendas of child discipline, see Christina Hardyment, *Dream Babies: Child Care from Locke to Spock*, Oxford: Oxford University Press, 1983, and Linda Gordon, *Heroes of their own lives*, London: Virago, 1989.

19 Helen Cresswell, *Classic Fairy Tales*, London: Harper Collins, 1993, p. 44.

20 Perhaps a genuine updating would feature a house made of Big Macs and fries. On anxieties about children and behaviour in the modern world, see Marina Warner, *Managing Monsters*, London: Vintage, 1994.

21 *The Orchard Book of Fairy Tales*, retold by Rose Impey, London: Orchard, 1992, p. 80.

22 Jack Zipes has recently suggested that 'Hansel and Gretel' works as a justification of paternal child-abuse; if so, it works by deflecting fear of the abusive parent onto fear of the abusive stranger, the witch; this is not the point made here. 'Hansel and Gretel: justifying child abuse', paper given at the University of Reading on March 12 1995. I am grateful to Tony Watkins for lending me his tape recording of Zipes's presentation.

23 Originally in Charles Dickens, 'Nurse's stories', *The Uncommercial Traveller*, 1860. Mary Weller told Dickens a number of frightening tales; she used to signal their onset by clawing the air and groaning. Dickens would beg her to stop, but she was relentless. Robert Louis Stevenson was also told his most frightening witch-story by his Scottish nanny Cunnie; the story is the horrible 'Thrawn Janet'. A good third to these is 'Jinny's Gibbet', a traditional gipsy folktale about a witch who cuts a hand of glory from a hanged man, only to realise that the same hand had gently touched her breast as the owner fed from it. The hanged man is her son. This story is retold in *Folktales of England*, ed. Katherine Briggs and Ruth Tongue, London: Routledge & Kegan Paul, 1965.

Index